T0083640

STUDIES IN WELSH HISTORY

Editors

RALPH A. GRIFFITHS   CHRIS WILLIAMS
ERYN M. WHITE

22

'A GLORIOUS WORK IN THE WORLD'

WELSH METHODISM AND THE INTERNATIONAL
EVANGELICAL REVIVAL, 1735–1750

Saturday, Oct. 17, 1741.　　　　　　　　　Numb. 28.

The WEEKLY HISTORY:

O R,

An Account of the most Remarkable Particulars relating to the present Progress of the Gospel.

London: Printed by *J. Lewis* in *Bartholomew-Close*, near *West-Smithfield*.
[Price One Penny.]

Those who are willing to take in this Paper Weekly, may have all the former Numbers; and such Persons are desired to send in their Names and Places of Abode to the Printer above mentioned, in order to be regularly served.

A Letter from Mr. HOWEL HARRIS *to Mr.* CENNICK.

Brinkworth, Oct. 7. 1741.

Dear Brother Cennick,

OUR dear Lord gives me to love you tenderly.---Thus far am I brought on my Journey.---I lay at my Brother's *Thursday* Night, and met Sir *Richard Ellison* on the way.---*Friday* I return'd to *London* again, so that *I* came only to *Maidenhead Friday* Night, and *Saturday* to *Newbury.*---I stay'd there till *Monday* Evening.---I discours'd *Sunday* Morning at 7 in the little Society of Methodists, went to Church and received the Sacrament.---*In* the Evening *I* went to Meeting to hear Mr. *Philips* and was ask'd to preach there in his Meeting at six, and so did, and *Monday* Morning in a Baptist Meeting, where *I* hope the Lord blessed me, to save my Soul from the Blood of all.---*I* would have preach'd in an Arian Meeting-house, but they (poor Souls) would not let such a Mad-man.---They long for your coming this way much, and *I* think it will be right for you to make it in your Road to *Wiltshire.*---I had a long discourse with them about having Satan bruis'd under our Feet, but they turn out all the Promises to Death and so lull themselves asleep and say, we must not expect to have Faith in exercise continually.

My dear *Brother*, what have we to do, but to such as never believ'd to shew them the absolute necessity of Faith, and to such as have it to shew the Necessity in order to bear Fruit, to keep it in continual exercise to look up still to Christ, and while we are continually looking to him, eyeing him! and feeding on him, we shall be chang'd to be more and more like him, and consequently bear more and more Fruit to him, then Sin will die and all Graces grow.---We must always wear our Shield, or we shall soon be wounded by some fiery Dart or other.---I am sure that my Misery and Bondage is, to forget Christ; to lose my watch, look from him aside.---While the Eye of my Soul is kept by his Spirit---fix'd on him; *I* am not then led away by the Lust of the Eye, the Lust of the Flesh, and the Pride of Life.

Then

A typical page from John Lewis's evangelical periodical, *The Weekly History*, from October 1741 when he was inundated with letters from many corners of the evangelical world. (By permission of Llyfrgell Genedlaethol Cymru/The National Library of Wales.)

'A GLORIOUS WORK IN THE WORLD'

WELSH METHODISM AND THE INTERNATIONAL EVANGELICAL REVIVAL, 1735–1750

by

DAVID CERI JONES

*Published on behalf of the
History and Law Committee
of the Board of Celtic Studies*

CARDIFF
UNIVERSITY OF WALES PRESS
2004

British Library Cataloguing-in-Publication Data
A catalogue record for this book is available from the British Library.

ISBN 0-7083-1870-3

Printed in Great Britain by Dinefwr Press, Llandybïe

EDITORS' FOREWORD

Since the Second World War, Welsh history has attracted considerable scholarly attention and enjoyed a vigorous popularity. Not only have the approaches, both traditional and new, to the study of history in general been successfully applied to Wales's past, but the number of scholars engaged in this enterprise has multiplied during these years. These advances have been especially marked in the University of Wales.

In order to make more widely available the conclusions of recent research, much of it of limited accessibility in post-graduate dissertations and theses, in 1977 the History and Law Committee of the Board of Celtic Studies inaugurated a new series of monographs, *Studies in Welsh History*. It was anticipated that many of the volumes would originate in research conducted in the University of Wales or under the auspices of the Board of Celtic Studies. But the series does not exclude significant contributions made by researchers in other universities and elsewhere. Its primary aim is to serve historical scholarship and to encourage the study of Welsh history. Each volume so far published has fulfilled that aim in ample measure, and it is a pleasure to welcome the most recent addition to the list.

CONTENTS

PREFACE

This study is intended to represent a significant reinterpretation of the eighteenth-century Welsh Methodist revival. Despite the extensive historiography relating to Welsh Methodism, modern historical scholarship has yet to illuminate a number of important areas. Both Eryn M. White in her *Praidd Bach y Bugail Mawr: Seiadau Methodistaidd De-Orllewin Cymru* (1995) and Geraint Tudur in his *Howell Harris: From Conversion to Separation, 1735–1750* (2000) have recently opened up new perspectives on the study of Welsh Methodism, but they have both approached the subject from decidedly Welsh points of view. This study adopts a more comparative approach and attempts to assess the role that the Welsh revival played in the wider evangelical enterprise, particularly between 1735 and 1750. In the historiography of the evangelical revival more generally, the current trend is to view the movement as a response to the collective trauma that engulfed the whole international Protestant community and that cut right across national and denominational boundaries. The Welsh revival must therefore be located within the context of this 'pan-Protestant' crisis. The focus of this study will be on the way the Welsh Methodists responded to this development and on the methods by which they communicated with their fellow evangelicals. It will trace some of the ways in which the Welsh revival influenced the wider evangelical movement and the manner in which involvement in an international evangelical community fundamentally affected the character and shape of Welsh Methodism.

The preparation of this work has naturally left me indebted to a number of people. I have been privileged to have as my doctoral supervisor and mentor, Dr Eryn M. White. Her unfailing support, encouragement and seemingly inexhaustible reserves of patience have consistently eased the research and writing of this work. The doctoral thesis on which this book is based was undertaken in the Department of History and Welsh History at the University of Wales, Aberystwyth. It was examined by Professor David W. Bebbington, and many of his penetrating comments and suggestions have refined my somewhat woolly thinking at a number of points. Subsequent discussions with him on the nature of early evangelicalism have also opened up a number of further highly productive avenues of enquiry. In addition, Dr Boyd Schlenther, Dr Michael F. Roberts, Dr Geraint Tudur and Professor Geraint H. Jenkins have either read parts of the original thesis or offered invaluable advice and direction at various point during its completion. Parts of the work have been developed and presented at conferences at the Universities of Lampeter, Bangor, Cardiff, Manchester, King's College, London and Northumbria at Newcastle, at the University of Wales, Centre for Advanced Welsh and Celtic Studies, Aberystwyth, and at the bi-annual conference of the Universities and Colleges Christian Fellowship (UCCF), Christianity and History Forum. Other scholars' responses to the work have been critical in crystallizing a number of points and clarifying ambiguities. Part of Chapter IV has been reworked in my ' "The Lord did give me a particular honour to make [me] a peacemaker": Howel Harris, John Wesley and Methodist infighting, 1739–1750', *Bulletin of the John Rylands University of Manchester Library* (2004, forthcoming), and similarly part of Chapter VI has been expanded in my ' "Transcripts of my Heart": Welsh Methodists, popular piety and the international evangelical revival, c.1758–50', in Joan Allen and Richard Allen (eds), *'Faith of our Fathers': Six Centuries of Popular Belief in England, Ireland and Wales* (Cardiff: Welsh Academic Press, 2004, forthcoming).

I am also grateful to the Historical Society of the Presbyterian Church of Wales for granting me access to Howel Harris's diaries and to the staff at the National Library of Wales, Aberystwyth, the Hugh Owen Library of the University of Wales, Aberystwyth, the Glasgow University Library and the John Rylands Library, Manchester, for their courteous help and efficiency. I received financial support from a number of sources during the completion of the doctoral thesis. I am indebted to the Glamorgan Further Education Trust Fund, the University of

Wales for receipt of the Thomas Ellis Memorial Award and to the James Pantyfedwen Foundation.

My greatest debts though are of an altogether different nature. To my parents I owe an incalculable debt for introducing me to the same evangelical faith as that practised by Howel Harris and George Whitefield and, secondly, for their constant support in innumerable ways throughout the course of the preparation of this work. My wife, Clare, has had to share the whole of our married life with Harris, Whitefield and various other Methodist interlopers. Without her love, interest, constant support and forbearance this work would have been deficient in so many ways. Finally, Carys Hanna and Celyn Rebekah, who both arrived during the preparation of this work, will now be able to reclaim their father from the eighteenth century, partially at least.

David Ceri Jones
Aberystwyth
August 2004

ABBREVIATIONS

Account   John Lewis (ed.), *An Account of the Most Remarkable Particulars of the Present Progress of the Gospel* (London, 1742–3)

BDE   Timothy Larsen (ed.), *Biographical Dictionary of Evangelicals* (Leicester, 2003)

BDEB   Donald M. Lewis (ed.), *Blackwell Dictionary of Evangelical Biography, 1730–1860*, 2 vols (Oxford, 1995)

CA   John Lewis (ed.), *The Christian's Amusement Containing Letters Concerning the Progress of the Gospel both at Home and Abroad* (London, 1740–1)

CCHMC   *Cylchgrawn Cymdeithas Hanes y Methodistiaid Calfinaidd* (Caernarfon, 1916–)

CH   John Lewis (ed.), *The Christian History or General Account of the Progress of the Gospel in England, Wales, Scotland and America* (London, 1743–7)

CMA   Calvinist Methodist Archive, National Library of Wales, Aberystwyth

DMBI   John A. Vickers (ed.), *Dictionary of Methodism in Britain and Ireland* (London, 2000)

DNB   Leslie Stephen and Sidney Lee (eds), *The Dictionary of National Biography*, 22 vols (London, 1908–9)

DSCHT   Nigel M. de S. Cameron (ed.), *Dictionary of Scottish Church History and Theology* (Edinburgh, 1993)

DWB   J. E. Lloyd and R. T. Jenkins (eds), *The Dictionary of Welsh Biography* (London, 1959)

ERF   Donald McKim (ed.), *Encyclopaedia of the Reformed Faith* (Louisville, KY, and Edinburgh, 1992)

HHD   Howel Harris's Diaries, Calvinistic Methodist Archive, National Library of Wales, Aberystwyth

JWRH   *Journal of Welsh Religious History* (Welshpool, 1993–2000; Bangor, 2001–)

NLW   National Library of Wales, Aberystwyth

ODCC   F. L. Cross and E. A. Livingstone (eds), *The Oxford Dictionary of the Christian Church* (Oxford, 1983)

ABBREVIATIONS

Trevecka   The Trevecka Letters, Calvinistic Methodist Archive, National
            Library of Wales, Aberystwyth

WH   John Lewis (ed.), *The Weekly History: Or an Account of the Most
            Remarkable Particulars Relating to the Present Progress of the
            Gospel* (London, 1741–2)

WHR   *Welsh History Review* (Cardiff, 1960–)

INTRODUCTION

In September 1751, Howel Harris (1714–73) set out on another of his extended visits to London, in the hope that he would be able to recapture some of the energy and fire that he felt he had lost. However, the circumstances in which he arrived in the city on this occasion were very different from those to which he had grown accustomed. There was no hero's welcome at George Whitefield's Tabernacle any longer and no crowded and expectant societies waiting to see him and hang upon his every word. A forlorn and dejected Harris, having recently been ostracized so publicly by his English and Welsh Methodist friends, had retreated to his home at Trefeca with only a small rump of supporters, while his old rival, Daniel Rowland (1711–90), had taken over the leadership of the revival in Wales. In his diary, Harris, now suddenly an outsider, tried to bestir himself by reminding himself of the heady days of the mid-1730s and 1740s when he, George Whitefield (1714–70) and John Wesley (1703–91) had stood at the apex of a genuinely international renewal movement that seemed, to them at least, to presage nothing less than the climax of the whole history of redemption. Harris therefore reminded himself of 'ye Universality of this last awakeng among many nations, in England, Scotland, Ireland, Wales, America, Germany, France, Swedeland &c.'[1] His ability to take such an all-embracing view of the evangelical revival was the result of his fifteen-year career as a revivalist, during which he had placed himself at the hub of a religious revival that was, in John Walsh's memorable phrase, 'an international and pan-Protestant phenomenon'.[2]

[1] National Library of Wales, Calvinistic Methodist Archive, Howel Harris's Diary (hereafter HHD) 152b: 9 September 1751.

[2] John Walsh, '"Methodism" and the origins of English-speaking evangelicalism', in Mark A. Noll, David W. Bebbington and George A. Rawlyk (eds), *Evangelicalism: Comparative Studies of Popular Protestantism in North America, the British Isles, and Beyond 1700–1990* (New York, 1994), p. 20.

The late 1730s and the early 1740s had witnessed exciting and highly charged outbursts of religious enthusiasm in countries as widely dispersed as Wales, England, Scotland, Ireland, many of the American colonies and parts of Germany. Together they gave birth to a revolutionary new religious movement. This 'new' religious force, according to David Bebbington's now widely adopted definition, united a vast array of religious awakenings by its stress on the four themes of conversionism, activism, biblicism and crucicentrism.[3] These were all interpreted within the context of a highly emotional and individualistic spirituality that emphasized voluntary commitment rather than religious dogma and confessional conformity,[4] thereby bringing about what Nathan Hatch has called the democratization of Christianity.[5] This is not to say that the evangelical revival was a single homogeneous movement. It could encompass Christians of many different persuasions, from Lutheran Pietists in Saxony, Presbyterians in Scotland, Anglicans and Dissenters, Calvinists and Arminians in England and Wales, and Puritan Congregationalists in New England, who each jealously guarded their distinctive identity. What the revivalists did was transcend these differences by emphasizing a set of core beliefs and elevating revivals of religion to central importance in an attempt to revitalize the flagging fortunes of the Protestant cause throughout much of western Europe and the American colonies.[6]

The self-identity of the first generation of Welsh evangelicals, or Methodists as all of the revival's converts were quickly nicknamed,[7] operated on a number of levels. They were, first and foremost, members of a local society and it was to this small body

---

[3] D. W. Bebbington, *Evangelicalism in Modern Britain: A History from the 1730s to the 1990s* (London, 1989), pp. 2–17.

[4] Frank Lambert, *'Pedlar in Divinity': George Whitefield and the Transatlantic Revivals* (Princeton, 1994) and Frank Lambert, *The Founding Fathers and the Place of Religion in America* (Princeton, 2003), pp. 127–58. For further discussion of the degree to which eighteenth-century evangelicalism was actually innovative see Robert Letham and Donald Macleod, 'Is evangelicalism Christian?', *The Evangelical Quarterly*, 67, 1 (1995), 3–33; Kenneth J. Stewart, 'Did evangelicalism predate the Enlightenment? An examination of the David Bebbington thesis', http://zondervanchurchsource.com/convention.parallel.htm; and Garry J. Williams, 'Was evangelicalism created by the Enlightenment?', *Tyndale Bulletin*, 53, 2 (2002), 283–312.

[5] Nathan O. Hatch, *The Democratization of American Christianity* (New Haven, 1989).

[6] W. R. Ward, *The Protestant Evangelical Awakening* (Cambridge, 1992).

[7] Richard P. Heitzenrater, *Wesley and the People Called Methodists* (Nashville, 1995), pp. 45–6.

that most felt the strongest allegiance.[8] However, each society
member was also part of a national awakening, initially under
the direct leadership of either Howel Harris or Daniel Rowland,
but quickly organized in a connexional system under the government of a ruling Association. But Harris's comments quoted
above indicate a further layer to Welsh Methodist identity.
Members were conscious of being part of a renewal movement
that was both deeply rooted within the particular traditions
of early Welsh Protestantism[9] and part of an international
evangelical movement that was simultaneously transnational,
transcontinental and transatlantic, aimed at re-energizing the
down-at-heel Protestant community. So, for example, the
evangelicals who gathered for their monthly update of revival
news at George Whitefield's Spa Fields Chapel in London on 8
November 1742 were typical of Methodists everywhere when, in
response to news of fresh outbreaks of enthusiasm in Scotland,
they sang:

> Great things in England, Wales and Scotland wrought,
> And in America to pass are brought,
> Awakened souls warn'd of the wrath to come,
> In numbers flee to Jesus as their home.[10]

The Welsh Methodists would also have been able to sing these
lines with great gusto, imbued as they were with a deep sense of
their place in the wider international evangelical community. At
the height of the revival in the early and mid-1740s, Howel
Harris customarily peppered his letters with confident statements
outlining the scope of the revival in places that to many a Welsh
ear would have sounded both exotic and exciting. To one
correspondent in late 1742 he wrote about the 'Progress of ye
Gospel in Scotland, Yorkshire, Lincolnshire, Warwickshire,
Wiltshire, Germany, Prussia, New England, Pennsylvania and

---

[8]   See Eryn M. White, 'The people called "Methodists": early Welsh Methodism and
the question of identity', *Journal of Welsh Religious History* (hereafter *JWRH*), 1 (2001),
6.
[9]   Glanmor Williams, 'Some Protestant views of early British Church history', in
Glanmor Williams, *Welsh Reformation Essays* (Cardiff, 1967), pp. 207–19.
[10]   'A call to the sleeping virgins, which was read in the society at the Tabernacle on
Monday, 8 November 1742', *The Weekly History or An Account of the Most
Remarkable Particulars Relating to the Present Progress of the Gospel* (ed. John Lewis)
(hereafter *WH*), 84 (Saturday, 13 November 1742).

many provinces'.[11] Other, more humble, Welsh Methodists
similarly recognized the magnitude of the revival and spoke of it
as 'the good work that is going on',[12] emphasizing the unity they
felt with Methodists everywhere. They echoed Harris's pride in
the 'glorious Work . . . in the world'[13] and were committed to
remembering 'To tell him [God] to humble and purify all his
Lambs, to send his Gospel over the world all the world. Put him
in mind of his Promises to [. . .] ye whole world'.[14]

The early Welsh Methodists' articulation of this world-view
was underpinned by a number of theological presuppositions,
shared by evangelicals everywhere. Firstly, they all justified their
existence in a similar way. They looked for no explanation
beyond the divine origin and inspiration of all their activities.
Indeed, so convinced were the pioneer revivalists of God's
intimate direction of every facet of their lives and careers that
they were often blinded to more worldly forces. For Jonathan
Edwards (1703–58) this new outbreak of religious enthusiasm
was a 'surprising'[15] work of God. In his writings on the revival he
repeatedly made use of terminology that stressed the immediacy
of the presence of the Holy Spirit, often using phrases such as the
'pouring out'[16] or the 'effusion'[17] of the Spirit to convey adequately the essence of the revival. George Whitefield continually stressed that it was the 'extraordinary presence of God
amongst us'[18] that was the overwhelming reason for the success
of his ministry and of the revival more generally. In Pembrokeshire, the exhorter Howell Griffith similarly spoke of the 'pouring

[11]   National Library of Wales, Calvinistic Methodist Archive, Trevecka Group, The
Trevecka Letters 2803 (hereafter Trevecka): Howel Harris to Herbert Jenkins (22
November 1742).
[12]   'Extract of a letter from a minister in the country to his friend in London (3
February 1742)', WH, 46 (Saturday, 20 February 1742).
[13]   Trevecka 708, Howel Harris to Marmaduke Gwynne (22 October 1742).
[14]   Trevecka 726, Howel Harris to Elizabeth Paul and Hetty Buckler (3 November
1742).
[15]   This adjective was used most tellingly in Jonathan Edwards's first work on the
revival, A Faithful Narrative of the Surprising Work of GOD in the Conversion of Many
Hundred Souls in Northampton, and the Neighbouring Towns and Villages of the
County of Hampshire, in the Province of the Massachusetts-Bay in New-England (1736).
See Clarence C. Goen (ed.), The Works of Jonathan Edwards, IV: The Great Awakening
(New Haven, 1972), pp. 99–211.
[16]   See Goen (ed.), The Works of Jonathan Edwards, IV, p. 110.
[17]   Quoted in Eifion Evans, Daniel Rowland and the Great Evangelical Awakening in
Wales (Edinburgh, 1985), p. 71.
[18]   See Iain H. Murray (ed.), George Whitefield's Journals (London, 1960), p. 251.

out of the Spirit among our Societies'[19] and Howel Davies
(1716–70) offered the opinion that 'the presence of God is with
us in a wonderful ravishing manner'.[20]

Their strictly spiritual interpretation of the awakenings that
they superintended was backed up by a thoroughly providentialist view of history. Their spiritual forebears, the seventeenth-
century Puritans, had schooled them to trace the finger of God in
every aspect of their daily lives. Since the Church was, in John
Calvin's (1509–64) words, 'the great *work-room* of God'[21] the
early Methodists were conditioned to pay particular attention to
religious history in order to establish a precedent for their
activities and thereby secure some measure of divine appro-
bation for their apparent innovations. They therefore mined the
history of the Church for examples of communities which shared
their enthusiastic outlook on the spiritual life and they constructed a model that enabled them to draw parallels between
their own revivals and the earliest apostolic communities,
focusing on every similar subsequent outbreak of religious
enthusiasm in the 1,700 years between the apostolic era and
their own day.[22]

This was an approach to history that was again articulated
most persuasively by the chief apologist of the revival, Jonathan
Edwards. In a series of sermons on just one brief scriptural
passage from Isaiah 51:8, originally preached in 1739 and
eventually published posthumously as *A History of the Work of
Redemption* (1774),[23] Edwards split the history of the Church,

---

[19] 'The Copy of a Letter from BRO HOWELL GRIFFITH, to BROTHER CENNICK (3 March
1743)', in *An Account of the Most Remarkable Particulars Relating to the Present
Progress of the Gospel* (ed. John Lewis) (hereafter *Account*), III, 1, 31.

[20] Trevecka 837, Howell Davies to John Cennick (no date).

[21] Quoted in Alexandra Walsham, *Providence in Early Modern England* (Oxford,
1999), p. 15.

[22] The early editions of the London-based religious magazines were filled with
accounts of 'revivals' that had occurred amongst the Waldensian communities
throughout various parts of Europe including the French Alps, the Holy Roman Empire
and the Albigensian communities in parts of southern France. See *The Christian's
Amusement: Containing Letter's Concerning the Progress of the Gospel Both at Home
and Abroad, &c. Together with an Account of the Waldenses and Albigenses: People that
Never Fell into the Popish Errors, but Retained the Truth of the Gospel from the Time of
the Apostles under all the Popish Persecutions Down to the Reformation* (ed. John Lewis)
(hereafter *CA*), issues 1, 2, 3 and 6 for examples. For more detail on the Waldenses see F.
L. Cross and E. A. Livingstone (eds), *The Oxford Dictionary of the Christian Church*
(Oxford, 1997), pp. 1714–15. For the Albigenses see ibid., p. 35.

[23] See John F. Wilson (ed.), *The Works of Jonathan Edwards, IX: A History of the
Work of Redemption* (New Haven, 1989).

and consequently of the world, into three distinct eras corresponding to the history of the accomplishment and application of redemption. The first era had begun with the fall of mankind in the Garden of Eden and had run up until the first advent of Christ. The second period focused on the brief course of Christ's earthly ministry, and the final era corresponded to the period from Christ's death until his millennial return – the so-called 'last days'. This theological compartmentalizing of history gave its devotees a sense of continuity and rootedness which enabled them to pinpoint exactly their place in God's grand cosmic design. Furthermore, a direct appeal was also made to the past in order to legitimize the apparent novelty of the new evangelical movement. Naturally, no period was exploited for examples as unrelentingly as that of the first generation of Christians. In the 'Preface' to Jonathan Edwards's 1741 tract, *The Distinguishing Marks of a Work of the Spirit of God*, William Cooper wrote:

> The dispensation of grace we are now under is certainly such as neither we nor our fathers have seen; and in some circumstances so wonderful, that I believe there has not been the like since the extraordinary pouring out of the Spirit immediately after our Lord's ascension. The apostolical times seem to have returned upon us: such a display has there been of the power and grace of the Divine Spirit in the assemblies of his people, and such testimonies has he given to the word of the Gospel.[24]

If first-generation evangelicals looked to the past to justify their activities, they also had an equally clear view of the future and, perhaps more importantly, of their own place in it. Their realization of their historical pedigree, their belief that God was intimately involved in every aspect of their lives, coupled with the knowledge that parallel revivals were occurring simultaneously in a wide variety of countries, naturally led them to make highly optimistic speculations about the future and the eventual culmination of the work of redemption with the commencement of the millennial reign of Christ on earth. Many first-generation evangelicals were sufficiently intoxicated with their own importance to suppose that their existence presaged the imminent

---

[24]   Goen (ed.), *The Works of Jonathan Edwards, IV*, p. 217.

return of Christ. In his *A History of the Work of Redemption* Jonathan Edwards reminded evangelicals everywhere:

> Tis not unlikely that this Work of God's Spirit, that is so extraordinary and wonderful, is the dawning, or at least a prelude, of the glorious Work of God so often foretold in Scripture, which in the progress and issue of it, shall renew the world of mankind.[25]

An anonymous contributor to the London-based edition of the revival magazine, *The Weekly History,* writing in October 1741, echoed Edwards's heightened expectations when he wrote: 'I hope God will arise and have mercy upon Zion, and make his Jerusalem yet a praise in the whole earth.'[26] Millennial speculations were of course not unique to the Methodists.[27] The members of new religious groups, in the euphoria of the early days of their movements, were invariably characterized by inflated expectations of their own place in God's programme for the world.[28] What gave the early Methodists' claims particular potency was that they were informed by the realization that despite being separately generated, their revivals were each interdependent parts of a considerably more widespread international event that in the late 1730s looked as though it was about to carry all before it.

This world-view was deeply rooted in the daily lives and experiences of the majority of the converts of the Welsh

---

[25] Wilson (ed.), *The Works of Jonathan Edwards, IX*, p. 353.
[26] 'Mr A M of Edinburgh to Mr S M of London (Edinburgh, 26 September 1741)', *WH*, 27 (Saturday, 10 October 1741).
[27] The literature dealing with the development of Protestant millenarianism in England and Wales is plentiful. However, there are fewer studies of Methodist eschatology. R. A. Knox in his *Enthusiasm: A Chapter in the History of Religion with Special Reference to the XVII and XVIII Centuries* (Oxford, 1950) is probably the best point at which to begin. On evangelical millenarianism more specifically see Kenneth G. C. Newport, 'Methodists and the millennium: eschatological expectation and the interpretation of biblical prophecy in early British Methodism', *Bulletin of the John Rylands University Library of Manchester*, 78 (1996), 103–22; and David Hempton, 'Evangelicalism and eschatology', *The Journal of Ecclesiastical History*, 31, 2 (1980), 179–94. For more on Jonathan Edwards's millenarian ideas see Wilson (ed.), *The Works of Jonathan Edwards, IX*, pp. 40–50 and 90–4; and John F. Wilson, 'History, redemption and the millennium', in Nathan O. Hatch and Harry S. Stout (eds), *Jonathan Edwards and the American Experience* (Oxford, 1988), pp. 131–41.
[28] See Jon Mee, *Romanticism, Enthusiasm and Regulation: Poetics and the Policing of Culture in the Romantic Period* (Oxford, 2003), pp. 25–37; David Lovejoy, *Religious Enthusiasm in the New World* (Cambridge, 1985); and Knox, *Enthusiasm*, passim.

Methodist revival, through their membership of what Susan O'Brien has called a transatlantic 'community of saints'[29] and their participation in an international communications network.[30] The individual awakenings were bound together by a complex web of relationships that existed across both national and cultural boundaries, throughout what is now called the British Atlantic world.[31] The various pioneer revivalists entered into close personal friendships with one another, regularly visited each other's revivals, frequently corresponded about every aspect of their ministries, wrote up their ideas and reflections on the key events in which they participated in their personal journals and diaries, patronized an extremely influential magazine, best known in its second incarnation as *The Weekly History,* and published books and sermons which explained their distinctive features in considerable detail. The primary purpose of much of the literature that was circulated in the network was utilitarian, as the pioneer revivalists used it to communicate with one another, to establish their converts in their newly discovered faith and to set the movement as a whole on a solid theological and organizational footing. But it also served another very different purpose. The revivalists quickly realized that if the individual awakenings were to be anything more than just a patchwork of loosely interconnected communities, some form of network binding them all together was necessary. The revivalists therefore used the diaries, letters, magazines and books that they produced in order to meld the various awakenings together, creating a community that became what Margaret Jones, in reference to the Wesleyan *Arminian Magazine* of the second half of the

---

[29]   Susan O'Brien, ' "A transatlantic community of saints": the Great Awakening and the first evangelical network, 1735–1750', *American Historical Review,* 91 (1986), 811.

[30]   The boundaries of this international evangelical communications network were first delineated by Susan Durden (née O'Brien). Much of her published work is based on her doctoral thesis, 'Transatlantic communications and influence during the Great Awakening: a comparative study of British and American revivalism, 1730–1760' (Ph.D., University of Hull, 1978). More accessible to the general reader are O'Brien, ' "A transatlantic community of saints" '; Susan Durden, 'A study of the first evangelical magazines, 1740–1748', *Journal of Ecclesiastical History,* 27 (1976), 255–75; and Susan O'Brien, 'Eighteenth-century publishing networks in the first years of transatlantic evangelicalism', in Noll, Bebbington and Rawlyk (eds), *Evangelicalism,* pp. 38–57.

[31]   See David Armitage and Michael J. Braddick (eds), *The British Atlantic World, 1500–1800* (Basingstoke, 2002), pp. 1–7.

eighteenth century, has called a 'public space'[32] in which all aspects of the evangelical movement were discussed and delineated, and in which there was a realistic expectation that anybody was free to contribute his or her insights. Much of the material that was produced was therefore penned in response to the actual day-to-day needs that arose within the revival and provides the historian of early Methodism with an alternative paradigm within which to interpret the early development of the Methodist movement.

From the very earliest days of their membership of the revival, the Welsh converts were introduced to the wider revival by Howel Harris, whose commitment to establishing the communications network was matched by no one, except perhaps George Whitefield. Any study which attempts to understand how the Welsh revival related to the wider evangelical movement must focus, initially at least, on the activities of these two men. Whitefield, 'the Grand Itinerant', was the one agent, above all others, who held the scattered awakenings together by, as Frank Lambert has traced in such painstaking detail, appropriating the marketing techniques of the commercial revolution to promote transatlantic revivalism.[33] His conspicuous position at the intersection of most of the evangelical awakenings ensured that anyone who had contact with him would inevitably be incorporated in the Anglo-American evangelical movement that he had, according to Harry S. Stout, almost single-handedly forged.[34]

Through his friendship with Whitefield, Harris became an integral part of the London evangelical scene. During his many extended visits to the London Methodists he found himself at the hub of the international community as news and information about the revival from throughout the British Atlantic world flooded in, was repackaged by Whitefield's trusted lieutenants and then fanned out to revival communities the length and breadth of the British Isles and beyond. Harris inevitably became

[32] Margaret P. Jones, 'From "the state of my soul" to "exalted piety": women's voices in the Arminian/Methodist magazine, 1778–1821', in R. N. Swanson (ed.), *Gender and Christian Religion*, Studies in Church History, 34 (Woodbridge, 1998), p. 273.

[33] Lambert, *'Pedlar in Divinity'*, pp. 52–95; Boyd Stanley Schlenther, 'Religious faith and commercial empire', in P. J. Marshall (ed.), *The Oxford History of the British Empire II: The Eighteenth Century* (Oxford, 1998), pp. 141–3.

[34] Harry S. Stout, 'George Whitefield in three countries', in Noll, Bebbington and Rawlyk (eds), *Evangelicalism*, p. 58.

one of the best-informed evangelicals of all and he ensured both
that his fellow Methodists back home were enabled to take
advantage of every opportunity that the wider revival afforded
them and that the progress of the Welsh revival was known
throughout the international revival. Many rank-and-file Welsh
Methodists took every opportunity to read revival news, and
some of them also began to write their own accounts of the
revivals in which they were themselves participating. For others
this kind of evangelical journalism was insufficient, and some of
the more ambitious and self-confident among them began to use
the network as a means of supplementing the religious diets
available to them more locally. They used the network in order
to obtain advice and counsel, evaluate the genuineness of their
experiences, learn and debate theology, share fellowship with
other like-minded individuals and get their hands on the latest
evangelical literature to come from the presses. By enthusiastically participating in all these activities the Welsh evangelicals
became some of the most vocal contributors to the international
communications network, priding themselves on the fact that
they were amongst the most consistently well-informed group of
saints anywhere in the evangelical world. For the historian their
participation opens a window on early Welsh Methodist
spirituality, making it possible to evaluate the difference between
the elite and lay experience of the revival.

This study is designed to place the Welsh Methodist revival into
the context of the international evangelical movement, by
analysing the way in which its members participated in this
communications network. The first two chapters provide the
context. Chapter I begins with a chronological survey of the
whole evangelical movement from its commencement in 1735
until the time in 1750 when meaningful cooperation between the
Welsh Methodists and the wider awakening was brought to an
abrupt conclusion. It then considers in detail some of the more
particular reasons for the emergence of evangelicalism in Wales,
before reflecting on some of the ways in which the historiography
of Welsh Methodism has, until fairly recently, prevented
historians from adopting the kind of comparative approach set
within the context of the eighteenth-century transatlantic world

that historians like John Walsh have recommended so persuasively.[35] Chapter II lays the necessary groundwork for the
unravelling of Welsh connections with the wider revival by
outlining the character and scope of the evangelical communications network. It examines how the revivalists used inter-
revival visits, letter-writing, the innovative genre of religious
magazines and an ambitious publication programme to draw the
scattered awakenings together. For many of those literate and
independently minded 'middling sorts' who were attracted to
evangelical religion in the 1730s, the highly participatory nature
of this communications network became an important outlet for
many of their energies and ambitions.

Chapters III, IV and V consider how the leaders of the Welsh
revival responded to being part of an international revival. The
chapters follow a broadly thematic approach, yet attempt to
reflect the chronology of the movement as closely as possible
within the confines of these themes. Chapter III concentrates on
the later 1730s and examines how the Welsh revivalists
responded to the surprising news of parallel revivals in other
localities and how they attempted to extend the fortunes of their
awakening to some of these other communities. It focuses mainly
on the relationship between Howel Harris and George Whitefield and demonstrates how this friendship became vital both to
the wider influence of Harris himself and to the Welsh
Methodists' integration into the evangelical movement. Chapter
IV uses the theme of division to analyse the changing nature of
the relationship between Wales and the wider revival. It demonstrates initially how Howel Harris and his Welsh followers sided
with George Whitefield and his Calvinism against John Wesley
in 1740 and 1741, but it goes on to analyse Harris's distinctive
role in these divisions, arguing that as he became a peacemaker
between the Calvinists, Arminians and Moravians he was able to
carve out a truly unique niche for himself.

---

[35] Walsh, ' "Methodism" and the origins of English-speaking evangelicalism', pp.
19–20. See also Leigh Eric Schmidt, *Holy Fairs: Scottish Communions and American
Revivals in the Early Modern Period* (Princeton, 1989); Marilyn J. Westerkamp,
Triumph of the Laity: Scots-Irish Piety and the Great Awakening, 1625–1760 (New
York, 1988); Michael J. Crawford, *Season of Grace: Colonial New England's Revival
Tradition in its British Context* (New York, 1991); and Ward, *The Protestant Evangelical
Awakening.*

Once the split between the Calvinists and the Wesleyans in England had taken effect in 1741, the Calvinistic Methodist movements of England and Wales were drawn closer together as Whitefield realized that his severely depleted revival needed both the resources and stability that the numerically much healthier Welsh Calvinistic revival could offer. This interdependence was expressed most obviously in January 1743 when the administrative structures of both revivals, which had been developing along broadly similar paths up to this point, were formally united under the oversight of the Joint Association of English and Welsh Calvinistic Methodism. Chapter V examines this development, tracing the events that led up to Whitefield's appointment as overall Moderator and Harris's as General Superintendent, with responsibilities split between Wales and the English Calvinists based at Whitefield's Tabernacle in Moorfields, London. It argues that the achievements of 1743 were not capitalized upon because the close interrelationship between the two revivals was never really sustained. Whitefield became a far less common sight in Wales, preferring to spend more and more of his time in the American colonies. Harris became more important in England, becoming the outright leader of English Methodism in 1748 when Whitefield, after his return from his longest stay in the colonies, renounced all desire to shoulder responsibility for the revival he had initiated.

The next two chapters shift the focus from the elite perspective of the revivalists and attempt to understand how rank-and-file Welsh Methodists responded to their evangelical counterparts around the world and how they took advantage of the opportunities afforded them by the communications network. The first of these chapters uses their contributions to the network to unravel some of the main features of early Methodist spirituality, focusing on the intricacies of the popular experience of the Methodist message to show how, for many of them, the international evangelical community played a very real role in their day-to-day lives. The final chapter widens the scope slightly and examines how much actual first-hand experience many ordinary Methodists had of revivals in countries other than England. It demonstrates how the colonial revival exercised a remarkably strong hold over the minds of many of them, as they read Jonathan Edwards for themselves, followed the course of

Whitefield's colonial travels avidly and supported his orphanage in Georgia with frequent financial contributions. It then takes up the issue of opposition and considers how the rank-and-file responded to the experience of overt persecution, particularly at times of acute national crisis like that which dominated the minds of most inhabitants of the British Isles in 1745.

These strands are drawn together in the Conclusion, which focuses on Howel Harris's dismissal from the international revival and his gradual retirement to Trefeca immediately after 1750. It argues that Harris's loss resulted in the mothballing of Welsh Methodist interaction with the wider revival, as the Welsh revivalists became far more interested in matters more closely related to their own survival. The ending of Harris's regular visits to London, the winding-up of the revival magazine, Whitefield's lack of interest in rebuilding his revival, and the obvious triumph of John Wesley's movement in England, meant that for most Methodists in Wales information about the progress of the revival elsewhere became almost impossible to come by. The remarkable inter-revival cooperation that had characterized relations between English and Welsh Methodism throughout the 1740s was never recovered.

I

'THE POURING OUT OF THE SPIRIT OF GOD': AN INTERNATIONAL EVANGELICAL AWAKENING

The Welsh Methodist revival sprang from the same soil as the rest of the evangelical revival, and Wales was, significantly, the first part of the British Isles to boast an indigenous evangelical renewal movement. From its commencement in 1735 until its disruption following the schism between Howel Harris and Daniel Rowland in 1750, every aspect of the development of the Welsh revival took place in a context far wider than that prescribed by Wales's own geographical boundaries. The revival in Wales had its immediate origins in the experience of the unordained Howel Harris, a schoolteacher from Talgarth near Brecon,[1] and Daniel Rowland, a Church of England curate in the two parishes of Llangeitho and Nantcwnlle in north Cardiganshire.[2] In 1735 both men experienced profound religious conversions that propelled them towards embarking upon highly dramatic preaching careers which quickly gained them a measure of fame and notoriety in their respective communities. Harris, ever conscious of his lay status, began his public ministry by reading the sermons of others in the homes of his immediate neighbours but soon developed a remarkable propensity for exhorting – an activity that he favoured over more formal preaching and which avoided the potential for embarrassment over his lack of clerical ordination. By the end of 1736, Harris had organized a small group of his most avid followers into a modest religious society at Y Wernos near Builth, and other similar groups followed quickly, so that by March 1739 he could boast that he had established a network of thirty religious societies in Breconshire[3] over which he exercised almost dictatorial control. He had also begun to preach

---

[1]   The best studies of Harris's early life and conversion are Geraint Tudur, *Howell Harris: From Conversion to Separation, 1735–1750* (Cardiff, 2000), pp. 13–37; Eifion Evans, *Howell Harris: Evangelist, 1714–1773* (Cardiff, 1974), pp. 1–10; and Geoffrey F. Nuttall, *Howell Harris, 1714–1773: The Last Enthusiast* (Cardiff, 1965).

[2]   For Daniel Rowland's early development as a revivalist see Evans, *Daniel Rowland*, pp. 27–35 and D. J. Odwyn Jones, *Daniel Rowland, Llangeitho* (Llandysul, 1938).

[3]   Evans, *Howell Harris*, p. 22.

in the open air slightly further afield wherever there happened to be a crowd large and eager enough to listen to him, and from an early stage he had realized the wider implications of his work. Daniel Rowland had no real need to develop such innovatory approaches to ministry. His position as a curate afforded him ample opportunities to hone the skills necessary to be an effective revivalist. He quickly began attracting sizeable crowds to his church at Llangeitho and on account of the numbers pressing to listen to him he too began preaching in the open air on Sundays and then holding additional services throughout the week in an attempt to cater to the demand. Within two years of the foundation of his first society, Harris could boast to George Whitefield that there was a 'great revival'[4] in Cardiganshire, 'a sweet prospect'[5] in Breconshire and Monmouthshire and some 'well-wishers to the cause of God'[6] in Montgomeryshire and Glamorgan.

Within a relatively short period of time, the Welsh revival became firmly established in its heartland areas in the south-west corner of the country and in Breconshire. Harris and Rowland amalgamated their awakenings in the immediate aftermath of their first meeting unexpectedly in the parish church at Defynnog, Breconshire, during August 1737,[7] turning a splintered collection of converts into something resembling a 'national' awakening under a more centralized control. In March 1739, George Whitefield, who at that stage was recognized as the undisputed leader of English Methodism, the Wesley brothers having only just begun their evangelical careers, visited Wales. Whitefield was deeply impressed with what he saw and as a result of his visit made every effort to promote the Welsh revival throughout the international revival community that had already begun to take shape.[8] From this time the fortunes of the English and Welsh revivals quickly became inextricably entwined. Howel

---

[4] Trevecka 136: Howel Harris to George Whitefield (8 January 1739).
[5] Ibid.
[6] Ibid.
[7] Tudur, *Howell Harris*, p. 42 and Evans, *Daniel Rowland*, p. 52.
[8] George Whitefield to Daniel Abbot (13 April 1739), in 'George Whitefield and friends: the correspondence of some early Methodists', ed. Graham C. G. Thomas, *National Library of Wales Journal* (hereafter *NLWJ*), 27, 3 (1992), 291–2; William Seward to Joseph Stennett (17 April 1739), ibid., 292–3; Murray (ed.), *George Whitefield's Journals*, pp. 229–30.

Harris became an influential figure in the two main centres of English Methodism – London and Bristol – playing a prominent part in the split between George Whitefield and the Wesley brothers in 1741, and after a further two years of close co-operation both revivals were finally united under the leadership of the Joint Association of English and Welsh Calvinistic Methodism in January 1743. Subsequently, Harris began to spend increasingly lengthy periods of time in London, battling to regain some of the ground that the Whitefieldians had lost to the more tightly regulated and energetic Wesleyans, who by this time were firmly in the ascendancy within English Methodism. In Wales itself events became more settled after 1743 as the converts came under the closer supervision of the Welsh Methodists' highly disciplined organizational structure. Towards the end of the 1740s Whitefield made repeated attempts to persuade Howel Harris to assume the sole leadership of the English Calvinistic movement because he wished to relinquish the responsibility in favour of a more loosely defined role that would allow him to travel between each of the revivals far more freely and spend more of his time in the American colonies. Harris, with unusual reluctance, had only recently accepted Whitefield's offer when controversy concerning his relationship with his prophetess and travelling companion, Madam Sidney Griffith, and his increasingly belligerent avowal of some of the more controversial elements of Moravian theology, led Whitefield to bar him from the English Calvinistic revival altogether. By the end of 1750, Daniel Rowland and the Welsh Methodists had taken similar action against Harris, separating from him and thereby splitting the movement between Harris's people and Rowland's people. Harris subsequently retreated to Trefeca with a small rump of his most committed supporters and looked on as Rowland attempted to take the revival forward by consolidating what had been achieved over the course of the previous fifteen years. This position persisted until the early 1760s and was only finally healed when a sufficiently chastened Harris was welcomed back into the Methodist fold and a new wave of enthusiasm, this time centred at Llangeitho, revivified the Welsh Methodists in 1762.[9]

    [9]   R. Geraint Gruffydd, 'Diwygiad 1762 a William Williams o Bantycelyn', *Cylchgrawn Cymdeithas Hanes y Methodistiaid Calfinaidd* (hereafter *CCHMC*), LIV, 3, (October 1969), 68–75; LV, 1 (March 1970), 4–13.

Despite being the first individuals in the British Isles to launch revivalistic careers, Harris, Rowland and their fellow Welsh Methodists were not the originators of the 'new' evangelical movement. The beginnings of the evangelical revival, as W. R. Ward has conclusively argued, must now be traced to events in continental Europe at the end of the seventeenth and the beginning of the eighteenth centuries.[10] In response to threats from a rejuvenated Catholic Church, beleaguered and perse-cuted Protestants, particularly in some of the larger German states, developed a new internalized, Pietistic vision of Christian-ity which laid all of its emphasis on the dynamics of each individual's direct relationship with God, rather than on religious dogma and confessional conformity.[11] Like early Methodism, which borrowed so much from it, Pietism cannot be reduced to any single denomination or body of doctrine. It was a renewal movement, 'fundamentally irenical'[12] according to Ernest Stoeffler, which functioned best within the parameters of the existing denominations.

This internalization of religion, as Ted Campbell has demon-strated, was not peculiar to Protestants but was 'part of a broad European cultural movement that included Catholics, Eastern Christians, and European Jews as well'.[13] Ernest Stoeffler's well-known and much quoted definition of pietism as 'venturesome [. . .] oriented towards life's vital concerns, and vibrant with spiritual and emotional dynamic',[14] does some justice to the new tone that was set by the Pietists, but their innovations must also be placed within a wider religious context. Their stress on the

---

[10]   Ward, *The Protestant Evangelical Awakening* and W. R. Ward, 'Power and piety: the origins of the religious revival in the early eighteenth century', *The Bulletin of the John Rylands Library*, 63 (1980), 231–52. For an indication of the wide acceptance with which Ward's views have been greeted see G. M. Ditchfield, 'Methodism and the evangelical revival', in H. T. Dickinson (ed.), *A Companion to Eighteenth Century Britain* (Oxford, 2002), 252–3.

[11]   The contribution of the Pietists to the later development of the evangelical revival has been examined most effectively in G. F. Nuttall, 'Continental pietism and the evangelical movement in Britain', in J. van den Berg and J. P. van Dooren (eds), *Pietism und Reveil* (Leiden, 1978) and Ted A. Campbell, *The Religion of the Heart: A Study of European Religious Life in the Seventeenth and Eighteenth Centuries* (Columbia, SC, 1991).

[12]   F. Ernest Stoeffler, *The Rise of Evangelical Pietism* (Leiden, 1965), p. 2.

[13]   Campbell, *The Religion of the Heart*, p. ix.

[14]   Stoeffler, *The Rise of Evangelical Pietism*, p. 246; also quoted and discussed in more detail in J. C. S. Mason, *The Moravian Church and the Missionary Awakening in England, 1760–1800* (London, 2001), p. 6.

'religion of the heart'[15] reflected broader religious trends that shifted the focus of theological perception away from the mind and the intellect and towards the affections and experience.[16] This shift led to a concentration on some of the fundamental questions of human existence and caused the Pietists to concentrate on the cultivation of personal piety, focusing on the means of entry into the spiritual life and the development of techniques designed to ensure its healthy nurture.

Initiation into this special direct relationship with God, according to their theological vision, was through an experience which they termed the 'New Birth' or conversion. They argued that each individual had to be brought to a crisis point at which he or she could then be born again and pass from a state of spiritual darkness to one of light.[17] This consequently made each individual responsible for his or her own spiritual life and forced Churches to develop techniques to bring people to the point of decision as they each competed for the same souls in the newly deregulated religious market-place.[18] No technique was more suited to creating an atmosphere in which people would feel ready to make such a commitment as the excitement and drama of the emotionally charged religious revival, backed up as it was by the novelties of open-air preaching and a support network of informal cell groups in which spiritual vitality could be maintained.

The need to adopt effective evangelistic strategies was made all the more urgent because the ranks of European Protestantism were being decimated by persecution in the wake of the Thirty Years War (1618–48).[19] The signing of the treaty of Westphalia in 1648 seemed, for a time, to guarantee Europe's Protestants some measure of stability and security against invasion by militant Catholic states.[20] These expectations were not fulfilled,

---

[15] Campbell, *The Religion of the Heart,* p. ix.
[16] Ibid., pp. 1–5.
[17] Stoeffler, *The Rise of Evangelical Pietism,* pp. 13–14.
[18] Lambert, *'Pedlar in Divinity';* Harry S. Stout, *The Divine Dramatist: George Whitefield and the Rise of Modern Evangelicalism* (Grand Rapids, 1991), pp. xvi–xviii, 35–6; and Schlenther, 'Religious faith and commercial empire', pp. 141–2.
[19] See Geoffrey Parker, *The Thirty Years' War* (London, 1984) and Ronald G. Asch, *The Thirty Years War: The Holy Roman Empire and Europe, 1618–48* (London, 1997).
[20] David J. Sturdy, *Fractured Europe, 1600–1721* (Oxford, 2002), pp. 70–5; Parker, *The Thirty Years' War,* pp. 172–89; and Ward, *The Protestant Evangelical Awakening,* pp. 18–21.

as the treaty did not protect Europe's Protestants from localized depredations on the part of ambitious and sufficiently well-motivated Catholic rulers. Events reached their climax in 1685 when the Edict of Nantes revoked the treaty of Westphalia, traumatizing an already nervous and fearful Protestant population. As a result of the new waves of persecution, European Protestantism, according to the estimate of Jonathan Edwards, had lost at least half of its adherents, as many nervous rulers led their territories back into the Roman Catholic fold.[21] Many of the newly revitalized and self-confident Catholic states then embarked on fresh purges, intended to secure confessional uniformity and the suppression and eradication of Protestant minorities. Yet far from eradicating Protestants and creating confessional conformity, W. R. Ward has argued that the 'experience of the process created bonds of sympathy among many European Protestants'.[22] The dispersal and migration of many of these groups to safer areas and the successful dispersion of their ideas was, therefore, made all the more likely and the experience of persecution ensured that the bonds of sympathy between them were bound still more tightly.

By 1692 two of the most influential Pietists, Philipp Jakob Spener (1635–1705)[23] and August Hermann Francke (1663–1727), had been expelled from Saxony and had taken up residence in Brandenburg-Prussia, where they were both afforded the freedom to implement their Pietistic theologies without interruption. Spener, from his position as the rector of the Nikolaikirche in Berlin, continued to develop many of the ideas which he had previously found so successful in encouraging a vibrant form of domestic piety – devices which included the use of networks of small intimate class meetings at which individuals met together for Bible reading, prayer and fellowship. Francke became professor of theology at Halle and from this base developed a Pietistic community that was to have profound implications for the

---

[21] W. R. Ward, *Christianity under the Ancien Régime, 1648–1789* (Cambridge, 1999), p. 6.
[22] Ward, *The Protestant Evangelical Awakening*, p. 353.
[23] W. R. Ward, 'Philipp Jakob Spener', in Timothy Larsen (ed.), *Biographical Dictionary of Evangelicals* (Leicester, 2003) (hereafter *BDE*), pp. 622–4; Stoeffler, *The Rise of Evangelical Pietism*, pp. 228–42; Richard L. Gawthrop, *Pietism and the Making of Eighteenth-Century Prussia* (Cambridge, 1993), pp. 104–20.

later development of the evangelical revival.[24] From his influential position at the university in Halle, Francke was able to publicize his Pietistic vision of Christianity throughout the Protestant world. His stress on individual piety led him to experiment with lay participation in local religious leadership, and to develop a highly efficient printing and literature distribution network; his establishment of schools and orphanages had widespread repercussions, as Halle rapidly became a byword for energetic and vigorous practical Christianity

However, the single most important contributory factor in the dispersion of Pietistic ideas occurred some years later when a group of migrants from Moravia sought refuge on the estate of Nikolaus Ludwig, Count Zinzendorf (1700–60)[25] at Berthelsdorf in Saxony in 1722. The exiles, descendants of the ancient Unitas Fratrum or Church of the Bohemian Brethren, established the Herrnhut community and, following a dramatic religious revival in 1727,[26] were reconstituted as the Moravian Church. At Herrnhut the Moravians developed an extremely close-knit community in which they attempted to revive many of the ideals of primitive Christianity. In common with all other Pietists they stressed the central importance of individual spirituality and sought to practise a 'community of goods'[27] – a kind of primitive Christian communism in which all members lived together on settlements and shared their possessions with one another, echoing the example of the original apostolic Christians.[28] This made

---

[24]   W. R. Ward, 'August Hermann Francke', *BDE*, pp. 237–9; Daniel L. Brunner, *Halle Pietists in England: Anthony William Boehme and the Society for Promoting Christian Knowledge* (Göttingen, 1993); Nuttall, 'Continental Pietism and the evangelical movement in Britain'.

[25]   Donald M. Lewis (ed.), *The Blackwell Dictionary of Evangelical Biography, 1730–1860* (Oxford, 1995) (hereafter *BDEB*), pp. 1226–7; Ward, *The Protestant Evangelical Awakening*, pp. 116–56; A. J. Lewis, *Zinzendorf, the Ecumenical Pioneer: A Study in the Moravian Contribution to Christian Mission and Unity* (London, 1962).

[26]   Colin J. Podmore, *The Moravian Church in England, 1728–1760* (Oxford, 1998), pp. 5–6; W. R. Ward, 'The renewed unity of the Brethren: ancient church, new sect or interconfessional movement?', *Bulletin of the John Rylands University Library of Manchester*, 70, 3 (Autumn 1988), 83–6.

[27]   John Walsh, 'John Wesley and the community of goods', in Keith Robbins (ed.), *Protestant Evangelicalism: Britain, Ireland, Germany and America, c.1750–1950: Essays in Honour of W. R. Ward*, Studies in Church History, Subsidia, 7 (Oxford, 1990), p. 25.

[28]   For more on the tendency of some of the early evangelicals towards various forms of Christian communism see John Walsh, 'John Wesley and the community of goods' and Eamon Duffy, 'Primitive Christianity revived: religious renewal in Augustan England', in Derek Baker (ed.), *Renaissance and Renewal in Christian History*, Studies in Church History, 14 (Oxford, 1977), pp. 287–300.

them amongst the most highly motivated and visionary of all of the early evangelical groups and propelled them into an aggressive evangelistic strategy that, despite their relatively small size, brought them to the attention of a far wider public. Also significant was the migration of the Salzburgers. In November 1731 the Catholic archbishop of Salzburg expelled all Protestants from his jurisdiction. He clearly thought that there were only very small pockets of Protestants in the city, but his miscalculation resulted in the expulsion of over 20,000 people.[29] Most of them migrated to Prussia but a small number arrived in England and were eventually granted permission to settle in the newly founded colony of Georgia in America,[30] a development that was later to have a significant impact on the lives of both George Whitefield and John Wesley in the mid-1730s.

These migrations were fundamental to the development of the evangelical revival because they spread many of the new evangelistic techniques with which these Pietistic groups had experimented so successfully. These devotional and evangelistic tools included camp meetings, open-air preaching and the organization of the earnest into small fellowship meetings for mutual support and encouragement, underpinned by an ambitious publishing and distribution network by means of which the Bible and the classics of Reformation and Puritan spirituality could be disseminated. In the fifty years immediately preceding the evangelical revival in the British Isles many of these devotional techniques had been adopted in the religious societies that had been established.[31] It was out of these societies that most of the revivalists emerged in the later 1730s, conditioned by the spirituality that they had acquired in them.

It was in the small town of Northampton in Massachusetts that the first indication was felt of what was to come. In 1734, Northampton's Congregational minister, Jonathan Edwards, preached a series of sermons in his church that focused on the

[29] Ward, 'Power and piety', 244–9; W. R. Ward, 'The relations of Enlightenment and religious revival in central Europe and in the English-speaking world', in Derek Baker (ed.), *Reform and Reformation: England and the Continent, c.1500–c.1750*, Studies in Church History, Subsidia 2 (Oxford, 1979), pp. 290–3.

[30] See Harold E. Davis, *The Fledgling Province: Social and Cultural Life in Colonial Georgia, 1733–1776* (New York, 1976), passim, and Kenneth Coleman, *Colonial Georgia: A History* (New York, 1976), pp. 40–8 and 156–8.

[31] Henry Rack, 'Religious societies and the origin of Methodism', *Journal of Ecclesiastical History*, 38 (1987), 582–95.

foundational evangelical themes of personal sinfulness and the need of urgent repentance. The sermons provoked an immediate and highly emotional response from Edwards's listeners, particularly among the young, and many conversions resulted – so much so that these events were thought widespread and significant enough to be accorded the title of a revival. However, the excitement remained fairly localized, extending to only a few of the surrounding towns and villages of eastern New England, and it was of relatively short duration.[32] Once the initial excitement had ebbed, Edwards sat down to record his own impressions of what had just happened, and his considered reflections were published in 1737 as *A Faithful Narrative of the Surprising Work of God in the Conversion of Many Hundred Souls in Northampton*.[33] The book was quickly reprinted in England at the end of 1737, carrying a commendatory introduction by two of England's most respected Dissenting ministers, Isaac Watts and John Guyse.

Yet, rather than providing the catalyst for a more widespread religious awakening in the colonies, the 'Great Awakening' as it later became known did not really get under way until George Whitefield arrived in America for the second time towards the end of 1739.[34] Whitefield's dramatic itinerant ministry, which occurred against the backdrop of his highly successful and well-publicized preaching in London in the preceding months, drew impressive crowds and he rapidly constructed a network of small, localized revivals throughout the colonies which he was then able to amalgamate to create an intercolonial movement.[35] Whitefield subsequently remained committed to the colonies throughout the rest of his life, dividing his time between them and the British Isles almost equally, supporting the revival communities that had been brought into existence by his earlier itinerancy, encour-

---

[32]   Goen (ed.), *The Works of Jonathan Edwards*, IV, pp. 19–25; George M. Marsden, *Jonathan Edwards: A Life* (New Haven, 2003), pp. 150–73; Michael J. Crawford, *Seasons of Grace: Colonial New England's Revival Tradition in its British Context* (New York, 1991), pp. 104–23.

[33]   The definitive edition of Edwards's work can be found in Goen (ed.), *The Works of Jonathan Edwards*, IV, pp. 99–201.

[34]   On Whitefield's colonial career, Lambert, *'Pedlar in Divinity'*; Stout, *The Divine Dramatist*; Arnold A. Dallimore, *George Whitefield: The Life and Times of the Great Evangelist of the Eighteenth-century Revival*, 2 vols (London, 1970 and Edinburgh, 1980), passim.

[35]   Frank Lambert, *Inventing the 'Great Awakening'* (Princeton, 1999), pp. 125–43.

aging sympathetic evangelical ministers and raising support for the orphanage which he had founded in the southern colony of Georgia.

Paradoxically, the most significant consequence of the Northampton awakening occurred outside the boundaries of the colonies themselves, as it became the catalyst for awakenings in other areas. Edwards's printed account had the effect of publicizing the awakening throughout the international network of evangelical ministers on the lookout for the beginning of something new.[36] Northampton quickly became the benchmark against which all other claims of revival were verified and Edwards's volume became a kind of textbook for many of the pioneer revivalists in England, Wales and Scotland. We know, for example, that Howel Harris had read about Jonathan Edwards's revival and had discussed it with Daniel Rowland by November 1738.[37] In the book's pages he would have been introduced to Edwards's carefully crafted model of a typical revival and would have learned about the sheer extraordinariness of the Northampton revival in terms like the following:

> God's work has also appeared very extraordinary in the degrees of the influences of his Spirit, both in the degree of awakening and conviction, and also in the degree of saving light, and love, and joy, that many have experienced. It has also been very extraordinary in the extent of it, and its being so swiftly propagated from town to town. In former times of the pouring out of the Spirit of God on this town, though in some of them very remarkable, yet it reached no further than this town; the neighbouring towns all around continued unmoved.[38]

From Edwards, Harris and his fellow revivalists could have honed, and in some cases even acquired, the vocabulary of revivalism. They would have observed Edwards's frequent use of adjectives such as 'surprising', 'remarkable' and 'unusual' in relation to what he perceived to be the activity of the Spirit of God and would have been presented with a paradigm that enabled them to interpret their own awakenings and fit them

---

[36] John Walsh, ' "Methodism" and the origins of English-speaking evangelicalism', pp. 20–1; Crawford, *Seasons of Grace*, pp. 3–138, passim.

[37] HHD 35: 27 November 1738.

[38] Goen (ed.), *The Works of Jonathan Edwards, IV*, p. 159.

into the far more widespread international phenomenon of evangelical Christianity.

Despite the prominence that both John and Charles Wesley have occupied in the historiography of the Methodist revival, they were both relative latecomers to the evangelical movement. In the first months of the English revival there was far more fluidity in the movement than subsequently became the case, particularly after 1740. Initially, the focus of the revival was the relatively small German society that met at Fetter Lane in London. By 1738 the society had been heavily infiltrated by Moravians and was superintended at this stage by Peter Böhler (1712–75).[39] Within its compass a diverse mix of individuals, from a variety of evangelical traditions, congregated to hear gospel sermons and share their religious experiences. All of the early revivalists, including both John and Charles Wesley, George Whitefield, Howel Harris and John Cennick (1718–55),[40] attended for various lengths of time between 1738 and 1740, drawn together because of their common experience of the New Birth and their desire to see a more widespread moral and spiritual reformation.[41]

George Whitefield was undoubtedly the pioneer of evangelicalism in England. Like both Howel Harris and Daniel Rowland in Wales, Whitefield experienced a life-changing evangelical conversion in 1735. He had graduated from the rigidly disciplined High Church piety of the Oxford 'Holy Club'[42] and had used his conversion as the springboard from which to seek ordination in the Established Church. Having been ordained as a deacon in 1736 by Bishop Benson of Gloucester, his home city, Whitefield preached his first sermon there in June of the same year and was censured by the

[39] T. S. A. Macquiban, 'Peter Böhler', *DEB*, pp. 60–1; Clifford W. Towlson, *Moravian and Methodist: Relationships and Influences in the Eighteenth Century* (London, 1957), pp. 47–65; Podmore, *The Moravian Church in England*, pp. 31–2 and 39–48.

[40] *BDEB*, p. 210; *DMBI*, p. 57; Podmore, *The Moravian Church in England*, pp. 49–50, 88–95 and 195–200.

[41] For more on the role of the Fetter Lane Society in the development of the evangelical revival see Podmore, *The Moravian Church in England*, pp. 29–71 and Tudur, *Howell Harris*, pp. 53–9.

[42] Dallimore, *George Whitefield*, I, pp. 67–72.

ecclesiastical authorities for allegedly driving fifteen people mad.[43] Whitefield's reference to this outbreak of 'madness' in his *Journals* is an indication of the dramatic effects that accompanied his preaching even in these earliest days. He quickly achieved a measure of notoriety as a popular preacher, earning the nickname of 'boy parson',[44] and large crowds gathered to listen to him both in London and in Bristol, particularly during the months in late 1736 and 1737 when he both served as a stand-in curate for Thomas Broughton (1712–77) at the chapel of the Tower of London[45] and deputized for an old friend from his days in the Holy Club, Charles Kinchin (d. 1742), who was rector at Dummer in Hampshire.[46] By this stage, scenes like those at Gloucester were being replicated in London and Bristol and wherever else he went and, with characteristic self-belief, Whitefield boasted in his *Journals* that 'the tide of popularity now began to run very high'[47] and that he was fêted with the 'hosannas of the multitude'.[48]

At the height of his popularity in 1737, Whitefield honoured a decision that he had made some time previously by sailing for the newly established colony of Georgia, where he hoped to be able to pursue a successful career as a colonial missionary. Georgia subsequently became central to Whitefield's life and career, as much of his energy was spent raising funds for the orphanage that he had established near Savannah.[49] When he returned to England a year later, in December 1738, the momentum that he had built up before his departure had been largely dissipated, and his absence had allowed the recently converted Wesley brothers to gain the upper hand and to snatch the initiative from him.

---

[43]   George Whitefield to Mr H. (30 June 1736), in Iain H. Murray (ed.), *George Whitefield's Letters, 1734–1742* (Edinburgh, 1976), p. 97.
[44]   Murray (ed.), *George Whitefield's Journals*, p. 77.
[45]   Ibid., p. 76. For more on Broughton see Luke Tyerman, *The Oxford Methodists: Memoirs of Rev. Messrs. Clayton, Ingham, Gambold, Hervey, and Broughton* (London, 1873), pp. 334–60 and John Walsh, 'The Cambridge Methodists', in Peter Brooks (ed.), *Christian Spirituality: Essays in Honour of Gordon Rupp* (London, 1975), pp. 251–83.
[46]   Murray (ed.), *George Whitefield's Journals*, pp. 78–9; Tyerman, *The Oxford Methodists*, pp. 363–70.
[47]   Murray (ed.), *George Whitefield's Journals*, p. 89.
[48]   Ibid.
[49]   Neil J. O'Connell, 'George Whitefield and Bethesda Orphan-House', *Georgia Historical Quarterly*, 54 (1970), 41–62 and Lambert, *'Pedlar in Divinity'*, passim.

Whitefield's return from the colonies therefore forced him to reassess his priorities. He clearly expected to arrive in London and to carry on where he had left off over a year previously. In an attempt to make up lost ground he returned to some of his old preaching haunts and, to his evident relief, once again discovered that, despite his apparent failure as a missionary in Georgia, he could still attract large crowds to Moorfields and Kennington Common.[50] While in the colonies, Whitefield's world-view was dramatically broadened. He had begun to realize that the awakening that he had started between 1736 and his departure for America was mirrored by very similar events in other countries. Consequently, after returning to England he attempted to establish contact with some of these other awakenings. He almost immediately wrote to Howel Harris. In his introductory letter he provided Harris with an account of his testimony and penned an up-to-the-minute report on his ministry before asking him for news of the Welsh revival and expressing the hope that the letter would be just the start of a much closer acquaintance with the Welsh revivalists.[51] The letter marked the beginning of Harris and Whitefield's close friendship and the beginning of the close interaction between the English and Welsh Calvinistic Methodists. It exemplified Whitefield's desire to maximize the potential of the various local awakenings by drawing them closer together and possibly developing some kind of structure that would create a united front, transcending national and denominational boundaries, creating a unified evangelical movement.

Neither of the Wesley brothers acquired decided evangelical convictions until over two years after Whitefield had begun his public ministry. Charles Wesley was converted[52] a few weeks before his brother John had his heart famously warmed at Aldersgate Street in May 1738.[53] John Wesley in particular had followed a remarkably similar path to Whitefield via Oxford, the Holy Club[54] and an ill-fated stint as a colonial missionary in

[50]   See Murray (ed.), *George Whitefield's Journals*, pp. 195 and 199–201.
[51]   Trevecka 136: George Whitefield to Howel Harris (8 January 1739).
[52]   Frederick C. Gill, *Charles Wesley: The First Methodist* (London, 1964), pp. 63–74.
[53]   Nehemiah Curnock (ed.), *The Journal of the Rev. John Wesley, A. M.*, vol. I (London, 1938), pp. 475–6.
[54]   Henry D. Rack, *Reasonable Enthusiast: John Wesley and the Rise of Methodism* (London, 1989), pp. 61–106.

Georgia,[55] before experiencing an evangelical conversion. From this experience he also discovered that he could preach and command the attention of remarkably large congregations by the force of his oratorical powers. Between 1738 and 1740 there existed a measure of harmony and cooperation between Wesley and Whitefield as they worked together and organized their converts into societies under their own immediate discipline. Yet this coexistence was shattered when John Wesley published a sermon, originally preached in April 1739, which he provocatively entitled *Free Grace*. In it he publicly stated his opposition to the Calvinistic theology preferred by George Whitefield and his followers. Whitefield, by this stage once again in the American colonies, was forced to issue a reply to the sermon[56] and for almost a year the English revival was thrown into turmoil by the bitter recriminations that these publications aroused. For a while it looked as if the revival would struggle to recover, but once the initial salvoes in the debate had been fired and its main combatants had taken up their entrenched positions, relationships settled and recrimination was replaced by a tacit recognition that in England at least there were, by this stage, three separate versions of the revival: the Wesleyan revival which was theologically Arminian, reflecting Wesley's eclectic spiritual development; the more traditional Calvinistic revival consisting of the followers of George Whitefield; and the Moravian revival, still focused on the Fetter Lane Society with which both the Wesley brothers and Whitefield had severed relations by the mid-1740s.[57]

Subsequently, the Calvinistic and Wesleyan revivals in England developed along entirely different lines. The Wesleyan revival went from strength to strength under the iron grip and discipline of John Wesley himself.[58] Whitefield, perhaps realizing

---

[55] See ibid., pp. 107–36.

[56] George Whitefield, *A Letter to the Rev. Mr John Wesley in Answer to his Sermon Entitled 'Free Grace'* (Bristol, 1741).

[57] Podmore, *The Moravian Church in England*, pp. 66–71.

[58] The historiography relating to the beginnings of Wesleyan Methodism is massive. Undoubtedly the most up-to-date scholarly study of the life of John Wesley remains Rack, *Reasonable Enthusiast*. Alongside this, Rupert Davies and Gordon Rupp (eds), *A History of the Methodist Church in Great Britain*, I (London, 1965) is still the most useful introduction to the first generation of Wesleyan Methodist development. Frank Baker, *John Wesley and the Church of England* (London, 1970) and Heitzenrater, *Wesley and the People Called Methodists* are also invaluable. The recent tercentenary of John Wesley's birth has also given rise to a number of interesting studies. See Roy Hattersley, *A Brand from the Burning: The Life of John Wesley* (London, 2002) and John Munsey Turner, *John Wesley: The Evangelical Revival and the Rise of Methodism in England* (London, 2002).

the strength of John Wesley's position in England, became increasingly committed to his transnational and transatlantic ministry. He came to rely more and more on his chief publicist, William Seward (1711–40), who ensured that his activities became as widely known as possible and that a sense of expectation and an impression of unrelenting progress always accompanied Whitefield's entourage.[59] After Seward died, as a result of being attacked by a mob during a preaching tour of Wales in 1740, Whitefield replaced him with John Lewis[60] and his revival magazine, *The Christian's Amusement*. The magazine had been printed intermittently by Lewis since early 1740, but in 1741 Whitefield, at Lewis's instigation, assumed editorial control. He began by renaming it *The Weekly History*[61] and packed it with up-to-the-minute reports from throughout the Calvinistic revivals, thereby turning it into the official mouthpiece of the Calvinistic Methodist movement. For the remainder of the 1740s, Whitefield divided his time between the British Isles and the American colonies, spending almost four years in the colonies between 1744 and 1748. He became, in effect, a self-styled international revivalist, and through this ministry he managed to bind together a complex community of saints who all looked to him as their spiritual father and leader. So at precisely the time that his hegemony in England was being challenged most seriously, he turned increasingly to his international responsibilities, divesting himself of sole responsibility for any single awakening, thereby minimizing opportunities for the kind of damaging and debilitating disputes that had damaged relations with the Wesley brothers so irreparably.

The English revival therefore became far less important to Whitefield, and so throughout the 1740s he sought to ensure its survival by tying its fortunes to the far stronger Calvinistic revival in Wales. In 1743, both revivals were formally unified under the administration of a joint Association and Whitefield himself was awarded the honorary title of Moderator, although in fact Howel

[59]   Lambert, '*Pedlar in Divinity*', pp. 52–5 and 229–31.
[60]   Very little is known about John Lewis. The editors of *The Dictionary of National Biography* (hereafter *DNB*) did not think that he deserved mention, and the only studies of him are the brief articles by M. H. Jones, 'John Lewis, the printer of "The Weekly History"', *CCHMC*, IV, 3 (June 1919), 84–92 and 'John Lewis, "Printer to the Religious Societies"', *CCHMC*, V, 1 (March 1920), 6–11.
[61]   Susan Durden, 'A study of the first evangelical magazines', 260–2.

Harris and Daniel Rowland largely carried out his duties. In England, Whitefield off-loaded responsibility for the Tabernacle, and with it the whole English Calvinistic movement, first to John Cennick, until he left in order to join the Moravians in 1745, and then to a number of other individuals, before finally deciding on Howel Harris, who had at last, after much heart-searching, reluctantly agreed to take the job just before he was expelled from the revival in January 1750. Subsequently, Whitefield spent more and more time in the colonies and battled with constant ill health throughout the remainder of his life. The countess of Huntingdon (1707–91), who later took up the leadership of Calvinistic Methodism in England, eventually brought some sort of order to the English Calvinistic revival by overseeing the registration of Calvinistic Methodist preaching houses after Whitefield's death in America in 1770.[62] The progress of English Calvinistic Methodism after 1750 was therefore very different from what had persisted throughout the 1740s. Whitefield was not able to 'settle' his converts as successfully as either John Wesley or the Welsh Methodists had done. He preferred the role of a roving revivalist, and therefore his main contribution to the subsequent development of evangelicalism remained his construction of a remarkably sophisticated international evangelical network that brought together like-minded revivalists that seemed, for a while, to intimate great things for the future of the Methodist movement.

The awakenings in England, Wales and the American colonies were the instigators of the wider evangelical movement. It was these revivals, emerging simultaneously in the mid-1730s, that were the inspiration for other smaller-scale and shorter-lived awakenings in a number of other countries. Whilst the Scottish evangelical revival was a decidedly indigenous awakening, centred on the parishes of Kilsyth and Cambuslang on the outskirts of Glasgow and led by two Church of Scotland ministers, James Robe (1688–1753)[63] and William McCulloch (1691–

---

[62] Boyd S. Schlenther, *Queen of the Methodists: The Countess of Huntingdon and the Eighteenth-Century Crisis of Faith and Society* (Durham, 1997), pp. 68–82.
[63] *BDEB*, p. 942; *DSCHT*, p. 721; Arthur Fawcett, *The Cambuslang Revival: The Scottish Evangelical Revival of the Eighteenth Century* (London, 1971), passim.

1771),[64] it owed much of its resilience to the active and enthusiastic participation of George Whitefield.

Even though the Scottish revival did not really get going until mid-1741, Whitefield had already developed links with Scottish evangelicals, Ebenezer (1680–1754)[65] and his brother Ralph Erskine (1685–1752).[66] They had seceded from the Church of Scotland in 1733 over what they perceived to be its doctrinal laxity and had founded their own doctrinally pure Associate Presbytery. Whitefield had begun a correspondence with Ralph Erskine in 1739, clearly in the hope that he and his brother would act as his agents in Scotland and introduce him to potentially sympathetic audiences north of the border. The Erskine brothers for their part assumed that Whitefield was in agreement with their strict secessionist stance, and when he arrived in Scotland for the first time in April 1741 it was at Ralph Erskine's church at Dunfermline that he first preached. When it became apparent that Whitefield would not relinquish his loyalty to the Church of England and come out in support of the Associate Presbytery, both Erskine brothers turned against him bitterly, becoming two of his most hostile opponents and outspoken evangelical critics.[67]

It was not until spring 1742 that events at Cambuslang began to dominate the minds of evangelicals throughout the extended revival community.[68] As early as February, William McCulloch had reported a heightening of spiritual interest in his congregations – more people were attending prayer meetings and there was more fervour in evidence at them than was usually the case.

[64]   *BDEB*, pp. 715–16 and *DSCHT*, pp. 507–8.
[65]   *DSCHT*, pp. 298–300 and A. T. N. Muirhead, 'Ebenezer Erskine', *BDE*, pp. 211–13.
[66]   *BDEB*, pp. 363–4 and *DSCHT*, pp. 301–2.
[67]   For more on Whitefield's relationship with the Erskine brothers and their Associate Presbytery, *DSCHT*, pp. 35–6; Dallimore, *George Whitefield*, II, pp. 83–92; and Andrew L. Drummond and James Bulloch, *The Scottish Church, 1688–1843: The Age of the Moderates* (Edinburgh, 1973), pp. 51–3.
[68]   In comparison with the rest of the evangelical revival little has been written about the Scottish revivals. Fawcett, *The Cambuslang Revival*, is a fairly uncritical hagiographical account. See instead Stewart J. Brown, 'Religion in Scotland', in H. T. Dickinson (ed.), *A Companion to Eighteenth Century Britain* (Oxford, 2002), pp. 261–7 and T. C. Smout, 'Born again at Cambuslang: new evidence on popular religion and literacy in eighteenth-century Scotland', *Past and Present*, 97 (1982), 114–27. For the wider context of religious developments in eighteenth-century Scotland: J. R. McIntosh, *Church and Theology in Enlightenment Scotland: The Popular Party, 1740–1800* (East Linton, 1998).

In a letter to Whitefield, McCulloch, adopting the fashionable terminology, reported that there appeared to be an extra-ordinary outpouring of the Spirit at Cambuslang and he urged Whitefield to come north to see it for himself and to help fan the small embers into a more powerful flame.[69] Whitefield, char-acteristically not wishing to miss this new wave of enthusiasm, arrived in Glasgow at the beginning of June and subsequently spent most of the summer encouraging and fuelling the Scottish awakening by his barnstorming sermons and extensive experi-ence of pastoring revival converts.

For a time it seemed as if the Scottish revival would outshine all previous awakenings, even eclipsing the one that had occurred at Northampton, Massachusetts, more than seven years earlier. The evangelical press was packed with the latest news from Scotland, so much so that John Lewis had to print a special double issue of the *Weekly History*[70] in July 1742 in order to satisfy demand. As a means of generating wider interest in events in Scotland, William McCulloch inaugurated his own religious magazine, *The Glasgow Weekly History*, which he published for the first time in 1741.[71] Clearly modelled on John Lewis's English version, McCulloch's magazine also included letters from sympathetic evangelicals, testimonies from new converts and accounts of revival occurrences from both Scotland and further afield. Like its London-based counterpart it also acted as a unifying force, locating the Scottish evangelicals within the international revival and informing interested parties throughout the evangelical world of the latest events at Cambuslang and Kilsyth.

Yet, despite its intensity and the interest that it generated, the Scottish revival was relatively short-lived. For a while it occupied centre stage and many evangelicals thought that it really did presage still more dramatic advances for the revival, occurring as it did after a lull in the excitement in England and Wales. However, by the time Whitefield left Scotland at the end of the

[69]   George Whitefield to William McCulloch (8 June 1742), in Murray (ed.), *George Whitefield's Letters*, pp. 401–2.
[70]   *WH*, 66 (Saturday, 10 July 1742).
[71]   William McCulloch's magazine was entitled *The Glasgow-Weekly-History Relating to the Late Progress of the Gospel at Home and Abroad; Being a Collection of Letters Partly Reprinted from the London-Weekly-History* (December 1741–December 1742). See also Durden, 'A study of the first evangelical magazines', 266–72.

summer of 1742, the revival was a spent force and both William McCulloch and James Robe were left with the responsibility of supervising and mentoring their new converts. Throughout the remainder of the 1740s, Scotland figured only intermittently in the wider revival. However, both McCulloch and Robe maintained a fruitful correspondence with some of their fellow revivalists in the British Isles and the American colonies, and it was among Scottish Presbyterians that Jonathan Edwards's plan for a 'Concert for Prayer', an international prayer network aimed at regenerating the revival and promoting evangelical unity, was most enthusiastically welcomed in 1747.[72]

Of the other countries that experienced indigenous religious awakenings only Ireland occasionally came to the attention of the international evangelical community.[73] Part of the explanation for Ireland's lack of prominence was the absence of enthusiasm with which Whitefield had been met on his first visit to the country in November 1738 as he returned to England from Georgia.[74] Whitefield's apparent failure to make much of an impression on the Irish in 1738 left the way wide open for Wesley and the Moravians. Wesley first visited in 1747 and subsequently made it an integral part of his regular tours, visiting roughly every other year and in 1748 he made it a separate circuit altogether. But of all the evangelical groups it was the Moravians who made perhaps the most significant impact in Ireland. John Cennick arrived in Ireland in 1746, after seceding from Whitefield's Calvinistic Methodists in 1745, and was instrumental in founding a number of important Moravian settlements in Dublin and the north of Ireland before his untimely death in 1755.[75] By this stage the Calvinistic communications network had atrophied to such an extent that the dissemination of news of fresh awakenings became

---

[72] Jonathan Edwards's plan for an international prayer network was outlined in a sermon published in 1748 as *A Humble Attempt to Promote Explicit Agreement and Visible Union of God's People in Extraordinary Prayer for the Revival of Religion and the Advancement of Christ's Kingdom on Earth.* See Fawcett, *The Cambuslang Revival*, pp. 210–35 and Marsden, *Jonathan Edwards*, pp. 333–40.

[73] David Hempton, 'Noisy Methodists and pious Protestants: evangelical revival and religious minorities in eighteenth-century Ireland', in George A. Rawlyk and Mark A. Noll (eds), *Amazing Grace: Evangelicalism in Australia, Britain, Canada, and the United States* (Grand Rapids, 1993), pp. 56–72 and David Hempton and Myrtle Hill, *Evangelical Protestantism in Ulster Society, 1740–1890* (London, 1992).

[74] Murray (ed.), *George Whitefield's Journals*, pp. 180–5.

[75] See *BDEB*, p. 210 and J. H. Cooper (ed.), *Extracts from the Journals of John Cennick: Moravian Evangelist* (Glengormley, 1996).

much slower, and for many Methodists, including those in Wales, news almost dried up altogether.

THE TAP ROOTS OF THE WELSH METHODIST REVIVAL

The use of the term 'evangelical revival' can be misleading, disguising as it does the sheer complexity of the early development of evangelicalism during the middle years of the eighteenth century. The upsurge of enthusiastic evangelical activity is notoriously difficult to define with precision chiefly because, as John Walsh has argued, in its first years it was 'more an attitude of mind than a considered plan of campaign'.[76] This problem of definition is made all the more difficult by the proliferation of terms used in reference to the revival. The movement that we know as the evangelical revival was called different things in different countries. From the broader perspective of the general history of Protestantism, the revival was just one aspect of the development of what later became known as evangelicalism. To confuse matters still further, evangelicalism itself does not fit easily into any of the models that have traditionally been used to define it. David Bebbington's fourfold definition, while not ideal, interpreting as it does the movement in terms of four broad distinctive themes, rather than in more narrowly defined theological or denominational terms, remains perhaps the most widely accepted.[77] Although not the exclusive preserve of evangelicals, biblicism, crucicentrism, conversionism and activism, when amalgamated, indicate the emergence of a new force within the religious life of many of the countries of western Europe and the American colonies. Furthermore, in the middle years of the eighteenth century, the distinction between evangelicalism and the evangelical revival was far from clear. Later in the century, evangelicalism was represented by a wide variety of groups and sects. In essence, evangelicalism became the basic underlying doctrinal and spiritual paradigm of groups as diverse as the Methodists, the Congregationalists and the Baptists, as

---

[76] John Walsh, 'Origins of the evangelical revival', in G. V. Bennett and John Walsh (eds), *Essays in Modern Church History: In Memory of Norman Sykes* (London, 1966), p. 161.
[77] Bebbington, *Evangelicalism*, pp. 1–19.

well as of some Anglicans and some Presbyterians, particularly in Scotland. In Wales, for example, evangelicalism and Methodism were not synonymous terms. There were many evangelicals who, though deeply influenced by the first generation of Methodist revivalists, strenuously avoided being labelled Methodists.

The emergence of a series of localized but unavoidably related awakenings during the middle years of the eighteenth century raises a number of important questions for the historian of the evangelical revival. Not the least of these is why a number of individuals, mainly within various Established Churches, turned to evangelical religion when they did and whether conditions in each of the countries in which evangelicalism took root were similarly conducive to its growth.[78] Questions relating to the origins and causes of the evangelical revival have been relevant ever since Élie Halévy[79] argued that the Methodist revival in England was little more than the re-emergence of a residual Puritanism. But it was John Walsh, in his landmark essay on the origins of the evangelical revival, who forced all subsequent historians of the early years of the revival to take the question of origins more seriously.[80] He suggested that there were, broadly speaking, three tap roots which led to the growth and success of evangelical religion, and that these tap roots were present, to a greater or lesser degree, in all of the communities in which the revival initially found such an enthusiastic response. He argued that the evangelical revival in England was a reaction against eighteenth-century rationalism, a revolt against the austerities of High Church piety and, echoing Halévy, a revival of a latent Puritan spirituality.[81] Significantly, he concluded that any discussion of the origins of Methodism that placed more stress on one or other of these tap roots was bound to lead to an unbalanced interpretation. What becomes clear is that rather than being a reaction to, or a protest against, wider intellectual or spiritual developments, evangelicalism was a movement that drew deeply from its Puritan, High Church and rational milieu and that, in the case of the Welsh revival, there was

---

[78] Walsh, 'Origins of the evangelical revival', p. 133.
[79] Élie Halévy's 'The birth of Methodism in England' was first published in French in 1909. For a translation and critical analysis of the work see É. Halévy, *The Birth of Methodism in England* (Chicago, 1971). See also John Walsh, 'Élie Halévy, and the birth of Methodism', *Transactions of the Royal Historical Society*, 25 (1975), 1–20.
[80] Walsh, 'Origins of the evangelical revival', pp. 132–62.
[81] Ibid., p. 138.

a large measure of continuity between the events of the mid-1730s and the developments that immediately preceded them.

The birth of Protestantism in Germany in 1517 was an event that sent shock waves throughout Europe and subsequently much further afield. The introduction of Protestantism to Wales occurred in the wake of its establishment by royal decree in England, and its success or failure was inextricably linked to the policies being pursued in London. Welsh Protestantism in the sixteenth century was something imported by a small band of highly committed Welshmen and was only later indigenized. Whilst the initiators of their own independent awakening, the Methodists were likewise reliant upon the support, in both direct and less obvious ways, of their international evangelical co-religionists. This pattern had been one of the defining characteristics of Welsh Protestantism since its beginning, and the emergence of the evangelical revival in the mid-1730s was in many senses the culmination of the previous two centuries of reforming and Puritan evangelization.[82]

Henry VIII's assumption of supremacy over the Church of England initially had very little impact in Wales. To the deeply conservative Welsh, Protestantism was the *ffydd saeson*, which had been imposed from without in a language and idiom that were entirely foreign. The first generation of Welsh Protestants, realizing that their newly discovered faith was perceived as being an alien imposition, recognized that it had to be presented to the Welsh people in Welsh dress.[83] They therefore rewrote the religious history of Wales and attempted to depict the Reformation as a movement that was intended to recapture earlier and purer forms of Welsh Christianity.[84] Alongside this they embarked on a policy of Cymricizing the basic texts of the Protestant faith. This was a policy championed most fervently by William Salesbury (?1520–?84)[85] and one that came to fruition with the publication of a magisterial Welsh translation of the

[82]   Glanmor Williams, 'Wales and the Reformation', in Williams, *Welsh Reformation Essays*, p. 30.
[83]   Ibid., pp. 23–4.
[84]   Glanmor Williams, 'Fire on Cambria's altar: the Welsh and their religion', in Glanmor Williams, *The Welsh and their Religion: Historical Essays* (Cardiff, 1991), pp. 35–7 and Glanmor Williams, *Reformation Views of Church History* (London, 1970).
[85]   R. Brinley Jones, *William Salesbury* (Cardiff, 1994) and Glanmor Williams, *Wales and the Reformation* (Cardiff, 1997), pp. 235–46.

entire Bible by William Morgan (?1545–1604), under the direct sponsorship of Elizabeth I, in 1588.[86] By 1603 the fortunes of the Church in Wales had been inseparably linked to those of its English counterpart and thereby allied to the fortunes of the Protestant enterprise throughout Europe.[87]

Christopher Hill has persuasively demonstrated how the influence of London grew increasingly pervasive throughout much of England and Wales during the century between the beginning of the Reformation and the outbreak of the Civil War.[88] In Wales metropolitan influences gained a firmer foothold.[89] When attempting to secure the evangelization of his fellow countrymen, John Penry (1563–93) had looked to London, and to Queen Elizabeth in particular, to give the lead in the Protestantization of the Welsh by making provision for a group of godly preachers and evangelists – an expectation that was to recur frequently from the majority of the small band of Welsh Puritans.[90] By the 1640s some Welsh Puritans, recognizing the magnitude of the task that they still faced, turned to petitioning Parliament still more zealously. Walter Cradock, in particular, made the precarious position of Protestanism in Wales abundantly clear when he preached before the House of Commons in July 1646.[91] When Parliament passed the Act for the Better Propagation of the Gospel in Wales in February 1650,[92] many Welsh Puritans felt that their hitherto largely unrewarded labours had at last received a measure of recognition. The Act proposed that each Welsh county should

[86]   Glanmor Williams, 'Bishop William Morgan and the first Welsh Bible', in Williams, *The Welsh and their Religion*, pp. 173–229 and J. Gwynfor Jones, 'Bishop William Morgan: defender of Church and faith', *Journal of Welsh Ecclesiastical History*, 5 (1988), 1–30.

[87]   Glanmor Williams, *Renewal and Reformation: Wales, c.1415–1642* (Oxford, 1987), p. 402.

[88]   Christopher Hill, 'Puritans and the "dark corners of the land" ', in Christopher Hill (ed.), *Change and Continuity in Seventeenth Century England* (London, 1974), p. 34.

[89]   See for example P. R. Roberts, 'The Union with England and the identity of "Anglican" Wales', *Transactions of the Royal Historical Society*, 22 (1972), 49–70 and Peter Roberts, 'Tudor Wales, national identity and the British inheritance', in Brendan Bradshaw and Peter Roberts (eds), *British Consciousness and Identity: The Making of Britain, 1533–1707* (Cambridge, 1998), pp. 8–42.

[90]   J. G. Jones, 'John Penry: government, order and the "perishing souls" of Wales', *Transactions of the Honourable Society of Cymmrodorion* (1993), 47–81.

[91]   Hill, 'Puritans and the "dark corners of the land" ', p. 34.

[92]   See Geraint H. Jenkins, *Protestant Dissenters in Wales, 1639–1689* (Cardiff, 1992), pp. 17–23 and Christopher Hill, 'Propagating the Gospel', in H. E. Bell and R. L. Ollard (eds), *Historical Essays, 1600–1750: Presented to David Ogg* (London, 1963), pp. 35–59.

have its own company of itinerant preachers and a body of commissioners was established which had the power to examine existing ministers and to dismiss those who were deemed less than orthodox. In reality, the Act promised far more than it actually delivered and after its initial three years on the statute book had passed it was not renewed. What is significant about these developments though, especially in the light of the later development of evangelicalism in Wales, is that much of the 'official' evangelistic activity undertaken by the Welsh Puritans emanated from London and was carried out with the backing of Parliament. The Welsh Puritans were acutely aware that without assistance from central government and the major centres of English Puritan strength, their work would only be marginally successful. Consequently, much of the Puritan activity in Wales was highly centralized and pervaded by an intensely Anglo-centric atmosphere, characteristics that largely account for its limited appeal and apparent failure.

Yet despite owing much to the wider Puritan community, 'the hotter sorts of Protestants' in Wales also had their own distinct emphases which they bequeathed to later generations of Welsh Protestants and particularly to the evangelicals. R. Tudur Jones has singled out two Welsh Puritans who, in his opinion, contributed decisively to the development of a distinctively Welsh Protestant spirituality.[93] Vavasor Powell (1617–70) was an early exponent of 'heart religion' and had championed the use of the cell group in which believers could meet in order to share and discuss together God's dealings with their souls. Morgan Llwyd (1619–59) took many of Powell's emphases a number of steps further. Heavily influenced by the writings of the German mystic Jakob Böhme (1575–1624), Llwyd, not unlike Powell, stressed that every person 'must seek God in his own heart'.[94] Though many of his Pietistic emphases meant that he eventually became more closely associated with the Quakers, Llwyd's stress on a direct confrontation with God in the inner recesses of one's personality was a direct precursor of the type of highly

---

[93]   R. Tudur Jones, 'The healing herb and the rose of love: the piety of two Welsh Puritans', in R. B. Knox (ed.), *Reformation, Conformity and Dissent: Essays in Honour of Geoffrey Nuttall* (London, 1977), pp. 154–79.
[94]   Ibid., p. 166.

individualistic spirituality championed by the evangelicals in the eighteenth century.[95]

The spirituality of many of the Welsh Puritans was characterized by an intensely affective experimental Calvinism. The Welsh Methodists built on this foundation, marrying traditional Calvinistic theology to profound and exciting charismatic experiences. Howel Harris in particular was aware of the debt that he owed to the Puritans and, when faced with accusations of deviance from orthodox Christianity, took immense pleasure in acknowledging his reliance on the writing of the 'good old orthodox Reformers and Puritans'.[96] The Welsh Puritans had developed still further the spiritual relationship that existed between England and Wales. To the Puritans, national boundaries held little significance when compared to the overriding importance of the onward march of the Kingdom of God. The Methodists stood four-square behind this tradition, confidently maintaining their Welshness while at the same time drawing upon the energies of their neighbouring revivalists in England and thereby placing themselves at the very centre of a revival that was genuinely international in its scope and ambitions.[97]

Evangelicalism in Wales also drew heavily on the second of John Walsh's three tap roots, High Church piety. By 1660, Protestantism had been the official faith of the Welsh for well over a century, and while the Welsh were not particularly enthusiastic about being Protestants they were certainly no longer Catholics. To Wales's small band of radical Protestants the mass evangelization of the Welsh still seemed a distant dream. Nonetheless, many of the foundations had been diligently laid and the evangelicals were to find that the reception of their message after 1735 was made all the easier as a result of the groundwork that had already been done. The years between 1660 and 1735 have traditionally been dismissed as decades during which Protestantism in Wales was characterized by

---

[95]   Ibid., p. 178.
[96]   Trevecka 1295: Howel Harris to James Erskine (19 February 1745).
[97]   Compare Eryn M. White, 'The people called "Methodists": early Welsh Methodism and the question of identity', *Journal of Welsh Religious History* (hereafter *JWRH*), 1 (2001), 1–14 and E. Wyn James, '"The new birth of a people": Welsh language and identity and the Welsh Methodists, c. 1740–1820', in Robert Pope (ed.), *Religion and National Identity: Wales and Scotland, c. 1700–2000* (Cardiff, 2001), pp. 14–42.

lethargy and stagnation.[98] Such a conclusion disguises the degree of continuity between the progress of the Protestant faith in Wales before and after 1660. With the apparent failure of the Puritan programme after the restoration of the Stuarts in 1660,[99] despite gaining freedom to practise their religion in 1689, Non-conformists in Wales became increasingly inward-looking, preferring to focus on personal spirituality rather than embark on ambitious strategies designed to effect some form of national evangelization. This new Pietistic strain, emanating, as W. R. Ward has shown in detail, from continental Europe,[100] introduced a more patient approach to evangelism, focusing attention on educational and literary provision, forcing godly Welshmen and women to use more persuasive evangelistic techniques.[101]

The upsurge of Pietist-inspired activity in Wales occurred within the context of an Established Church that was held in affection and loyally supported by the overwhelming majority of Welsh people.[102] Its condition and effectiveness in this period have been unfairly pilloried, particularly by those historians naturally sympathetic to the evangelicalism of the Methodists.[103] In reality, the spirituality of the Church in England and Wales, according to John Spurr, was 'far from tepid';[104] many clergy-men were doing a fairly conscientious job in very disadvan-tageous circumstances. They were not completely incompetent, and some of the bishops, though often neither Welsh nor Welsh-speaking, seemed, on the surface at least, to be genuinely committed to their duties. A similar situation prevailed among

---

[98] Geraint H. Jenkins, *Literature, Religion and Society in Wales, 1660–1730* (Cardiff, 1978), pp. 305–9.

[99] For the Welsh response to the Restoration see Jenkins, *Protestant Dissenters in Wales*, pp. 39–56 and Craig D. Wood, 'The Welsh response to the Glorious Revolution of 1688', *JWRH*, 1 (2001), 15–33.

[100] See Ward, *The Protestant Evangelical Awakening*, passim and below, pp. 17–21.

[101] Rack, 'Religious societies and the origins of Methodism', 589–90.

[102] Eryn M. White, 'The Established Church, Dissent and the Welsh language c. 1660–1811', in Geraint H. Jenkins (ed.), *The Welsh Language before the Industrial Revolution* (Cardiff, 1997), p. 236.

[103] For contemporary examples of this tendency see Eifion Evans, 'Spirituality before the Great Awakening: the personal devotion of Griffith Jones, Llanddowror', in Eifion Evans, *Fire in the Thatch: The True Nature of Religious Revival* (Bridgend, 1996), pp. 57–74; Evans, *Daniel Rowland*, pp. 9–17; and, from an English perspective, Dallimore, *George Whitefield*, I, pp. 19–32.

[104] See for example John Spurr, 'The Church, the societies and the moral revolution of 1688', in John Walsh, Colin Haydon and Stephen Taylor (eds), *The Church of England c.1689–c.1833: From Toleration to Tractarianism* (Cambridge, 1993), pp. 127–42.

the ordinary parochial clergy who, despite their poverty, preached regularly[105] and, more often than not, conducted their services in the language of the majority of their parishioners.[106] One of the most remarkable developments in the Established Church in Wales during these years was the notable revival in preaching that occurred. Sermons became a more important part of worship and were delivered more frequently.[107] Characterized by plainness of style, they were invariably pastoral in their application and born of an increasing desire among the laity for some of the agencies of popular piety. By the eve of the Methodist revival, the general rule in rural areas was for sermons to be preached on at least alternate Sundays.[108] A healthy awareness of the many weaknesses of the Established Church in the years preceding the birth of Methodism in Wales should not prevent us from accepting that for the overwhelming majority of Welsh people the Church was their natural spiritual home[109] and, for the godly, it remained the most advantageous platform from which to launch an effective evangelistic campaign. It was this fact, perhaps, more than any other that accounted for the Methodists' dogged determination to remain loyal to the Church throughout the eighteenth century.

Between 1660 and 1730, the initiative for the evangelization of the Welsh therefore came from within the Church itself. It owed its success to a small group of London-based Welshmen who had been deeply influenced by Pietistic theology. Through their inspirational activity the Welsh people benefited from a wide-ranging programme of educational and literary reform. The Welsh Trust was founded by Thomas Gouge (?1605–81) in 1674. Though not a Welshman himself, he looked upon Wales as a mission field and its people as ripe for the Gospel.[110] He set about his evangelistic mission by using the Trust to establish

[105] Jenkins, *Literature, Religion and Society in Wales*, p. 12.
[106] White, 'The Established Church, Dissent and the Welsh language', p. 269.
[107] Jenkins, *Literature, Religion and Society in Wales*, p. 12.
[108] Jenkins, *The Foundations of Modern Wales*, p. 181.
[109] Philip Jenkins, 'Church, nation and language: the Welsh Church, 1660–1800', in Jeremy Gregory and Jeffrey S. Chamberlain (eds), *The National Church in Local Perspective: The Church of England and the Regions, 1660–1800* (Woodbridge, 2003), pp. 83–4.
[110] Eryn M. White, 'Popular schooling and the Welsh language', pp. 318–20; M. G. Jones, *The Charity School Movement: A Study of Eighteenth Century Puritanism in Action* (Cambridge, 1938), pp. 277–89.

charity schools and circulate godly literature. By the autumn of 1675 over 2,225 children[111] had passed through the doors of the Trust's schools. Despite this, the active life of the schools was relatively short, as they unbendingly stuck to their policy of providing education exclusively through the medium of English, even in monoglot Welsh-speaking areas. Their attempts at providing pious literature were somewhat more successful. Stephen Hughes (1622–88)[112] ensured that a new edition of the Welsh New Testament was published, followed by an edition of the whole Bible in 1678. They were supplemented by the reprinting of numerous Pietist and Puritan devotional works, including the writings of John Bunyan, as well as works by indigenous Welsh writers like Vicar Rhys Prichard (?1579–1644) and Lewis Bayly (d. 1631).[113] In 1678 alone, the Welsh Trust was responsible for circulating 5,185 books[114] among Welsh readers, and its activities represented the first coordinated attempt in this period to raise the moral and spiritual fortunes of the Welsh people. The Trust was also successful in consolidating the spiritual link between England and Wales still further and setting the agenda for what was by far the most successful Pietistic venture in Wales, the Society for Promoting Christian Knowledge (SPCK).

The SPCK was founded in 1699[115] and, like the Welsh Trust, concerned itself with the twin objectives of setting up schools and publishing godly literature. Between 1699 and 1740 the society established ninety-six schools in Wales, sixty-eight of which were opened in the years up to 1715.[116] Like the Welsh Trust before it, the SPCK's schools also resolutely stuck to using English as the only language of instruction and so, despite admirably attempting to redress what the Society regarded as the Welsh people's

---

[111] Jenkins, *The Foundations of Modern Wales*, p. 199.
[112] See 'Apostol Sir Gaerfyrddin: Stephen Hughes, c. 1622–1688', in Geraint H. Jenkins, *Cadw Tŷ Mewn Cwmwl Tystion: Ysgrifau Hanesyddol ar Grefydd a Diwylliant* (Llandysul, 1990), pp. 1–28.
[113] See J. Gwynfor Jones, 'Some Puritan influences on the Anglican Church in Wales in the early seventeenth century', *JWRH*, 2 (2002), 25–6, 30–3 and 35–43.
[114] Jenkins, *The Foundations of Modern Wales*, p. 199.
[115] Jones, *The Charity School Movement*, pp. 36–109; Eamon Duffy, 'The long Reformation: Catholicism, Protestantism and the multitude', in Nicholas Tyacke (ed.), *England's Long Reformation, 1500–1800* (London, 1998), pp. 55–70; Craig Rose, 'The origins and ideals of the SPCK, 1699–1716', in Walsh, Haydon and Taylor (eds), *The Church of England*, pp. 127–42; Mary Clement, *The S.P.C.K. and Wales, 1699–1740* (London, 1954); White, 'Popular schooling and the Welsh language', pp. 320–4.
[116] White, 'Popular schooling and the Welsh language', p. 320.

indifference and immorality, born of the lack of an integrated system of popular education, the success of its schools was inevitably limited. The SPCK's most enduring legacy, however, was its ambitious programme of printing and distributing godly literature. Between 1546 and 1660, only 108 books had been published in Welsh, a figure that contrasted sharply with the 545 books that were published, largely at the instigation of the SPCK, between 1660 and 1730.[117] Perhaps its greatest single achievement was the publication of 10,000 copies of a new edition of the Welsh Bible in 1718, produced under the supervision of Moses Williams (1685–1742).[118] Of the religious books published by the Society, almost all of them concentrated on theological and devotional themes that stressed subjective, inward religion, self-examination and the highest standards of holy living, themes that characterized much of the popular devotional literature of the day and contributed to the sense of depressed failure that paralysed so many of those who eventually found evangelicalism to be such a liberating release from the stringencies of High Church piety.[119] When taken together with the activity of the Welsh Trust, the work of the SPCK contributed substantially to the development of the religious life of Wales. It was during these decades that Wales began to make the transition from being an oral-based to a print culture.[120] In the slightly longer term this activity, particularly the reprinting of bibles and devotional works, carried on the work that had been commenced by the early Welsh Protestants, but it also laid the foundations for the mass evangelization of the Welsh that was to make its first major impact with the Methodist revival in 1735 and culminate in the middle years of the nineteenth century.

While much of the activity carried out by Pietist-influenced individuals in this period occurred within the Established Church, the Dissenters were no mere bystanders. In the same way as the history of the Established Church between 1660 and

---

[117] Jenkins, *Literature, Religion and Society in Wales*, p. 34.
[118] *DWB*, p. 1060 and Meic Stephens (ed.), *The New Companion to the Literature of Wales* (Cardiff, 1998), p. 799.
[119] Walsh, ' "Methodism" and the origins of English-speaking evangelicalism', pp. 25–6.
[120] Richard Suggett and Eryn White, 'Language, literacy and aspects of identity in early modern Wales', in Adam Fox and Daniel Woolf (eds), *The Spoken Word: Oral Culture in Britain, 1500–1800* (Manchester, 2002), pp. 67–77.

1730 has been misrepresented, so the Dissenters have been practically written off as lacklustre and largely ineffective.[121] Though it would be true to say that the Dissenters in general were not as energetic as they had been prior to the Restoration, they were not entirely inactive either, having entered on a period of quiet, inward-looking consolidation after having achieved toleration in 1689. Their numbers grew markedly in these years. For example, in 1676 the 'Compton Census' recorded that there were 4,248 members in Dissenting congregations in Wales,[122] a figure that had grown by 1718 to 17,779 in eighty-nine individual congregations.[123] It is likely that these figures disguise the actual numbers of attendees at Dissenting meeting houses in these years as they do not include the large number of adherents and casual listeners who also usually attended. Whilst naturally cautious about active involvement with Anglican religious societies like the SPCK, the Society for the Propagation of the Gospel (SPG) and the Society for the Reformation of Manners (SRM), the Dissenters profited indirectly from many of their achievements. Their heavily word-orientated congregations benefited from the increase in the levels of basic literacy, and the inexpensive publication of numerous theological and devotional books made the discharge of their pastoral responsibilities far easier. The culture of the Dissenting meeting house in these interim years was characterized by earnestness and simplicity, with the Scriptures placed firmly at the centre of all their activities. Sermons were usually warm and lively occasions calculated to bring about the conversion of sinners and the edification of saints. Despite obvious signs of life, it is still true to say that the Dissenters had lost some of the vitality and vigour that had ensured their survival during the decades of repressive and restrictive government legislation. The direct descendants of the Welsh Puritans therefore required revival and reinvigoration rather than a root-and-branch reformation like their rivals in the Anglican Church.

---

[121]   For instances of the low esteem in which the Dissenters in Wales were held in these years see Derec Llwyd Morgan, *The Great Awakening in Wales* (London, 1988), pp. 3–4, and Jenkins, *Literature, Religion and Society in Wales*, pp. 308–9. Also useful is Michael Watts, *The Dissenters, I: From the Reformation to the French Revolution* (Oxford, 1978), pp. 438–45.

[122]   Jenkins, *The Foundations of Modern Wales*, p. 192.

[123]   Ibid., p. 195.

The single most important link between the Pietistic spirituality of these years and the pioneers of the Methodist revival was Griffith Jones (1683–1761), Llanddowror.[124] Jones, an Anglican clergyman in southern Carmarthenshire, was largely responsible for passing on many of the practices that were to become some of the distinguishing features of Welsh Methodism and of evangelicalism more generally. In 1713 he had led a small-scale local awakening at Laugharne when he experimented successfully with preaching in the open air, attracting large and enthusiastic crowds. Alongside his work as a clergyman, Jones's greatest contribution lay in his foundation of a system of Circulating Schools. Although he had enthusiastically supported the educational work of the SPCK, Jones recognized the inadequacy of the English-language-based educational system which it had attempted to implement in Wales. Jones's schools were tailored to suit the specific educational requirements of his parishioners, meeting in the evenings and at times of the year when the agricultural community was not at full stretch. They were designed with relatively modest aims, to teach people of all ages to read in Welsh; writing came later. They used the most readily available texts, most importantly the Bible and the Prayer Book as well as a few devotional works like Lewis Bayly's *The Practice of Piety* (1611). Jones set up his first school in 1731, and by his death in 1761 3,325 schools had been established and at least 250,000 students had passed through their doors.[125] From the perspective of the beginnings of the Welsh Methodist revival, Griffith Jones's schools provided a literate constituency, conditioned to accept with a greater measure of understanding than ever before the Bible-orientated religion which the evangelicals had to offer.

The years between 1660 and 1730 laid the foundations for the subsequently more rapid development of Protestantism in Wales. The spiritual, educational and literary advances of the period were the context in which the early pioneers of the Welsh revival were nurtured. They were years when Welsh Protestantism was dragged further into the mainstream of English and European

---

[124] *DWB*, pp. 463–4; Geraint H. Jenkins, ' "An old and much honoured soldier": Griffith Jones, Llanddowror', *Welsh History Review* (hereafter *WHR*), 11 (1983); F. A. Cavanagh, *The Life and Work of Griffith Jones of Llanddowror* (Cardiff, 1930); Glanmor Williams, 'Religion, language and the circulating schools', Glanmor Williams, *Religion, Language and Nationality in Wales* (Cardiff, 1979), pp. 200–16.
[125] Jenkins, *The Foundations of Modern Wales*, p. 377.

Protestant developments as the impact of the persecution and migration of Protestants from all parts of Europe touched Wales through the higher profile that these migrations afforded Pietistic theology. In Wales, the London-based religious societies became the conduit through which Pietistic spirituality found a willing response, and the Welsh became beneficiaries of an unprecedented amount of educational and literary provision that brought the central themes of Protestantism to a far wider audience than ever before. Geraint H. Jenkins has argued that the period witnessed a number of 'seminal factors at work . . . which helped to nourish the religious, educational and cultural revivals of the eighteenth century'.[126] However, these factors did not, in themselves, lead directly to the evangelical revival. They were preparatory factors, but no more. What was required, as John Walsh has pointed out, was a catalyst that would, taking advantage of these developments, ignite the flames of revival.[127]

That catalyst duly arrived in the life-changing conversion experiences that a number of individuals passed through in 1735, firstly in Wales and then in England. These immediate experiences of God's grace were the single most significant motivating factor turning otherwise relatively insignificant individuals into national revivalists. This stress on the significance of the conversion experience tallies neatly with the third of John Walsh's tap roots – the influence of rationalism and the Enlightenment. Traditionally, it has been assumed that evangelicalism, with its stress on non-rational experience, was the antithesis of the cool dispassionate rationalism of the Enlightenment, to which it emerged as a reaction.[128] Yet, in reality the relation between the two was far more complex. Evangelicalism was, by its very nature, deeply imbued with the spirit of the Enlightenment.

The evangelical stress on the centrality of the Bible, the atoning death of Christ and the necessity of individual conversion was not unique. What was innovative was the stress on activity, a focus which marked the evangelicals out from their most immediate and closest spiritual predecessors, the

---

[126] Ibid., p. 212.
[127] See Walsh, ' "Methodism" and the origins of English-speaking evangelicalism', p. 21.
[128] See Bebbington, *Evangelicalism in Modern Britain*, p. 51.

Puritans.[129] Whereas the Puritans devoted much of their attention to the internal struggles of the Christian life and to ensuring that the believer was indeed numbered among the elect, the evangelicals, imbued with considerably more confidence and self-belief, turned their attention to the far wider concerns of evangelism and mission. According to David Bebbington, this change of emphasis was the result of a massive epistemological change in attitude to the way in which an individual could know and experience God.[130] Evangelicals were utterly convinced that they had been the recipients of God's grace and favour because they could adduce bona fide evidence in support of their claims.

This development stemmed directly from Enlightenment notions of rationality. Among the evangelicals it was Jonathan Edwards who did most to marry the empiricism of the Enlightenment with enthusiastic religion. Edwards was influenced by the epistemology of John Locke who, in his *Essay Concerning Human Understanding* (1690), had dismissed the concept of innate ideas and had argued that reason was dependent on ideas drawn from the senses,[131] a theory which located the source of true knowledge within the realm of experience.[132] Edwards christianized much of Locke's epistemology and argued that individuals could receive a definite assurance regarding spiritual matters through a 'new sense',[133] whereby the Holy Spirit created 'a new inward perception or sensation'[134] in the mind of each converted person.[135] Each individual's joy and confidence therefore came to be based upon the degree to which he or she possessed and enjoyed assurance of salvation. According to Jonathan Edwards, such assurance was warranted only if an

---

[129] David W. Bebbington, 'Revival and enlightenment in eighteenth-century England', in Edith L. Blumhofer and Randall Balmer (eds), *Modern Christian Revivals* (Chicago, 1993), pp. 21–2.

[130] Ibid., p. 22.

[131] Maurice Wiles, *Archetypal Heresy: Arianism through the Centuries* (Oxford, 1996), p. 70.

[132] See also Iain McCalman (ed.), *An Oxford Companion to the Romantic Age: British Culture, 1776–1832* (Oxford, 1999), pp. 585–6 and Roy Porter, *Enlightenment: Britain and the Creation of the Modern World* (Oxford, 2000), pp. 60–71.

[133] Bebbington, *Evangelicalism in Modern Britain*, pp. 47–8.

[134] Ibid,. p. 48.

[135] For more on Edwards's debt to John Locke see Marsden, *Jonathan Edwards*, pp. 60–4; Norman Fiering, 'The rationalist foundations of Jonathan Edwards's metaphysics', in Nathan O. Hatch and Harry S. Stout (eds), *Jonathan Edwards and the American Experience* (New York, 1988), pp. 73–7 and Leon Chai, *Jonathan Edwards and the Limits of Enlightenment Philosophy* (New York, 1998).

individual could confidently pass the tests that he had deduced from Scripture and outlined in his revival manifesto, *The Distinguishing Mark of a Work of the Spirit of God* (1741),[136] and which he regarded as infallible indicators of genuine Christian experience. Practically, this development led to a complete change of emphasis and enabled evangelicals to argue that true Christianity was not to be characterized by morbid introspection and protracted soul-searching but by confidence, joy, security and an outward-looking evangelistic concern for the spiritual well-being of one's neighbours. The relationship between the Enlightenment and evangelicalism was therefore not entirely negative, as the Enlightenment, in its English guise at least, was not an exclusively secular and irreligious movement.[137]

In Wales, the conversions of Howel Harris and Daniel Rowland in 1735 sparked the revival. They occurred against the backdrop of considerable unease within Protestantism and were the result of the accumulated influence of Puritan spirituality, a reaction against the rigid austerities of aspects of the extremely popular strain of High Church piety and the rationality of the Enlightenment. Like the awakenings that occurred in other countries, the Welsh Methodist Revival drew its inspiration from those same springs and emerged in response to the sense of crisis pervading European Protestants who felt that their future was bleak. This tangible sense of crisis largely explains why, in 1735, Harris and Rowland, together with George Whitefield in England, turned to evangelical religion, and, from the sense of release that they discovered within its deeply emotional spiritual experiences, they also turned to spread that message as widely as they could, employing every technique which they could realistically utilize.

THE PROBLEM OF THE 'METHODIST VIEW OF HISTORY'

When Christopher Hill, in reference to the writing of sixteenth- and seventeenth-century English religious history, talked about

[136] For a critical edition see Goen (ed.), *The Works of Jonathan Edwards*, IV, pp. 214–88.
[137] Martin Fitzpatrick, 'Enlightenment', in McCalman (ed.), *The Oxford Companion to the Romantic Age*, p. 300.

the problem of too many predecessors,[138] he could equally well have been talking about the evangelical revival. Every student of Methodism in Wales has to grapple with some of the entrenched opinions that have prevented it from being subjected to the critical scrutiny that is its due. Approaching the study of the Welsh Methodist revival with the assumption that it was an event of international significance and an important part of the wider development of international Protestantism remains a novelty. Primarily in reference to English Wesleyan Methodism, John Walsh has commented that until relatively recently the evangelical awakenings of the 1730s and 1740s were treated in 'splendid isolation – as disparate movements, with their own principles of momentum, geographically contained by the bounds of a region or state'.[139] Perhaps in no case has this criticism been more appropriate than with reference to the Welsh revival, which has been bedevilled by denominational and hagiographical studies.[140]

Traditionally, much of the historiography of the Welsh Methodist revival has been content to stress the uniqueness of the Welsh experience of the evangelical revival. Whilst there has been some recognition of the simultaneous existence of renewal movements in other countries, there has been a spectacular failure to realize that some sort of relationship must have existed between them. Welsh Methodist historiography has until comparatively recently been dominated by the all-pervasive 'Methodist view of history'. It originated with the Welsh revival's chief apologist, William Williams, Pantycelyn, who, after the initial excitement of the revival had abated, began to construct a distinctively 'Methodist' interpretation of both recent events and of the more distant past, in much the same way as Jonathan Edwards had done for the colonial awakening. His interpretation gained in popularity as Calvinistic Methodism became more permanent and made the transition from being just a faction within the Established Church to become Wales's largest religious

[138] Christopher Hill, 'History and denominational history', in Christopher Hill, *The Collected Essays of Christopher Hill, II: Religion and Politics in Seventeenth Century England* (Brighton, 1986), p. 3.
[139] Walsh, 'Methodism and the origins of English-speaking evangelicalism', p. 19.
[140] Jenkins, *Protestant Dissenters in Wales*, pp. 1–8. For a comparison with similar developments in the historiography of the Great Awakening see Allen C. Guelzo, 'God's designs: the literature of the colonial revivals of religion, 1735–1760', in Harry S. Stout and D. G. Hart (eds), *New Directions in American Religious History* (New York, 1997), pp. 141–72.

denomination in the nineteenth century.[141] In the present century, those evangelical historians who regard themselves as the direct spiritual heirs of the Calvinistic Methodists have also done their utmost to perpetuate it.[142]

There were two main strands in William Williams's view of history. Firstly, he argued that the beginning of the Welsh revival in 1735 was akin to the dawning of a new day after a long, dark and cold winter's night. In other words, before 1735 Wales was trapped in spiritual darkness, a darkness which was only dispelled by the clarion call of Howel Harris and Daniel Rowland. In *Atteb Philo-Evangelius* (1763), he used the contrasting metaphors of darkness and light in order to convey something of Harris's and Rowland's impact. He wrote that before 1738, 'Ignorance covered the face of Wales, hardly any Gospel privilege could stand against the corruptions of the day, until about 1738 light broke forth as the dawn in many parts of the world . . . and O wonderful morning! The Sun shone on Wales.'[143] Williams clearly adopted a cyclical view of Church history and argued, as Jonathan Edwards had done in his posthumously published sermons, *A History of the Work of Redemption* (1774),[144] that the sun which had shone so brightly on the apostolic Church had faded dramatically over subsequent centuries and had only been kept alight by radical sects like the Waldensians, the Albigensians and the Lollards in England. Since the Reformation the cycles had been completed far more frequently and the emergence of the evangelicals and the Methodists seemed to so many of their number to be like yet another new dawn for the Kingdom of God.

---

[141] Some of the most influential nineteenth-century works that reinforced the 'Methodist view of history' include John Hughes, *Methodistiaeth Cymru*, 3 vols (Wrecsam, 1851–6); William Williams, *Welsh Calvinistic Methodism: A Historical Sketch of the Presbyterian Church of Wales* (London, 1872); Hugh J. Hughes, *Life of Howell Harris: The Welsh Reformer* (London, 1892); J. Morgan Jones and William Morgan, *Y Tadau Methodistaidd* (Abertawe, 1895, 1897); and Beriah Gwynfe Evans, *Diwygwyr Cymru* (Caernarfon, 1900).

[142] See Evans, *Howel Harris: Evangelist*, pp. 1–4. Despite a very positive interpretation of Griffith Jones's evangelistic ministry and his work for the SPCK, Eifion Evans does not seem to think that this seriously alters the traditional interpretation of the parlous religious condition of pre-Methodist Wales. See Evans, 'Spirituality before the Great Awakening', in Evans, *Fire in the Thatch*, pp. 57–74. See also Evans, *Daniel Rowland*, pp. 9–25 and, to a lesser extent, George E. Clarkson, *George Whitefield and Welsh Calvinistic Methodism* (New York and Lampeter, 1996).

[143] English translation quoted in Evans, *Daniel Rowland*, p. 75.

[144] Marsden, *Jonathan Edwards*, pp. 193–6.

The second aspect of William Williams's view of the revival concerned the place that he accorded its international dimensions. This is an emphasis that comes increasingly to the fore in some of the elegies that he wrote to commemorate the deaths of some of the early leaders of the revival.[145] In his elegy on the death of George Whitefield, he ranged through all of the countries in which Whitefield operated, demonstrating his own intimate familiarity with many of the communities in which the revival had taken root. He wrote:

> Urania sing, let equal numbers flow,
> And trace his footsteps everywhere they go:
> . . .
> To thousand souls within the western land.
> Thro' Pennsylvania, and each country round,
> Great Philadelphia his blessed mission own'd;
> New England where the pious Boston rise
> Her stately towers to the vaulted skies:
> And Newbury, where the blessed seraph dies,
> And Caroline's, the Jersies, and Long Isle,
> And on New York, his glorious doctrines smile;
> . . .
> Old England mourn, if any love remains,
> A Gloomy grave thy WHITEFIELD now contains;
> Who once invited to the Gospel feast
> The British Isle from western shore to east;
> Wales, England, Scotland, and the Irish isle
> Should not forget that blessed man awhile . . .[146]

Williams clearly expected his readers to be as familiar with the international dimensions of the evangelical revival as he showed himself to be. His writing therefore had a definite utilitarian purpose. Through it he gave his readers a sophisticated understanding of the past that enabled them to locate themselves within the context of the illustrious history of Christianity in Wales and at the centre of a community of grace that transcended national, cultural and denominational boundaries.

---

[145] These elegies have recently been subjected to critical analysis in R. Geraint Gruffydd, 'Marwnadau William Williams Pantycelyn', *Llên Cymru*, 17 (1993), 254–71 and Cathryn Charnell-White, 'Galaru a Gwaddoli ym Marwnadau Williams Pantycelyn', *Llên Cymru*, 26 (2003), 40–62.
[146] N. Cynhafal Jones (gol.), *Gweithiau Williams Pantycelyn*, I (Treffynnon, 1887), pp. 652–9 (translated).

Subsequent historians within the Welsh Calvinistic Methodist Connexion enthusiastically subscribed to Williams's rewriting of history. They saw it as their duty to perpetuate his legacy, but in reality they took up only one aspect of his thesis – his view of the revival's origins – excluding his international perspective. By therefore distorting Williams's interpretation, they perpetuated a circumscribed view of the early years of the Welsh revival that placed it within an extremely narrow historical, cultural and national context, ignoring the wider context in which it occurred. Perhaps this is, to some extent, understandable, as the historians of religion in the mid-nineteenth century wrote from a position of strength, supremely confident in the hegemonic position that Nonconformity had attained in Welsh society. When they wrote about the events of the 1730s, they tended to portray Harris, Rowland and Williams, Pantycelyn, in semi-heroic terms, as religious pioneers acting almost alone, albeit under the direct guidance of God, against the prevailing spiritual torpor in which they found themselves. Cast in such terms, it became almost impossible to embark on any critical discussion of early Methodism and extremely difficult to set the awakening within its broader Welsh, British, evangelical and Protestant context. In order to reintegrate the Welsh Methodist revival into the wider evangelical movement it is necessary to clear away some of the prejudices of Welsh Methodist historiography before constructing a view of the awakening that does considerably more justice to its transnational and transatlantic character.

In some of the more recent work on the evangelical revival more generally, there has been greater readiness to question the traditional shibboleths of evangelical historiography. Perhaps one of the earliest to do this, as has been pointed out on a number of occasions already, was John Walsh. Focusing on the origins of the revival, a controversial subject in itself, especially amongst those evangelical historians who can only think of the revival in strictly providentialist terms, Walsh recognized that the narrowness of traditional sectarian histories presented a significant obstacle to understanding the real nature of the evangelical movement. He was particularly concerned about historians' over-preoccupation with the career of John Wesley and, by implication, with the school of thought that magnified the importance of the revival's leading personalities to the detriment of other equally significant factors. For Walsh, such histories resulted in a 'diversion of historical attention from the study of the Revival as a whole, and in particular, from the complex of influences that fed it'.[147] When he came to re-examine the subject of the origins of the revival again, almost thirty years later, he was able to reflect on the far healthier way in which the revival had come to be approached and to reiterate the indispensability of adopting both a comparative and an international approach, in addition to the current propensity to concentrate on highly localized studies.[148]

The change in the way the evangelical revival has been studied between Walsh's first and second article has been due to the pioneering work of a number of historians. In her doctoral thesis, Susan Durden[149] attempted to deconstruct the revival and examine the specific means by which the pioneer revivalists created what she imaginatively called a 'transatlantic community of saints'.[150] Her published writings on the revival are in effect an examination of methods of communication in the north Atlantic world in the middle decades of the eighteenth century. The network that the pioneer revivalists created, based on the inter-revival activities of a select band of revivalists and backed up by a vast array of correspondents and publications, combined the otherwise disparate individual awakenings and created the impression that the revival would continue to expand exponentially. Durden's work has ensured that every historian approaching any part of the revival must take account of this communications network and must do justice to the international world-view that was an ingrained feature of so many of the first-generation evangelicals.

---

[147] Walsh, 'The origins of the evangelical revival', p. 132.

[148] See for example J. D. Walsh, 'The Yorkshire evangelicals in the eighteenth century with special reference to Methodism' (Ph.D., University of Cambridge, 1956); J. Obelkevich, *Religion and Rural Society: South Lindsey, 1825–75* (Oxford, 1976); D. Luker, 'Revivalism in theory and practice: the case of Cornish Methodism', *Journal of Ecclesiastical History*, 37 (1986), 603–19; K. Leese, 'The impact of Methodism on Black Country society, 1743–1860' (Ph.D., University of Manchester, 1972); and Eryn M. White, *Praidd Bach y Bugail Mawr: Seiadau Methodistaidd De-Orllewin Cymru* (Llandysul, 1995).

[149] Susan Durden, 'Transatlantic communications and influence during the Great Awakening: a comparative study of British and American revivalism, 1730–1760' (Ph.D., University of Hull, 1978).

[150] Susan O'Brien, ' "A transatlantic community of saints" ', 811–32.

Alongside Durden's work stands that of W. R. Ward. Like Durden, Ward has been preoccupied with the wider context within which the evangelical revival first emerged and then developed. Ward, as has already been pointed out, concentrated on the role that events within European Protestantism, particularly the development of Pietism, had on the collective Protestant mentality.[151] Yet, whereas Durden was content to outline the existence and main parameters of the international communications network, Ward has gone a number of steps further by demonstrating how the creation of this network became not only possible but also absolutely necessary and even unavoidable. By locating the impetus for the revival in the crisis afflicting the European Protestant community in the 1730s, Ward has argued that the persecution and consequent migration of Pietistic Protestants led to the spread of many of the techniques that the pioneer revivalists found particularly effective in their efforts to arrest their numerical decline. Taken together with the work of Susan Durden, it is easy to see how the networks which many of these Protestant minorities had created to keep in touch with their widely scattered co-religionists could be used and copied by the evangelicals when they needed to maximize their numbers and present a position of strength and uniformity to their many detractors.

Historians have also attempted to rescue George Whitefield from the hagiographers by reassessing the vital role he played in the construction of the international revival. Frank Lambert, in his biography of Whitefield, controversially portrayed him as a religious salesman, a proto-tele-evangelist even,[152] who went about 'organising, promoting and explaining his evangelical mission'.[153] According to Lambert, Whitefield peddled his evangelistic message to the masses by using the opportunities presented to him by the burgeoning north Atlantic market that was being transformed by a consumer revolution.[154] Whitefield

---

[151] See Ward, *The Protestant Evangelical Awakening*, passim and Ward, 'Power and piety', 231–52.

[152] Frank Lambert, '*Pedlar in Divinity*', pp. 226–31.

[153] Frank Lambert, ' "Pedlar in divinity": George Whitefield and the Great Awakening, 1737–1745', *Journal of American History*, 77 (1990), 813.

[154] Neil McKendrick, 'The consumer revolution in eighteenth-century England', in Neil McKendrick, John Brewer and J. H. Plumb (eds), *The Birth of a Consumer Society: The Commercialisation of Eighteenth-Century England* (Bloomington, 1982), pp. 9–33.

was able to deploy advertising and popular print to address a mass audience and knit together disparate individuals and awakenings into a broader movement, creating a sense of collective solidarity.[155] Complementing Lambert's biography, Harry Stout has similarly argued that Whitefield was a 'religious celebrity'[156] who consciously worked at 'forging a new Anglo-American evangelical paradigm that was revival-driven, non-denominational and international in scope'.[157] For Stout, Whitefield was primarily an actor who used his celebrity status to command an audience and sustain a following that ultimately came to transcend national and denominational divisions.[158]

These three alternative approaches represent just a few of the ways in which traditional approaches to the study of the evangelical revival have been challenged and largely replaced by critical and comparative explorations of the internal dynamics of early evangelicalism and the forces that fed it. Predictably, within Welsh Methodist historiography much work still needs to be done to catch up with some of these alternative perspectives. In his brief study of Howel Harris, Geoffrey Nuttall recognized that Harris 'worked in a context, in a company, wider than "the Evangelical Revival in England and Wales"'.[159] In a sense Nuttall's attitude was typical of much that was written on Welsh Methodism in the twentieth century. Recognizing the existence of an international dimension, writers like Nuttall failed to take the next logical step and to demonstrate the interconnectedness of the various awakenings and how they fed off one another.[160]

These historians were still hampered to some extent by the all-pervasive influence of the 'Methodist view of history', which remained deeply ingrained in all those who ventured to write about Welsh Methodism until Geraint H. Jenkins published his *Literature, Religion and Society in Wales, 1660–1730* (1978).

---

[155] Lambert, ' "Pedlar in divinity" ', 837.
[156] Stout, *The Divine Dramatist*, p. xiv.
[157] Stout, 'George Whitefield in three countries', p. 58.
[158] Ibid., p. 69; Harry S. Stout, *The New England Soul: Preaching and Religious Culture in Colonial New England* (New York, 1986), pp. 189–92; Stout, *The Divine Dramatist*, pp. xix–xxiv.
[159] Nuttall, *Howell Harris*, p. 18.
[160] See also R. W. Evans, 'The eighteenth century Welsh awakening with its relationships to the contemporary English evangelical revival' (Ph.D., Edinburgh, 1956) and, to some extent, Derec Llwyd Morgan, *The Great Awakening in Wales* (London, 1988).

Jenkins has sought, almost iconoclastically, to discredit the Methodists' approach to their own history. By focusing on the years immediately preceding the revival, he has argued that an overconcentration on the events of 1735, and the lives of Howel Harris and Daniel Rowland in particular, has given rise to 'a dangerous and misleading mystique about the providentially-inspired rôle of the early Methodist leaders'.[161] The Welsh Methodist revival was a far more complex movement than its chief defenders have often been prepared to admit. It did not suddenly burst on the scene in 1735 and sweep all before it in the following decades. The early history of Welsh Methodism is a catalogue of personality clashes and infighting accompanied by fitful growth, until at least the 1762 Llangeitho revival, if not much later. The Welsh Methodist revival needs to be earthed in the context of the events that were occurring throughout society. This is why a discussion of its origins is so important. The Methodist revival did not take place in a historical vacuum but emerged during a period of momentous change when many of the foundations of modern Wales were being laid.[162] The rise in literacy rates, the rejuvenation of Dissent and the emergence of Methodism all occurred simultaneously and all fed off one another. The years between 1660 and 1730 were years of remarkable religious activity that conditioned many individuals to respond to the heart-searching and exciting message pro-claimed with such urgency by the early Methodists.[163]

If the Methodist revival is now seen as more of an evolutionary phenomenon,[164] then those evolutionary forces must also have been present in countries other than Wales, and if it is possible to trace common forces at work which gave rise to Methodism, then it must be equally logical to assume that these forces binding the various awakenings together continued to influence

---

[161] Jenkins, *Literature, Religion and Society in Wales*, p. 307.
[162] Jenkins, *The Foundations of Modern Wales*, p. vii.
[163] Jenkins, *Literature, Religion and Society in Wales*, p. 309.
[164] See White, *Praidd Bach y Bugail Mawr*. For those who do not read Welsh some of her conclusions have been summarized in '"The world, the flesh and the devil" and the early Methodist societies in south west Wales', *Transactions of the Honourable Society of Cymmrodorion*, 3 (1997), 45–61. Geraint Tudur's recently published study of Howel Harris's early career, whilst not intended to be a complete history of early Welsh Methodism, does offer some insight into the way in which Harris took advantage of some of the opportunities that participation in the wider revival offered. See Tudur, *Howell Harris*, passim.

the growth and shape that the revival eventually assumed. At the most fundamental level, the Welsh Methodist revival was an indigenous movement, deeply rooted in the peculiar characteristics of Welsh society. Yet it was also conditioned by wider evangelical developments. The origins of the revival lay in the crisis of confidence affecting the whole of western European Protestantism, and it was the discovery of the potential benefits of revivals of religion that led many pious individuals, in a variety of countries, to look for fresh outpourings of the Spirit of God in an attempt to arrest the seemingly inexorable decline in their fortunes.[165]

---

[165] See W. R. Ward, 'Was there a Methodist evangelistic strategy in the eighteenth century?', in Tyacke (ed.), *England's Long Reformation*, pp. 285–305; David Hempton, 'Established Churches and the growth of religious pluralism: a case study of Christianisation and secularisation in England since 1700', in Hugh McLeod and Werner Ustorf (eds), *The Decline of Christendom in Western Europe, 1750–2000* (Cambridge, 2003), pp. 82–90; and the analysis of the rise in popularity of revivals in Scotland first, then in America, in Schmidt, *Holy Fairs*.

II

PROMOTING THE 'COMMUNION OF SAINTS UPON EARTH'

By adopting a comparative approach to the early history of the Welsh Methodist Revival it is very easy to lose sight of what being a Methodist actually meant for the majority of its early converts. As has already been argued, Welsh Methodist identity operated on a number of levels. Each individual Welsh Methodist was at one and the same time a member of a local society, a national revival and an international Protestant renewal movement. It was a complex identity that such individuals were able to maintain by the successful operation of a sophisticated and multi-layered communications network which became the means by which evangelicals and Methodists from England, Wales, Scotland, the American colonies and further afield communicated with one another and shared their views about every aspect of propagating the revival. The friendships, letters, magazines and books that enabled the early Methodists to communicate with one another also acted as links in a complex chain, drawing the widely scattered awakenings into something approaching a coherent and unified evangelical movement.

In Wales the successful operation of the communications network was firmly rooted in the religious societies that were established during the late 1730s and early 1740s. Before 1743, the Welsh revival consisted of little more than a relatively *ad hoc* patchwork of tightly knit societies, which had sprung up under the inspiration of Howel Harris and Daniel Rowland, to meet the immediate spiritual needs of their small groups of converts. John Wesley, George Whitefield and Howel Harris were equally firm believers in the absolute indispensability of religious societies[1] but

[1] For details on the foundation of Methodist societies in England see John Walsh, 'Religious societies: Methodist and evangelical, 1738–1800', in W. J. Shiels and Diana Wood (eds), *Voluntary Religion*, Studies in Church History, 23 (Oxford, 1986), pp. 279–302 and Rack, 'Religious societies and the origins of Methodism', 582–95. Whitefield's views on their necessity may be traced in his sermon, 'The nature and benefits of religious Society', in John Gillies (ed.), *The Works of the Reverend George Whitefield*, V (London, 1772), pp. 107–22 and his *A Letter from the Rev. Mr George Whitefield, to the Religious Societies Lately Set on Foot in Several Parts of England and Wales* (Edinburgh, 1739).

in the first years of the revival none of them matched Harris for his energetic founding of them. Soon after his conversion in 1735, he began exhorting members of his own immediate family and some of his neighbours in his own home before quickly branching out and holding meetings in some of the neighbouring farmhouses, exhorting people to take their religion more seriously. Those who responded to his message were organized into small informal cells where they met regularly, encouraged one another in their spiritual lives and subjected themselves to the close supervision and discipleship of those who had greater spiritual experience and insight. By the end of 1736, Harris had adopted the term 'society' in reference to them[2] and by March 1739, he had established thirty societies[3] in Breconshire and its immediate hinterland.[4]

John Wesley's definition of the purpose and remit of his societies, apart from his reference to their male-only membership, can be just as easily applied to those founded by Harris. He defined them as

> A company of men, having the form and seeking the power of godliness, united in order to pray together, to receive the word of exhortation and to watch over one another in love, that they may help each other to work out their own salvation.[5]

The societies were therefore necessarily highly demanding institutions as membership necessitated a commitment to the exacting disciplines of evangelical spirituality. They required a high degree of literacy, the ability to discuss theology and religious experience at a relatively high level, the confidence to participate publicly in meetings and the self-belief necessary to be encouragers of fellow society members. It was within the context of these close-knit religious societies that news about awakenings in other parts of Wales was first heard and that the events occurring in Bristol,

---

[2]   Trevecka 87, Howel Harris to Griffith Jones (8 October 1736).
[3]   Evans, *Howell Harris*, p. 22.
[4]   For more on Harris's experiments in founding societies during these early months of the revival, see W. G. Hughes-Edwards, 'The development and organisation of the Methodist Society in Wales, 1735–1750' (MA, University of Wales, 1966), pp. 63–78 and Tudur, *Howell Harris*, pp. 63–9.
[5]   Quoted in Hughes-Edwards, 'The development and organisation of the Methodist Society in Wales', p. 63.

London, Cambuslang, Northampton and Herrnhut were followed most closely. For the Welsh Methodists the international communications network that came into existence in the late 1730s was mediated through the local societies. It was in the societies that the Welsh Methodists heard news about the revival, listened to readings from the religious magazines and prayed most fervently for the spread of God's Kingdom throughout the world.

Meaningful participation in the wider evangelical revival demanded skills still relatively rare in mid-eighteenth-century Welsh society. Evangelical religion took for granted both a degree of literacy and an access to godly literature that had been largely alien to the overwhelming majority of Welsh people before the beginning of the eighteenth century. The word-orientated nature of evangelicalism therefore restricted its appeal to those groups which had successfully taken advantage of some of the educational opportunities recently presented to them. The Welsh Methodists, recognizing the patchy nature of their compatriots' understanding of some of the basic tenets of the Protestant and evangelical faith, launched the first concerted Protestant mass-evangelization programme witnessed in Wales.[6] They took full advantage of the achievements of their immediate predecessors but departed from them significantly by widening their scope and vision beyond serving the needs of their own immediate evangelical subculture. The success of evangelicalism during these years stemmed in large part from the commitment of the highly motivated 'middling sorts', who despite their relatively small number fuelled profound changes in Welsh society. These 'middling sorts'[7] were people of 'modest means

[6] Williams, *Wales and the Reformation*, pp. 402–4 and Williams, *Welsh Reformation Essays*, p. 30. Compare with Ward, 'Was there a Methodist evangelistic strategy in the eighteenth century?', pp. 285–305.

[7] There is an ever-growing literature on the emergence and contribution of the 'middling sorts'. By way of introduction see Keith Wrightson, *English Society, 1580–1680* (London, 1982), passim and J. R. Rule, *Albion's People: English Society, 1714–1815* (London, 1992), pp. 72–84, 85–104. Of the more specific literature, Jonathan Barry and Christopher Brooks (eds), *The Middling Sort of People: Culture, Society and Politics in England, 1550–1800* (London, 1994), is indispensable and will guide the interested reader to other relevant works. The literature on the 'middling sorts' in Wales is more manageable. See Jenkins, *The Foundations of Modern Wales*, passim and on the link between the 'middling sorts' and literacy see Geraint H. Jenkins, 'The eighteenth century', in Philip H. Jones and Eiluned Rees (eds), *A Nation and its Books: A History of the Book in Wales* (Aberystwyth, 1998), pp. 109–22.

and humble circumstances'.[8] They were an extremely diverse group, occupying the place between the gentry and the labouring classes, and included among their number representatives from such occupations as shopkeepers, manufacturers, wealthy independent artisans, civil servants; professionals such as doctors, schoolteachers and lawyers; lesser merchants and representatives from other ambitious, upwardly mobile professions. They were invariably men and women whose wealth and status had provided them with sufficient independence to be able to act outside the terms dictated by the traditional hierarchical establishment. However, despite their *nouveau riche* status, the 'middling sorts' were more often than not renowned more for their advocacy of the puritanical attributes of industriousness, frugality and prudence. Though usually moderately wealthy, they stressed the importance of financial perspicacity and of the efficient or godly management of one's time and resources, attributes that were largely the product of their religious commitments. Already godly and in earnest about their religion well before the 1730s, they were drawn to the complementary mentality of evangelical religion that satisfied their thirst for knowledge and education and which, with its emphasis on the personal experience of the New Birth, made each individual responsible for his or her religious life.[9] By requiring such people to take hold of their own religious destinies, evangelicalism appealed to the individuality of the 'middling sorts' and at last seemed to afford them the opportunity, for which they had long sought, to use their wealth and influence to effect some sort of 'godly' reformation.

The 'middling sorts' were perhaps the most literate and well-read members of Welsh society. The acquisition of literacy in much of western Europe in the early modern period was inevitably related to social status. Keith Wrightson has argued that the advances that had occurred in the basic levels of literacy in the sixteenth and seventeenth centuries had not succeeded in producing a fully literate society but had given rise to the development of a 'hierarchy of illiteracy which faithfully mirrored the hierarchy of status and wealth'.[10] The 'middling sorts' had been

---

[8]   Watts, *The Dissenters*, p. 408.
[9]   Bebbington, *Evangelicalism*, pp. 5–10 and Hatch, *The Democratization of American Christianity*.
[10]   Wrightson, *English Society*, p. 190.

some of the most fortunate beneficiaries of the acquisition of the basic elements of literacy. For them the ability to read and write was usually an essential requirement of their professions, but it became a necessary prerequisite for the consolidation of their position in society. David Cressy has calculated that over the course of the early modern period illiteracy rates in England gradually declined.[11] In 1500, 90 per cent of men could not sign their name, a figure that had dropped significantly to 55 per cent by 1714. Among women the decline in illiteracy was similar, though far less dramatic. In 1500, 90 per cent of women could not sign their name, but by 1714 the proportion had fallen to 75 per cent.[12] In Wales the situation was worse. Illiteracy figures remained stubbornly high until, as a result of the educational initiatives of Griffith Jones, perhaps as many as 250,000 adults and children, out of a total population of about 450,000, were taught the basic rudiments of literacy.[13]

The acquisition of literacy naturally set off a chain reaction that had far-reaching consequences. It fuelled the almost insatiable desire of the 'middling sorts' for knowledge that, in turn, created a market for books. During the second half of the seventeenth century the number of books printed in Welsh and for a Welsh readership increased dramatically,[14] despite Wales not getting its own printing press until 1714.[15] Much of this literature was preoccupied with religious and moral issues aimed at instilling the rigid devotional disciplines of evangelical religion, and it slaked the thirst of the 'godly' middling ranks.[16] By the mid-1730s a distinct body of people had emerged in Welsh

---

[11] See David Cressy, *Literacy and the Social Order: Reading and Writing in Tudor and Stuart England* (Cambridge, 1980). Cressy's calculations are based on individuals' ability to sign their names. Keith Thomas has argued that this method of measurement is too crude an indicator for this period. There was a marked distinction between the ability to read and being able to write and, according to Thomas, it is probable that more people had basic reading skills than could actually sign their name. He argues that early modern England was therefore a partially literate society in which there coexisted people living at very different levels of intellectual sophistication. See Keith Thomas, 'The meaning of literacy in early modern England', in Gerd Baumann (ed.), *The Written Word: Literacy in Transition* (Oxford, 1986), pp. 97–131.

[12] Cressy, *Literacy and the Social Order*, p. 176.

[13] White, 'Popular schooling and the Welsh language, 1650–1800', p. 331.

[14] Jenkins, *Literature, Religion and Society in Wales*, p. 34.

[15] Eiluned Rees, 'The Welsh book-trade before 1820', in Eiluned Rees, *Libri Walliae: A Catalogue of Welsh Books and Books Printed in Wales, 1546–1820* (Aberystwyth, 1987), pp. xxii–xxv.

[16] Ian Green, *Print and Protestantism in Early Modern England* (Oxford, 2000), pp. 34–9.

society who were literate, inquisitive, ambitious, unremittingly godly and, significantly, committed to experiential religion. They themselves had benefited from the drive to increase the levels of literacy in Wales and, imbued with missionary zeal, they had responded to the perceived spiritual ignorance of their fellow countrymen and -women in imaginative and highly effective ways. They were therefore sufficiently well prepared to respond to a message that infused their already disciplined spirituality with new and exciting charismatic experiences.

The pioneer Welsh Methodists exemplified many of the traits of the devout 'middling sorts'. Both Howel Harris and Daniel Rowland were literate from an early age and unremittingly earnest about their religion, both before and after their evangelical conversions in 1735. They both recognized that their vision of a movement based on the experience of the New Birth and intense fellowship in small groups struck a chord with many from the middling orders. The early membership of the Welsh revival was largely drawn from the ranks of the lower middling orders. Its members were overwhelmingly young, the number of women was slightly more than the number of men, they were usually moderately well off, possibly with some stake in property and invariably animated by a sense of pride in their much-vaunted self-sufficiency. W. G. Hughes-Edwards's analysis of the background of some the early Methodist exhorters has shown that among the twenty-three whose occupations are noted were farmers, schoolmasters, carpenters, blacksmiths, farm labourers, a weaver, a physician, a bookbinder and a clockmaker.[17] Apart from the obvious sense of spiritual fulfilment that these individuals gained from participation in the revival, membership, and in some cases leadership, enhanced their independent status because they took responsibility for their religious lives into their own hands.

In a sense membership of a Methodist society also acted as a social leveller since access was based not on social status but on one's spiritual condition.[18] Within the society itself there was a degree of equality since each member was felt to have a valuable

[17] Hughes-Edwards, 'The development and organisation of the Methodist Society', p. 132.
[18] White, 'The world, the flesh and the devil', 47–9; White, *Praidd Bach y Bugail Mawr*, pp. 79–116.

contribution to make to the spiritual well-being of the whole. Significantly, during the first years of the movement, even the division between the sexes could sometimes be blurred. Whilst women did not usually assume a leadership role in any of the societies, many women were attracted to the vital piety and intimate support network that membership offered. Many of these women were individuals of independent means, who found within evangelicalism an outlet by means of which they too could make a telling contribution in a society where nearly all other avenues of influence outside the household remained firmly closed to them.[19] Evangelicalism took full advantage of the aspirations of the lower middling ranks by creating what Eryn M. White has called 'a literate, serious-minded, Bible-orientated group, who took to discussing theological questions with great gusto'.[20]

The character and preoccupations of the early Welsh Methodists also predisposed them to participate fully in the wider awakening. The fact that so many of them were literate, had an almost insatiable appetite for knowledge and were enthusiastic about their religion, ensured that they grasped wholeheartedly every opportunity for further fellowship and interaction that being part of the international revival offered. They eagerly made use of all the means of communication that the pioneer revivalists brought into being in the early months of the revival. Between 1739, when Howel Harris met George Whitefield for the first time, and 1750, the Welsh Methodists drew on the common forces that were coursing throughout the wider evangelical movement, and channelled their energies into amplifying the collective understanding of genuine evangelical experience. For the historian of the evangelical revival, these

---

[19]   The study of women and religion in early modern England and Wales is another rapidly developing historiographical field. The best overviews of the status of women in this period are J. Eales, *Women in Early Modern Europe, 1500–1700* (London, 1998) and Olwen Hufton, *The Prospect Before Her: A History of Women in Western Europe, I: 1500–1800* (London, 1995). On the role of women in religion see Patricia Crawford, *Women and Religion in England, 1500–1720* (London, 1993); Merry E. Wiesner, *Women and Gender in Early Modern Europe* (Cambridge, 1993), pp. 179–217; and Marilyn Westerkamp, *Women and Religion in Early America, 1600–1850* (London, 1999). On the Welsh context see Eryn M. White, 'Women, religion and education in eighteenth-century Wales', in Michael F. Roberts and Simone Clarke (eds), *Women and Gender in Early Modern Wales* (Cardiff, 2000), pp. 210–33; and Eryn M. White, 'Women in the early Methodist Societies in Wales', *JWRH*, 7 (1999), 95–108.

[20]   White, 'The world, the flesh and the devil', 45–6.

means of communication are the entry point into the world of a substantial body of mid-eighteenth-century evangelicals.

In the months immediately following their conversions the pioneer revivalists established networks of communication, based on what Susan O'Brien has called a vibrant 'print culture'.[21] The majority of these networks were centred in London and were initiated by George Whitefield. Throughout the later 1730s and the 1740s these networks mushroomed. As the communication links proliferated, Whitefield delegated responsibility for their day-to-day administration to a few hand-picked secretaries. His first and subsequently best-known assistant was William Seward (1711–40).[22] According to Frank Lambert, Seward acted as Whitefield's 'chief reporter and press agent'[23] between 1737 and his premature death at the hands of a mob at Hay-on-Wye in 1740.[24] Seward was Whitefield's chief publicist, ensuring that his itinerary was well advertised and that up-beat reports of his preaching regularly appeared in the press. By manipulating news about Whitefield and concentrating only on his successes, Seward was able to infuse Whitefield's ministry with an air of inevitability and inexorable progress. Seward also coordinated the development and growth of the inter-revival print network. The majority of Whitefield's letters passed through his hands, and from his position at the hub of the revival Seward was able to initiate the forging of links between Whitefield's English converts and their counterparts in Wales and beyond.

Seward's early death in 1740 was therefore a great loss to the whole of the revival. In its aftermath, Whitefield turned increasingly to John Lewis, the London-based printer and bookseller, to fill the void that had been left. Lewis handed over his evangelical magazine, *The Christian's Amusement*, which had been struggling to capture a large enough readership to maintain its financial viability, to Whitefield's Calvinistic Methodists in 1741. Under Whitefield's guidance, and rebranded as *The Weekly History*, it became the public voice of his revival. From his print shop,

[21] Durden, 'Transatlantic communications and influence during the Great Awakening', p. 51.
[22] See *BDEB*, p. 996; Lambert, *'Pedlar in Divinity'*, pp. 51–5; and Dallimore, *George Whitefield*, I, pp. 251–2.
[23] Lambert, *'Pedlar in Divinity'*, p. 57.
[24] See Dallimore, *George Whitefield*, I, pp. 582–6 and Geoffrey L. Fairs, 'Notes on the death of William Seward at Hay, 1740', *CCHMC*, LVIII, 1 (March 1973), 12–17.

Lewis produced and distributed throughout the international evangelical community a remarkable amount of literature in support of Whitefield until, disillusioned and nearly bankrupt, he defected to the Moravians in 1745.[25] His work was picked up, albeit more spasmodically, by some of Whitefield's assistants at the Tabernacle. John Syms played an important role, acting as Whitefield's book secretary and ensuring the cheap production, printing and distribution of most of Whitefield's writings and the works of other evangelicals such as Jonathan Edwards and the Erskine brothers, until he too defected to the Moravians in 1745.[26] Syms was replaced first by Howel Harris himself[27] and then, soon after, by Thomas Boddington.[28] Harris worked very closely with each of these individuals but it was his relationship with John Lewis that was most fruitful. Lewis became the source of much of the evangelical literature, whether in the form of letters or printed material, that reached Wales. It was usually sent to Harris, who then distributed what he thought most suitable to exhorters and societies throughout south Wales. In this relatively simple way Harris was able, almost single-handedly, to educate the Welsh Methodists about the wider revival and expose them to many of the ideas that were circulating around the evangelical world. The behind-the-scenes activities of individuals like Seward and Lewis kept Whitefield's ministry at the forefront of evangelical attention, and their administration of a sophisticated print culture engendered a remarkably unified sense of purpose between Calvinistic revivalists in England, Wales, Scotland and the American colonies.

At first the community came together as a result of the friendships that the pioneer revivalists made with one another between 1736 and 1738. In Wales, the two local awakenings were fused when Harris and Daniel Rowland met for the first time at Defynnog, Breconshire, in August 1737.[29] These connections were the essential platform from which Harris was able to establish links between the revival in Wales and similar awakenings under way elsewhere. At the beginning of 1739 he exchanged

[25] Podmore, *The Moravian Church in England*, p. 92.
[26] Trevecka 1607, John Syms to Howel Harris (18 January 1747).
[27] CMA 2946, p. 37. See also Edwin Welch (ed.), *Two Calvinistic Methodist Chapels 1743–1811: The London Tabernacle and Spa Fields Chapel* (London, 1975), pp. 12–3.
[28] Trevecka 1674, Thomas Boddington to Mrs Doyle (29 June 1747).
[29] Tudur, *Howell Harris*, p. 42.

correspondence with, and then met, George Whitefield for the first time. Whitefield visited Wales for the second time in April 1739 and he persuaded Harris to return with him to London to witness the rapidly developing awakening there. Harris spent over two months in London and was introduced to all of the main personalities of the English revival who, at that stage, were still attending the Moravian-dominated Fetter Lane Society. These months set a precedent for the rest of the 1740s. Harris remained a regular visitor to London as well as to the revival centres in other parts of England, in some years spending up to six months touring the scattered awakenings. The friendships that he made on this occasion were all of long standing and bore fruit when figures like Whitefield, John and Charles Wesley, William Seward, John Cennick, Joseph Humphreys and later the countess of Huntingdon made regular visits to Wales.

One of the most obvious difficulties when analysing the relationship between the Welsh revival and the wider evangelical movement is the dominant position occupied by Howel Harris. Harris was clearly the most active of the Welsh revivalists on the international evangelical stage, but his dominance can be exaggerated because of the nature of much of the manuscript evidence that remains about the early years of Welsh Methodism. Nearly all of the sources relating to the early months and years of the revival stem from Harris's pen. His massive collection of diaries and letters reflects his own highly prejudicial view of the events of the late 1730s and the 1740s, and in the absence of any of the personal papers of Daniel Rowland and William Williams it is often difficult to avoid uncritically accepting Harris's version of events.

Welsh Methodist interaction with the wider evangelical community was clearly something that operated on a number of levels. Nobody else in Wales matched Harris's commitment to developing links with evangelicals in other countries. The absence of any substantial body of papers relating to the career of Daniel Rowland[30] makes it difficult to trace whether he played any meaningful role in the wider revival. Although he did occasionally visit the English revival – he was in Bristol in April 1748[31] for

---

[30] It is likely that Rowland's papers were given to the countess of Huntingdon by his son Nathaniel and subsequently lost. See Evans, *Daniel Rowland*, pp. 2–3 and Edwin Welch, 'The correspondence of Nathaniel Rowland and Lady Huntingdon, 1781–90', *CCHMC*, 2 (1978), 26–37.

[31] 'From a Friend at Bristol to Mr J—s R—ll—y (May 2, 1748)', *CH*, pp. 215–16.

example – from the evidence in Harris's diaries and letters it seems that Rowland was always reluctant to take on additional commitments outside Wales. Whilst he was as aware of the international dimension of the movement as anybody in Wales and was on very good terms with both George Whitefield and John Cennick, Rowland rarely visited England himself and his only face-to-face contact with the English Methodists occurred when they visited Wales. As far as we know, his only direct contacts with England were a few letters to members of his congregation who had moved to London.[32] Rowland's own overriding commitment to Wales eventually led to tensions between him and Harris over the latter's frequent and protracted absences from what, in Rowland's view, were his chief responsibilities. His comments to Harris in October 1742, at a time when the initial fervour of the revival in Wales had abated and when there was pressing work to be done organizing the converts, are indicative of his concern and indicate his growing impatience with Harris's gallivanting: 'Don't you hear all the Brethren in Wales crying out loudly, Help! Help! Help Help! Brother Harris! [. . .] What is London now, in the Day of Battle! [. . .] Must poor Wales afford an Assistant to England?'[33] Below the level of Harris and his fellow revivalists, there was a body of more locally known figures who were also committed to wider evangelical participation. In Wales, individuals like Thomas Price of Watford, James Beaumont (d. 1750), John Oulton and Herbert Jenkins (1721–72) relished news of the progress of the revival and wrote their own letters, adding to the pool of revival knowledge. James Beaumont also served some of the English Methodist societies in Wiltshire[34] and Herbert Jenkins was a frequent face in Bristol and at Whitefield's Tabernacle in London throughout the 1740s.[35]

---

[32]   Trevecka 625, Daniel Rowland to Mr W.G. (6 September 1742) and 'Letter; Daniel Rowland to member of his flock in London', *Account*, II, I, 7–9.

[33]   Trevecka 705, Daniel Rowland to Howel Harris (20 October 1742).

[34]   'At an Association held at Gloucester, 11 October 1747', CMA 2946, p. 41; 'At a meeting at Gloucester, 23 December 1747', CMA 2946, p. 44; 'At an Association at Bristol, 27 January 1748', CMA 2946, p. 49. For more on James Beaumont's role in the revival see Dallimore, *George Whitefield*, II, pp. 234, 255 and Geraint Tudur, '"Like a right arm and a pillar": the story of James Beaumont', in Robert Pope (ed.), *Honouring the Past and Shaping the Future: Religious and Biblical Studies in Wales: Essays in Honour of Gareth Lloyd Jones* (Leominster, 2003), pp. 133–58.

[35]   On Herbert Jenkins's contribution to the life of Whitefield's Tabernacle see 'Association held at Tabernacle House, 11 December 1745', CMA 2946, p. 13. On his responsibilities in other parts of England see 'Association held at London, 18 June 1746', CMA 2946, p. 16. For more details of his role in the revival see Tudur, *Howell Harris*, pp. 89–90.

Such inter-revival visits were usually only the prerogative of the pioneer revivalists. Even then only George Whitefield exercised a genuinely international ministry by means of his regular transatlantic trips. Howel Harris, despite giving serious consideration to accompanying Whitefield to America,[36] never visited the colonies, Scotland or the Moravian settlement at Herrnhut, as John Wesley had done in 1738.[37] By dividing his time between Wales and London, Harris in effect let the wider revival come to him. He was fortunate because during these years London was at the intersection of a vast north Atlantic empire, undergoing a consumer revolution that brought more goods and commodities within the range of more people than ever before.[38] It also supported a print trade that had flourished after the repeal of the Licensing Act in 1695, ensuring the free flow of information between the colonies and the British Isles.[39] The evangelicals were able to take full advantage of these propitious circumstances. By regularly visiting London, Harris placed himself at the hub of this fluid community of news and ideas. Harris's experience was therefore very different from that of the majority of the rank-and-file converts of the revival in Wales for whom visiting London was unrealistic. Travel from Wales was still hazardous, roads were poor and few people possessed either the time or the spare cash to travel very far from their own immediate localities.[40] Their contact with such exotic figures as Whitefield or John Wesley was either reserved for those rare occasions when they happened to be passing close by, or limited to the itinerancy of Howel Harris whose news of the international revival connected them with the burgeoning north Atlantic community of belief and experience.

[36]   HHD 73, 6 June 1741 and Trevecka 376, Griffith Twyning to Howel Harris (28 August 1741).
[37]   Baker, *John Wesley and the Church of England*, p. 55 and Herbert Boyd McGonigle, *Sufficient Saving Grace: John Wesley's Evangelical Arminianism* (Carlisle, 2001), pp. 108–10.
[38]   McKendrick, Brewer and Plumb (eds), *The Birth of a Consumer Society*, pp. 1–6; T. H. Breen, ' "Baubles of Britain": The American and consumer revolutions of the eighteenth century', *Past and Present*, 119 (1988), 73–104.
[39]   See Ian K. Steele, *The English Atlantic, 1675–1740: An Exploration of Communication and Community* (New York, 1986), pp. 132–64 and Hugh Amory and David D. Hall (eds), *A History of the Book in America, I: The Colonial Book in the Atlantic World* (Cambridge, 2000), pp. 152–98.
[40]   Jenkins, *The Foundations of Modern Wales*, pp. 127–8 and 296–8.

The primary purpose of the communications network was the discussion and analysis of evangelical experience. In its earliest years it consisted mainly of familiar letters and revival narratives. The communications network was built on the foundational beliefs shared by almost all the revivalists. The inter-revival itinerancy of the pioneer revivalists and some of their more gifted co-workers would have been meaningless had they not been able to step from revival to revival in the knowledge that there were certain core beliefs held in common throughout the movement. Whilst all the revivalists gave allegiance to the summaries of orthodox belief contained in the various official doctrinal statements of the particular Church or denomination to which they belonged, the single most important unifying factor was not theological but experiential – an experience of the New Birth underpinned by a shared understanding of the conversion process. In the lives of all of the revivalists, conversion was the catalyst that had led to the beginning of their public ministries and the outbreak of their revivals. The near-identical conversions of Howel Harris, Daniel Rowland, George Whitefield and the Wesley brothers became the axis linking the Methodisms of England, Wales and beyond.

The Methodists' understanding of the conversion experience had been adapted in a number of areas from that which had been commonly assumed by their nearest evangelical predecessors, the Puritans. Conversion was no less central to the spiritual pilgrimage of the Puritans, but they tended to lay stress on its more progressive nature. They argued that conversion invariably began with a period of intense conviction of sin that only eventually terminated in the convert obtaining a measure of forgiveness and assurance, after a long-drawn-out 'dark night of the soul'. Like the Methodists after them, the Puritans stressed the importance of testing the genuineness of each testimony by the presence of the 'fruits of the Spirit' in each convert's life.[41] Whilst the early evangelicals did not dispute any of the elements of this process – indeed both Harris and Whitefield experienced

<hr />

[41] See Michael C. Questier, *Conversion, Politics and Religion in England, 1580–1625* (Cambridge, 1996), pp. 12–39; Norman Pettit, *The Heart Prepared: Grace and Conversion in Puritan Spiritual Life* (New Haven, 1966); and Charles E. Hambrick-Stowe, *The Practice of Piety: Puritan Devotional Disciplines in Seventeenth-Century New England* (Chapel Hill, 1982).

long periods of intense conviction of sin – in their preaching they often compressed the various phases into a far tighter time frame and stressed the immediate attainability of the New Birth. When preaching Whitefield would urge his congregations to 'see that you receive the Holy Ghost before you go hence'[42] and experience an immediate conversion. It was this tone that rang so loudly and so startlingly in the ears of many who were more accustomed to the more cultured tones of the Puritans and their successors among the ranks of the Dissenters. Their stress on the immediate attainability of New Birth was supported by an equally strong emphasis on the tests that each individual was to apply to ascertain whether his or her experience was genuine or not. Though it departed from the schema of the Puritans in its time-scale the evangelical model of conversion was no less well defined. It quickly became one of the overriding purposes of the evangelical communications network to expound and explain this theology of conversion and thereby ensure that evangelicals everywhere, despite many of their other divisions, were at least united on the very core elements of their identity.

This was why the revivalists recorded their spiritual experiences in such painstaking detail. John Wesley, George Whitefield and Howel Harris kept detailed journals in which they recorded the details of their lives in excruciating detail. In this they were following in the tradition of the Puritans once again. Puritanism had, of course, placed particular emphasis on the experiential nature of Christian faith[43] and their fixation with judging whether spiritual experience was genuine or not had led them into producing stylized models of genuine spirituality. By locating the essence of religion in the personal interaction between each individual and God, they encouraged a highly personalized interpretation of Christianity. This accounted for the Puritan practice of keeping confessional diaries that, in the absence of a mechanism of auricular confession as persisted in the Catholic tradition, enabled them to keep a careful watch on their spiritual temperatures.[44] The practice of keeping such diaries had increased

---

[42]   Quoted in Lambert, 'Pedlar in Divinity', p. 22.
[43]   Owen C. Watkins, The Puritan Experience (London, 1972), pp. 14–6.
[44]   For more detail on the tradition of Puritan autobiographies see Watkins, The Puritan Experience; Patricia Caldwell, The Puritan Conversion Narrative: The Beginnings of American Expression (Cambridge, 1983); and C. Lloyd Cohen, God's Caress: The Psychology of Puritan Religious Experience (Oxford, 1986), pp. 201–41. For an analysis of

markedly in the second half of the seventeenth century, particularly among some of the more radical Protestant groups, who required a satisfactory personal testimony before they granted individuals membership of their gathered Churches,[45] and by the eighteenth century the fashion for directly autobiographical works[46] created an ideal climate for the publication of personal religious narratives.

Many of the pioneer revivalists kept detailed spiritual diaries. In the revival's earliest days George Whitefield's *Journals*[47] was perhaps the single most influential textbook on the parameters of genuine conversion and revival. Whitefield penned his diary with a definite eye to publication. It appeared from the press in easily digestible segments at regular intervals in the later 1730s and outlined Whitefield's activities in the months immediately preceding the publication of each instalment. His *Journals* represented Whitefield's immediate thoughts and impressions about the revival and acted as the official interpretation of the movement, often being the first contact that many converts had with the revival outside their own immediate localities. Whitefield's *Journals* was avidly read in Wales. By November 1738 Harris had read the *Journals* through for the second time and confessed to being deeply 'affected' by its contents.[48] For Harris, Whitefield's *Journals* held such significance because it was the first tangible indication that his work, and that of Daniel Rowland in Cardiganshire, was part of a far more extensive movement of God's Spirit.

Howel Harris was also a fanatical diarist. Although he began keeping his diary as a private devotional tool and a means whereby he could confess his faults to God,[49] he soon began to harbour hopes that one day his diaries would be published like Whitefield's. In 1738 he wrote: 'I think I write this Diary that I

Howel Harris's debt to the Puritan conversion narrative tradition see Geraint Tudur, 'A critical study, based on his own diaries, of the life and labours of Howell Harris and his contribution to the revival in Wales between 1735 and 1750' (D.Phil., University of Oxford, 1989), pp. 5–8. Also important on the wider Pietist and Methodist debt to this tradition is W. R. Ward's introduction in R. P. Heitzenrater and Frank Baker (eds), *The Works of John Wesley, XVII: Journals and Diaries*, I (Nashville, 1988), pp. 1–36.

  [45] Hindmarsh, *John Newton and the English Evangelical Tradition*, p. 36.

  [46] Michael Mascuch, *Origins of the Individualist Self: Autobiography and Self-Identity in England, 1591–1791* (London, 1997).

  [47] See Iain H. Murray (ed.), *George Whitefield's Journals* (London, 1960).

  [48] HHD 35, 27 November 1738.

  [49] Tudur, *Howell Harris*, pp. 3–4.

may see the secret workings of Grace, sin, corruption and nature and if possibly it may be useful to others.'[50] Whether at this stage Harris envisaged quite how extensive his diary would actually become is unlikely. The 248 individual volumes of the diary in the National Library of Wales at Aberystwyth, covering the years between 1735 and Harris's death in 1773, amount to a massive legacy. Each entry was usually written at intervals throughout each day, the events of the evening being written either late at night or first thing the following morning. Harris must have spent a considerable portion of each day completing his diary. The entries are long, at times well over ten closely written pages per day. They were often written in a minute hand, at first in Latin and Welsh and at times even in code and in various directions on each page, giving the impression of the frenetic pace at which Harris seemed to live. Despite his optimistic wishes nothing but excerpts from them have ever been published[51] and nothing appeared from the presses during his own lifetime. In reality, Harris's diary would not have been suitable for publication because of its sheer bulk and the fact that its contents are intermixed with much personal and extraneous material reflecting his fluctuating religious moods, swinging between ecstatic highs and dark depressions. Whilst the diary contains masses of detail on the development of Methodism in Wales and elsewhere, much of this material is intermixed with long confessional passages in which Harris analysed his spiritual state over and over again in tortuous detail. Whilst Whitefield's *Journals* is more polished and very obviously written for a wide readership, and representative of his interpretation of the early years of the revival, Harris's diaries have to be approached more cautiously. In many ways this makes them more valuable than those of either Whitefield or John Wesley. They offer an unparalleled insight into the mind of the revivalist and allow us to eavesdrop on Harris's thought-processes. Fortunately for the historian of Welsh Methodism, the personal records of both Harris and Whitefield are fairly easily accessible. They enable us

---

[50]   HHD 34, 1 November 1738.
[51]   See John Thickens, *Howel Harris yn Llundain* (Caernarfon, 1934) and the trilogy edited by Tom Beynon: *Howel Harris: Reformer and Soldier, 1714–1773* (Caernarfon, 1958), *Howel Harris's Visits to London* (Aberystwyth, 1960) and *Howel Harris's Visits to Pembrokeshire* (Aberystwyth, 1966).

to piece together the manner in which the Welsh revival and its counterpart in England were drawn together in the later 1730s, and Harris's diary in particular allows us to trace the Welsh response to the international revival in considerable detail.

Few Methodists dreamt of keeping such painstaking records of their daily lives. Those who did put pen to paper usually adopted the mode of the familiar letter. Correspondence became the foundation of the international communications network, and in many ways the history of the evangelical revival is unintelligible without a detailed study of the letters of the revivalists and their followers. Letter-writing was the means by which the pioneer revivalists made contact with one another for the first time. After they had subsequently met face to face their letter-writing invariably became both more frequent and more sophisticated. For the revival's rank-and-file converts writing letters, reading the correspondence of fellow evangelicals and hearing letters read aloud publicly were the chief means by which they obtained first-hand knowledge of the progress of the international revival. Letters therefore acted as a gel melding the national awakenings together, the most important way in which evangelicals interacted with brethren from further afield.

The early Methodists were able to exploit letter-writing to its full potential because of the advances that had been made in the delivery of mail throughout the British Isles in the early part of the eighteenth century. In 1711 the postal systems of England and Wales, Scotland and Ireland had finally been merged[52] which significantly improved the efficiency of the service, the safe delivery and reception of letters, the speed of communication and, perhaps most important, the expense involved.[53] The imaginative use of letter-writing was not an evangelical innovation. Once again evangelicals followed a well-defined apostolic, Protestant and, more immediately, Puritan tradition. A large

[52]   See Howard Anderson and Irvin Ehrenpreis, 'The familiar letter in the eighteenth century: some generalisations', in Howard Anderson, Philip. B. Daghlion and Irvin Ehrenpreis (eds), *The Familiar Letter in the Eighteenth Century* (Lawrence, Kansas, 1966), pp. 269–70.

[53]   For more on the development of the postal service in the early part of the eighteenth century and its importance for the Methodists see Frank Baker (ed.), *The Works of John Wesley, 25: Letters, I: 1721–39* (Oxford, 1980), pp. 20–3.

proportion of the New Testament itself is, of course, made up of
the letters of the apostles Peter, Paul and John. By means of these
letters, the apostles, especially Paul, were able to supervise the
widely scattered network of infant Christian communities. A
limited transatlantic communications network had also been
developed by those Puritans who had emigrated to the American
colonies in the seventeenth century. Naturally much of this
correspondence was the result of the strong ties that existed
between the migrants and their families back in their homeland,
but there was also a spiritual dimension to it. For many Puritan
émigrés the New World offered an opportunity to implement the
radical religious programme that had proved to be almost
impossible at home. Those Puritans who had chosen to remain
at home were kept informed about the progress of their efforts to
build a 'city on a hill' in the New World and were able
symbolically to unite with them in a prayer network that spanned
the Atlantic.[54] By the early decades of the eighteenth century this
transatlantic flow of correspondence had, to some degree, dried
up. A severely attenuated triangular correspondence between
some English Dissenters including Philip Doddridge (1702–51)
and Isaac Watts (1674–1748), a small number of colonial
Puritans and some Scottish Presbyterians had survived,[55] and it
was through this group that news of Jonathan Edwards's
awakening at Northampton in 1735 first reached a wider
audience. The pioneer revivalists, particularly Whitefield, initially made use of this transatlantic network to spread information
about their activities, but when it proved incapable of coping
with either the type or the quantity of information that
Whitefield and his friends wished to trade, they replaced it with
their own more flexible version, based on a new alignment of
correspondents who were either for or against the revival.

The pioneer revivalists encouraged all of their converts to put
any gifts that they possessed to full use by contributing letters to
the correspondence network. The only barrier to active
participation was illiteracy. The early Methodists' genuinely all-
inclusive attitude stemmed in part from their radical imple-

---

[54] See David Cressy, *Coming Over: Migration and Communication between
England and New England in the Seventeenth Century* (Cambridge, 1987), pp. 213–34.
[55] Walsh, '"Methodism" and the origins of English-speaking evangelicalism', pp.
20–2 and Crawford, *Seasons of Grace*, pp. 82–6.

mentation of the 'priesthood of all believers', but it also owed as much to the thirst for knowledge that characterized many of those who had initially been drawn to the empowering message of the revivalists. The independent spirit of the 'middling sorts' thus found a companion in the individualism inherent in the evangelical message, and this was amply demonstrated by the enthusiasm with which many Welsh Methodists responded to the new opportunities which participation in the international dimension of the revival presented.

In Wales, the most regular correspondents were obviously the pioneer revivalists. In Howel Harris's correspondence the names of Daniel Rowland, William Williams, Howel Davies (1716–70), George Whitefield, the Wesley brothers, John Cennick, William McCulloch and James Erskine (1679–1754) predominate. Below the level of the leading revivalists there are many letters from other more locally known figures such as Thomas Price, James Beaumont, Herbert Jenkins, Thomas Bowen and John Oulton in Wales, Joseph Humphreys, John Lewis, Thomas Boddington and John Syms in England, and Ebenezer and Ralph Erskine in Scotland. There were also many other Methodists, not directly involved in the leadership of the revival locally or nationally, who wrote to Harris and sometimes to one another. In this group there were many women, including Elizabeth Thomas, Anne Dutton, Elizabeth Paul, Sarah Mason and Elizabeth Clifford. These figures, and others like them, usually contacted Harris after having heard him preach, after he had visited their societies or, in the case of the English-based correspondents, as a result of his high-profile ministry at Whitefield's Tabernacle at Moorfields, and their first foray into the letter-writing network was invariably the beginning of a more long-term commitment.

This correspondence took a number of different forms and served a wide variety of purposes. The overriding aim of many of these letters, especially during the early days of the revival, was the circulation of news. Many of them are therefore somewhat impersonal, containing very little introductory material and little or no discussion of private matters. For many correspondents letters were merely the most convenient and efficient method of transmitting the latest news about the progress of the revival. They were often written in haste, conveying the tangible excitement that participation in these events entailed, and were sent to the revivalist who was most likely to ensure that their contents were publicized as widely as possible. Many more humble Methodists took advantage of these opportunities to report on the progress of the awakenings in their respective localities.[56] The vital importance of letter-writing is reflected in the fact that even when people wrote letters for other purposes, they almost always included at least one paragraph summing up the latest progress of the awakening in which they participated.[57] In a society in which travel was still relatively slow the letter-writing network became the ideal means of disseminating news about the progress of the revival. The frequent interchange of up-to-date news created an air of expectancy and conveyed to readers a sense of the inexorable progress of the revival.

Yet the letters also served other equally important purposes. They quickly became the chief means by which many of the rank-and-file members of the revival articulated their spiritual experiences. By recounting their experiences in a letter to one of the pioneer revivalists or a prominent exhorter, converts could seek verification of their experiences from those who were supposed to be experts in matters of the soul, compare their experiences with those of contemporaries and seek guidance on areas where they were still uncertain. For others their letters could serve a more didactic purpose. By recording their experiences they could instruct others and point the way forward for many who still languished in unbelief or struggled with doubts about the reality of their testimonies. To those 'middling sorts' who had so recently acquired the basic tools of literacy, such participation in the revival seemed to be the opportunity to extend their influence and develop a more public profile for which they had sought. The letter-writing network also became one of the most important means whereby many of the ordinary members of the revival gained answers to their most pressing

---

[56] See Trevecka 426, anon. to George Whitefield (26 November 1741); 'From a gentleman in the country to his friend in London, concerning the Rev. Mr Whitefield (28 February 1741)', *WH* 12; and 'Letter, Thomas James (exhorter in Wales) to Howel Harris (London) (9 October 1742)', *Account*, II, I, pp. 47–52.

[57] Trevecka 316, Sarah Mason to Howel Harris (28 February 1741) and Trevecka 401, Thomas Price to Howel Harris (24 October 1741).

worries and problems. A wide range of problems were dealt with in the letters, including personal difficulties, spiritual struggles and temptations, and occasionally more practical and mundane concerns. Used in this way the network became a living resource into which the ordinary members of the revival could tap at any time, thereby supplementing the pastoral care which they received more locally in the societies to which they belonged.

Finally, the letter-writing network came into its own when the evangelical movement was faced with internal dissension and opposition from those in positions of authority. When theological divisions came to dominate the revival in 1740 and 1741 the letter-writing network proved to be an invaluable forum in which theological issues could be discussed and the issues at stake brought to the attention of the widest possible constituency. Later in the 1740s, when the divisions between the Calvinists, Arminians and Moravians had taken effect and positions had hardened, the network, following its realignment along strict Calvinistic lines, began to reflect some of the other problems that the movement faced. It became one of the means by which the stories of persecution and violence that many converts endured with stoical resignation were retold. By so doing, a feeling of collective solidarity was engendered as the revivalists and their followers sought to usher in the Kingdom of God. By analysing the contents of the letter-writing network it is possible to piece together what membership of the revival meant for some of its rank-and-file members and to judge whether their experiences differed markedly from those of their leaders.

Whilst the subject matter of these letters varied from correspondent to correspondent and usually reflected the preoccupations of the individual revivalists themselves, the style of the letters largely mirrored that which Whitefield, Wesley and Harris had adopted in their own diaries and journals. The Methodist prized plainness in all things; the writing of letters was no exception. For John Wesley, a plain style characterized by 'perspicuity and purity, propriety, strength and easiness'[58] was

---

[58]   Isabel Rivers. *Reason, Grace and Sentiment: A Study of the Language of Religion and Ethics in England, 1660–1780, I: Whichcote to Wesley* (Cambridge, 1991), p. 216.

most suitable to the discussion of experiential and practical religion. Profound spiritual realities were to be expressed in easily understandable language or, as Wesley put it, 'if we think with the wise, yet must [we] speak with the vulgar.'[59] Anything that gave the impression of 'stiffness, apparent exactness, [or] artificialness of style'[60] was to be avoided. Plainness of style suited the utilitarian purpose of much Methodist correspondence. Since their letters were invariably designed to be used for the edification of others any attempt at literary or theological innovation was to be avoided.[61] John Lewis, the editor of the Calvinistic religious magazine in the 1740s, went to great lengths to explain both the purpose of letter-writing and the style that he expected his fellow Methodists to adopt:

> The best way then is for every person Simply to write what he once was in a state of nature, how and by what means he came to have the dawnings of light and grace upon his soul, and how it has been with him since this time. This may be done in a brief manner; and I am persuaded would be very useful as well as entertaining. The distress'd, tempted soul will hereby see that many of his brethren and Sisters in the kingdom and patience of Jesus, have walked in the same road before him. What will heaven be, but searching into and comparing of one anothers experiences, joined with praising God for the same. And shall we be backward to begin the work of heaven now.[62]

Personal references were therefore usually kept to a minimum. Spontaneity was tempered by the somewhat formulaic style that many of the correspondents adopted. Whether they were reporting on the latest news of the revival in their own community, relating their experiences of God's grace or seeking advice and help, directness and simplicity were most prized. For many, a plain style was simply equated with a scriptural style, and,

---

[59]   Ibid.

[60]   Ibid.

[61]   For more on the genre of epistolary narratives see Elizabeth Heckendorn Cook, *Epistolary Bodies: Gender and Genre in the Eighteenth-Century Republic of Letters* (Stanford, 1996); Isabel Rivers, ' "Strangers and Pilgrims": sources and patterns of Methodist narrative', in J. C. Hilson, M. M. B. Jones and J. R. Watson (eds), *Augustan Worlds: Essays in Honour of A. R. Humphreys* (Leicester, 1978), pp. 189–203; and D. B. Hindmarsh, 'The Olney autobiographers: English conversion narrative in the mid-eighteenth century', *Journal of Ecclesiastical History*, 49, 1 (January 1998), 61–84.

[62]   *WH* 13 (anonymous letter).

following Wesley's practice of 'express[ing] Scripture sense in Scripture phrase',[63] they expressed themselves through the language, idioms and tropes of the Bible.[64] Many correspondents also seem to have been aware that what they were writing might be read aloud publicly, perhaps in Whitefield's Tabernacle or in any number of local societies scattered about the Welsh countryside. This could also create problems and prevent some people putting pen to paper. Richard Thomas Bateman, for example, seems to have been embarrassed at the possibility of his private thoughts and feelings being paraded before his fellow Methodists.[65] Bruce Hindmarsh has argued that these letters 'existed ambiguously somewhere between the private and public document'.[66] Some of their letters seem to be too impersonal to be private letters whereas others seem too informal to be compositions intended primarily for public consumption. Methodist letters needed to be personal enough to answer the immediate needs of the recipient, but they also had to contain enough material to give them a wider application and relevance, as they were often returned to again and again throughout a recipient's pilgrimage.[67]

The Welsh Methodists were dedicated participants in the letter-writing network. Indeed they have bequeathed perhaps the fullest and most complete body of correspondence from any of the individual revivals, including letters touching on every aspect of the development of the evangelical revival.[68] Naturally, the Welsh letters represent the world-view and concerns of Howel Harris and, like his diaries, need to be treated with an equal amount of caution. Harris was usually the conduit through which much of the information regarding the international revival was circulated in Wales. His own letters were vital to the

[63] Quoted in Rivers, *Reason, Grace and Sentiment*, p. 223.
[64] White, 'The Established Church, Dissent and the Welsh language c. 1660–1811', pp. 266–7.
[65] Trevecka 1017, John Lewis to Howel Harris (26 October 1743).
[66] Hindmarsh, *John Newton and the English Evangelical Tradition*, p. 32.
[67] Ibid., pp. 245–6.
[68] Howel Harris's letters make up a substantial part of the Trevecka Letters collection which forms an integral part of the Calvinistic Methodist Archive, housed in the National Library of Wales in Aberystwyth. The collection contains almost 3,000 letters and covers the whole period of Harris's adult life from 1725 to 1773. For a published calendar of these letters see M. H. Jones, *The Trevecka Letters* (Caernarfon, 1932) and B. S. Schlenther and E. M. White, *A Calendar of the Trevecka Letters* (National Library of Wales, Aberystwyth, 2003).

success of the entire communications network. He was one of its most enthusiastic and committed supporters and, apart from Whitefield himself, its most frequent participant. He worked closely with William Seward, John Lewis and John Syms to ensure that his own letters were circulated as widely as possible, that those of his converts got to their required destinations and that ample supplies of letters from other revivals reached Wales.

However, the distribution of letters and the relation of news from the revival at large were never as coordinated in Wales as they were in England. The practice of holding specific days for the reading of letters, as the Moravians had done at Fetter Lane[69] and as happened regularly at Whitefield's Tabernacle[70] and Wesley's Foundery,[71] had no obvious parallel in Wales. These Letter Days were high points in the life of Whitefield's Tabernacle. At the height of the revival they took place monthly, often lasting for hours at a time, and they involved the reading of the latest correspondence received about the revival, interspersed with prayers, exhortations from Whitefield and on occasion the singing of hymns which summarized the progress and scope of the revival and which had been composed specially for these days.[72]

Given Howel Harris's special interest in all things relating to the international dimensions of the revival it is somewhat surprising that he never attempted to introduce such a day into the regular programme of the Welsh revival. Whitefield had recommended these days to Harris in 1741 as an ideal means whereby 'Unity would [. . .] be promoted, love increased, and our hands strengthened'.[73] Despite their reluctance to act on

[69]   Podmore, *The Moravian Church in England*, p. 44

[70]   O'Brien, 'A transatlantic community of saints', 825–6.

[71]   John Wesley's institution of a monthly Letter Day at the Foundery owed much to the Moravians. See Podmore, *The Moravian Church in England*, p. 76

[72]   John Lewis included an account of one of these Letter Days in the revival magazine. See 'The order of the Letter Day at the Tabernacle, on Monday, May 30, 1743', *Account*, III, I, 73–83. See also O'Brien, 'A transatlantic community of saints', 826–7.

[73]   George Whitefield to Howel Harris (28 December 1741), in Murray (ed.), *George Whitefield's Letters*, p. 512.

Whitefield's advice, the Welsh Methodists took a keen interest in the proceedings of the Letter Days that occurred at the Tabernacle. Letters from Wales were regularly sent up to London in time for the monthly letter-reading gathering[74] and news of their proceedings regularly percolated back to Wales.[75]

In Wales the letter-writing network tended to operate in a far more informal manner and much depended on the initiative of Howel Harris. For those societies that were fortunate enough to see Harris on a regular basis, news from around the revival and the latest letters were relatively easy to come by. Harris would report on the latest events in London, Scotland or the American colonies, particularly if he had just returned from one of his visits to London, in an informal way at society meetings. For others, perhaps living in more remote areas where access to Howel Harris or Daniel Rowland was more fitful, much depended on the interest of their local exhorter. If he was interested in the progress of the revival in other parts of the world, then his society members also tended to be fairly well informed about international evangelical events. If he was not particularly interested, or perhaps had very little knowledge of English, news could be far more difficult to obtain.

For most Welsh Methodists the biggest handicap to their participation in the letter-writing network was linguistic. The network operated almost exclusively in English whereas most Welsh Methodists were native Welsh-speakers.[76] Whilst there were many who had a measure of understanding of English, this was often insufficient to enable them to participate fully in the communications network. To remedy this Harris improvised by maximizing the potential of those society members and local leaders who had some understanding of English. Many of these individuals, often exhorters involved in the local administration of the revival, were asked to write letters which could be sent to London and from there circulated throughout the revival.[77] We

---

[74] Trevecka 644, Howel Harris to Daniel Rowland (14 September 1742) and Trevecka 697, Howel Harris to Howel Davies (15 October 1742).

[75] Trevecka 626, Howel Harris to Thomas James (7 September 1742); Trevecka 723, Howel Harris to Thomas James (2 November 1742); and Trevecka 1088, Howel Harris to James Beaumont (21 January 1744).

[76] White, 'The Established Church, Dissent and the Welsh language', pp. 264–5.

[77] Trevecka 695, Howel Harris to Daniel Rowland (15 October 1742) and Trevecka 697, Howel Harris to Howel Davies (15 October 1742).

know that substantial numbers of letters from evangelicals from other awakenings reached Wales. Harris ensured that all of Whitefield's business managers looked out for letters that could be forwarded to Wales[78] and which he then ensured were distributed among the exhorters either to be read aloud at society meetings or distributed to those sufficiently literate to be able to read them for themselves.[79] In these ways the letter-writing network became a living reality in Wales. Whilst the language barrier militated against its successful operation to some extent, the creative way in which Howel Harris and his bands of committed exhorters were able to make use of them ensured that large numbers of Welsh Methodists were well informed about the latest revival news.

Despite the strenuous efforts of both Howel Harris and George Whitefield to ensure that the contents of the inter-revival letter-writing network reached as wide an audience as possible in Wales, they still only managed to reach a comparatively limited number of readers. Harris and Whitefield recognized from an early date that if the international communications network was really going to flourish and encompass as wide an audience as possible it would require a more efficient and popular vehicle of transmission. By the end of the 1730s, Whitefield had recognized that the revival movement had already grown too large to be adequately covered by the limited resources and range of the letter-writing network alone.[80]

The evangelicals were able to take full advantage of the boom in the print trade that had occurred in the wake of the repeal of the Licensing Act (1662) in 1695.[81] Its repeal had led to a flood of inexpensive and semi-popular newspapers and magazines from the proliferation of small-scale print shops in London and other English cities.[82] Magazines with an overtly evangelical content were a

---

[78]   Trevecka 1227, John Syms to Howel Harris (8 September 1744).
[79]   See for example Trevecka 155, Howel Harris to Thomas James (24 April 1739).
[80]   Stout, *The Divine Dramatist*, p. 144.
[81]   Michael Treadwell, 'The stationers and the printing acts at the end of the seventeenth century', in John Barnard, D. F. McKenzie and Maureen Bell (eds), *The Cambridge History of the Book in Britain, IV: 1557–1696*, (Cambridge, 2000), pp. 755–76 and Green, *Print and Protestantism in Early Modern England*, pp. 553–90.
[82]   See Jeremy Black, *The English Press in the Eighteenth Century* (London, 1987), pp. 12–22 and John Brewer, *The Pleasures of the Imagination: English Culture in the Eighteenth Century* (London, 1997), pp. 131–4.

highly innovative undertaking by the early Methodists, and the three publications that they were able to support established a new genre of spiritual writing. John Lewis edited the English and Welsh edition. It was published regularly – for a few years weekly – between 1740 and 1748 and appeared in a number of different guises with four different names during its eight-year print run. It was first published with the title *The Christian's Amusement* in September 1740, at the sole initiative of Lewis and under his exclusive editorial control. He attempted to print it weekly until March 1741, but financial difficulties forced him to abandon the project. It was at this point that Whitefield came to the rescue. Having recently returned from the American colonies, Whitefield discovered that his revival had completely dissipated as a result of the competitiveness of John Wesley and his followers. With his patronage the magazine was relaunched a few weeks later bearing the title *The Weekly History*. Officially Lewis remained the editor but the contents of the magazine reflected the course of Whitefield's itinerancy far more closely than its predecessor had done. In this format the magazine appeared every week until November 1742, when it was again superseded, appearing more spasmodically with the rather cumbersome title *An Account of the Most Remarkable Particulars Relating to the Present Progress of the Gospel in England, Wales, Scotland and America, as far as the Rev. Mr Whitefield, his Fellow Labourers and Assistants are Concerned.* After running for another year in this format the final version of the magazine appeared in 1743 and again appeared at more irregular intervals, this time with the title *The Christian History*.[83]

In Scotland, James Robe and William McCulloch copied John Lewis's example. McCulloch edited *The Glasgow Weekly History* between December 1741 and December 1742. Its contents were borrowed largely from the London magazine, though it also contained a substantial amount of Scottish material, information from the American colonies and a number of letters from Wales.[84] It was superseded by *The Christian*

---

[83] The only remaining complete copy of the magazine is at the National Library of Wales in Aberystwyth. Extended discussion of its significance and influence can be found in Susan Durden, 'A study of the first evangelical magazines, 1740–1748', *Journal of Ecclesiastical History*, 27, 3 (1976), 255–75; O'Brien, 'A transatlantic community of saints', 823–9; Lambert, *'Pedlar in Divinity'*, pp. 69–75; and Lambert, *Inventing the 'Great Awakening'*, pp. 165–71.

[84] Lambert, *'Pedlar in Divinity'*, pp. 73–4.

Monthly History in November 1743. This version focused more narrowly on conversion narratives written by Scottish evangelicals, and remained in circulation until January 1746.[85] In the American colonies there was only one edition of the magazine. In March 1743, *The Christian History, Containing Accounts of the Revival and Propagation of Religion in Great Britain and America* was begun under the editorial oversight of Thomas Prince Jr.[86] Unlike the Scottish and English magazines, the colonial version concentrated on events in the colonies themselves, paying particular attention to the course of Whitefield's colonial itinerancy.

All versions of the magazine followed a very similar pattern. When the revival was at its peak and demand was almost insatiable, they appeared weekly, each issue running to four pages and printed on inexpensive paper. The magazines were not, either in content or purpose, a marked departure from any of the other methods that had been utilized to bind the individual awakenings together. They grew out of the success of the letter-writing network and most issues contained material that had already been circulating in the letter-writing network for some time. Pieces written specifically for the magazine tended to be the exception, as the magazine contained just a sample of the best material from the wider network.

Those who took the initiative in the publication of the magazine and were its most regular contributors and supporters sought to ensure that all its readers clearly understood its aims and purpose. In the American colonies, Jonathan Edwards, perhaps the most articulate exponent of an international interpretation of the revival, recognized that the existing letter-writing network needed to be significantly expanded if its full potential were to be thoroughly utilized. He wrote:

> One thing more I would mention which . . . would tend to promote the revival and that is, that an history should be published once a month, or once a fortnight of the progress of it. It has been found by experience, that

---

85   The contents of these narratives have been analysed by T. C. Smout, 'Born again at Cambuslang: new evidence on popular religion and literacy in eighteenth-century Scotland', *Past and Present*, 97 (1982), 114–27.

86   J. E. van de Wetering, 'The Christian history of the Great Awakening', *Journal of Presbyterian History*, 44 (1966), 122–9; Amory and Hall (eds), *A History of the Book in America, I: The Colonial Book in the Atlantic World*, pp. 415 and 450.

the tidings of the remarkable effects of the power and grace of God in any place, tends greatly to awaken and engage the minds of persons, in other places.[87]

Similarly, James Robe thought that the religious magazines were 'a choice Means to promote the Communion of Saints upon the Earth'.[88] However, the most articulate explanation of the rationale behind the magazine came from the two key figures behind the London-based enterprise. John Lewis scattered comments throughout the magazines that give some indication of the reasons why he felt that they were a strategic weapon in the propagation and advance of the revival. In 1741 he hoped that the magazine would 'both edify and please all the Brethren'.[89] Its publication was clearly intended to bind the various evangelical communities in England and Wales closer together. In using a magazine in this way, Lewis was exploiting still further the resources that had been offered to the Methodists by the burgeoning transatlantic print culture. Newspapers and magazines had proliferated owing to the cheapness of the most modern printing techniques and the increase in disposable income of the middling sorts. [90] Speaking through a letter sent to the magazine by an anonymous writer, Lewis compared the Methodist magazines with those enjoyed by polite society:

Shall the polite world have their Spectators, Tatler's, Guardians and Comedies: Shall the curious Reader have his daily and Weekly News, his Advertiser, Gazetteer, Miscellany, &c. And shall not the Children of God also have their proper entertainment, their weekly amusement, their Divine Miscellany, and the historical account of the progress of the Lord's kingdom.[91]

---

[87]   Quoted in Durden, 'A study of the first evangelical magazines', 257.
[88]   Quoted in Lambert, 'Pedlar in Divinity', p. 75.
[89]   CA 14.
[90]   Black, The English Press in the Eighteenth Century, pp. 25–49; Michael Harris and Alan Lee (eds), The Press in English Society from the Seventeenth to Nineteenth Centuries (London, 1986); and, despite its mostly political concerns, Hannah Barker, Newspapers, Politics, and Public Opinion in Late Eighteenth Century England (Oxford, 1998), which contains much background detail on the growth of the popular newspaper press in London.
[91]   (Anonymous letter), WH 13.

Yet he was also keen to point out that the evangelical magazines had a far higher purpose than other publications. The contents of his magazine were intended to encourage the saints by demonstrating to them, with first-hand accounts, the success of the revival. In a note inserted in *The Weekly History* in 1742 John Lewis wrote:

> If Ministers, and other Discerning People of God, in England (or wheresoever the Lord is pleased to direct this Paper) will be so kind as to send Accounts of the Progress of the Gospel, and the Powerful Operation of the Holy Spirit, to the Printer: he humbly hopes (and has by Experience found) that such Accounts are and have been very comfortable and encouraging to those who have an Opportunity of reading the same: And for that Reason, such letters wou'd be gladly received, and carefully inserted by their Humble Servant.[92]

Such accounts he firmly believed would galvanize the resolve of his readers and, perhaps more importantly, 'prepare our minds against a time of suffering, if it should please God to call us to it'[93] – a possibility that seemed increasingly likely in 1741.

Throughout its eight years in print, John Lewis's magazine was never wholly free from uncertainties about its long-term viability. Part of the problem stemmed from the very nature of the magazine itself. Its profitability depended on the success of the revival. When things were going well the magazine prospered. When the revival seemed to be foundering, particularly after the divisions of 1740 and 1741, the magazine struggled to maintain its place in the regular reading of many Methodists. Its success depended on the enthusiastic commitment of Whitefield and Howel Harris. When the magazine became *The Weekly History* in April 1741, Whitefield's direct input increased dramatically and his editorial control ensured that the magazine became more narrowly focused on publishing accounts of the success of the revival and therefore more successful.[94] What has not been so well documented is the extent to which Howel Harris devoted considerable time and energy in support of the magazine and in encouraging John Lewis to persist with its publication, despite seemingly insurmountable problems.

---

92   *WH* 46 (Saturday, 20 February 1742).
93   Ibid.
94   *WH* 4.

Harris had been an enthusiastic reader of *The Christian's Amusement* since it had first been published. In a letter to John Lewis in March 1741 he assured him that the magazine had been 'sweet and edifying to me and to others'[95] and offered his services as a promoter and distributor of the magazine in Wales.[96] From this date Lewis and Harris seem to have developed a very close working relationship, and Lewis sought Harris's opinion on a number of occasions regarding the magazine's publication. Shortly after Harris had written to him in March 1741, Lewis confided to Harris that he was struggling to keep the magazine going, as he was barely selling enough copies each week to cover the basic costs of printing and paper.[97] It was in response to this crisis that Whitefield stepped in and rescued the magazine by giving it a new role as the official mouthpiece of the Calvinistic revival. Later, when the magazine faced even more serious crises, Lewis once more turned to Howel Harris for advice and encouragement. When in 1743 Lewis was again considering changing the format of the magazine it was to Harris that he turned for advice. He hoped that his decision to change its layout, printing it in a neat pocket-sized version and producing it less frequently, would enable him to include more material in each volume and meet more of his readers' needs. By also adopting more aggressive marketing techniques, lowering its price and offering to deliver copies of the magazine to addresses in London, he hoped that he would be able to recoup some of his losses. Harris was kept closely informed of these decisions.[98] Later, after these marketing ploys had failed to arrest the decline in the magazine's sales figures, it was to Harris that a dejected Lewis first signalled his intention to quit printing the magazine altogether.[99] Harris, as always, sought to be as practical and encouraging as possible, promising that the Welsh Methodists were prepared to do all they could to assist him in keeping the magazine afloat.[100] Despite his efforts, Lewis

[95] Trevecka 319, Howel Harris to John Lewis (19 March 1741).
[96] Ibid.
[97] Trevecka 235, John Lewis to Howel Harris (no date) and Trevecka 311, John Lewis to Elizabeth James (31 January 1741).
[98] Trevecka 853, John Lewis to Howel Harris (8 April 1743) and Lambert, 'Pedlar in Divinity', pp. 81–2.
[99] See Trevecka 1364, John Lewis to Howel Harris (21 October 1745).
[100] Trevecka 1368, Howel Harris to John Lewis (5 November 1745).

found it almost impossible to make the magazine a financial success. When the revival was at its height and Whitefield was most closely involved in the magazine's production there was sufficient momentum to keep the magazine in print. When the progress of the revival became more fitful in the mid-1740s and the Calvinistic revival struggled to maintain its position in the face of repeated secessions from its ranks after Whitefield had departed for a four-year visit to America, the demise of the magazine was inevitable. In addition, it is possible that Lewis's own disillusionment with the Calvinistic movement and his desire to join the Moravians may have contributed significantly to his decision finally to relinquish responsibility for the loss-making magazine.

Howel Harris's friendship with John Lewis and his obsession with everything relating to the international dimensions of the revival ensured that the magazine was widely circulated in Wales and that its pages were regularly stocked with items dealing with Welsh events. Yet Harris was conscious that in the same way as many of the letters that circulated throughout the revival were beyond the reach of many monoglot Welsh-speaking Methodists, so the magazine, also only printed in English, had limited appeal to those Welsh Methodists whose only language was Welsh. In 1741 Harris had expressed his concerns to John Lewis and apologized for the relatively small number of issues that he felt could be circulated in Wales as a result of the language barrier.[101] Yet such was the value of the magazine, particularly in the early 1740s, that the Welsh Methodists seriously considered funding the translation of some of the most useful issues and printing them at the recently established provincial press at Pontypool.[102] Despite initial interest in the idea, Harris's apparent lack of enthusiasm for the enterprise ensured that nothing more concrete materialized.[103]

Notwithstanding the language barrier, there seems little doubt that many of the Welsh Methodists had some form of access to the magazines. Howel Harris, having decided against translating large sections of the magazine into Welsh, became the chief

---

[101] Trevecka 319, Howel Harris to John Lewis (19 March 1741). See also Trevecka 1368, Howel Harris to John Lewis (5 November 1745).
[102] Rees, 'The Welsh book-trade before 1820', p. xxiv.
[103] Trevecka 319, Howel Harris to John Lewis (19 March 1741).

distribution officer of the magazine in Wales, a position that he was able to occupy with comparative ease because of his intimate knowledge of both the London and the Welsh Methodist communities. Using his London links and his friendship with John Lewis, he was able to develop a network of distribution centres throughout south and west Wales that roughly corresponded to the areas covered by his fellow revivalists and the larger band of exhorters.[104] In 1741 he tried to interest Richard Jenkins, an exhorter at Llandinam, to take *The Weekly History* and distribute it among the societies that he served in Montgomeryshire.[105] Similarly, he urged William Richard to take copies of the magazine with him when he visited the societies in his care in south Cardiganshire and western Pembrokeshire.[106] In southwest Wales more generally, Daniel Rowland acted as the main distributor. He made it readily available to the large numbers who gathered regularly at Llangeitho and ensured that it was distributed from that centre to many of the local leaders of the revival scattered throughout the south-west. In September 1742, for example, he received a consignment of magazines from Howel Harris, complete with detailed instructions for their wider circulation. Harris advised him to send copies to Elizabeth Thomas at Longhouse, who would then be able to distribute them throughout Pembrokeshire with the help of Howel Davies; he then requested that he forward the remainder to Griffith Jones who, he hoped, would distribute them on his own travels in Carmarthenshire.[107]

Precise distribution figures for the magazine in Wales are difficult to establish. With reference to its circulation in England, Frank Lambert has estimated that George Whitefield's itinerant preachers delivered at least 500 copies of the magazine on their regular circuits.[108] The minutes of the Tabernacle give slightly more concrete figures. On 6 July 1747, right at the end of its run, the following entry was made:

---

[104] See the list of recipients on the inside of the front cover of HHD 105, 29 November–24 December 1743 and Trevecka 1315, Howel Harris to John Lewis (19 April 1745).

[105] Trevecka 372, Howel Harris to Richard Jenkins (17 August 1741).

[106] Trevecka 668, Howel Harris to William Richard (29 September 1742).

[107] Trevecka 644, Howel Harris to Daniel Rowland (14 September 1742).

[108] Lambert, *'Pedlar in Divinity'*, p. 70.

> Brother Blake see that the Monthly Hystory be sent about according as they are subscribed for, vizt. 150 to the west, Exeter; 60 to Plymouth and 80 to Gloucester, and 40 to Portsmouth, Oulney, etc., 50 to Essex, Chatham, Chinner, and 50 to Staffordshire, Salop, Ludlow.[109]

The following November another more detailed entry was included in the minutes; it stated:

> Agreed again with John Lewis as more calls come in for the Weekly Hystory that we take 400 from him att bookseller's price, vizt. At 4s. 0d., and he take care to send them punctually att the month's end (after being revised by Brother Boddington and corrected) by the proper wagons as follows – 150 to Mr Kennedy at Exeter and the brother that goes first there to bring up the money, 60 to Plymouth to Mr Kinsman near the Tabernacle there, 80 to Alderman Harris att Gloucester sent to Mr Awstin near Newgatestreet, 50 to Mr Pearsal by the Welch Cross, Birmingham, 40 to Portsmouth and the rest to the Tabernacle house to be sent – 18 to Essex, 5 to Chatham and [gap], and to be payd by Brother Shergold.[110]

Whilst neither entry relates directly to Wales it does give some indication of the number of magazines that were still being circulated. It would be safe to assume that circulation figures for 1741 and 1742, when the revival was at its height, would have been far in excess of the 400 ordered from John Lewis in November 1747. Whilst these entries do not give any indication of the number of issues that Howel Harris carried back to Wales after his trips to London, they demonstrate how substantial numbers of the magazine entered Wales via towns on the Welsh border like Gloucester, Ludlow and Shrewsbury.

As with the contents of the letter-writing network, Harris found ways of circumventing the language barrier and making the magazine relevant to monoglot Welsh-speakers. Again he made use of the societies to disseminate the contents of the magazine. Where societies possessed a bilingual exhorter, issues could be read aloud in their meetings by means of *ad hoc* or précised translations. Issues of the magazine could also be circulated informally among friends and it is not too difficult to imagine society members with some rudimentary understanding

---

[109] CMA 2946, 2, part 2, 6 July 1747, p. 38.
[110] Ibid., p. 39.

of English gathering their Welsh-speaking friends to hear the latest news about the progress of the revival. Despite Howel Harris's concern that the number of subscribers to the magazine in Wales was small, there is sufficient evidence to suggest that there was a real hunger for it among many Welsh Methodists. Such was the demand that in 1743 Harris requested John Lewis to send any spare back-issues; he felt confident that they would be eagerly snapped up by the Welsh Methodists if the price was right![111] There was also some interest in receiving copies of the colonial version of the magazine in 1746,[112] and a few Welsh evangelicals were sufficiently aware of *The Glasgow Weekly History* to send William McCulloch details about the progress of the revival in Wales.[113] Their insatiable thirst for the latest news about the revival ensured that the Welsh Methodists benefited from the contents of the magazines, even if their access to them was at times reliant on the second-hand translations of a sympathetic English-speaking brother or sister. Sufficient numbers of Welsh Methodists wrote to Lewis and Harris expressing their gratitude for the issues of the magazine that they had received for us to conclude that it fulfilled an extremely valuable role for many in Wales, particularly in the early 1740s. An anonymous Welsh brother, probably Howell Griffith, wrote in a letter printed in *The Weekly History* in 1742: 'I have found great unity in my Soul with yours; and have had great sweetness in reading your Papers; they are dear and refreshing to my poor Soul.'[114] Similarly, the comments of John Oulton, a sympathetic Independent minister from Leominster on the Welsh border, written in a letter to Howel Harris in March 1742, reinforce his testimony: 'Blessed be God, with pleasure and refreshment I read ye experimental Gospel Letters In the weekly history (and hope

---

[111]   Trevecka 853, John Lewis to Howel Harris (8 April 1743).

[112]   Trevecka 1424, John Syms to Howel Harris (4 March 1746).

[113]   See William McCulloch (ed.), *The Weekly History: or, An Account of the most Remarkable Particulars relating to the present Progress of the Gospel*, 48 and 49.

[114]   See 'Brother at Treverig-Ucha to John Lewis', *The Christian History: Or a General Account of the Progress of the Gospel in England, Wales, Scotland and America: So Far as Mr Whitefield, his Fellow Labourers, and Assistants are Concerned* (ed. John Lewis) (hereafter *CH*), VII, 1, 75–8.

they will be continued) Especially as they are a transcript of my own heart respecting sin and grace.'[115]

The evangelical magazines have not received the attention they merit from serious students of the evangelical revival. Whilst historians like Susan O'Brien and Frank Lambert have drawn attention to the important role that they played in the creation of the international communications network, their actual contents have not so far been subjected to closer analysis. This is surprising, since their contents provide an almost unparalleled insight into all aspects of the international revival, and in many respects the viewpoints put forward in the magazine can be taken as the official interpretation of the early history of the Methodist movement and the clearest indication of the pioneer revivalists' understanding of the key events of the late 1730s and 1740s. The magazines clearly acted as a unifying agent binding the various national awakenings together by building on the foundation of the letter-writing network and widening its scope through the creation of a public mouthpiece by means of which the converts of the revival could be more adequately shepherded, and the revival more closely defined.

For these reasons the magazines are an invaluable resource for the historian of the Welsh Methodist revival. The letters that appeared in them provide still more evidence of the reality of the international dimension of the revival in the experience of the average Welsh Methodist. Their contents lend themselves to almost endless analysis and can be used by historians seeking answers to a range of questions. However, the nature of the letters means that they do not lend themselves easily to detailed quantitative analysis. A single letter, for example, may contain information and commentary on a wide range of subjects and events in a relatively short compass, and sometimes in only a cursory manner. Very few letters focus on just one issue. The letters therefore lend themselves most naturally to a consideration of some of the main themes that occupied the minds of the members of the international evangelical community during the late 1730s and the early 1740s. In the present study they have

---

[115] Trevecka 504, John Oulton to Howel Harris (27 March 1742). For examples of the premium that the Welsh Methodists placed on regularly receiving copies of the magazine see the letter 'From a brother at Treverig-Ucha, in Llantrisant Parish, Glamorganshire in Wales to the Printer of this Book', *CH*, VII, 1, 75–8.

been used more narrowly to demonstrate the existence of an international communications network, based on the shared experience of the New Birth and the outpouring of the Holy Spirit and to deconstruct the Welsh Methodists' role within it. It remains for others to deploy the letters in other ways and to subject them to a different range of questions.

The contents of the letter writing network, the correspondence reprinted in the evangelical magazines and the published versions of both Whitefield's and Wesley's diaries are closely related stylistically in that they are all highly personal responses to the evangelical approach to Christianity and the events of the early years of the evangelical revival. Whether they were Whitefield's accounts of his international itinerancy or the personal experience of fairly insignificant evangelicals, they were all very similar pieces of literature designed to fulfil the early evangelicals' craving for the latest news, support, fellowship and the discussion of more practical issues. Whilst analysing this material is vital to unravelling the Welsh Methodists' interaction with the wider revival, it is easy to overlook the primary place that all the revivalists gave to the more transitory activity of preaching. All the revivalists were, first and foremost, charismatic preachers accustomed to preaching to exceptionally large crowds of eager and animated listeners. Preaching tended to be the first point of contact with the revivalists' message for the majority of individuals, and it was as an immediate response to such preaching that many people experienced their conversions.[116] The experience of the sermon and the drama of being involved in one of these sermonic events tended to encourage some of the more outlandish emotional excesses of the revival.[117] The didactic content of the sermon often

---

[116] On the role of preaching in the evangelical revival see Stout, *The New England Soul*, pp. 185–258; Horton Davies, *Worship and Theology in England: From Watts and Wesley to Maurice, 1690–1850* (Grand Rapids, 1966), pp. 146–50; and Ned Landsman, 'Evangelists and their hearers: popular interpretations of revivalist preaching in eighteenth-century Scotland', *Journal of British Studies*, 28 (1989), 120–49.

[117] Very little work has been done on the development of preaching in Wales during the eighteenth century. For some reflections on the nineteenth century see Sioned Davies, 'Performing from the pulpit: an introduction to preaching in nineteenth-century Wales', in Joseph Falaky Nagy (ed.), *Identifying the Celtic* (Dublin, 2002), pp. 115–40 and W. P. Griffith, ' "Preaching second to no other under the sun": Edward Matthews, the Nonconformist pulpit and Welsh identity during the mid-nineteenth century', in Pope (ed.), *Religion and National Identity*, pp. 61–83.

took second place to the emotionalism of the preaching event. Sermons came into their own as they were printed and distanced from the excesses of the context in which they were first delivered. They eventually played as important a role in the nurture and development of the converts as many of the letters and religious magazines created specifically for this purpose. They were one of the chief methods of doctrinal instruction, the source of much spiritual and practical advice and the principal means of encouragement for those converts who found it too difficult to maintain the rate of development that they had managed to attain in the very first days and months of their evangelical lives.

To maximize the potential of the best of these sermons the revivalists sought to ensure that as many of them as possible went into print and were circulated as extensively as possible. Again, George Whitefield took advantage of the expansion of the provincial book trade during the early part of the century to make some of the best evangelical literature available to a wide readership at fairly accessible prices.[118] As a result of the sheer number of them that became available, Whitefield's printed sermons, according to Frank Lambert, came to assume an 'important, symbolic significance'[119] throughout the revival, representing as they did all of its most important principles and themes. Harris, despite producing a massive amount of literature in the form of diaries and letters, would not have regarded publishing his sermons as an appropriate venture for someone who persisted in styling himself as nothing more than a layman and an exhorter – definitely not a preacher![120] Daniel Rowland only published two small collections of sermons in Welsh in the early 1770s.[121] It was not until almost twenty years after the beginning of the Welsh revival that William Williams first emerged as its main theologian, and not until after the fresh outbreak of revival in 1762

[118] John Feather, *The Provincial Book Trade in Eighteenth-Century England* (Cambridge, 1985); John Feather, *A History of British Publishing* (London, 1988), pp. 93–105; and Brewer, *The Pleasures of the Imagination*, pp. 136–8.

[119] Lambert, 'Pedlar in Divinity', p. 76.

[120] For more on Harris's view of his own role as a layman in the leadership of the revival see Tudur, *Howell Harris*, pp. 21–2 and 28–32. Despite this, Harris was amongst the best-read of all of the early Methodists. For an indication of the scope of his personal reading see Geoffrey F. Nuttall, *Howel Harris, 1714–1773: The Last Enthusiast* (Cardiff, 1965), pp. 63–4; and, for a more detailed discussion, Eifion Evans, 'Howel Harris and the printed page', *CCHMC*, 23 (1990), 33–62.

[121] See Daniel Rowland, *Pum Pregeth* (Caerfyrddin, 1772) and Daniel Rowland, *Tair Pregeth* (Caerfyrddin, 1772).

did he publish any of his main apologetic works.[122] In this vacuum the Welsh Methodists made use of the best material published by evangelicals such as Whitefield, Jonathan Edwards and Ebenezer and Ralph Erskine, a policy which demonstrated their solidarity with what was being produced by these figures and reinforced the sense of common purpose among all the awakenings.[123]

The priority that George Whitefield attached to the provision of godly literature in Wales was in evidence on the very first occasion when he visited Howel Harris in March 1739. Among the things that they discussed together to advance the revival none seemed as important as the reprinting of a new edition of the Welsh Bible and the translation of some of Whitefield's best sermons into Welsh.[124] Whitefield's own published work attained something verging on apostolic authority in Wales. His close working relationship with Howel Harris had led to his becoming a frequent visitor; the Welsh Methodists had sided with him against the Wesley brothers in the early 1740s, and following this he had become privy to all the discussions aimed at bringing a measure of order to the Welsh societies. His writings played an important role in this process and they were widely read in Wales. Those with some understanding of English read them soon after they were published and tended to be the most enthusiastic voices urging their translation into Welsh. By 1740, four of Whitefield's most important works had appeared in Welsh. Among these, his sermon on the New Birth[125] and his defence of the Methodist societies[126] were translated very soon after they had appeared in English.[127]

[122] His *Llythyr Martha Philopur* was not published until 1762 and its sister work, *Ateb Philo-Evangelius*, not until a year later. His work on the Methodist societies themselves, *Drws y Society Profiad*, was published in 1777. Copies of these works can be found in Gomer Morgan Roberts (gol.), *Gweithiau William Williams Pantycelyn* (Caerdydd, 1964 and 1967). For more on the context of the works see the brief overview of his life and work in Glyn Tegai Hughes, *Williams Pantycelyn* (Cardiff, 1983), pp. 510–75.

[123] Morgan, *The Great Awakening in Wales*, p. 9.

[124] George Whitefield to Daniel Abbot (10 March 1739), in Thomas, 'George Whitefield and friends: the correspondence of some early Methodists', *NLWJ*, XXVII, 2 (1991), 176.

[125] See George Whitefield, *Nodau'r Enedigaeth Newydd. Sef Pregeth a Bregethwyd yn Eglwys Plwyf St. Mary, Whitechapel* (Bristol, 1739).

[126] See George Whitefield, *Llythyr Oddiwrth y Parchedig Mr G. W. at Societies neu Gymdeithasau Crefyddol a Osodwyd yn Ddiweddar ar Droed Mewn Amriw Leodd yng Nghymru a Lloegr* (Bristol, 1740).

[127] A complete list of books authored by George Whitefield which were either translated into Welsh or printed in Wales can be found in Rees, *Libri Walliae*, pp. 642–3.

The way in which Whitefield's writings were received and circulated in Wales illustrates many of the difficulties faced by Harris as he tried to ensure that the best evangelical literature produced by supporters of the revival reached Wales. Realizing the importance that many of his co-revivalists attached to his printed works, Whitefield attempted to satisfy demand by setting up a book room at the Tabernacle.[128] Initially the task of printing Whitefield's writings had been given to the Moravian bookseller, James Hutton (1715–95),[129] and their distribution was undertaken by William Seward.[130] After Seward's death, Whitefield centralized the distribution of his works at the Tabernacle book room. He appointed John Syms as his agent and from this centre he was able to distribute effectively both his own works and those of many of his contemporaries throughout the revival, using the networks that had already been established to facilitate the circulation of letters and *The Weekly History*. After Syms joined the Moravians in 1745, he was eventually replaced by Thomas Boddington who was able to carry on Syms's work along the same lines.[131] In the same way as Howel Harris had developed a close working relationship with John Lewis, he cultivated an equally profitable friendship with Syms, and their friendship acted as a nexus whereby godly evangelical literature was introduced and circulated throughout Wales. In 1743, for example, he offered Harris nine bound copies of Whitefield's *Journals* for the Welsh Methodists at a 16 per cent discount,[132] and between 1744 and 1746 he regularly sent large parcels of books to Wales via Howel Harris.[133] The precise number of books is difficult to ascertain with any degree of accuracy. In many of his letters to Harris, Syms seems to have simply informed Harris of the latest publications and expected him in his reply to order substantial numbers of the recommended

[128] Lambert, 'Pedlar in Divinity', p. 85.
[129] Podmore, *The Moravian Church in England*, pp. 34–6.
[130] Lambert, 'Pedlar in Divinity', pp. 84–5.
[131] Trevecka 1475, Thomas Boddington to Howel Harris (21 June 1746); Trevecka 1687, Thomas Boddington to Howel Harris (18 August 1747); and Trevecka 1699, Thomas Boddington to Howel Harris (29 September 1747).
[132] Trevecka 1035, John Syms to Howel Harris (5 November 1743) and Lambert, 'Pedlar in Divinity', p. 91.
[133] Trevecka 1188, John Syms to Howel Harris (9 June 1744); Trevecka 1211, John Syms to Howel Harris (11 August 1744); and Trevecka 1424, John Syms to Howel Harris (4 March 1746).

works.[134] In June 1744, for example, Syms sent Harris 200 copies of Whitefield's *Letter to the Rev. Mr Thomas Church*[135] and forty-three copies of a volume containing twenty-three of Whitefield's sermons.[136]

Once they reached Wales the books were distributed through the distribution centres that Harris had previously established.[137] Sometimes the distribution of literature worked in the opposite direction, as local exhorters took the initiative by placing orders with Howel Harris that were then relayed to London. Thomas Bowen from Tyddyn, Montgomeryshire, wrote to Harris in 1743[138] requesting a copy of the first volume of the recently published Welsh translation of Ralph Erskine's *Law-Death Gospel-Life*[139] and five copies of the second volume which he judged to be 'more choice'[140] than the first, and a volume of John Cennick's hymns.[141]

Yet in the same way as Harris had complained to John Lewis about the lack of interest in his magazine because of the inability of many Welsh Methodists to understand its English-language contents, so Harris seems to have been frustrated by the often slow response which he received from some quarters when he tried to arouse interest in the latest publications to roll from the evangelical presses. When, in August 1744, John Syms unexpectedly sent Harris a parcel containing a large number of copies of Whitefield's sermons and *Journals*, Harris, in his reply, doubted whether he would be able to dispose of even half of them because 'ye people are so poor & so welchly'.[142] Rather than requesting that he send the books that he could not sell back to London, Syms, in his reply, audaciously offered Harris advice

---

[134] Trevecka 1211, John Syms to Howel Harris (11 August 1744).

[135] Thomas Church was vicar of Battersea and prebendary of St Paul's. In 1744 he wrote *A Serious and Expostulatory Letter to the Rev. Mr Whitefield*, criticizing Whitefield for his irregular practices and particularly for his frequent absences from Georgia which he felt had resulted in the neglect of his Orphan House. *DNB* and Luke Tyerman, *The Life and Times of the Rev. George Whitefield*, II (London, 1876), pp. 95–6.

[136] Trevecka 1188, John Syms to Howel Harris (9 June 1744).

[137] Trevecka 811, Howel Harris to George Whitefield (1 March 1743).

[138] Trevecka 826, Thomas Bowen to Howel Harris (24 March 1743).

[139] The two volumes of Ralph Erskine's sermons were translated by John Morgan from Pontypool and printed by Felix Farley at Bristol in 1743 with the title, *Traethawd am Farw i'r Ddeddf, a Byw i Dduw*.

[140] Trevecka 826, Thomas Bowen to Howel Harris (24 March 1743).

[141] This was probably John Cennick's, *Sacred Hymns for the Use of Religious Societies* (Bristol, 1743).

[142] Trevecka 1220, Howel Harris to John Syms (29 August 1744).

on the best way to advertise and stimulate interest in the books. His letter is revealing for the insight it gives into the way in which the evangelical book trade operated. Importantly, Syms first stressed that the books were sent for the 'Use of the People & not to make a gain of'.[143] He cautioned Harris against 'taking them abt with You to peddle Them off',[144] but in characteristic fashion he counselled that Harris need only tell people about the availability of the books and leave it to the Holy Spirit to motivate people to buy them. Those that remained unsold, he thought, would be best placed in the hands of designated stockists to whom people could resort if they wished to purchase copies. This somewhat innovative commercial approach illustrates the tension that many Methodists often felt about employing the worldly techniques of the market-place to further evangelical religion. Far from ruthlessly exploiting every available opportunity afforded by the thriving commercial market, as Frank Lambert has argued,[145] Syms's letter highlights the reluctance with which many Methodists often entered the world of advertising and commerce and how aware they were of the apparent inconsistency between their message of salvation by free grace through complete reliance on the direct work of the Holy Spirit and their reliance on sophisticated communication techniques to maintain the momentum of their movement.

Yet, as has already been stressed, much of this literature was beyond the reach of many Welsh-speaking evangelicals. Much of it was produced in England to meet the needs of the English evangelicals, and it was written in the English language. Harris, Daniel Rowland and the other leaders of the revival in Wales were all proficient readers of English and could read and assimilate with apparent ease all the godly books that rolled off the London revival presses. Whereas the problems posed by the language barrier could be fairly easily overcome with relatively small pieces of literature like letters and the religious magazines, printed books presented a whole range of different logistical problems. Apart from the impact which writers such as Whitefield, Jonathan Edwards, the Erskine brothers and others had on the views of the Welsh revivalists and thus indirectly on many of their followers,

---

[143]   Trevecka 1227, John Syms to Howel Harris (8 September 1744).
[144]   Ibid.
[145]   Lambert, 'Pedlar in Divinity', pp. 11–51.

more specific interaction for the majority of Welsh evangelicals was more problematic. Spontaneous translations of printed sermons and more substantial theological works in society meetings were obviously impractical and, as a result, the Welsh revivalists were forced to invest considerable time and effort in translating the works which they felt would be most relevant to their converts. Throughout the 1740s the provision of suitable evangelical literature in the Welsh language became one of the most frequently recurring issues at the Welsh Methodists' regular Association meetings. In 1743, for example, the Association decided to translate and print Ralph Erskine's *Law-Death Gospel-Life* into Welsh,[146] and in July 1745 they decided to translate and print Elisha Coles's *A Practical Discourse on God's Sovereignty*.[147] For many of the ordinary Methodists these translations were the only access they had to the work of evangelicals from other cultures and countries. The enthusiasm with which they were purchased and read once again demonstrates the insatiable thirst of many Methodists in Wales for the latest material analysing the revival and offering spiritual instruction and support. Of course reading such material, like reading the evangelical letters and magazines, was another tangible expression of the international world-view of many Welsh evangelicals and evidence of their commitment to participation in the wider evangelical movement.

As well as being committed letter-writers and voracious readers, the Welsh Methodists, like their Wesleyan and Calvinistic counterparts in England, kept meticulous records of all aspects of the administration and oversight of their revival. As the revival grew beyond the small groups of societies under the direct oversight of Harris and Daniel Rowland, the revivalists became increasingly preoccupied with issues relating to the consolidation of their converts and the perpetuation of the movement. In their practical responses to administrative problems the Welsh revivalists unwittingly began to develop a form of Church order closely akin to a loose form of Presbyterian connexionalism, albeit within the

---

[146] Trevecka 878, Howel Harris to George Whitefield (25 May 1743).

[147] See 'Association held at Blaen-y-Gwyn, 3 July 1745', in CMA 2945, p. 145. Coles's treatise had first been translated into Welsh and printed in 1729 with the title *Traethawd ar Benarglwyddiaeth Duw*. See Rees, *Libri Walliae*, pp. 161–2.

confines of the Church of England during the eighteenth century. Their system was based on the division of the country into different areas, each under the oversight of a superintendent, who in turn was governed by monthly, quarterly and annual Associations, under the overall guidance of their 'Elder Brother',[148] George Whitefield, who was given the title of Moderator by both the English and Welsh Calvinistic Methodists in January 1743.

Detailed minutes were kept of all the organizational meetings held by the Welsh Methodists in the late 1730s and the 1740s. This documentation consists of the minutes of their various Associations and the reports on the activities of the societies written by the superintendents and the exhorters and sent to the relevant Association. The society meeting reports, which usually focused on reporting the spiritual condition of members, tended to be written in Welsh. The Association minutes, by contrast, were written in English. English was the language of the international revival and as a result of Whitefield's frequent contributions to the deliberations of the Associations, the keeping of records in English seems to have been natural and entirely uncontroversial.[149]

These administrative records obviously differ from the letters and printed literature which the early evangelicals produced. They were not intended to be read by every member of the revival and so did not function as unifying agents between Welsh Methodism and international evangelicalism in the way that letters did. They do however highlight the manner in which the Welsh revival was administered, and they make it possible to decipher the way in which the Welsh revivalists, with the support and input of Whitefield, attempted to create a more tangible structure that could give expression to their desire to be seen as both Welsh Methodists and participants on the wider evangelical stage. For the historian anxious to trace the interplay between the revival in Wales and coexistent movements in England,

---

[148] Howel Harris usually began his letters to Whitefield by calling him 'My dearest Elder Brother' or some similar variation. See, for example, Trevecka 607, Howel Harris to George Whitefield (21 August 1742) and Trevecka 788, Howel Harris to George Whitefield (25 January 1743). The term is indicative of the advisory role that Whitefield came to occupy in Wales. On the significance of the title see Jones, *The Trevecka Letters*, pp. 280–1, and on what it actually meant see below, pp. 192–3.

[149] For more on the Welsh Methodists' adoption of the English language in their official records see White, 'The Established Church, Dissent and the Welsh language', pp. 264–5.

Scotland, the American colonies and contexts further afield, the literature that the early evangelicals produced is invaluable. The diaries, letters and magazines that the Methodists produced or patronized, and the printed works which they saw through the presses, created the impression that God was doing something extraordinary in their day and that he was using the Methodists to carry it out.

III

'OUR DAYS ARE REFORMING DAYS': ESTABLISHING THE INTERNATIONAL REVIVAL

When, in November 1742, Howel Harris wrote to one of his co-workers in Wales 'about the Progress of ye Gospel in Scotland, Yorkshire, Lincolnshire, Warwickshire, Wiltshire, Germany, Prussia, New England, Pennsylvania and many other provinces',[1] he did so against the backdrop of almost four years of continuous interaction between his own Welsh revival and many of the evangelical communities included in his brief overview. Interpreting the Welsh Methodist revival as merely one element in what has been called a 'pan-Protestant phenomenon'[2] is deeply rooted in the daily experience of many of the first generation of evangelical converts. Soon after learning of one another's existence the pioneer revivalists sought to form meaningful friendships with each other and, on the basis of these relationships, began to share their experiences and their ideas about the propagation of their work.

It was Howel Harris who made the first tentative contacts with his fellow revivalists, and throughout the whole of his time at the head of the Welsh revival he consistently kept his followers in the minds of their fellow evangelicals and relentlessly publicized his revival among those evangelicals with whom he came into regular contact. He was able to do this because of the close relationship that existed between himself and the leader of the English revival in the late 1730s, George Whitefield. Whitefield was the pivot around which the majority of Welsh participation revolved. It was Harris who ensured that Whitefield was kept regularly up to date with the progress of the revival in Wales, that news from the other revivals regularly reached the Welsh Methodists and that the events occupying the minds of the revivalists filtered down to the level of the humblest convert in Wales. In the later 1740s especially, he became an indispensable

---

[1] Trevecka 2803, Howel Harris to Herbert Jenkins (22 November 1742).
[2] Walsh, 'Methodism and the origins of English-speaking evangelicalism', p. 44.

figure in the leadership of the English Calvinistic revival, particularly during Whitefield's extended absence in the American
colonies between 1744 and 1748.

Harris's responsibility for ensuring that the Welsh revival
remained robustly committed to its international obligations does
not necessarily mean that the other leaders of the Welsh awakening were uncommitted to the international aspects of the revival.
Daniel Rowland, Howel Davies and, later, William Williams
were enthusiastic followers of the progress of the evangelical
movement and keen to interpret it as the precursor of the
imminent arrival of Christ's millennial reign.[3] Yet, Daniel
Rowland in particular became gradually more irritated at
Harris's fondness for spending long periods of time in London,
particularly during the periods when Rowland felt that the
Welsh revival needed his undivided attention.[4] Although the
majority of them never quite matched Harris's enthusiasm, all of
the Welsh Methodists, to a greater or lesser degree, were committed to the maintenance of their participation in the transnational revival, ensuring that the Welsh revival remained at the
cutting edge of wider evangelical developments.

Harris's introduction to the wider revival occurred when a
letter from Whitefield arrived at Trefeca in January 1739. The
letter heralded the dawn of a remarkable four-year period,
during which the Welsh and English revivals enjoyed a remarkable sense of common purpose. Though this unity was preserved,
to some extent, throughout the 1740s, after 1741 it never proved
to be as strong or as mutually rewarding as it was during the two
years that immediately preceded the revival's descent into the
infighting that precipitated its polarization along theological
lines. However, it would be misleading to assume that, before
Whitefield first wrote to Harris, neither of them had had any
previous contact with their respective countries or awakenings.
Whilst the importance of the letter must be acknowledged and its
contents given due weight and prominence, Whitefield did not
write to Harris in a vacuum with no prior knowledge of him or
his work, and similarly Harris would not have received the letter

---

[3]   Dewi Arwel Hughes, 'William Williams Pantycelyn's eschatology as seen in his
Aurora Borealis of 1774', *Scottish Bulletin of Evangelical Theology*, IV, I (1986), 49–63.
[4]   Trevecka 705, Daniel Rowland to Howel Harris (20 October 1742). See also
below, pp. 205–6 for more detail.

in total ignorance and unaware that there were other awakenings in the British Isles and in the American colonies. There were definite antecedents to this initial contact which, from Harris's point of view at least, predisposed the Welsh Methodists to adopt a transnational view of their revival.

Before his conversion in 1735 and the beginning of the Welsh awakening shortly afterwards, Howel Harris had been precon-ditioned by his upbringing and education to adopt a world-view that went far beyond the confines of his neighbourhood and homeland.[5] Despite M. H. Jones's insistence that his parents were 'simple, peasant folk, illiterate to all intents and purposes',[6] Harris's formative years can hardly be regarded as representative of the majority of the inhabitants of early and mid-eighteenth-century Wales. He was one of three brothers, each of whom reached a measure of prominence in his chosen profession and in London society.[7] As a youth Howel enjoyed a good general education, financed chiefly by his eldest brother, Joseph, who seems to have assumed responsibility for counselling him at many of the important crossroads in his early life. Though later overshadowed by his younger brother, Joseph was prominent in London society. He had accompanied the astronomer royal, Edmond Halley (1656–1742), on trips to the West Indies,[8] and in 1737, after a short period as a domestic tutor, he became deputy assay-master at the Royal Mint. Through Joseph, the young Howel achieved a far more rounded and exciting window on the world than did most of his neighbours. Many of Joseph's letters to his family in Wales during the 1720s and early 1730s are remarkable in the details about national and international

---

[5]   Jenkins, *The Foundations of Modern Wales*, pp. 88–9.

[6]   Jones, *The Trevecka Letters*, p. 44.

[7]   For Joseph Harris (1704–64) see *DWB*, pp. 341–2 and Jones, *The Trevecka Letters*, pp. 44–7; for Thomas (1707–82) see *DWB*, pp. 342–3 and Jones, *The Trevecka Letters*, pp. 48–51. For other Welshmen who made good in London in the seventeenth and eighteenth centuries see Emrys Jones (ed.), *The Welsh in London, 1500–2000* (Cardiff, 2001), pp. 46–50.

[8]   Trevecka 15, Joseph Harris to his parents (15 August 1730); Trevecka 18, Joseph Harris to his parents (13 October 1730); Trevecka 19, Joseph Harris to his parents (12 November 1730).

events.[9] In April 1735, for example, Joseph, in a letter to his mother, told her about the battles being fought by British soldiers in the Rhineland and Italy[10] and the proposed marriage of the Prince of Wales to the daughter of the King of Prussia.[11] Whilst it would be unwise to claim too much for Joseph's influence, there is little doubt that from a young age Howel Harris was accustomed to thinking of himself within both a Welsh and a wider British, if not an international, context. His interest in international affairs, planted by his brother, was carried into his evangelicalism and was reflected in his almost insatiable appetite for information about the revival in far-flung places. When Harris learned that both he and Wales were not alone in witnessing revivals of religion, it must have seemed perfectly natural for him to extend his gaze beyond the Welsh border and place his own activities within the broadest possible context.

By the end of 1737, Howel Harris, having begun his own revival in Breconshire, had also learned that he was not alone in trying to bring about a moral and spiritual reformation in Wales. Daniel Rowland had initiated his revival at Llangeitho and they had both met for the first time at Defynnog in the summer of 1737.[12] In September of that year Harris had also struck up a friendship with Howel Davies who, when employed as a schoolmaster at Talgarth, had been converted whilst listening to Harris preach.[13] The two became close friends in the work of revival and Davies's subsequent labours in Pembrokeshire became well known throughout the international revival.[14] With these two friends Harris widened the scope of his ministry and branched out beyond the immediate locality of his home, taking the first

---

[9] Trevecka 26, Joseph Harris to his mother (10 March 1733); Trevecka 37, Joseph Harris to his mother (4 May 1734); Trevecka 44, Joseph Harris to his mother (19 April 1735); Trevecka 47, Joseph Harris to Howel Harris (31 May 1735); Trevecka 55, Joseph Harris to Howel Harris (27 August 1735).

[10] These battles were part of the much more extensive War of the Polish Succession fought between 1733 and 1735. See J. O. Lindsay (ed.), *The New Cambridge Modern History, VII: The Old Regime, 1713–63* (Cambridge, 1957), pp. 204 and 379–80.

[11] Trevecka 44, Joseph Harris to his mother (19 April 1735).

[12] Evans, *Daniel Rowland*, pp. 51–2.

[13] Tudur, *Howell Harris*, pp. 40–1.

[14] Howel Harris to George Whitefield (5 December 1742), *Account*, II, II, 24–5, and Anne Thomas to Howel Harris (3 September 1742), *WH* 80 (16 October 1742). For more on Howel Davies see *DWB* and Tom Beynon, *Howell Harris's Visits to Pembrokeshire* (Aberystwyth, 1966). Readers of Welsh may also wish to consult Rhidian Griffiths, 'Howel Davies: Apostol Sir Benfro', *CHMCC*, 11 (1987), 2–14.

tentative steps towards drawing together a number of hitherto small-scale localized awakenings.

Although these two friendships became the foundation upon which the Welsh revival was subsequently built, in the awakening's early days it was Harris's relationship with Griffith Jones, Llanddowror,[15] which proved to be the most fruitful both in Harris's own experience and in his rapidly developing awareness of the wider significance of events under way in Wales. Though not always the Welsh Methodists' most enthusiastic supporter, Griffith Jones was Harris's main counsellor and adviser in the earliest months and years of the revival. Throughout 1736 Harris was a regular visitor to Llanddowror, and through Griffith Jones's patient mentoring, Harris's horizons were gradually broadened as he came into close contact with many of the ideas and theologies that were subsequently to mould his career. Whilst at Llanddowror, Harris witnessed Griffith Jones's wide range of contacts and correspondents and was introduced to some of the earnest and godly friends whom he had made as a result of his work with the Society for Promoting Christian Knowledge.

Griffith Jones's most committed patron was Sir John Philipps (?1666–1737),[16] one of the most devoted members of the SPCK, a regular correspondent with many of the most prominent Pietistic leaders of the day and an enthusiastic early supporter of John Wesley and his Oxford Methodists.[17] Through Sir John's influence and encouragement, Griffith Jones became a member of the SPCK and enjoyed frequent correspondence with both August Herman Francke and Jakob Böhme. It was undoubtedly from Griffith Jones that Howel Harris first learned of Francke's philanthropic activities at Halle and of the obvious debt which

[15]   For an indication of the influence which Griffith Jones exerted on Harris during the early months of the revival see Trevecka 78, Howel Harris to Griffith Jones (27 June 1736); Trevecka 80, Howel Harris to Griffith (31 July 1736); and Trevecka 87, Howel Harris to Griffith Jones (8 October 1736). See also Jenkins, ' "An old and much honoured soldier" ', 451–2.

[16]   *DWB* and Geoffrey F. Nuttall, 'Continental Pietism and the evangelical revival', pp. 217–18; Clement, *The SPCK and Wales,* is useful for many of Sir John's philanthropic interests and Peter D. G. Thomas, *Politics in Eighteenth-century Wales* (Cardiff, 1998), pp. 178–99 has a detailed discussion of his political activities.

[17]   Nuttall, 'Continental Pietism and the evangelical movement', p. 217.

the SPCK owed to Francke.[18] Such was Jones's influence that, before the end of 1736, Harris had read Böhme's English translation of Francke's *Pietas Hallensis* (1705)[19] and had already had thoughts of building 'an Alms House and School House and employ[ing] as many as I could have of followers'.[20] Sir John Philipps's patronage of George Whitefield at Oxford[21] and his support of the Oxford Methodists ensured that Harris would also have heard about the evangelical and philanthropic activities which they undertook in Oxford, and of the beginnings of Whitefield's preaching activities in Gloucester and London. At the same time as he was learning of other similarly enthusiastic evangelicals in Wales, he was introduced to the Pietistic theology which was to have such a profound effect on his future development and which represented one element of his increasing awareness of the international dimensions of the evangelicalism of which he was becoming such an important part.

Harris's interest in the development of the international revival was fuelled still further when, in February 1738, he received a copy of Jonathan Edwards's recently published account of the awakening that had occurred at Northampton in 1735, *A Faithful Narrative of the Surprising Work of God in the Conversion of Many Hundred Souls in Northampton* (1736).[22] He observed the similarity of this revival to his own work in Wales and recorded how 'reading of the conversion of many in New England, had heart boiling with love to Christ . . . with great joy in hearing of that God visits the world'.[23] For Harris, Edwards's work was the first tangible indication that he was caught up in a far more widespread renewal movement than he had previously anticipated. It showed him, even more clearly

[18]   The influence of Böhme and Francke on the evangelical revival is dealt with in detail in Brunner, *Halle Pietists in England*. Also important are Nuttall, 'Continental Pietism and the evangelical movement in Britain', passim; Campbell, *The Religion of the Heart,* pp. 86–7, 119–20; and Ward, *The Protestant Evangelical Awakening*, pp. 303–8.

[19]   HHD, 28 December 1736.

[20]   Ibid.

[21]   Murray (ed.), *George Whitefield's Journals*, pp. 69–70 and 76–7.

[22]   Edwards's account of his Northampton revival was first published in New England in 1736. It first appeared in Britain with a commendatory introduction by two of the most prominent Dissenters in the country, John Guyse and Isaac Watts, in October 1737. However, no Welsh translation of any of Edwards's writings was attempted until John Roberts's in 1809. See his *Cyfarwyddiadau ac Annogaethau i Gredinwyr* [. . .] *A Gasglwyd, yn Benaf, Allan o Waith* [. . .] *Jonathan Edwards* (Bala, 1809).

[23]   HHD 25 (27 November 1738).

than Griffith Jones had done the previous year, that the awakening that he superintended was part of a movement that was not only transnational but even stretched across the Atlantic.

Harris's discovery of the work of the Pietists and of the Northampton awakening, at such a formative period in his development as a revivalist, led him to make his own contacts with like-minded enthusiastic evangelicals outside Wales. Before he received his first letter from George Whitefield in January 1739, Harris had begun to correspond with a number of other English evangelicals, some of whom were later to become prominent in the English revival, and among his closest associates. In November 1738, Harris wrote what seems to have been his first letter to a fellow evangelical in England, an individual identified only by his initials, M.P. from Bristol. In the letter Harris immediately adopted the style of the familiar letter, including in it many elements that were later to become such marked features of Methodist correspondence.[24] He began, by way of introduction, with the customary words of exhortation: 'Pray let us strengthen each others hands, against this villain and enemy of our souls, Self. So likewise, let us assist each other, to stir up our drowsy Spirits, so to talk, think of, and speak to this glorious Prince of Peace.'[25] He then went on to recommend a number of evangelical books, before turning to the main purpose of the letter, the transmission of the latest news from Wales. He informed his correspondent about the latest successes of the revival in Wales:

> our days are reforming days; there is a hopeful prospect in some places, that would rejoice your souls; we have several societies in some places, in this and other countries . . . you have heard of the Rev. Mr Griffith Jones of Carmarthenshire, and the Rev. Mr Rowlands of Cardiganshire, and some other clergymen in this county, who preach CHRIST powerfully, there is also in these parts, a Baptist preacher[26] that God has owned very much, together with some other Dissenting ministers.[27]

---

[24]   Rivers, '"Strangers and pilgrims"', pp. 189–201 and Hindmarsh, *John Newton and the English Evangelical Tradition*, pp. 243–6.
[25]   Trevecka 129, Howel Harris to Mr M.P. (21 November 1738).
[26]   Probably a reference to John Powell, Abergwesyn. See *DWB*, p. 774.
[27]   Trevecka 129, Howel Harris to Mr M.P. (21 November 1738).

By writing in this way and concentrating on the main centres of Welsh Methodist strength, Harris became accustomed to delivering optimistic accounts of the Welsh revival to English readers. These accounts were designed to promote the Welsh work and advertise its existence, its firmly rooted foundation and, perhaps more importantly, its permanence. The letter demonstrates that even as early as 1738 Harris had begun to talk about a national Welsh revival, whose three strands – his own work in Breconshire, Daniel Rowland's preaching in Cardiganshire and Griffith Jones's work in Carmarthenshire – despite their independent origins, were patently part of the same movement.

Many of Harris's other letters in these months followed a very similar pattern, one that was also reflected in the letters of some of the individuals who wrote to Harris. During November 1738, Harris received a letter from a London-based evangelical, Mrs J. Godwin. Like Harris's own correspondence, her letters contained many of the main elements of Methodist letter-writing. After beginning her letter with the usual general spiritual exhortations she launched into the latest news she had received about the wider revival. Her letter also included a vital additional element. At its conclusion she recommended a number of evangelical books, lately published in London, which she felt would be of interest and use to the Welsh Methodists and offered Harris her services as a book distributor. She wrote:

> I called at Mr Hutton's[28] the night I came to town as desired and beg'd him to send me those journals or anything else for you the Friday following [. . .] if at any time you want anything here, be free in sending me, whose pleasure is in serving such servants of my Lord.[29]

By doing this Mrs Godwin fulfilled an important function during the early months of the revival, particularly in the months before George Whitefield set up his own book room at the Tabernacle in 1740. Mrs Godwin became a valuable link between the Welsh Methodists and the English revival, and her recommendations of evangelical literature together with her willingness to send copies of books to Wales ensured that the Welsh Methodists were

---

[28] James Hutton, the Moravian bookseller. Podmore, *The Moravian Church in England*, pp. 34–6.
[29] Trevecka 130, Mrs J. Godwin to Howel Harris (24 November 1738).

exposed to many of the same influences as their English counter-parts, and consequently both were drawn more closely together. These developments had all contributed to Howel Harris's rapidly developing understanding of the revival, and he had already tentatively formulated an interpretation of the revival which rooted it firmly in the context of developments occurring within European Protestantism more generally.

The gradual awakening of Howel Harris's world-view was also mirrored in the early experience of George Whitefield. From the beginning of his evangelical career, Whitefield seemed more aware than any of his contemporaries of the international dimensions of the revival, and became almost immediately the movement's most prominent international personality. As such, he became committed to fostering links between each of the awakenings that constituted the wider movement, and he realized that, to a very large extent, the success of the revival depended on its inclusivity and its ability to maximize the scattered resources that lay at the disposal of its leaders. On Trinity Sunday 1736, for example, Whitefield preached a sermon in Bristol in which he expounded his vision of the nature of genuine Christian fellowship[30] and indicated his concern to draw together as many evangelicals as possible into some sort of loose confederacy in which otherwise widely dispersed awaken-ings could be made to feel part of a more ambitious evangelical movement. He wrote:

> It is necessary, therefore (at least GOD's dealing with us hath shewed it to be so) that we should be drawn with the cords of a man. And that a divine revelation being granted, we should use one another's assistance under GOD, to instruct each other in the knowledge, and to exhort one another to the practice of those things which belong to our everlasting peace.[31]

---

[30] The sermon was based on some words from Ecclesiastes 4: 9–12: 'Two are better than one . . . if they fall, the one will lift up his fellow.' The sermon was published in 1737 with the title *The Nature and Necessity of Society in General, and of Religious Society in Particular.*

[31] John Gillies (ed.), *The Works of the Reverend George Whitefield*, V (London, 1772), p. 110.

His desire to create a fellowship of revival-minded saints across national and denominational boundaries was the main reason why Whitefield remained intimately involved in the progress and development of the Welsh revival from 1739 until his split with Howel Harris in 1750. His close involvement with Wales was perfectly natural and should come as no surprise. Wales was England's nearest neighbour and there were obvious similarities in the revivals in both countries. Furthermore, before making his first contact with Howel Harris, Whitefield had already established links with a number of pious and influential Welshmen. Whilst at Oxford and during his time as a curate immediately following his ordination in 1736, Whitefield had been the recipient of the enthusiastic support and encouragement of Sir John Philipps. Philipps had provided Whitefield with a small bursary of £30 a year which had enabled him to complete his studies at Oxford,[32] and he had been 'a great encourager of the Oxford Methodists'.[33] Sir John had also been influential in securing Whitefield's ordination. He had provided him with the necessary financial support to defray the expenses, and when Whitefield acted as a stand-in at the congregation which met at the Tower of London during 1736, Sir John became one of his most regular listeners.[34]

From his *Journals* it is also clear that Whitefield was well acquainted with the work of Griffith Jones before he made contact with Howel Harris. His knowledge of Jones's activities undoubtedly stemmed from their mutual friend and patron, Sir John Philipps. Whilst returning from Georgia in November 1738, Whitefield's ship docked in Ireland for a short time. His impression of the Irish was not good. To Whitefield they appeared 'of the Romish Profession, and seem to be so very ignorant that they may well be termed the wild Irish'.[35] Whitefield's comments are relevant because of the comparison that he drew between them and the Welsh. Whitefield attributed the ignorance of the Irish to their lack of education and concluded that the best way to overcome this ignorance would be to set up schools as Griffith Jones had done in Wales. He wrote in his *Journals*:

[32]   Murray (ed.), *George Whitefield's Journals*, p. 67.
[33]   Ibid.
[34]   Dallimore, *George Whitefield*, I, pp. 103–5.
[35]   Murray (ed.), *George Whitefield's Journals*, p. 181.

> I can think of no likelier means to convert them from their erroneous principles, than to get the Bible translated into their own native language, to have it put in their houses, and charity schools erected for their children, as Mr Jones has done in Wales, which would insensibly weaken the Romish interest.[36]

Thus, before Whitefield had learned of the activities of Howel Harris and the beginnings of the revival in Wales, he had been favourably disposed, through some of his previous contacts with sympathetic pious Welshmen, to the particular emphases and practical applications of Welsh evangelicalism.

Whitefield's first intimation of the beginning of a religious awakening in Wales seems to have come from a letter written in November 1738 between two English evangelicals, Thomas Cole of Gloucester to the Revd Westley Hall, which is included in a recently rediscovered collection of Whitefield's letters.[37] In the letter Cole broke the news of 'the unusual labours of the Welsh reformer, Mr Howel Harris'[38] to the English evangelical community. Given the fact that, even at this early stage in the revival, letters were being circulated amongst interested fellow evangelicals and read aloud at their frequent meetings, it can be safely deduced that Whitefield's knowledge of Harris, hitherto mainly second-hand from Sir John Philipps, would have been further deepened. Thomas Cole's letter bristled with excitement as he related the details that he had garnered about events in Wales:

> Is it not pleasant to hear as the effects of his [Howel Harris] exhortation of whole parishes being like to excel in seriousness . . . Is it not surprising to hear of a valley of about 30 or 40 houses where a serious impression has been so general that, if there should be an immoral or profane person there, he was not like to meet with company or countenance?[39]

---

[36] Ibid.

[37] This recently discovered collection of 109 letters written between 1737 and 1739 has been edited by Graham C. G. Thomas, 'George Whitefield and friends: the correspondence of some early Methodists', *National Library of Wales Journal*, 26, III (Summer 1990), 251–80; 26, IV (Winter 1990), 367–96; 27, I (Summer 1991), 65–96; 27, II (Winter 1991), 175–203; 27, III (Summer 1992), 289–318; 27, IV (Winter 1992), 431–52.

[38] 'An abstract of a letter to the Reverend Mr Westley Hall by the Reverend Mr Thomas Cole of Gloucester Concerning Mr Howel Harris (November 1738)', in Thomas (ed.), 'George Whitefield and friends', *NLWJ*, 26, IV, 394.

[39] Ibid.

Cole's letter demonstrates the way in which evangelicals in England immediately assumed that Harris's revival was of the same nature as their own revivals. Cole himself went a step further by recommending that Harris's work should be made known as widely as possible and resolved himself to 'collect a particular history of the man'.[40]

By the end of 1738, before the beginning of Whitefield's correspondence with Howel Harris, a confused and somewhat *ad hoc* web of transnational contacts between pious evangelicals was already in place. In December 1738 Philip Doddridge, the evangelical Dissenting minister from Northampton, had written to Whitefield to express his delight at the new movement that seemed to promise the renewal and revivification of the whole of English Protestantism:

> A truly generous and catholic spirit is prevailing in different denominations and I trust will still prevail till we come all to the unity of the Spirit and the stature of a perfect man. Oh what little things are those that divide us, with those many strong, endearing bands which will bind us close to Christ and one another for every Christians glorious title! Oh that every sectarian name were lost in that![41]

It was against such an expectant and religiously optimistic background that Whitefield's exploratory letter to Howel Harris, written almost immediately after he had arrived back in England from his first visit to the American colonies, eventually reached Trefeca on 7 January 1739.

From Howel Harris's standpoint the timing of Whitefield's letter was impeccable. Harris had reached something of an impasse in his exhorting ministry and had begun to doubt the appropriateness of carrying on as an unordained layman without the sanction of the Church. Both his own local vicar, Pryce Davies,[42] and his mentor, Griffith Jones, had tried to caution him against continuing to exhort if he wished to secure Anglican

---

[40]   Ibid.
[41]   'Philip Doddridge to George Whitefield (23 December 1738)', in Thomas (ed.), 'George Whitefield and friends', *NLWJ*, 27, I, 72–3.
[42]   Trevecka 54, Howel Harris to Pryce Davies (16 August 1735) and Trevecka 65, Pryce Davies to Howel Harris (27 February 1736).

ordination.[43] When Whitefield's letter arrived it therefore found Harris at a crossroads in his career, unsure whether to continue exhorting and risk the opprobrium of the ecclesiastical authorities or to return to his duties as a schoolmaster and make himself into a more plausible candidate for the Church. As he read Whitefield's opening remarks many of his fears must have evaporated. Whitefield greeted him as a highly esteemed brother and co-worker. He paid tribute to Harris's labours and drew the obvious parallels between what he himself had been doing in London and Bristol. Whitefield drew no distinction between his own work as a clergyman and Harris's unofficial lay activities. He wrote: 'Though I am unknown to you in person, I have long been united to you in spirit, and have been rejoiced to hear how the good pleasure of the Lord prospered in your hand.'[44] One of the most striking characteristics of the letter is the extent to which Whitefield was prepared to be totally open and honest with Harris about the work of the revival and about his own feelings and emotions. By so doing, he revealed to Harris that many of the problems and doubts that Harris himself was facing were not unique but were fairly common among the English evangelicals, as they struggled with the resentment that their ambiguous relationship to the Established Church aroused. Following these general exhortations, Whitefield's letter followed the accepted pattern of Methodist letter-writing. Whitefield launched into a detailed discussion of the 'great pouring out of the Spirit in London'[45] and confidently reported that the converts 'walk in the comfort of the Holy Ghost and are edified'.[46] By including in his letter a summary of the progress of the English awakening, Whitefield indicated his intention to ensure that Methodist letters remained focused on the relaying of news. His letter clearly necessitated a response and Whitefield was not slow in requesting an immediate reply, thereby strengthening his foothold in Wales. He wrote:

> You see my dear Brother, the freedom I have taken in writing to you. If
> you would favour me with a line or two, by way of answer, you would

---

[43]   Trevecka 78, Howel Harris to Griffith Jones (27 June 1736); Trevecka 80, Howel Harris to Griffith Jones (31 July 1736); and Evans, *Howell Harris*, pp. 28–32, 48.

[44]   Trevecka 133, George Whitefield to Howel Harris (20 December 1738).

[45]   Ibid.

[46]   Ibid.

greatly rejoice both me and many others. Why should we not tell one another what God has done for our souls.[47]

By writing in this way, Whitefield was attempting to establish a tangible link between the English and Welsh revivals and to create a channel by which information about both revivals could be more easily and widely circulated. Whitefield evidently believed that by initiating a correspondence with Howel Harris he would be able to instil, within his fellow revivalists and their respective converts, an awareness of the scope of the awakenings in which they were all participating.

Harris's enthusiasm for Whitefield's vision of an international revival is evident in the tone and content of his immediate reply to the letter. After conveying his gratitude to Whitefield for writing, Harris expressed his solidarity by stressing the spiritual unity that he felt with Whitefield and his converts. He wrote:

When I first heard of your labours and successes, my soul was united to you, and engaged to send addresses to heaven on your behalf. When I read your Diary, I had uncommon influence of the Divine presence shining on my poor soul almost continually.[48]

This spiritual or mystical unity formed the basis of their relationship. Reading Whitefield's letter must have been an intensely spiritual experience for Harris. It confirmed many of his thoughts about the revival, addressed many of his uncertainties and provided him with the confidence necessary to carry on with his work in spite of the threats from the Church. For Harris the letter had almost scriptural authority and the 'sense' of the presence of God that accompanied its reading must surely have seemed like a recommissioning. It ensured that the necessary groundwork was in place for closer interaction between the respective awakenings.

After these comments, Harris's response continued in almost mirror image to Whitefield's. He went on to provide Whitefield with a county-by-county summary of the Welsh awakening, and in so doing demonstrated his own enthusiasm for the vision of a

---

[47] Ibid.
[48] Trevecka 136, Howel Harris to George Whitefield (8 January 1739). A printed copy of this letter can also be found in Benjamin LaTrobe, *A Brief Account of the Life of Howell Harris* (Trevecka, 1791), pp. 112–14.

transnational revival that Whitefield had begun to construct in his introductory letter. From Harris's reply it is obvious that he was also aware of the scope of the religious awakening that was under way and conscious of the need to establish some form of infrastructure that would link the various awakenings to one another. In some ways Harris's awareness of the potential of the revival appears to have been even more well developed than Whitefield's. He characteristically grasped the opportunity to correspond regularly with Whitefield and used their friendship to publicize the Welsh work and integrate it into the mainstream of evangelical and Methodist influence. After admitting that it was 'ravishing'[49] to hear of the revival in London, Harris swept into a highly emotive rehearsal of events in Wales. The receipt of Whitefield's letter seems to have inspired him to look at the work in Wales in a entirely new light. Harris wrote in a way that indicated renewed self-confidence and a greater awareness of his own important part in the commencement and propagation of the Welsh revival. He wrote:

> I have some good news to send you from Wales. There is a great revival in Cardiganshire, through one Mr D. Rowland, a church minister, who has been much owned and blessed in Carmarthenshire also. We have also a sweet prospect in Breconshire and part of Monmouthshire and the revival prospers in this county [Glamorgan] where I am now. There is also here a very useful dissenting minister[50] [. . .] There is another of the same character in Montgomeryshire[51] [. . .] There are two or three young

---

[49]   Ibid.
[50]   By 1739 Harris was corresponding with two Glamorgan Dissenting ministers, Henry Davies, Blaen-gwrach (?1696–1766), minister at Cymer, and David Williams, Pwll-y-pant (1709–84), minister at Watford near Caerphilly. For Henry Davies see *DWB*, p. 136; Trevecka 115, Henry Davies to Howel Harris (11 July 1738); and Trevecka 122, Henry Davies to Howel Harris (21 September 1738). On David Williams see *DWB*, pp. 1030–1; Trevecka 116, David Williams to Howel Harris (14 July 1738); and Trevecka 125, David Williams to Howel Harris (17 October 1738).
[51]   Possibly a reference to Lewis Rees, Llanbrynmair, with whom Harris was in contact by 1739. See Trevecka 139, Lewis Rees to Howel Harris (20 January 1739) and Trevecka 186, Lewis Rees to Howel Harris (1 September 1739).

curates in Glamorganshire[52] who are well-wishers to the cause of God, and we have an exceedingly sweet and valuable clergyman[53] in Breconshire.[54]

Harris's account is significant in a number of respects. He refers to the various Welsh awakenings as 'the revival' indicating that even by the beginning of 1739 the Welsh revival was sufficiently well established and permanent to enable its pioneers to begin to act as the leaders of a national movement. Secondly, it was wide-ranging in its scope, covering most of the counties of south and west Wales, and, significantly, in these early months and years it was still interdenominational. The revival's stress on the New Birth and moral and spiritual reformation had clearly struck a chord with a number of sympathetic Dissenting ministers with whom Harris was in regular contact, and it had managed to enlist the support of a number of like-minded individuals within the Established Church. It was only later when the true nature of Methodism emerged that many of the Dissenters, disappointed at the revivalists' persistent allegiance to the Church, refused to support it with as much enthusiasm and that many churchmen, alarmed at the apparent disregard the Methodists had for the Church's authority, withdrew their public support.

These two letters were the means by which George Whitefield and Howel Harris, and through them the English and Welsh revivals, were drawn into a closer working relationship. However, Harris remained far from satisfied. Having been introduced to Whitefield he took the obvious next step, closing his reply with a tentatively optimistic request that he must have known would elicit a positive reply: 'I could not miss this opportunity of obliging you; and were you to come to Wales I trust it would not be labour in vain. I hope the faithful account I have given you will excite you.'[55] Whitefield's response was immediate and enthusiastic. Having so recently become thoroughly acquainted with the beginning of renewal movements in the American

[52]   It is almost impossible to identify who these curates were. One was probably Philip Thomas, Gelligaer. In 1742, Harris listed five beneficed clergy and five curates among the Methodists in Wales, so it seems unlikely that there would have been as many as three sympathetic curates at such an early stage in the revival. Trevecka 694, Howel Harris to George Whitefield (15 October 1742).
[53]   This is undoubtedly a reference to Thomas Lewis, Merthyr Cynog. See *DWB*, p. 561, and Tudur, *Howell Harris*, p. 39.
[54]   Trevecka 136, Howel Harris to George Whitefield (8 January 1739).
[55]   Ibid.

colonies, Whitefield was now anxious to add the Welsh Methodist revival to his slowly emerging international revival movement. Writing to a friend at the beginning of March 1739, Whitefield, pre-empting John Wesley, began to refer to the 'whole world'[56] as his parish and assume the role of the premier inter-revival evangelist, the self-styled 'Grand Itinerant'.[57]

Before arriving in Wales in March 1739, Whitefield met Griffith Jones in Bath on two separate occasions. Deeply impressed by Jones and 'much edified by [his] conversation',[58] Whitefield, like Harris, seems to have regarded Griffith Jones as a father-like figure on account of the breadth of his pastoral experience and the 'many obstructions he had met with in his ministry'.[59] Possibly the most valuable result of these meetings with Griffith Jones was the added sense of expectancy which they engendered in Whitefield. It seems, at this stage, that Whitefield anticipated that Griffith Jones would become unavoidably drawn into the day-to-day life of the revival and perhaps fulfil the role of mentor to the more inexperienced 'young soldiers just entering the field'.[60] That this never happened stemmed chiefly from Griffith Jones's reluctance to jeopardize the work of his Circulating Schools by aligning himself too closely with a revival which challenged the lethargy of the Established Church, upon which Jones relied so heavily for support, rather than from the hesitancy of either Whitefield or Harris.

On the morning of 7 March 1739, Whitefield and his business manager, William Seward, crossed the river Severn at the New Passage and on the following day met Howel Harris in Cardiff. On their first meeting the relationship between the 'official' leaders of the English and Welsh revivals, begun so promisingly three months earlier, blossomed into the most productive transnational friendship of the whole revival. In order to provide Whitefield with the most rounded picture of the work in Wales, Harris arranged a short preaching tour which saw Whitefield and Seward visit some of the most important evangelical communities in the Cardiff and Newport areas. Whitefield 'took

[56]   George Whitefield to Daniel Abbot (3 March 1739), in Thomas (ed.), 'George Whitefield and friends', *NLWJ*, 27, I, 82.
[57]   Stout, *The New England Soul*, p. 189.
[58]   Murray (ed.), *George Whitefield's Journals*, p. 220.
[59]   Ibid.
[60]   Ibid.

account'[61] of the Welsh revival, though there is no recorded mention on this occasion of Daniel Rowland or of the revival beyond the south-east corner of Wales, and he discussed with Harris some practical issues relating to the wider propagation of the Welsh revival and the closer synchronization of their respective revival communities.[62] For Whitefield the visit had been a great success, and he was particularly heartened by the 'divine and strong sympathy' [63] he felt with Harris. He returned to London resolved to publicize the Welsh revival still more widely and to introduce Harris and his Welsh evangelicals to the wider evangelical community.[64]

For Howel Harris, Whitefield's visit began an important period of transition in his development as a revivalist. Through his relationship with Whitefield and as a result of Whitefield's readiness to introduce him to the rest of the revival as a much-valued co-worker, Harris's low opinion of himself was, at least temporarily, alleviated. Whitefield's obvious approval of Harris's activities was reflected in the highly emotive descriptions of Harris and his work that he recorded in his *Journals* and circulated in his letters. On first meeting him, for example, Whitefield wrote: 'my heart was knit closely to him. I wanted to catch some of his fire, and gave him the right hand of fellowship with my whole heart.'[65] By testifying to the unity that he felt with him in such a public way, Whitefield undoubtedly did more to raise Harris's morale and self-confidence than almost any other event in the late 1730s. By admitting that Harris was possessed of a fire that he himself did not possess in quite the same measure, Whitefield was able to carve out a niche for Harris as the inspirational exhorter, lacking the recognition of the Church establishment perhaps, but possessed of the greater recognition and

[61]   Ibid., p. 230.
[62]   Infuriatingly neither Whitefield's *Journals* nor his correspondence nor Harris's diary and letters for March 1739 give any concrete idea of the particular practical issues pertaining to the organization and furtherance of their revivals that were discussed over the course of these three days. For an insight into their respective responses to Whitefield's first preaching tour see Murray (ed.), *George Whitefield's Journals*, pp. 227–31; Trevecka 146, George Whitefield to Samuel Mason (3 March 1739); and Trevecka 148, William Seward to Daniel Abbott (10 March 1739). For an indication of Howel Harris's response see HHD 41, Thursday, 8 March and Friday, 9 March 1739.
[63]   Murray (ed.), *George Whitefield's Journals*, p. 230.
[64]   Trevecka 146, George Whitefield to Samuel Mason (3 March 1739) and Trevecka 147, George Whitefield to Daniel Abbott (10 March 1739).
[65]   Murray (ed.), *George Whitefield's Journals*, pp. 228–9.

obvious approval of God himself. In offering him the right hand of fellowship, Whitefield was recognizing Harris's pre-eminence as the originator of the Welsh revival and offering him a position at the very apex of the international evangelical community.

For Harris this recognition could not have been better timed. His lack of official recognition by the Church had resulted in repeated bouts of depression in which he lamented his inferiority to individuals like Griffith Jones, Daniel Rowland and Howel Davies, and at times he even doubted whether he was a Christian at all.[66] It was out of respect for the offices of the Church and as a result of his own sense of inferiority that Harris chose to call himself an exhorter[67] rather than a preacher or an evangelist, both terms which implied a measure of recognition by the ecclesiastical authorities. Whitefield seems to have been aware of the problems that might arise on account of Harris's lay status and consequently dealt with them obliquely in his first reports on the Welsh revival. At the end of his first visit, after some typically hyperbolic comments on Harris's activities, he emphasized that Harris had taken on this role 'not authoritatively, as a minister, but as a private person exhorting his Christian brethren'.[68] Whitefield, like both Daniel Rowland and Howel Davies, did not regard Harris as an oddity or with suspicion. In Whitefield, Harris discovered a friend and co-worker who was prepared to overlook his lay status and regard him with the equality and respect for which he so incessantly craved.

Whitefield's recognition of the office of the 'exhorter' had major repercussions for the wider Methodist movement. In a recently published introductory essay on the evangelical revival, Grayson Ditchfield has argued that the Methodists' acceptance of a lay ministry was as significant a defining characteristic of the movement as any of the four hallmarks of the movement outlined by David Bebbington.[69] In many ways it was one of the most

---

[66]   HHD 41, 10 March 1739, and HHD 41, 15 March 1739.

[67]   On the development of the office of the exhorter and the development of a lay ministry in Methodism more widely see Baker, *John Wesley and the Church of England*, pp. 79–84; Geoffrey Milburn and Margaret Batty (eds), *Workaday Preachers: The Story of Methodist Local Preaching* (Peterborough, 1995), pp. 15–8; Paul Wesley Chilcote, *'She Offered them Christ': The Legacy of Women Preachers in Early Methodism* (Nashville, TN, 1993); and Evans, *Howell Harris*, pp. 11–14.

[68]   Murray (ed.), *George Whitefield's Journals*, p. 229.

[69]   G. M. Ditchfield, 'Methodism and the evangelical revival', in H. T. Dickinson (ed.), *A Companion to Eighteenth Century Britain* (Oxford, 2002), p. 252.

dramatic innovations that the Welsh Methodists ever made, inspired by the fact that their most charismatic leader was not ordained and seemed destined unlikely ever to be so. It followed that if Harris could lead, preach, exhort and superintend societies, then the way to do likewise could be open for other suitably gifted individuals who had no desire to enter Anglican orders or indeed would never be accepted because of poor education and lack of English. There was also an element of inevitability in the Methodists' support of lay leadership. For many years it was a small-scale movement which did not have sufficient resources in terms of sympathetic clergy to take on its leadership, and furthermore, as the societies were chiefly intended for fellowship rather than for worship, the revivalists did not allow the somewhat draconian strictures of the Established Church to stand in their way.[70] However, Whitefield's acceptance of Harris's lay ministry did not altogether cure him of his inferiority complex. Throughout the course of the later 1730s and the 1740s, Harris struggled with his lack of clerical status and felt at times that his contemporaries regarded him in a lesser light and that his leadership was impaired because of it. Despite this, it would none the less be true to say that from this time onwards Harris became more content with his status, better prepared to deal with his bouts of depression, and outwardly at least more self-confident and assured. Involvement in the international revival community therefore provided him with a further source of recognition. If his beloved Church of England was not prepared to recognize him and accord him its official backing then he would be forced to look elsewhere. It was fortunate for Harris that the evangelical movement was sufficiently strong and self-confident to enable its leaders to continue in their chosen paths in spite of the censures of the Church to which they, despite everything, remained firmly loyal. It was only when problems regarding Harris's leadership of the Welsh revival became more prominent in the later 1740s that his old doubts resurfaced and he once more began to assume that both Daniel Rowland's and George Whitefield's problems with him resulted

---

[70] Eryn M. White, 'Women in the early Methodist societies in Wales', *JWRH*, 7 (1999), 104–5. See also Timothy D. Hall, *Contested Boundaries: Itinerancy and the reshaping of the American Religious World* (Durham, NC, 1994), and for a comparison with some of the reasons encouraging itinerancy among the Dissenters, Deryck W. Lovegrove, *Established Church, Sectarian People: Itinerancy and the Transformation of English Dissent, 1780–1830* (Cambridge, 1988).

not from any theological or moral deficiencies but from their pride in their status and their scorn of Harris's inferior position.

In addition to observing and reporting on events in Wales, Whitefield's first visit also marked the beginning of his practical contribution to the development of the organizational structure of the Welsh Methodist movement. By taking an active part in the organization of the revival in Wales, Whitefield moved from being merely an onlooker, albeit a passionately interested and committed one, to being a vital part of the Welsh revival's leadership – almost a Welsh Methodist by adoption. For White-field, one of the most abiding impressions of his first contact with the Welsh Methodists was of the unity which he observed among them and, in particular, their willingness to tolerate those with whom they had significant theological differences, but who were none the less committed to a renewal of the Protestant faith in Wales. This observation was of the utmost significance as by 1739 Whitefield had already realized that the English revival had the potential to be as divisive as it could be invigorating. Tensions had already surfaced between Anglicans and Dissenters, and between those who favoured Arminianism rather than the traditional moderate Calvinistic orthodoxy shared by most early eighteenth-century evangelicals. Whitefield pin-pointed Harris's 'most catholic spirit'[71] as the root cause of this unity, and in his *Journals* it was to this aspect of the Welsh revival that he drew most attention in the hope that the rest of the move-ment would take heed and learn from its example. He wrote:

> [Howel Harris] loves all who love our Lord Jesus Christ and therefore he is styled by bigots, a Dissenter [. . .] Blessed be God, there seems to be [a] noble spirit gone out into Wales [. . .] What inclines me strongly to think so is, that the partition wall of bigotry and party-zeal is broken down, and ministers and teachers of different communions, join with one heart and one mind to carry on the kingdom of Jesus Christ. The Lord make all the Christian world thus minded![72]

Although the irenic spirit that characterized the Welsh revival in the later 1730s was, for George Whitefield, one of the most impressive and encouraging features of the whole revival, it

---

71   Murray (ed.), *George Whitefield's Journals*, p. 229.
72   Ibid.

predictably did not last long. Whitefield's admiration of Harris's ecumenism, based on his readiness to make contact with a wide array of evangelicals from various denominational traditions and his openness to new and different theologies, also waned. By the mid-1740s, Harris's domineering personality and his fondness for some of the more controversial aspects of Moravian theology had begun to create tensions within the leadership of Welsh Methodism. Yet in England, the full ramifications of this development did not become immediately apparent. In London, Harris acted as an intermediary between the various factions of the revival throughout the 1740s as he came to enjoy prominence as a vital peaceable force and possibly the key factor in ensuring fairly amicable, if at times somewhat strained, relations between the Wesleyans, the Whitefieldians and the Moravians.

Whitefield took a particularly close interest in the more than thirty societies that Harris had established in south-east Wales by March 1739.[73] Whilst in Wales he discussed with Harris issues relating to them and decided 'on such measures as seemed most conducive to promote the common interest of our Lord'.[74] The significance of this discussion lies in the fact that, even at this early stage, Harris was prepared to listen to the advice of an outsider – albeit one whose prominence in the wider revival movement was unparalleled. These discussions marked the beginning of Whitefield's close involvement in the decision-making processes of the Welsh revival. To Harris, Whitefield became his 'dearest and Elder Brother'[75] and a constant source of advice and counsel in his own leadership of the Welsh revival. At times of transition and crisis in Wales, Harris continually looked to Whitefield and often summoned him to Wales to arbitrate on potentially divisive matters and give his seal of approval to the decisions that both he and Daniel Rowland reached. For example, in August 1742, Harris typically wrote to Whitefield begging his attention on behalf of his fellow Welsh

---

[73] Evans, *Howell Harris*, p. 22.
[74] Murray (ed.), *George Whitefield's Journals*, p. 230.
[75] Trevecka 788, Howel Harris to George Whitefield (25 January 1743). This was invariably the way in which Harris began his letters to Whitefield and indicates something of the nature of the relationship between them both. For further examples see Trevecka 607, Howel Harris to George Whitefield (21 August 1742); Trevecka 650, Howel Harris to George Whitefield (16 September 1742); and Trevecka 775, Howel Harris to George Whitefield (10 January 1743).

Methodists: 'I am at a loss Dr Dr Bro Whitefield what to do [. . .] Did not the Lord once set Wales much upon your Heart, and does he now withdraw your Heart from us.'[76] In many ways Harris intended Whitefield's first visit to Wales to act as an introduction to as much of the Welsh revival as possible. Neither Harris nor Whitefield provide any further details of the specific issues relating to the oversight of Harris's societies which they discussed. Our knowledge of what they decided is limited to some comments that Whitefield wrote in a letter to Daniel Abbott in which he reported that they had decided to translate some of Whitefield's sermons into Welsh and 'get a new translation of a Welsh Bible'.[77] Such a decision demonstrates the importance that both Harris and Whitefield attached to the provision of godly evangelical literature at the very outset of the revival. It was a decision that had far-reaching consequences, and their wish to forge ahead with these publications ensured that the close working relationship that was beginning to develop between them began to be extended beyond the narrow confines of their personal friendship. The Welsh Methodists' reliance on George Whitefield does not of necessity mean that they were incapable of taking decisions on their own, as Roy Hattersley has recently implied in his study of John Wesley.[78] Rather, it demonstrates the extent to which the Welsh Methodists regarded Whitefield as their final source of authority and is indicative of the high regard in which he was held throughout the revival. In Wales, the ties forged in 1739 reaped significant dividends as both English and Welsh Calvinistic Methodism developed hand in hand, and as each was able to support the other in a variety of ways. Indeed it could be argued that it was ultimately Harris who became more indispensable to Whitefield's revival in the later 1740s when Whitefield wished to divest himself of responsibility for the London societies and take up a more informal international role.

Whitefield left Wales in 1739 with renewed zeal for his own ministry and encouraged by the fact that Howel Harris had independently reached similar conclusions about the best means

---

[76]   Trevecka 592, Howel Harris to George Whitefield (9 August 1742).
[77]   'George Whitefield to Daniel Abbott (10 March 1739)' in Thomas (ed.), 'George Whitefield and friends', *NLWJ*, 27, II, 175–6.
[78]   Hattersley, *A Brand from the Burning*, p. 196.

by which to propagate their revivals. For Whitefield, his first visit to Wales came at a critical juncture in his development as a revivalist. He had in the days immediately preceding his arrival in Wales begun preaching in the open air in Bristol[79] and despite confiding in his *Journals* that he had never felt 'more acceptable to my Master than when I was standing to teach those in the open fields',[80] he still felt unsure about the propriety of his highly controversial actions. He seems to have been helped by discussions with Griffith Jones at Bath during February 1739,[81] when they discussed their respective ministries and Jones seems to have shared his own experiences of preaching out of doors with Whitefield.[82] It is inconceivable that their conversation would not also have included some discussion of Howel Harris's open-air ministry in Wales, especially as Whitefield's visit was so close.

The discussions with Griffith Jones, together with the example of Howel Harris, finally convinced Whitefield about the effectiveness of preaching in the open air whenever circumstances demanded. Harris's stress on the necessity of exhorting out of doors where more people could be reached convinced Whitefield of the wisdom of his recent actions in Bristol. His comments about Harris seem to bear this out. In his *Journals*, he focused on Harris's readiness to exhort and preach 'in a field [. . .] at other times in a house, from a wall, a table, or any thing else'[83] and expressed a desire to imitate him and to 'catch some of his fire'.[84] In many ways this was one of the most significant contributions which Howel Harris made to the whole of the wider evangelical movement. Though staunchly loyal to the Church of England, both Harris and Whitefield were acutely aware of the opposition that their 'enthusiastic' repackaging of Protestantism would generate from both the Church and the traditional Dissenting denominations. Preaching outside the walls of church or meeting house was, of course, only one element in this new evangelicalism. The individualism that stemmed from their relocation of

---

[79]   Dallimore, *George Whitefield*, I, pp. 249–69 and Stout, *The Divine Dramatist*, pp. 66–74.

[80]   Murray (ed.), *George Whitefield's Journals*, p. 216.

[81]   Ibid., p. 220.

[82]   Jenkins, 'An old and much honoured soldier', 455–9 and Eifion Evans, 'Spirituality before the Great Awakening: the personal devotion of Griffith Jones, Llanddowror', in Evans, *Fire in the Thatch*, pp. 57–74.

[83]   Murray (ed.), *George Whitefield's Journals*, p. 229.

[84]   Ibid.

genuine Christianity within the realm of experience and the climactic event of the New Birth was backed up by an equally individualistic emphasis on the preaching event. The ability to preach was not necessarily dependant on ordination but upon the power of the Holy Spirit conveyed immediately, something that could be experienced equally by lay and ordained individuals.[85] By venturing into the open air the early Methodists were taking the Gospel to the people, placing the onus on the individual to respond, and thereby attempting to reach the unchurched masses in mid-eighteenth-century England and Wales.[86]

Within three weeks of his first visit to Wales, Whitefield returned. This time he stayed longer and undertook a tour beyond the small area around Cardiff and Newport that he had seen three weeks earlier. His preaching, usually translated on the spot by Howel Harris in monoglot Welsh-speaking areas, was once again greeted with an enthusiastic response.[87] William Seward, always ready to report the latest news surrounding Whitefield as positively as possible and create maximum publicity for his leader's activities, reported to the small group of London evangelicals who followed Whitefield's international wanderings closely that they had 'met with great success in Wales and carry all before us [. . .] Indeed, we go from place to place as Joshua did when he took Canaan, from conquering to conquer.'[88] This second visit[89] reinforced the positive impression of the Welsh revival and of Howel Harris that he had received three weeks earlier. Following the visit Whitefield regularly spoke of wanting to spend increasing periods of time in Wales –

---

[85]   Stout, *The New England Soul*, pp. 189–94.

[86]   John R. Guy, 'An investigation into the pattern and nature of patronage, plurality and non-residence in the old diocese of Llandaff between 1660 and the beginning of the nineteenth century' (Ph.D., University of Wales, 1983); S. R. Thomas, 'The diocese of St David's in the eighteenth century: the working of the diocese in a period of criticism' (MA, University of Wales, 1983); and Peter Virgin, *The Church in an Age of Negligence: Ecclesiastical Structure and Problems of Church Reform, 1700–1840* (Cambridge, 1989).

[87]   See for example HHD 99, 14 April 1743.

[88]   'William Seward to Joseph Stennet (5 April 1739)' in Thomas (ed.), 'George Whitefield and friends', *NLWJ*, 27, II, 196.

[89]   Between 1739 and 1743, Whitefield paid five extended visits to Wales. After the two visits in 1739, he returned again after his return from America in November 1741. In early 1743, he came to Wales on two occasions, once in January, when he oversaw the foundation of Calvinistic Methodism in England and Wales, and then in April he came to attend a further Welsh Association.

admitting that the longer he stayed the more attracted to the country he became.[90]

Whitefield's more considered judgements about his experiences in Wales came a few weeks after he had left, in some letters written to some of his closest associates in London. His abiding impression was that Wales was a 'noble soil for Christianity'[91] and that the Welsh seemed 'much readier to receive the Gospel than [the people] in England'.[92] The reason for this, he believed, was the presence of larger numbers of 'spiritual clergy'[93] than in England and, perhaps somewhat patronizingly, their 'primitive simplicity'.[94] The most productive consequence of Whitefield's two visits, though, was his friendship with Howel Harris. By April 1739, their relationship had been cemented and Whitefield had come to regard Harris as a co-worker and one of his closest associates. Despite Whitefield not having met Daniel Rowland, Harris had ensured that he was introduced to as wide a constituency as possible in the short time spent in Wales, and he had already become party to some of the discussions relating to the revival's future direction. Whitefield's abiding impression of the Welsh, a view he ensured was transmitted throughout the burgeoning international evangelical community, was that they

> seem a people sweetly disposed to receive the Gospel. They are simple and artless. They have left bigotry more than the generality of our Englishmen and through the exhortation of Howel Harris, and the ministry of others, they are hungering and thirsting after the righteousness of Jesus Christ.[95]

It was a view typical of that held by many English visitors to Wales and reflected in much of the literature produced in England about Wales and the Welsh.[96] Whitefield's admiration for the innocence and simplicity of the Welsh was in marked contrast to the hitherto traditional image of Taffy, who was

---

[90] Murray (ed.), *George Whitefield's Journals*, p. 246.
[91] 'George Whitefield to Samuel Mason (7 April 1739)', in Thomas (ed.), 'George Whitefield and friends', *NLWJ*, 27, II, 197.
[92] Ibid.
[93] Ibid.
[94] Ibid.
[95] Murray (ed.), *George Whitefield's Journals*, p. 246.
[96] Moira Dearnley, *Distant Fields: Eighteenth-Century Fictions of Wales* (Cardiff, 2001), p. xvi.

invariably poor, dishonest and smelly![97] His views were undoubtedly informed by his own disdain of life in English cities like
London and Bristol and his growing realization that the revivals
in those cities were slowly beginning to disintegrate. Visiting
Wales seemed to re-energize Whitefield. Its receptiveness to the
evangelical message offered him fresh hope and seemed to point
the way out of the mire in which the English revival seemed
irretrievably sunk.

During both visits to Wales, Whitefield, under the coordinating hand of William Seward, maintained his practice of
reporting back to friends in London. Seward usually sent letters
by 'every post'[98] to James Hutton, who then circulated them to
the expectant Methodists gathered in Fetter Lane eager to hear
about Whitefield's Welsh exploits.[99] In these letters he relayed
up-to-the-minute information on the places he visited, the people
he met and the conversations he held. However, he seems to
have realized very early on that such correspondence, whilst indispensable, was also insufficient if the various awakenings were
to be drawn closer together into a more meaningful relationship.
Consequently, at the end of his second visit to Wales, in April
1739, Whitefield invited Howel Harris to return with him to
London.[100] Harris spent almost six weeks away from Wales, and
whilst lodging with James Hutton[101] he was able to observe the
English revival at close quarters and begin to carve out a niche
for himself within it. His time in England took him to the four
key centres of the English revival – Gloucester, Oxford, Bristol
and London – though most of his time was spent in London.

Harris's first experience of the English revival proved one of
the most dramatic and defining experiences of his life. It had a
profound effect on his own outlook and eventually on the wider
Welsh revival. Initially the most significant result of his visit was

---

[97]   Dearnley, *Distant Fields*, pp. xiii–xxi, 1–11 and Peter Lord, *Words with Pictures:
Welsh Images and Images of Wales in the Popular Press, 1640–1860* (Aberystwyth,
1995), pp. 33–74. On the extent to which the Welsh Methodists celebrated their
Welshness see James, 'The New Birth of a people', pp. 27–30.
[98]   William Seward to Samuel Mason (7 July 1739), in Thomas (ed.), 'George
Whitefield and friends', *NLWJ*, 27, III, 312.
[99]   George Whitefield to Samuel Mason (21 February 1739), in Thomas (ed.) 'George
Whitefield and friends', *NLWJ*, 27, I, 81–2; George Whitefield to Daniel Abbot (24
February 1739), ibid., 83–4; and George Whitefield to Samuel Mason (23 March 1739),
in Thomas (ed.), 'George Whitefield and friends', *NLWJ*, 27, II, 182–3.
[100]   See Appendix 1, p. 343.
[101]   Podmore, *The Moravian Church in England*, p. 61.

the new contacts and friendships that he made. The focal point of the English revival at this time was still the Moravian-dominated Fetter Lane Society. Its members included such figures as John and Charles Wesley, John Cennick and the countess of Huntingdon, as well as the Moravians, James Gambold (1711–71)[102] and James Hutton. Count Zinzendorf, who happened to be visiting London at the time, had taken a particularly keen interest in the progress of the Welsh revival whilst at home in Saxony, by means of regular letters received from James Hutton who, as Whitefield's literary agent at this time, had immediate access to the most up-to-date evangelical news.[103]

By meeting such a wide variety of English evangelicals, by discussing his experiences with them and by telling them about the revival in Wales, Harris was able to piece together his own network of like-minded evangelicals, independent of the patronage and initiative of Whitefield. These new friends included such influential figures as William Seward and John Lewis, as well as less prominent figures like Mrs Judith Godwin,[104] Anne Dutton,[105] Isabel Allen,[106] Samuel and Sarah Mason[107] and John Acourt.[108] These new contacts, amongst numerous others, became the means by which the Welsh revival was drawn closer to the English revival and thereby drawn into the broader resurgence of evangelical religion. Harris returned to Wales established on the international stage with renewed confidence and a far clearer idea of where the future of his revival lay.

In the same way as Whitefield had taken account[109] of the Welsh societies, Harris was given access to the inner core of the English revival and learned about the issues affecting its future prosperity at first hand. By the time that Harris arrived in London, tensions in the Fetter Lane Society were already

---

[102] See *DWB*, pp. 273–4; *BDEB*, pp. 422–3; and Podmore, *The Moravian Church in England*, passim.

[103] Nuttall, *Howell Harris*, p. 24.

[104] Trevecka 202, Mrs J. Godwin to Howel Harris (23 November 1739) and Trevecka 209, Mrs J. Godwin to Howel Harris (17 January 1740).

[105] Trevecka 215, Anne Dutton to Howel Harris (4 February 1740).

[106] Trevecka 160, Isabel Allen to Howel Harris (5 May 1739).

[107] Trevecka 246, Sarah Mason to Howel Harris (22 May 1740) and Trevecka 266, Samuel Mason to Howel Harris (14 August 1740).

[108] Trevecka 238, John Acourt to Howel Harris (no date).

[109] Murray (ed.), *George Whitefield's Journals*, p. 230.

beginning to jeopardize the unity of the English revival.[110] The most damaging disagreement related to concerns over some of the more innovatory aspects of Moravian theology, but beneath these grievances lurked deeper and far less principled personality clashes. Harris had taken a particular interest in the theological innovations of the Pietists ever since his mentor, Griffith Jones, had introduced him to them in 1736. Throughout his life he maintained an ambivalent attitude towards the Moravians. From the earliest days of his spiritual pilgrimage he had been a regular subscriber to Griffith Jones's *Welch Piety*[111] and had read some of the best known writings of Böhme and Francke.[112] Despite this, when occasion demanded he could be as stern in his con-demnations of the Moravians as both John Wesley[113] and George Whitefield, who became bitter opponents of Moravian-ism in the 1740s.[114] At other times, Harris resembled them so closely that many of his fellow Methodists, particularly in Wales, feared that he had actually joined them.[115]

The roots of this ambivalent attitude are to be found in Harris's indebtedness to the Moravians during his first visit to London. Despite arriving in the city on something of an emotional crest after Whitefield's euphoric second preaching tour of south Wales, Harris's emotional insecurities soon resur-faced. There is little doubt that Harris felt intimidated by the spiritual maturity of the Fetter Lane evangelicals. His low opinion of himself and the nagging uncertainties he still har-boured about the suitability of his leadership of the Welsh revival were further compounded when he learned of the Moravian doctrine of 'stillness' that was then prominent in the society. As a theological innovation, 'stillness' shifted the emphasis in the schema of redemption away from justification by faith towards a

[110] For the Fetter Lane Society see Podmore, *The Moravian Church in England*, pp. 29–71.

[111] Nuttall, *Howell Harris*, p. 64.

[112] Ibid., pp. 63–4 and Evans, 'Howel Harris and the printed page', passim.

[113] On John Wesley's attitude and debt to the Moravians see Rack, *Reasonable Enthusiast*, pp. 202–7 and Podmore, *The Moravian Church in England*, pp. 73–80.

[114] Whitefield's relations with the Moravians after the break-up of the Fetter Lane Society are dealt with in detail in Podmore, *The Moravian Church in England*, pp. 80–8.

[115] See HHD 130, 30 April 1748 and HHD 144, 30 May 1748. The most helpful study of the Moravians' influence in Wales remains R. T. Jenkins, 'The Moravian brethren in north Wales: an episode in the religious history of Wales', *Y Cymmrodor*, XLV (London, 1938).

more passive understanding of faith that stressed the individual's need to wait until God bestowed the gift directly.[116] Practically, those who advocated 'stillness' tended to relegate the means of grace, such as preaching, prayer and Bible reading, to a secondary status, preferring to stress the necessity of waiting passively for the gift of salvation. This teaching threw Harris into confusion and uncertainty. He had struggled with doubts about his spiritual condition for a number of years and had passed through an agonizing conversion experience before going on to agonize for a number of months until he received his equally intense baptism with the Holy Spirit.[117] Faced with a theology that seemed fundamentally to contradict his own experience, articulated by individuals whose personal holiness seemed unimpeachable, Harris questioned the whole reality of his Christian profession. His diaries for these months are littered with entries that betray his confusion. On 30 April 1739, for example, he confided in his diary:

> I did not know what to do. I was afraid to write these convictions down least it was 'working'. I was afraid to pray, though I had desires put in me, least it was 'doing' [. . .] I went along (much humbled inwardly) fearing every step [. . .] dreading the name of 'doing' or anything like it.[118]

Naturally, Harris's depression dragged him further into despair and despondency until, whilst in London, he reached crisis point, doubting both the reality of his conversion and the validity of his work in Wales.

It was the Calvinistically inclined English evangelicals, and Whitefield in particular, who came to Harris's rescue. They, together with the Wesley brothers, had become dissatisfied with Moravian teaching and had become concerned about the pernicious influence of the emphasis on 'stillness'. The Wesley brothers had already begun to distance themselves from the Moravians when Harris arrived in London.[119] Charles Wesley

---

[116] *DMBI*, p. 337; Podmore, *The Moravian Church in England*, p. 60.

[117] See Evans, *Howell Harris*, pp. 1–10 and Tudur, *Howell Harris*, pp. 15–19. Also useful, because it is largely based on extracts from Harris's own diaries, is Richard Bennett, *Howell Harris and the Dawn of Revival* (Bridgend, 1987), pp. 19–27.

[118] HHD 44, 30 April 1739.

[119] These debates and divisions are discussed at length in Podmore, *The Moravian Church in England*, pp. 59–71 and Rack, *Reasonable Enthusiast*, pp. 202–5.

publicly disagreed with John Shaw, a member of the society who
had questioned the validity of the priesthood and claimed to be
as qualified as any man to administer the sacraments.[120] By the
end of 1739 the Wesley brothers had practically separated from
the Moravians, having established their own headquarters in
London, and taken the first step towards purchasing the
Foundery, which John Wesley hoped would act as a focus for
their own rapidly developing brand of Methodism.[121] After a
period in which Harris's moods fluctuated between ecstatic
spiritual 'highs' and the depths of despair, the patient counsel of
Whitefield – and we may presume his observation of the
misgivings of the Wesley brothers – gradually 'enlightened [him]
more and more'.[122] Through their instruction and constant
reiteration of the doctrine of justification by faith alone, he came
to understand that 'faith is the fundamental Grace in the spiritual
work and the genuine spring of all our obedience'.[123] These
comments, though, underestimate the extent to which Harris's
discussions with Whitefield revolutionized his theological development. Prior to meeting Whitefield in March 1739, Harris had
read a substantial amount of Puritan literature but had not
adopted decidedly Calvinistic convictions about the order of
salvation. His relative susceptibility to the insights of both the
Wesleys and the Moravians is indicative of the uncertainty with
which he reacted to their particular theological innovations.
Whitefield, sensing Harris's wavering adherence to the orthodoxy of the Church of England, ensured that, throughout his
stay in London, Harris was given a never-ending supply of
Calvinistic literature. Indeed, Harris seems to have spent an
inordinate amount of his time in London studying, so much so
that he complained of spending more time reading the Puritans
than Scripture itself.[124] By plying him with godly Reformed literature Whitefield ensured that Harris was made aware of the
precise ways in which he thought the Wesleys and the Moravians
had deviated from Anglican orthodoxy and ensured his adherence to a modified form of Calvinism that did justice to the

[120] Rack, *Reasonable Enthusiast*, p. 202.
[121] See ibid., p. 204.
[122] HHD 44, 30 April 1739.
[123] Quoted in Tudur, *Howell Harris*, p. 54.
[124] See Evans, 'Howel Harris and the printed page', 40–1.

parallel doctrines of God's ultimate sovereignty and mankind's responsibility to respond to the free offer of the Gospel.[125]

Reflecting on this period of testing, with the benefit of hindsight, Harris recognized the danger he had been in during his dalliance with 'stillness' teaching and precisely how important the whole experience had been to his spiritual development. In his diary he confided:

> Sure the Lord alone did bring me here to London [. . .] seeing every thing concurring [. . .] to supply all my want; His servants made to speak to my purpose, their words working on me and sending more and more to build me in faith in Christ.[126]

Neither was he slow to acknowledge who was responsible for his deliverance and his renewed sense of assurance. In 1740 he admitted that it had been his meeting with George Whitefield and his wise guidance that had finally saved him from complete despair.[127] Despite the difficulties that Harris had encountered meeting the Moravians at Fetter Lane and the way in which he had seen both Whitefield and John and Charles Wesley distance themselves so markedly from them, he always harboured a secret admiration for them. Even in the middle of his gravest spiritual trials, he remained enamoured of their spirituality and could still wish them every success. In May 1739, for example, he wrote in his diary:

> Hearing of ye Moravian Brethren my soul was made inwardly to rejoice in their success (more than if it had been given my self – least self shd take a share in it) & to pray for their preservation – & found ye highest esteem in my soul for them Xt honrs them – an humble longg att a Distance to see them &c.[128]

From the perspective of Harris's subsequent development, his meeting with the Moravians was highly significant. Despite being closely associated with Whitefield, Harris never publicly con-

[125] See Tudur, *Howell Harris*, p. 55 and Evans, 'Howel Harris and the Printed Page', 47–8 for contrasting views on the rapidity of Harris's theological development.
[126] HHD 45, 27 May 1739.
[127] HHD 56, 25 May 1740.
[128] HHD 45, 27 May 1739.

demned the Moravians, and certainly never formally separated from them. Throughout the 1740s, when both Whitefield and the Wesleys had practically ostracized them, Harris remained on good terms with many of the Moravian leaders in London and consistently longed for the 'Ld [to] bless the Moravian Church, [and to] [. . .] keep them pure'.[129]

Much the same relationship existed between Harris and the Wesley brothers. Although Harris did not meet John Wesley on this particular visit to London, his meeting with Charles was sufficient to cement the bond that had already begun to form as a result of what he had already heard about both of them. Harris first met John Wesley in Bristol as he returned to Wales in June 1739. Reflecting on the meeting in his *Journals*, John Wesley wrote:

> About nine that faithful soldier of Christ, Howell Harris, called upon me. He said he had been much tempted not to do it at all; that many had told him I was an Arminian, a Free-willer, and so on; so that he could hardly force himself to come [. . .] 'But' he added, 'I had not been long there, before my spirit was knit to you, as it was to dear Mr Whitefield, and before you had done, I was so overpowered with joy and love that I could scarce stand, and with much difficulty got home.'[130]

Despite misgivings about aspects of John Wesley's theology and having, no doubt, been warned to keep his distance from them, Harris's admiration for the Wesleys' spirituality overcame all his other concerns. In his relations with the brothers, the Moravians and some of the various other groups in Wales who were sympathetic to the revival, Harris was able to be genuinely ecumenical. His desire for spiritual life and vitality, and his detection of these qualities in many of the groups with which he personally had significant theological differences, allowed him to overcome minor differences and to move amongst these groups with comparative ease. This was something that not even George Whitefield, usually famed for riding roughshod over traditional denominational boundaries, could always achieve. Harris was able to use these relationships to maximum effect by keeping the lines of communication between the various factions open and, throughout the

---

[129] Ibid.
[130] A. H. Williams, 'The leaders of Welsh and English Methodism, 1738–1791', *Bathafarn*, 16 (1961), 37.

1740s, he was able to act as a voice of moderation, preventing the revival from collapsing into petty wrangling and damaging recriminations. Paradoxically, this was a role that Harris was able to fulfil in England but not in Wales. It remains one of the ironies of the early history of the Methodist revival in England and Wales that a figure who eventually became so divisive in Wales was able to become a powerful unifying force in England.

In many respects the Howel Harris that returned to Wales was very different from the one who had made his way to London three and a half months previously. Whitefield, having observed Harris at close quarters during his two visits to Wales, had had sufficient foresight to realize the positive benefits that Harris would reap from being in London. What he could not have foreseen was the extent to which Harris would begin to act independently of his patronage. Harris used all of the opportunities with which he was confronted in England to create his own network of evangelical friends and correspondents, realizing that this was essential if the Welsh revival was to become a fully integrated part of the international evangelical community. From this date the Welsh revival became a far more newsworthy subject, accounts of its progress appeared far more frequently in the evangelical press, and Harris himself became a more visible figure on the evangelical stage. Harris had arrived in London depressed and suffering from chronically low self-esteem, even wondering whether to continue his work. He left the capital recommissioned and with a new sense of purpose and destiny – more sure of his own role as a layman, theologically better educated, and more determined to advance the cause of the revival in Wales.

The relationship that existed between Harris and Whitefield was the foundation for the further interaction of the Welsh and the English awakenings and it set the agenda for contact with some of the other more distant evangelical communities. Yet it would be a mistake to assume that Harris's contact with awakenings beyond Wales was dependent on the initiative or patronage of George Whitefield alone. As has been already pointed out, Harris was aware of many of the wider developments in the evangelical movement long before he met Whitefield but there is no doubt that he would not have been able to forge as many meaningful relationships with these other awakenings without the kind of access that his contacts with Whitefield gave him or without the degree of evangelical respectability that associating with him brought. By becoming more closely associated with the English revival, Harris's disjointed contacts with some of the other revival communities were rationalized and placed in the context of the whole evangelical movement. But the tension between being able to act alone as one of the leaders of the Welsh revival, and therefore enjoying a rank ostensibly the same as Whitefield's, and his dependence on Whitefield's patronage characterized Harris's contacts with evangelicals outside England and Wales where he had not been able to establish a physical presence.

The way in which the Welsh Methodists developed their relationship with the colonial awakening is illustrative of this tension. Jonathan Edwards's account of the 1735 Northampton revival, *A Narrative of Surprising Conversions*, had come into Harris's hands shortly after it was first published in Britain towards the end of 1737. We know that by the end of 1738 both Harris and Daniel Rowland had read Edwards's work and were able to discuss its contents in detail when the two of them met in Breconshire.[131] In its pages they would have read Edwards's graphic descriptions of the awakening at Northampton, and witnessed his carefully nuanced theological explanation of the revival. Despite significant differences relating to the different social and religious characters of New England and Wales, they would have been able to understand and agree with Edwards's main theological concepts – particularly his theology of the outpouring of the Spirit which lay at the heart of the book.

The Welsh Methodists' interest in the colonial revival was subsequently intensified by means of their close working relationship with George Whitefield, who as early as 1737 had already begun to divide his time between the British Isles and the American colonies.[132] Although the Welsh Methodists had no

---

[131]   HHD 35, 27 November 1738 and Evans, *Daniel Rowland*, pp. 69–72.
[132]   Between 1737 and the early 1750s, Whitefield spent a total of eight years in the American colonies. His first visit lasted from December 1737 until December the following year. Within eight months he was again in American, on this occasion staying until March 1741. In August 1744 he again set out for the colonies and did not return to Britain until July 1748. He then remained in England for three years before embarking on a shorter visit lasting from September 1751 until May 1752.

direct links with the colonies, the colonial revival was to have a disproportionately significant impact on the development of the revival in Wales, in much the same way as it did in many other countries.[133] George Whitefield's prolonged absences from England, as a result of his transatlantic wanderings, meant that Howel Harris's expertise and experience were heavily utilized in England, resulting in his eventual assumption of the leadership of the Tabernacle Society in 1748. This indirect impact of Whitefield's colonial activities had far-reaching consequences for the Welsh revival. It meant that the responsibility for much of its day-to-day oversight often fell to Daniel Rowland; and within the Welsh movement, though Harris was always held in high esteem and commanded a significant following, it was often to Rowland that most felt the stronger loyalty.

When in London, Harris stood at the intersection of the international evangelical community. All the news about the progress of the revival was mediated to the scattered evangelical communities through Whitefield's network of booksellers and press agents. Harris was perhaps one of the most energetic contributors to the success of this network. Whilst in London, he was almost always one of the first to hear about revival events in far-flung places and, significantly, was particularly susceptible to the different opinions and influences that were vying for attention. Harris's position in London ensured that events in the American colonies, particularly those associated with Whitefield, were kept at the forefront of the minds of many evangelicals in Wales. They learned of Whitefield's colonial itinerancy through the regular flow of journalistic letters that Whitefield and his wife sent back to their evangelical supporters in England and Wales[134] and there is some evidence to suggest that a few Welsh Methodists were readers of the colonial evangelical magazine edited by Thomas Prince, *The Christian History*.[135] Whitefield was also able to exploit the Welsh Methodists' passion for news from America by ensuring that they remained committed to his chief

[133] See Crawford, *Seasons of Grace*, pp. 197–222, 226–8 and Harold P. Simonson, 'Jonathan Edwards and his Scottish connections', *Journal of American Studies*, 21, 3 (1987), 353–70.

[134] Trevecka 1359, Elizabeth Whitefield to Howel Harris (29 September 1745); Trevecka 1562, George Whitefield to Howel Harris (8 November 1746); and Trevecka 1660, Elizabeth Whitefield to Howel Harris (30 May 1747).

[135] See Trevecka 1424, John Syms to Howel Harris (4 March 1746).

colonial venture – his orphanage in Georgia. By supporting the Orphan House financially throughout the 1740s, many Welsh Methodists acquired a financial stake in the colonial revival which led them to follow the course of Whitefield's itinerancy with párticular care in order to ensure that their gifts to the work in Georgia, often at considerable personal sacrifice, were being properly utilized.[136]

The Welsh Methodists' relationship with revival communities in Europe operated in a much more oblique way. There were very few direct contacts with German Pietists. Links with them came chiefly through some of Harris's other Moravian friends in London. Harris does not seem to have expressed any desire to fellow John Wesley's lead by visiting Herrnhut or Halle. Exposure to Pietism was therefore much more indirect, as its influence permeated back to Wales, particularly as Harris moved closer and closer to the Moravians as the 1740s progressed. Despite being one element in the Wesleyan, Calvinistic and Moravian triumvirate that made up the English revival, for most Welsh Methodists the Moravians were very much fringe figures. The only tangible links between the Welsh Methodists and Europe came during the mid-1740s when a number of English Methodists serving in the British armies in northern France and the Low Countries wrote letters to their evangelical friends, keeping them up to date with their spiritual progress, and they reported any inklings of revival activities among the soldiers.[137]

The only other awakening to figure prominently in William Williams's overview of the revival in his *Aurora Borealis* (1774)[138] was that which occurred in Ireland. At first surprising because of the almost complete lack of Calvinistic involvement, the Irish awakening probably enjoyed prominence because of the role played by the sometime Calvinist and close friend of Howel Harris, John Cennick. Cennick came to Ireland at the invitation of some Dublin Baptists and quickly sprang to prominence

---

[136] On the Welsh Methodists' interest in Whitefield's Orphan House see below, pp. 294–302.

[137] See below, pp. 324–6.

[138] Garfield H. Hughes (gol.), *Gweithiau William Williams Pantycelyn*, II (Caerdydd, 1967), p. 179.

among the religious societies that had been established in the city.[139] Disputes within these societies led him to leave Dublin for the life of a roving evangelist, and he enjoyed considerable success among Moravian societies in parts of Ulster.[140] Cennick kept in occasional contact with Howel Harris[141] and we can be sure that among Harris's closest followers there was some knowledge of Cennick's activities in Ireland. Cennick was one of the few evangelicals outside Wales with whom Harris kept in intermittent contact even after his expulsion from the English revival in 1750.[142]

Despite William Williams's 'strong thoughts of going to Ireland' in June 1746,[143] Harris does not seem to have had any wish to visit John Cennick or any of the Methodist societies in Dublin. By the mid-1740s part of the truce that had been reached between the Calvinists and the Wesleyans involved their agreement to refrain from proselytizing in areas where either group had already established a foothold. Wesley's dominance in Irish Methodist circles by this time,[144] more than any other factor, probably dissuaded Harris from establishing contacts in Ireland himself. So again the Welsh Methodists' contact with Irish Methodism came second hand through Whitefield and, to a lesser extent, Cennick. Before Wesley had made his own inroads in Ireland, Whitefield had attempted to establish a foothold in Dublin. Having travelled through Ireland, from Limerick in the west to Dublin, on his return from the American colonies at the end of 1738, Whitefield had been shocked to discover the poverty of the Irish and seemed genuinely moved to do what he could for them.[145] Despite subsequent visits during the 1740s, the Irish seemed immune to Whitefield's powers of persuasion, and his efforts did not usually meet with an enthusiastic response. The Methodists in Wales followed the course of his Irish missions with avid interest. There was a flurry of interest and considerable prayer in Wales during September 1742 when Whitefield made

---

[139] Hempton, 'Noisy Methodists and pious Protestants', pp. 61–2.
[140] Hempton and Hill, *Evangelical Protestantism in Ulster Society*, pp. 7–8.
[141] Trevecka 1757, Howel Harris to John Cennick (15 January 1748) and Trevecka 1849, John Cennick to Howel Harris (5 March 1749).
[142] Trevecka 1938, Howel Harris to John Cennick (5 June 1750).
[143] Trevecka 1471, William Williams to Howel Harris (5 June 1746).
[144] Hempton, 'Noisy Methodists and pious Protestants', pp. 64–6.
[145] Murray (ed.), *George Whitefield's Journals*, pp. 180–1.

a concerted effort to establish himself first in the Isle of Man and then in Ireland.[146] Then in January 1744 there was a similar response as Whitefield tried again in vain![147]

Interest in the progress of the awakening in Scotland was of an altogether different order. By 1739, the only part of the evangelical community that did not figure in the thoughts of the Welsh Methodists was the Scottish awakening which, despite intimations of revivals, did not really get going until 1741 when Whitefield made his first preaching tour of Scotland, gathering a number of local awakenings into something resembling a national Scottish revival. For the majority of Methodists in Wales news of events in Scotland came chiefly through the letters that passed between Harris and some of the Scottish evangelicals and through the detailed revival narratives that appeared in the pages of *The Weekly History* during the summer of 1741.[148] Direct Welsh contacts with Scottish evangelicals were limited to those correspondents with whom Howel Harris was able to remain in contact by virtue of his role at the centre of the revival in London. Unlike the American revival, Harris depended on George Whitefield for his introduction to Scottish evangelicals, and one of the most fruitful friendships to emerge from Whitefield's extended visit to Scotland in the summer of 1741 was that between Harris and William McCulloch.

McCulloch had clearly heard of Harris and his work in Wales from Whitefield and seems to have asked Whitefield to introduce him to Harris. Although they never actually met and Harris never visited Scotland himself, Whitefield passed on McCulloch's request for a letter to Harris. Harris, probably still not cured of his inferiority complex, confessed to being surprised and humbled at McCulloch's request.[149] His first letter to McCulloch is typical of many similar letters that he wrote to other revivalists, introducing both himself and his work and interspersing it with

---

[146] Trevecka 510, Howel Harris to Thomas Bowen (no date); Trevecka 644, Howel Harris to Daniel Rowland (14 September 1742); Trevecka 656, Howel Harris to Thomas James (21 September 1742); Trevecka 658, Howel Harris to George Whitefield (23 September 1742); and Trevecka 669, Howel Harris to George Whitefield (29 September 1742).

[147] Trevecka 1087, Howel Harris to Anne Bowen (21 January 1744); Trevecka 1096, Howel Harris to Daniel Rowland (31 January 1744); and Trevecka 1101, Howel Harris to Griffith Jones (2 February 1744).

[148] See *WH* 64 (Saturday, 26 June 1742) and *WH* 66 (Saturday, 10 July 1742).

[149] Trevecka 637, Howel Harris to William McCulloch (11 September 1742).

appropriate exhortations. In its opening sentences he confessed that 'the account of the work with you at Cambuslang has made me rejoice indeed and bless ye Lord for coming to tabernacle among you'.[150] From this customary beginning, Harris launched into a minutely detailed account of the progress of the Welsh revival and his own role in it. The purpose in rehearsing these details was made clear in his concluding exhortations to McCulloch that he 'recommend all the Welsh lambs I earnestly beg of you to ye Prayers of all as Pray in faith and desire their Lord'.[151] Whitefield was delighted to hear that Harris had responded positively to his encouragements to make contact with McCulloch. Writing from Scotland in September 1742, he assured Harris that his letters had borne fruit and that he had become 'much beloved here'.[152]

Knowledge about the Welsh Methodists from Harris's letters and Whitefield's dissemination of news whilst in Scotland had the result of bringing Harris into contact with some other Scottish evangelicals. At around the same time as he wrote to McCulloch, Harris received a letter from Lady Jane Hume Campbell. In it she thanked Harris profusely for his letters printed in some of the recent issues of *The Weekly History* that had reached Scotland and assured him that his writing had been blessed 'in a Peculiar Manner to my Heart'.[153] The positive response that his work had elicited in Scotland seems to have made Harris wonder whether it would be worth visiting Scotland himself, accompanying Whitefield in a supporting capacity. In response to a request from an anonymous Scottish minister, Harris, obviously attracted by the idea of physically extending the borders of his ministry, decided against it, citing his lack of an 'immediate call amidst so many worthy labourers in Scotland'.[154] There is little doubt that the unordained Harris was put off going to Scotland by the prospect of having to work with so many ordained ministers. Once again, Harris's sense of inferiority surfaced. Whilst he had by this time developed a niche for himself in London and had overcome many of the misgivings

---

[150]   Ibid.
[151]   Ibid.
[152]   'The copy of a letter from the REV. MR WHITEFIELD in SCOTLAND, to MR HOWEL HARRIS, in HOXTON, near LONDON' (16 September 1741), *WH* 81 (23 October 1742).
[153]   Trevecka 666, Lady June Hume Campbell to Howel Harris (28 September 1742).
[154]   Trevecka 736, Howel Harris to minister in Scotland (23 November 1742).

that some of the revivalists with whom he worked might have harboured, he was not prepared to enter an atmosphere where his gifts and status would again be called into question and where he would once more have to justify his ministry to staunch high Presbyterians.

Harris's most fruitful other Scottish contact was the influential Scottish Member of Parliament, James Erskine, Lord Grange. Erskine, a regular face at Whitefield's Tabernacle when in London, proved to be an ideal ally for the Methodists, particularly when they faced opposition from the mob and the hostility of the authorities in the mid-1740s.[155] Harris maintained a regular correspondence with him throughout the decade and he became an enthusiastic supporter of the Welsh Methodists and a particular source of advice and counsel to Howel Harris.[156] Both men were committed to maintaining some form of unity among the various English Methodist sects and it seems that throughout the 1740s both Harris and Erskine worked closely together as they attempted to reintegrate the Calvinists, the Wesleyans and the Moravians. These Scottish contacts contributed the final piece to the Welsh evangelicals' transnational and transatlantic world-view. Although the Scottish revival did not always loom as large in the minds of the Welsh Methodists as the English or the colonial revivals, many of them were kept in close touch with events in Scotland in the pages of the evangelical press. Again it was only Harris who enjoyed regular direct contact with Scottish evangelicals, but there were a significant number of individuals in Wales who felt that the fresh outbreaks of evangelical enthusiasm in 1741 and 1742 in and around Glasgow represented a fresh fillip for the revival at precisely the time when it appeared to be running out of steam.

By the end of 1739, therefore, the Welsh revivalists' perception of themselves had undergone a significant revolution. Both Howel Harris and Daniel Rowland had joined forces, linking their revivals to create something more closely resembling a national awakening, and they had then moved from having only

---

[155] This theme is developed in considerably more detail in Chapter VI.
[156] For an indication of the nature of their correspondence that was most frequent in 1743 and 1744, see Trevecka 1127, James Erskine to Howel Harris (25 February 1743); Trevecka 1156, James Erskine to Howel Harris (26 March 1744); Trevecka 1186, James Erskine to Howel Harris (23 May 1744); and Trevecka 1285, James Erskine to Howel Harris (26 January 1745).

the vaguest inkling that they were part of a more significant development within international Protestantism, to being enthusiastic members of an evangelical renewal movement which encompassed many parts of England, Wales, Ireland, continental Europe and the American colonies. Despite the varying degrees of contact that they had with each of these awakenings during the late 1730s and early 1740s, the future of the movement seemed certain. To its most committed members it appeared to presage the beginning of a golden age for the Gospel – maybe even the dawn of the millennium itself. They could hardly have imagined that their expectations would soon be dashed and their energies seriously dissipated.

IV

DIVIDING TIMES: CONCENTRATING ON THE 'SHADOWS OF RELIGION'

The creation of the transnational revival network had been made possible because, as John Walsh has written, in its first formative decade the revival was 'more an attitude of mind than a considered plan of campaign'.[1] The revivalists' stress on the New Birth, brought about by the immediate intervention of the Holy Spirit, and their shared commitment to the evangelization of their communities enabled them to subdue many of their theological and denominational differences. Reflecting on the first years of the revival, Whitefield, in a letter to John Powell from Philadelphia in 1739, rejoiced in the:

> Divine Attraction [. . .] between all ye members of ye Misticalle Body of [which] J X is ye Head [. . .] love is so far shedd abroad in our Hearts as to cause us to love one another tho we a little differ in Externals for my part I hate to mention them.[2]

Yet, he must have realized that his hyperbolic evaluation was over-optimistic, as problems had already begun to surface, especially in London. As early as the end of 1738, even before he had visited London for the first time, Harris had observed that in Wales:

> Satan by a Spirit of Bigotry in all parties, as well as with us, has affected to do great mischief in many places among CHRIST'S little flock, to embitter their spirit, against others, of a different persuasion, and each directing their thoughts, from the substance to the shadows of religion.[3]

The seeds of dissension were present from the earliest days of the revival. It was not long before a concentration on the 'shadows of religion' became a spirit of bigotry and suspicion that was then closely followed by bitter recrimination.

---

[1] Walsh, 'Origins of the evangelical revival', p. 161.
[2] Trevecka 200, George Whitefield to John Powell (9 November 1739).
[3] Trevecka 129, Howel Harris to Mr M.P. (21 November 1738).

The differences that emerged among the pioneer revivalists should come as no great surprise. They had been drawn together from a variety of national contexts, denominational traditions and social backgrounds and, though initially they found common ground in their experience of the New Birth, it was perhaps inevitable that these differences would eventually come to be mirrored in the movement they led. Their divisions were of a number of kinds. At the most fundamental level there was a clash of personalities. Howel Harris, Daniel Rowland, George Whitefield and John Wesley were uncompromising leaders who, though they were each indispensable to the revival, found it at best difficult, and at times virtually impossible, to work with one another. They were also extremely committed members of the Church of England and struggled against the pressure that was put on them by their fellow Anglicans, who resented their enthusiasm and the irregularities that arose from their itinerant ministries,[4] and the Dissenters, who could not understand the reasons for the strength of their allegiance to the Church and thought that the compromises that resulted from it far outweighed any perceived benefits.[5] Theologically, a diverse cross-section of opinions was found among them and it was over these issues that tensions boiled over most fiercely. The early

[4]   On the Welsh Methodists' relationship with the Established Church see Tudur, *Howell Harris*, pp. 92–150; R. Buick Knox, 'Howell Harris and his doctrine of the Church', *CCHMC*, XLIX, 3 (September 1964), 61–78; *CCHMC*, L, 1 (March 1965), 1–18, and 2 (July 1965), 34–44; and White, 'The Established Church, Dissent and the Welsh language, c.1660–1811', 264–9. For their relations with traditional Anglican spirituality see J. Gwynfor Jones, 'Some Puritan influences on the Anglican Church in Wales in the early seventeenth century', *JWRH*, 2 (2002), 19–50 and Morgan, *The Great Awakening in Wales*, pp. 30–45. On the state of the Church of England in the eighteenth century see John Walsh and Stephen Taylor, 'Introduction: the Church and Anglicanism in the "long" eighteenth century', in John Walsh, Colin Haydon and Stephen Taylor (eds), *The Church of England, c.1689–c.1833: From Toleration to Tractarianism* (Cambridge, 1993), pp. 1–64 and Peter Virgin, *The Church in an Age of Negligence* (Cambridge, 1989). Also useful, if introductory, is William Gibson, *The Church of England, 1688–1832: Unity and Accord* (London, 2001). The best analyses of the English Methodists' clash with the Church tend to concentrate on Wesley. See Baker, *John Wesley and the Church of England*; A. Brown-Lawson, *John Wesley and the Anglican Evangelicals of the Eighteenth Century* (Durham, 1994), pp. 81–131; Rack, *Reasonable Enthusiast*, pp. 275–81, 291–313; and David Hempton, 'Methodism and the law, 1740–1820', *Bulletin of the John Rylands University Library of Manchester*, 70, 3 (Autumn 1988), 101–3.

[5]   On the Welsh Methodists' relationship with Dissenters see Tudur, *Howell Harris*, pp. 92–150 and Knox, 'Howell Harris and his doctrine of the Church', 76–8. For the wider context see Watts, *The Dissenters*, I, pp. 434–45 and G. F. Nuttall, 'Methodism and the older Dissent: some perspectives', *The Journal of the United Reformed Church History Society*, II (1981), 259–74.

1740s were dominated by heated debates about the relative strengths and weaknesses of Moravianism, Arminianism and Calvinism.[6] The amorphous and fairly inclusive renewal movement of the later 1730s and 1740s[7] became a more multifaceted movement, assuming a different nature under the superintendence of each of its leaders and in each of the countries in which it took root. Yet despite these divisions, it would be a mistake to assume that the revival lost any sense of overall unity or that the revivalists stopped regarding themselves as co-workers in the same work. Despite there being many Methodisms there was still very definitely only one evangelical revival, though unity was manifested in a variety of different para-institutional ways.

The polarization of the revival that occurred in the early months of 1740 represents the second stage in the development of the international evangelical movement. On the basis of the friendships that had been established in the later 1730s, the leaders of the Welsh revival, and Howel Harris in particular, continued to participate in the evangelical community, even though the manner in which they did so altered significantly. In the first months of their awakenings the revivalists craved friendship and mutual support most of all, and their correspondence largely reflected this in their excited accounts of the events which they were inspiring and in their desire to meet one another regularly in order to share the ideas and techniques that would help propagate the movement. By 1740 this excitement had largely abated, and the communications network was forced to adapt to meet the new needs of the revival. Although journalistic letters still predominated, a new tone was often introduced into them, as individuals began to decide for themselves which interpretation of the revival they favoured.

---

[6]   Historians have tended to pay very little attention to the details of this controversy. Those who have discussed it have favoured a Wesleyan perspective and have downplayed its significance. Studies of this kind include Rack, *Reasonable Enthusiast*, pp. 198–202; Herbert Boyd McGonigle, *Sufficient Saving Grace: John Wesley's Evangelical Arminianism* (Carlisle, 2001), pp. 107–27; and Frank Baker, 'Whitefield's break with the Wesleys', *The Church Quarterly*, 3, 2 (1971), 103–13. For accounts more favourable to the Whitefieldians see Dallimore, *George Whitefield*, II, pp. 19–62; Irwin W. Reist, 'John Wesley and George Whitefield: a study in the integrity of two theologies of Grace', *The Evangelical Quarterly*, XLVII, 1 (1975), 26–40; and A. P. F. Sell, *The Great Debate: Calvinism, Arminianism and Salvation* (Worthing, 1982), pp. 59–76.

[7]   Trevecka 626, Howel Harris to Thomas James (7 September 1742); Trevecka 628, Howel Harris to Marmaduke Gwynne (7 September 1742).

Howel Harris played a vital role in all of these divisions and in the discussions and debates that they fuelled. His presence in London at all the critical moments in the early development of the revival ensured this and also meant that his followers in Wales were able to follow closely the various controversies, and in some instances make their own telling contributions to them. Harris's role in them demonstrates the remarkably different way in which he operated outside Wales. In Wales he continually stressed his own supremacy and indispensability. He was 'Called first, [and] sent out first'[8] and therefore deserved to be given pre-eminence among his fellow Methodists.[9] As the revival progressed, Harris began to gain a reputation for stubbornness and arrogance and, in the opinion of none other than George Whitefield himself, an insatiable 'desire for power'.[10] By the mid-1740s, Daniel Rowland had grown particularly weary of him having found him difficult to work alongside ever since they had first disagreed publicly, at the Talyllychau Association in March 1742, over the precise nature of God's covenant with mankind.[11] As tensions became more prominent, so Harris's insistence that he was in charge because he had been evangelizing a 'long time ere I heard of Mr Rowland'[12] became more frequent and he quickly became a divisive figure, the root cause of many of the Welsh revival's weaknesses and the reason for its eventual disruption in 1750.

In England, Harris's public profile was very different. Daniel Rowland's reluctance to network among English evangelicals as extensively as Harris meant that he was a much less prominent figure on the international evangelical stage.[13] Harris was able to take centre stage and allowed many of the less well-informed English evangelicals to think that the revival in Wales was largely of his own making. In some circles in London he was known as 'the Bishop',[14] whilst in Bristol, particularly in 1747, he was

---

[8]   HHD 117, 15 May 1745.
[9]   See also HHD 122, 1 April 1744; HHD 125, 20 January 1747; and HHD 132a, 30 November 1748.
[10]   HHD 146a, 7 December 1750.
[11]   HHD 86, 17 March 1742.
[12]   HHD 121, 9 February 1746.
[13]   For Daniel Rowland's contacts in London and visits to the city, see Evans, *Daniel Rowland*, pp. 199–207.
[14]   HHD 106, 14 January 1744.

called the 'Pope'.[15] Whilst Harris confessed to being 'humbled to the dust'[16] at these titles, there can be little doubt that the un-ordained Harris, always very conscious of his lack of ecclesiastical recognition, would have taken immense pride – albeit secretly – in his status among the English evangelicals. His role as a trouble-shooting revivalist allowed him to take a bird's-eye view of the English revival and there is no doubt that when in London he was able to adopt a similar role to that which Whitefield assumed when he came to Wales. In England, Harris had the type of access to all factions of the revival that not even Whitefield could match. The friendships that he had made with many of the most prominent London Moravians and with many of Wesley's followers, during his first visit to London in the summer of 1739, enabled him to move between each faction with relative ease and acceptance. This was vital for the long-term future of the revival. For a while after 1740, it appeared that the divisions between the Whitefieldians and the Wesleyans would irrevocably damage the whole revival, and perhaps even precipitate its complete dissolution. That they did not was in large measure a result of the tireless work of Harris who, when he visited London and Bristol, was able to act as the go-between among the warring factions. This was Harris's most lasting contribution to the English revival. In 1746 he confided to his diary: 'the Lord did give a particular honour to me to make a peacemaker of me.'[17] If, when in Wales, his voice was often a discordant one, in England Harris came to be seen as the voice of toleration and reason.

Howel Harris was probably the first of the revivalists, in both England and Wales, to provoke both the displeasure of the Established Church and the suspicion of the Dissenters. By 1740 he had reached a fairly well-defined position in his relations with both groups – a position which developed very little throughout the rest of his career. Almost immediately after his conversion, Harris had begun to 'exhort', the term he preferred to 'preaching', in the homes of his nearest neighbours around

[15] HHD 127, 4 June 1747.
[16] Ibid.
[17] HHD 127, 19 June 1746.

Trefeca and Talgarth, entirely of his own volition and without the prior approval of his local vicar, Pryce Davies. At first, Harris attempted to maintain amicable relations with Davies, stressing that he 'sincerely endeavoured to practice those excellent doctrines we have from you',[18] but it was not long before Harris's irregular activities aroused Davies's suspicion and disapproval. In an exchange of letters in 1735 and 1736, Pryce Davies warned him:

> since you have advanced so far as to have your public lectures from house to house, and even within the limits of the church, its full time to let you know the sin and penalty you incur in so doing. The office you've fondly undertaken belongs not to the layity any farther than privately in your own families.[19]

In the face of the disapprobation of his local vicar, Harris turned to Griffith Jones, who had himself flouted parish boundaries in 1714, when he had initiated a mini-revival in southern Carmarthenshire. Jones's counsels during these months proved to be vital to Harris's development and to the formulation of his position in the Church. Jones advised him to be cautious and to take care not to arouse the opposition of the Church, if he still wished to stand a chance of being ordained. When the bishop of St Davids, Nicholas Clagett (d. 1746), turned down his first application in 1736,[20] Harris, though initially depressed and uncertain whether to continue exhorting or not, eventually emerged from the episode more resolute in his determination to carry on. To Griffith Jones he belligerently protested that he had done more good by his itinerating than he ever could if he was confined to a single parish, and that, in any case, the success of his exhorting was evidence enough of God's approval of his work![21]

Harris's early experience of the cumbersome and restrictive rules of the Established Church was deeply frustrating. Despite his protestations that God's approval of his work was of far more importance than the approval of the Church, he remained

---

[18] Trevecka 54, Howel Harris to Pryce Davies (16 August 1735).
[19] Trevecka 65, Pryce Davies to Howel Harris (27 February 1736).
[20] Trevecka 80, Howel Harris to Griffith Jones (31 July 1736).
[21] Ibid.

deeply scarred by his rejection and throughout his career protested his loyalty to the Church at every conceivable moment. He made sure that he communicated in the Church as often as possible and he continually urged all his followers to do the same,[22] protesting that he was 'much for the Church'.[23] This is not to say that Harris was not acutely aware of the many weaknesses of the Church, particularly its clergy's reluctance to preach the evangelical gospel,[24] a view that even led him on one occasion to conclude: 'light has taken its leave of this Church and Christ is lost.'[25] Yet he judged that even this was an insufficient ground for leaving a Church whose foundations he believed to be thoroughly biblical. In the face of compelling evidence suggesting otherwise, Harris never gave up hope of seeing 'a reformation in this poor benighted church'.[26] Throughout his career, Harris never really moved beyond this ambivalent and at times contradictory view of the Church – on the one hand openly flouting its rules while on the other vociferously protesting his affection for it and his loyalty towards it.[27]

Harris's early contacts with the Dissenters in Wales led to his adoption of an equally ambivalent attitude. In the early years of the revival he was befriended by a number of prominent Dissenting ministers,[28] including both Edmund Jones, Pontypool,[29] and David Williams, Pwll-y-Pant, who clearly hoped to be able to influence him and possibly channel his energies into the revitalization of the Dissenting cause. Bound together by their shared moderate Calvinism, Harris and his Dissenting sympathizers

---

[22]   See 'An account of the proceedings at the Association held at Waterford, Jany 5th and 6th, 1743', CMA 2945, pp. 5–6; 'At the Association at Llanvihangel, May 3d 1744', CMA 2945, pp. 86–7; Trevecca 562, Howel Harris to Griffith Jones (24 May 1742); and Knox, 'Howell Harris and his doctrine of the Church', 73.

[23]   HHD 23a, 1 April 1737.

[24]   See Trevecka 562, Howel Harris to Griffith Jones (24 May 1742) and HHD 235, 27 March 1761.

[25]   HHD 108, 4 March 1744.

[26]   Trevecka 602, Howel Harris to John Cennick (17 August 1742).

[27]   See Trevecka 562, Howel Harris to Griffith Jones (24 May 1742); Trevecca 674, Howel Harris to Herbert Jenkins (2 October 1742); and Trevecca 694, Howel Harris to George Whitefield (15 October 1742).

[28]   Trevecca 136, Howel Harris to George Whitefield (8 January 1739).

[29]   See Trevecca 119, Edmund Jones to Howel Harris (10 August 1738); Trevecka 162, Edmund Jones to Howel Harris (21 May 1739); and Trevecka 243, Edmund Jones to Howel Harris (9 May 1740). For more on Edmund Jones's relationship with the Methodists see Edgar Phillips, *Edmund Jones: The Old Prophet* (London, 1959).

seemed, on the surface, to be natural allies, and Harris clearly hoped that they would be able to work in partnership to further the task of spiritual renewal in Wales.[30] He reiterated his love to all Dissenters on numerous occasions and paid tribute to their faithfulness to the Gospel over many decades, often in the face of considerable persecution.[31] However, despite his admiration for their faithfulness and resilience, he felt that many of them had 'sunk from ye Ld.',[32] lost much of their vitality and become legalistic and moribund.[33] When the Baptists, in particular, later began to poach some of his converts, Harris became increasingly disillusioned with them and disturbed by their readiness to 'reap a harvest for which they had done so little to prepare'.[34] For the Dissenters, Harris's loyalty to the Church proved to be too much of a stumbling block, and, as it became increasingly clear that he had no intention of leaving the Established Church, they began to distance themselves from him, becoming bitingly critical of both his enthusiasm and his seemingly blind loyalty to the Church.[35] Harris seems to have quickly reached the conclusion that if he threw in his lot with the Dissenters his revival would be marginalized and its decline into irrelevancy would be both inevitable and rapid. By early 1740 he had come to the conclusion that the Church was the most advantageous platform from which to reach the maximum number of people and to ensure that the revival would not be tainted by accusations of disloyalty and revolutionary intent in the way that some of the Nonconformist denominations had been throughout the seventeenth century. Some comments in his diary in 1740 reflect this fear: 'Had I been a Dissenter, I should not have done the 20th part of the good I do!'[36] Practical considerations related to the public image of the revival were undoubtedly among the most significant factors that led Harris to reiterate constantly, in public at least, his unswerving allegiance to the Church and his distance from the Dissenters.

---

[30]   HHD 21, 10 April 1737 and HHD 25, 21 September 1737.
[31]   HHD 52, 9 February 1740 and HHD 54, 7 March 1740.
[32]   HHD 135a, 23 July 1749.
[33]   HHD 54, 7 March 1740; HHD 62, 30 August 1740; and HHD 132a, 11 October 1748.
[34]   Quoted in Knox, 'Howell Harris and his doctrine of the Church', 76.
[35]   See Trevecka 694, Howel Harris to George Whitefield (15 October 1742) and Trevecka 2799, Howel Harris to George Whitefield (16 November 1742).
[36]   HHD 52, 10 February 1740.

Harris's arrival at this highly ambivalent position had considerable repercussions on the future course of the revival. In Wales it ensured that Methodism, for most of its first eighty years at least, remained in the Church of England. Harris's discovery that both George Whitefield and John Wesley also wished to keep the revival firmly within the Church, and at the same time maintain amicable relations with evangelicals of other denominational affiliations, ensured that they were able to pool their energies into holding their converts to this policy. On numerous occasions the policy brought them into direct collision with the Church and the Dissenters, as well as with other individuals within the revival itself who were unhappy and frustrated with their leaders' position, which to many of them appeared to be too much of a compromise, neither loyal enough to the Church for many Anglicans, nor critical enough of it for many Dissenters.

Harris's conciliatory policy was brought into sharper focus during his first visit to London in 1739. His arrival in April proved to be fortuitously significant. It coincided with the controversy that was undermining the unity of the Fetter Lane Society over the same issue with which he had grappled during the previous months – the validity of the ministry of laymen. Harris's ecumenical spirit had been one of the things that had most impressed Whitefield when he had first visited Wales a few weeks earlier,[37] and there is little doubt that Whitefield felt that Harris might have a valuable contribution to make to the preservation of the unity of the Fetter Lane Society. Harris fitted into the London revival perfectly and was immediately called on to offer leadership and counsel. On his first night in London he witnessed John Shaw in open dispute with Charles Wesley, having rejected the principle of a Christian priesthood, claiming that he himself, and any other layman, could both baptize and administer the sacrament.[38] Whitefield had faced similar problems with Charles Kinchin (1711–42) [39] who had resigned his fellowship of Corpus Christi College, Oxford, and seemed to be on the verge of seceding from the Church of England altogether,

---

[37]   See Murray (ed.), *George Whitefield's Journals*, p. 229.
[38]   Podmore, *The Moravian Church in England*, pp. 52–3; Baker, *John Wesley and the Church of England*, p. 80; Rack, *Reasonable Enthusiast*, pp. 202 and 211.
[39]   See *BDEB*, p. 646 and *DMBI*, pp. 191–2.

only to be dissuaded by Whitefield at what was patently the final hour.[40] Shaw was subsequently expelled from the Fetter Lane Society, a move which Harris, himself a layman, wholeheartedly supported.[41]

Harris's attitude to the cases of Shaw and Kinchin raises important questions about his status in the English revival. As a layman who had struggled with the ecclesiastical authorities over his right to exhort and establish religious societies,[42] it might be thought that Harris would have been more sympathetic to their views than he in fact turned out to be. However, Harris seems to have regarded himself in a very different light from either Shaw or Kinchin and was not prepared to think of his own activities as a challenge to either the priesthood or the Church. He had justified his lay ministry while in Wales by appealing to the Holy Spirit's obvious attestation of his work, demonstrable by the numbers who regularly listened to him and professed conversion under his ministry. Secondly, he used the fact that he was the 'first of all the Brethren'[43] as proof that God had singled him out as a special case. Harris was at pains to avoid the impression that he intended to challenge the Church of England in any way, and to allay any suspicions he continually strove, as much as he could, to ensure that his loyalty to the Church was clearly reiterated to both the Church itself and his followers. Like John Wesley, Harris did not see his acceptance of lay ministry as a direct threat to the Church and never suggested that unordained laymen should compete with the priesthood by administering the sacraments.[44] Harris was able to deploy this somewhat tortuous logic to justify his own position both to himself and to his contemporaries, who, recognizing his obvious contribution to the revival, especially in the 1740s, were reluctant to challenge him openly on the issue.

The incidents with Shaw and Kinchin were probably even more important to the developing ecclesiology of Whitefield and

---

[40] See Murray (ed.), *George Whitefield's Journals*, pp. 255–7 and Luke Tyerman, *The Life and Times of the Rev. John Wesley: Founder of Methodism*, 2 vols (London, 1876–7), vol. 1, pp. 363–70.

[41] HHD 43, 25 April 1739.

[42] Trevecka 65, Pryce Davies to Howel Harris (27 February 1736); Tudur, *Howel Harris*, pp. 28–32, 58–9, 63–4, 128–9.

[43] HHD 125, 20 January 1747.

[44] See Brown-Lawson, *John Wesley and the Anglican Evangelicals of the Eighteenth Century*, pp. 81–131.

John Wesley. Both were forced to pay more careful attention to their relationship with the Church after the two incidents and it is inconceivable that Whitefield, in particular, was not helped by Harris to define his position more clearly. The standpoint at which he arrived during these weeks was identical to that which Harris had developed in the months when both the Anglicans and Dissenters in Wales were doing their best to undermine his ministry. In his published *Journals*, clearly expounded for all to read, Whitefield outlined his new position:

> For my own part, I can see no reason for my leaving the church, however the corrupt members and ministers of it treat me. I judge of the state of the church, not from the practice of its members, but its primitive and public constitutions; and so long as I think the Articles of the Church of England are agreeable to Scripture, I am resolved to preach them up without bigotry or party zeal.[45]

Fundamentally, this was a position that rested not on what the Church of England was but what the revivalists felt it ought to be. When it contravened their wishes or restricted them in any way, they were prepared to go beyond its bounds without compunction whilst still protesting that they were loyal to it because they were the only ones who were truly representative of its primitive simplicity according to its original creeds and confessions. It was an ingenious position and one that commanded the adherence of the vast majority of revivalists in both England and Wales.

The policy was repeatedly challenged from a number of quarters during the early years of the revival. As early as the end of April 1739, Whitefield was drawn into conflict with the Church by taking a decision that was to affect the pattern of his whole ministry. He had been impressed with Howel Harris's readiness to exhort anywhere, 'in a field, [. . .] at other times in a house, from a wall, a table, or any thing else',[46] and had eventually mustered the courage to take his own first step into the open air in Bristol during February 1739, shortly before he visited Wales for the first time. The account of the sermon and its

---

[45] See Murray (ed.), *George Whitefield's Journals*, pp. 255–6.
[46] Ibid., p. 229.

effect on the miners at Kingswood has passed into Methodist folklore,[47] but his indebtedness to the example of Howel Harris has not been so readily acknowledged.

Harris was prepared to defend his itinerant and open-air preaching in much the same way as he had defended himself against those who were ready to criticize him for his lack of clerical ordination. Apart from appealing to his favourite defence – the incontestable divine attestation of his ministry[48] – Harris appealed to well-known scriptural precedents, particularly to the example of Apollos,[49] to support his apparently irregular activities, and he repeatedly claimed that it was an evangelistic necessity, rather than a lack of respect for the authority of the Church, that had propelled him into the open air. He also had Anglican precedents, particularly Griffith Jones,[50] on which to call for support much closer to home. In these circumstances, Harris attempted to claim that the Church, in its most catholic sense, had always allowed the ministry of lay people in pioneer missionary situations, and he was prepared to argue that much of Wales was still untouched by the Gospel and therefore virgin territory for the Church. Harris and many of the other revivalists were undoubtedly helped by the Church's inability to meet the changing needs of the populations that it was supposed to serve. In Wales, the Church had been unable to adapt to changes in demographic patterns. Creating new parishes and erecting new church buildings was a laborious process, usually requiring an Act of Parliament and the slow response to these challenges left the way wide open for the Methodists. Methodism in Wales thrived in the large, poorly managed rural parishes, and later in some of the new semi-industrial communities that did not have a strong Anglican presence.[51] The weaknesses of the Church therefore allowed Harris to argue that open-air preaching was essential because people in these widely dispersed and often

---

[47]   Ibid., pp. 215–16. See also Robert W. Malcolmson, ' "A set of ungovernable people": the Kingswood colliers in the eighteenth century', in J. Brewer and J. Styles (eds), *An Ungovernable People: The English and their Law in the Seventeenth and Eighteenth Centuries* (London, 1980), pp. 118 and 125–6.

[48]   HHD 18, 3 February 1737.

[49]   Evans, *Howell Harris*, pp. 13–14.

[50]   Jenkins, 'An old and much honoured soldier', 455–6.

[51]   White, 'The Established Church, Dissent and the Welsh language c.1660–1811', pp. 261–3; Ward, *The Protestant Evangelical Awakening*, pp. 320–4; Ward, 'Was there a Methodist evangelistic strategy in the eighteenth century?', pp. 285–305.

sparsely populated rural parishes did not have access to evangelical preaching.[52]

Harris's rationale of open-air preaching was clearly influential in the personal development of both Whitefield and John Wesley.[53] Whitefield similarly argued that the main reason for going to Kingswood in February 1739 was his concern for the spiritual condition of the miners. The Kingswood miners were, in his opinion, 'little better than heathens',[54] and if the Church was ill equipped and unprepared to deal with them, then necessity determined that he himself was forced to fill the void. Meeting Harris the following month in Wales confirmed Whitefield in his desire to continue preaching in the open air and to become still more provocative by venturing into the open air in London itself. On 27 April 1739, Whitefield, having been denied access to the pulpit of a church in Islington, preached in the graveyard outside proclaiming: 'And since the self-righteous men of this generation count themselves unworthy, I go out into the highways and hedges, and compel harlots, publicans, and sinners to come in, that my Master's house may be filled.'[55] There can be little doubt that Harris's presence in London during these weeks was a vital contributory factor to Whitefield's determination to make field preaching a successful means of mass evangelization in the city. Although neither Whitefield's *Journals* nor Harris's private diaries make any reference to discussions between them as to how best to preach in the open air, it is inconceivable, given Whitefield's many admissions of indebtedness to Harris, that he would not have drawn upon his extensive experience and sought to learn from him at first hand how best to capture the attention of congregations and ensure that his message was best suited to the different constraints of field preaching. In the weeks immediately following, Whitefield repeated his Islington performance time and again, honing his skills, in consultation with Harris, and witnessing the crowds becoming ever larger and open-air field preaching one of the most important innovations of the whole revival.

[52]   Trevecka 343, Howel Harris to David Lloyd (14 June 1741).
[53]   On Whitefield's debt to Harris's example as a field preacher and for a useful analysis of some of the similarities between them see Stout, *The Divine Dramatist*, pp. 66–70.
[54]   Murray (ed.), *George Whitefield's Journals*, p. 222.
[55]   Ibid., p. 259.

Predictably, Whitefield's new venture aroused the displeasure of the ecclesiastical authorities. The bishop of London, Edmund Gibson (1669–1748),[56] published a virulent pamphlet against him: *A Pastoral Letter by Way of Caution against Lukewarmness on the One Hand and Enthusiasm on the Other* (1739).[57] In it he railed against Whitefield and, by implication all other Methodists, for their 'enthusiasm' and irregular behaviour. More specifically, he brought nine charges against Whitefield ranging from his supposedly claiming direct divine inspiration and the gift of prophecy, to preaching a new Gospel and attacking the spirituality of the clergy.[58] Whitefield thought the attack damaging enough to respond with a letter of his own, and before the end of 1739 his *An Answer to the Bishop of London's Pastoral Letter* was rushed into print and almost immediately translated into Welsh by John Lewis.[59] The Welsh translation was undoubtedly undertaken at the suggestion of Harris and the work can be taken to represent the official position of the revival in relation to the Church in 1740. It reflected Harris's views, and it could conceivably be argued that its conclusions owed more to him than to Whitefield. Whitefield constructed his reply as a reasoned point-by-point rebuttal of the charges levelled by Gibson, but it was in his response to Gibson's accusation of disloyalty to the Church that Whitefield made some of his most important remarks. He boldly argued that his criticisms of the clergy were entirely valid and challenged the bishop to rebuke those who fell short of their high calling. Whitefield, and thereby the wider Methodist community, took the opportunity to proclaim their loyalty to the Church, but they also ensured that the price of their loyalty and its limits were clearly understood. Whitefield remained an Anglican for practical and perhaps entirely selfish reasons – the Church of England was the best vantage point from which to reach the unchurched majority. He was prepared to remain loyal to it on condition that it did not attempt to circumscribe his evangelistic activity.

[56]   *DNB*, XXI, pp. 274–5 and Norman Sykes, *Edmund Gibson, Bishop of London, 1669–1748: A Study in Politics and Religion in the Eighteenth Century* (Oxford, 1926).
[57]   The work was translated into Welsh by Theophilus Evans and published in 1740 with the title, *Llythyr-addysg Esgob Llundain at y bobl o'i Esgobaeth* (Gloucester, 1740). See Rees (ed.), *Libri Walliae*, p. 264.
[58]   Dallimore, *George Whitefield*, I, pp. 389–90.
[59]   See *Ateb y Parchedig Mr Whitefield, i Lythyr Bugeiliaidd diweddaf Esgob Llundain* (Pontypool, 1740) and Rees, *Libri Walliae*, p. 642.

Although as a layman Howel Harris appeared to many of the London evangelicals to be something of a godsend as they attempted to justify their extra-parochial activities, he did not emerge from his first visit to London entirely free from doubts about his own role and his continued membership of the Church. He had been particularly impressed by some Baptists whom he had met, and at one point seems to have seriously considered joining them. Though he resisted the temptation he admitted that he had never 'permitted [. . . his] thought to turn so favourable this way before'.[60] Yet his attitude to the Baptists – and we may assume other Nonconformist groups – was softened by this experience to such an extent that he was able to recognize that 'There is much carnality in me & others of my side wn we oppose our Brethren ye Baptists, as if it had been ye party & not Xt we were to be zealous for!'[61]

Harris also used his time in London to make further inquiries about the possibility of securing ordination in the Church of England, on this occasion at the hands of the bishop of London. His reasons for doing so are difficult to fathom, particularly in the light of the bishop's passionate antipathy towards the Methodists. Predictably, Gibson declined his application, citing his field preaching and his reputation for consistently flouting the parochial rules and regulations of the Church.[62] By the conclusion of Harris's first visit to London, the revivalists' policy on relations with both the Church of England and the Dissenters had been severely tried and tested. Whitefield had maintained his nerve under pressure from the bishop of London and some within the London revival, and Harris had resisted the temptation to throw in his lot with the Baptists, even though yet another application for ordination had been rejected. Despite the Church's hostile attitude towards them, the revivalists had come to the conclusion that remaining within the Church was their only option if they wished to bring about the kind of national revival that many of them clearly expected in 1739. There was widespread agreement that 'people were more likely to promote the reformation by continuing in the Church of England than by

---

[60] HHD 44, 4 May 1739.
[61] Ibid.
[62] Harris's account of this meeting with Gibson was recorded in his diary. See HHD 44, 11 May 1739.

separating from it while they can with peace of conscience'.[63] Their allegiance to the Church was not without its limits, however. They were all ready to admit that the Church had 'fallen from her pure and holy Doctrine'[64] and clearly hoped that their presence in the Church would act as the catalyst for its reformation along more evangelical lines. In a letter to Charles Wesley, who was perhaps the most consistently loyal of all of the revivalists, Harris expanded on his hope that they would be able to bring about a renewal in the Church and hoped that like-minded individuals within the Dissenting denominations would emulate their activities: '[I do] not confine [my] Desires for her (the Church of England) only nor make me bitter toward ye other reformed Churches abroad, but secretly longing we may all have sweet union and fellowship here on Earth all of our Sects.'[65] In order to demonstrate their loyalty Harris urged all of his followers to communicate in their local parish churches as regularly as possible, even in situations when the local incumbent was known to be unsympathetic to their views. Harris had established societies in order to supplement the activities of the Church, by providing the spiritual support and encouragement necessary to those individuals who did not receive sufficient spiritual sustenance from their parish minister, rather than to replace it altogether. Harris was also less cautious about society members meeting with the Dissenters than some of his co-revivalists, and he repeatedly urged his followers to meet evangelicals whether they happened to be members of the Church of England or not. This position was explained and reiterated time and again in the writings of all the revivalists and in Wales the position was defined still further at the Association meetings that began to be held more frequently after 1739.[66] In his correspondence Harris also attempted to explain the position in more detail and invariably sought to offer guidance to those who were considering leaving the Church or were facing difficulties because of the oppressive measures being taken against them. In a letter to John Cennick in February 1742, for example, he outlined the position in detail:

[63] Trevecka 2805, John Oulton to Howel Harris (April 1743).
[64] *CA* 18.
[65] Trevecka 613, Howel Harris to Charles Wesley (28 August 1742).
[66] See for example 'At the Association at Llanvihangel, May 3d 1744' in CMA 2945, pp. 86–7 and the Monthly Association at Nantmel, 18 October 1744 in CMA 2945, p. 127.

Most receive the Sacrament in the Church: and hear sermons only where they may be benefited; others that can't have it in their parish Churches monthly, or that may have scruples that can't be removed have the liberty of concerning with the Dissenters; but not so as to adhere to any party so as to leave their brethren of the Church, or of any other spirit, but to retain their liberty of partaking everywhere that they have freedom and opportunity with Christ's lambs.[67]

The first generation of evangelical leaders were prepared to walk this tightrope between the Church and the Dissenters and throughout their lives they largely succeeded in doing so, in spite of the protests of some of their more vociferous supporters. By 1740, Harris in Wales and Whitefield and the Wesley brothers in England had arrived at the same position and had through conflict and debate honed it still further. None contributed more to the development and successful implementation of the policy than Howel Harris, and in the years between 1739 and his dismissal from the revival in 1750 he consistently urged restraint among his followers, defended the Church and sought to ensure that the revival in both England and Wales did not wholly disintegrate over the rights or wrongs of any particular form of Church government. Although a theological realignment did take place in 1740 and 1741, it is remarkable that the policy of maintaining membership of the Church whilst still striving to be genuinely interdenominational emerged from these disagreements remarkably unscathed.

The extent to which the international dimension of the movement strengthened the revivalists' commitment to the policy has also not been adequately appreciated. The fact that the evangelical revival occurred in a wide variety of denominations – among Anglicans in England and Wales, Presbyterians in Scotland, Presbyterians and Congregationalists in the American colonies and amongst Moravians and members of the Lutheran state Church in the German provinces – meant that those revivalists who were committed to maintaining an international profile could not afford to become enmeshed in denominational politics. Whitefield's experience in Scotland illustrates this perfectly. He arrived in Scotland for the first time in July 1741

---

[67]   Trevecka 471, Howel Harris to John Cennick (4 February 1742).

and honoured the invitation of Ebenezer and Ralph Erskine, the leaders of the controversial 'Associate Presbytery', by preaching at Ralph Erskine's congregation at Dunfermline. Quickly realizing that their secessionist group was not the most advantageous platform from which to launch a successful evangelistic campaign in Scotland,[68] Whitefield was forced to distance himself from them and throw in his lot with a small group of sympathetic Church of Scotland ministers who had closely followed the progress of the revival elsewhere and were keen for him to venture north of the border and fan the flames of their nascent revival.[69] Whitefield was profoundly impressed by what he witnessed taking place in the Church of Scotland parishes around Glasgow, where his new friends, William McCulloch and James Robe, ministered, and, in spite of all his efforts to enforce loyalty to the Church of England, it seems that he was even tempted at one point to declare himself enthusiastically in favour of the Presbyterian form of Church government. To John Willison of Dundee he wrote: 'I have often declared, in the most public manner, that I believe the Church of Scotland to be the best constituted National Church in the world.'[70]

Howel Harris was kept closely informed of the progress of Whitefield's visit to Scotland and took a keen interest in these developments in his ecclesiology. Harris strongly advised him against making any unwise remarks about Church government and warned him that 'declaring for Presbytery against Prelacy or for Prelacy against Presbytery is not of God'.[71] Harris's reasoning rested on his conviction that declaring for any single form of ecclesiastical government would drag the revivalists into endless disputes with those who took a different view from them and would therefore jeopardize the long-term sustainability of the revival. Whitefield's impetuosity seems to have been controlled by Harris as he successfully dragged Whitefield back to the

---

[68]   See George Whitefield to Thomas Noble (8 August 1741) in Murray (ed.), *George Whitefield's Letters*, pp. 307–9; George Whitefield to John Willison (15 October 1742), ibid., pp. 514–15; and Murray (ed.), *George Whitefield's Journals*, p. 312.
[69]   See George Whitefield to William McCulloch (8 June 1742), in Murray (ed.), *George Whitefield's Letters*, pp. 401–2 and 'The Rev. Mr McK—t writes thus to Mr Whitefield (21 June 1742)', *WH* 67 (Saturday, 17 July 1742).
[70]   See Trevecka 626, Howel Harris to Thomas James (7 September 1742); Trevecka 644, Howel Harris to Daniel Rowland (14 September 1742); and George Whitefield to John Willison (15 October 1742), in Murray (ed.), *George Whitefield's Letters*, p. 515.
[71]   Trevecka 694, Howel Harris to George Whitefield (15 October 1742).

position that they had previously occupied of benevolent neutrality towards all denominations.[72] Ultimately, Whitefield's visits to Scotland provided him and the rest of the revival with further confirmation of the essential wisdom of their ecumenical policy and he emerged from it resolved to 'bear and converse with all others, who do not err in fundamental[s], and who give evidence that they are true lovers of the Lord Jesus'.[73]

Whitefield's experience of the revival in the American colonies illustrated the relevance of this policy. On his colonial preaching tours Whitefield had grown accustomed to balancing the conflicting demands of the Presbyterianism of the Tennant brothers[74] in Pennsylvania and the Congregationalism more prevalent in New England. Again Whitefield tried to retain his independence, conscious of the detrimental effect of being closely associated with any single group. Yet again it was Howel Harris who seemed to grasp most clearly the importance of ensuring that the revival remained genuinely interdenominational, by highlighting the fact that God had not distinguished between the denominations when he had sent the revivals in the first place. He wrote to Whitefield: 'God speaks for each of these [denominations], in Scotland He owns Presbyterians, in America, Independency, here [England] and in Wales, Episcopacy.'[75]

With a settled policy in place, the middle and later years of the 1740s saw a fairly widespread recognition among the Methodists of the desirability of maintaining their status within the Church whilst still being accommodating to those who differed from them over matters of Church government but who were none the less committed to experiential religion. This is not to say that there were not some who remained deeply suspicious of the revival, or that there were none within the revival itself who protested vociferously against the policy. Many mainstream Anglicans found it difficult to distinguish between the enthusiasm

---

[72]   See ibid; Trevecka 638, Howel Harris to George Whitefield (11 September 1742); and Trevecka 650, George Whitefield to Howel Harris (16 September 1742).

[73]   George Whitefield to John Willison (15 October 1742), in Murray (ed.), *George Whitefield's Letters*, p. 515.

[74]   Ward, *The Protestant Evangelical Awakening*, pp. 269–73; Lambert, *Inventing the 'Great Awakening'*, pp. 47–8. For a more detailed analysis of Gilbert Tennant's role in the Great Awakening, see M. J. Coalter, *Gilbert Tennant, Son of Thunder: A Case Study of Continental Pietism's Impact of the First Great Awakening in the Middle Colonies* (New York, 1986).

[75]   Trevecka 694, Howel Harris to George Whitefield (15 October 1742).

of the revival and what they knew about the radical Puritan sects of a century earlier – fears that became more pronounced in the mid-1740s when the Methodist societies were suspected of being covert organizations for Jacobite sympathizers.[76] These suspicions forced the Methodists into repeatedly protesting that they were loyal to the state, the Church and King George II, thereby putting further pressure on their links with the evangelical Dissenters.

At the opposite extreme the Dissenters remained uneasy about the Methodists' apparent blind loyalty to the Established Church and lost no opportunity to criticize them for their inconsistency. Harris, in response, usually appealed to them to

> show that you see that Jesus is no Respector of persons but that he still has a few that have not bowed the knee to Baal even in this benighted church, and show that it is the advancement of his cause and not of our own Parties you have at heart, by rejoicing to see him reformed among us![77]

Harris's attitude to the Dissenters throughout the 1740s remained just as ambivalent as was his attitude to the Church of England. He was as ready as ever to praise them for their spirituality, and whenever he attended their meetings he invariably left them convinced that 'the power of God is among them, and they have the truth'.[78] Yet his overriding allegiance to the Church resulted at times in his taking a somewhat harsher line, particularly when it appeared that he was about to lose converts to them. Geraint Tudur discusses this development in reference to the Caeo Association of 1745, at which Harris was forced into declaring publicly against the Dissenters because of the demands of five Glamorgan exhorters for ordination.[79] This Association and the one that followed it shortly afterwards at Watford seemed to mark a turning-point in relations with the Dissenters and went some way towards settling the issue for the Welsh Methodists. Those who wanted the Methodist societies to remain within the Church of England finally triumphed and renewed their commitment to remain within it until they were either

---

[76] See below, pp. 324–7.
[77] Trevecka 480, Howel Harris to the Tabernacle Society (12 February 1742).
[78] HHD 115a, 18 December 1744.
[79] Tudur, *Howell Harris*, pp. 112–16.

thrown out or shown the way out by God himself. But despite the uncharacteristic adoption of this hard-line position, once the threat of mass defections had passed and controversy had died down, Harris's more positive opinions of the spirituality of the Dissenters once again surfaced and he continued to enjoy meaningful fellowship with them.

It was probably against the backdrop of these developments in Wales that Harris was able to take such a firm line against those threatening the unity of the Calvinistic revival in London. Whitefield's absence from the British Isles between 1744 and 1748 fundamentally weakened his English work. In his place he had left John Cennick in charge of the Tabernacle, but it soon became clear that he was both unable and probably uninterested in presiding over the increasingly fractious Tabernacle Society. When he decided to leave and join the Moravians in December 1745, taking almost 400 members with him,[80] the leadership of a decimated Tabernacle fell, almost by default, to Howel Harris. The prosperity of the Tabernacle was also undermined by the activities of one of its former members, William Cudworth (1717–63).[81] Cudworth had been, until his secession, in charge of the Tabernacle school, but had left the Tabernacle shortly after Whitefield's departure to the American colonies in August 1744. He then founded a rival preaching house at Spitalfields, taking with him a substantial number of members from the original Tabernacle. It seems that the threat from Cudworth's rival meetings, despite Cudworth's own Antinomian leanings, caused considerable unrest within Whitefield's Tabernacle for some months. In addition to the steady stream of people drifting from it throughout 1745, there was also a more widely felt unease in the Tabernacle about its long-term future. Whitefield's pro-longed absences left it directionless, and the gap does not seem to have been adequately directionless by Cennick. Howel Harris laid the blame for the restlessness in the Tabernacle squarely at the door of Cudworth,[82] but it is probably more accurate to say that Cudworth's secession from the revival was just a symptom of

---

[80]   Podmore, *The Moravian Church in England*, p. 93.
[81]   *DMBI*, p. 84; *BDEB*, pp. 278–9; Dallimore, *George Whitefield*, II, p. 231; J. C. Whilebrooke, 'Wesley and William Cudworth', *Proceedings of the Wesley Historical Society*, XII, 2 (June 1919), 34–6.
[82]   HHD 117, 31 May 1745.

the lack of leadership that was putting the future of the Calvinistic revival in grave doubt.

Harris's confidence in the Church and his unrelenting opposition to those who expressed a wish to secede from it was born of
the fact that during the middle and later 1740s he, together with
Whitefield and some of the other leading London-based evangelicals, believed that they were on the verge of gaining the recognition – or at the least the benevolent toleration – of the Church.
Their confidence arose from their participation in the countess of
Huntingdon's ambitious evangelistic strategy aimed at securing
the conversion of some of the most influential members of
English high society. From 1744 until the early 1750s, the
countess held weekly evangelistic meetings at her home in
Chelsea, to which she invited all of the main evangelical
preachers of the day, including Whitefield, the Wesley brothers,
Howel Harris and Philip Doddridge. Their congregations varied
from week to week, but often included such well-placed individuals as Lord Lothian, the Earl of Chesterfield, Countess Delitz,
Lord Bolingbroke, James Erskine, Lord North and Charles
Stanhope.[83] Although these meetings resulted in only one
genuine conversion, that of the countess's aunt, Lady Frances
Shirley, the countess does not seem to have been overly concerned, as the meetings had what she regarded as an even more
important function. Those who gathered were not primarily
drawn together by their shared evangelicalism but because of
their opposition to the king and his Whig ministers, and their
support for Frederick, Prince of Wales, and his Leicester House
circle.[84]

The Methodists clearly hoped that their contacts with this
opposition group would result in more influence at court and
kinder treatment from the Church of England that would give
them the freedom and space to carry out their top-down
reformation of both the Church and wider society. Their
fortunes seemed to focus on their expectation that, on becoming
king, the Prince of Wales would make Whitefield a bishop.
Whitefield himself appears to have harboured ambitions of this

[83]   For a more complete list see Schlenther, *Queen of the Methodists*, pp. 40–1.
[84]   See H. D. Rack, 'Religious societies and the origins of Methodism', 591–3 and
Linda Colley, *In Defence of Oligarchy: The Tory Party, 1714–60* (Cambridge, 1982), pp.
221–5, 239–40.

sort from the very beginning of his career. He had taken particular pleasure in learning that the Methodists were 'talked of at Court'[85] in 1739, and as early as 1735 he had reported to John Wesley that God had told him that one day he would be made a bishop.[86] His ambitions seemed to be nearing reality when the king, albeit in jest, had recommended to Lord Bolingbroke (1678–1751) that making Whitefield a bishop would put an end to his preaching![87] The hopes of the countess of Huntingdon and her group disappeared with the death of the Prince of Wales in 1751, the dissipation of the Calvinistic revival with the loss of Howel Harris, and Whitefield's lack of interest in its leadership when he returned from America in 1748.[88]

Howel Harris was one of the most regular preachers at the countess's parlour meetings and therefore privy to all the discussions that took place around her 'Grand Table'.[89] His attitude to Whitefield's ambitions of elevation to the bench of bishops was as contradictory as were many of his other opinions. He was not averse to praying that God would reward the Methodists with a 'Christian bishop',[90] but at other times he does not appear to have been as convinced, and he argued with Whitefield that becoming a bishop would severely 'cramp [his] usefulness'.[91] Rather than use the countess's noble and influential friends to press for an evangelical bishop, Harris appears to have used his new-found influence to press the claims of his fellow Welsh Methodists for special protection from those who were intent on persecuting them out of existence. In December 1744, on one of his first visits to the countess's home, he took the opportunity to bring her up to date with the progress of the revival in Wales.[92] His conversation would doubtless have included an

---

[85] Quoted in Rack, 'Religious societies and the origins of Methodism', 592.
[86] Ibid.
[87] Ibid.
[88] The political ambitions of the countess of Huntingdon and the circle that gathered at her home have received more detailed attention in some recent writing on the revival. See Geoffrey F. Nuttall, 'Howell Harris and "The Grand Table": a note on religion and politics, 1744–50', *Journal of Ecclesiastical History*, 39, 4 (1988), 531–44; Rack, 'Religious societies and the origins of Methodism', 591–3; Schlenther, *Queen of the Methodists*, pp. 38–44; and Ward, 'Was there a Methodist evangelistic strategy in the eighteenth century?', pp. 288–91.
[89] HHD 135, 3 May 1739.
[90] HHD 140, 17 January 1750.
[91] HHD 131a, 30 June 1748.
[92] HHD 115a, 24 December 1744.

account of how the revival had begun with the ministries of
Daniel Rowland and himself, and would have gone on to discuss
the growth and development of the societies, especially in the light
of the recently held Joint Association of English and Welsh
Calvinistic Methodism at which the societies had been brought to
order and George Whitefield had been established as their
Moderator.[93] Harris's potted history of the revival would have
been designed to win the countess's support and through her the
sympathy of some of her more influential friends. By 1744 the
Welsh revival had reached an impasse. The enthusiasm associated
with its early years had died down and the revival had become a
more permanent fixture on the Welsh religious scene. The
problems that it now faced were substantially different from those
it had faced in its first years. These new problems were, in a sense,
ones associated with growth. The revivalists had become more
concerned about organizing their existing converts than winning
new ones, and this focus had resulted in a certain degree of
dissatisfaction with the way in which the revival was being led.
Many were unhappy with the policy that had been adopted
towards relations with the Church and the Dissenters, and there
were enough people who felt that maintaining their Anglican
status was detrimental to the wider cause of the revival to create
significant unrest among the Welsh Methodists.

The Church's hostile policy towards the Methodists remained
as virulent as ever, and it is likely that Harris began to use his
contacts with the countess of Huntingdon to seek redress of some
of the grievances of his converts in the hope that this would allay
any desire to turn their backs on the Church of England
altogether. Problems seem to have been particularly acute, for
example, when the Welsh Methodists attempted to gain a
foothold in north Wales during the mid-1740s. In 1745 Lewis
Evan (1720–92)[94] had been commissioned to itinerate in north
Wales,[95] but in 1746 he was imprisoned at Dolgellau for
exhorting at Bala. In an attempt to secure his release from
prison, Harris petitioned some of the countess's closest associates

[93]   The significance of this Association is dealt with in considerable detail in the
following chapter. See below, pp. 214–17.
[94]   *DWB*, p. 247 and Richard Bennett, 'Lewis Evan, Llanllugan', *CCHMC*, VI, 3
(November 1921), 42–51.
[95]   See 'Monthly accounts at Trevecka, Jan. 16 1745', CMA 2945, p. 141.

and friends, particularly Mrs Abigail Edwin, the wife of John Edwin MP, on Lewis Evan's behalf.[96] Harris again used some of the countess's influential contacts to draw attention to the way in which Sir Watkin Williams Wynn (1692–1749)[97] had been persecuting some of the first generation of north Walian Methodist converts in the later 1740s.[98] There is little doubt that Harris looked upon his meetings around the countess of Huntingdon's 'Grand Table' as an important step in the revival's progress towards respectability. Yet, in many ways Harris's attempt to maintain the policy of staying loyal to the Church whilst on good terms with evangelical Dissenters was fraught with difficulties. In reality, Harris was fighting against some of the innate contradictions of the Methodist movement which, on the one hand, castigated the Church for its failings and flouted its laws, and, on the other, continually reaffirmed its loyalty to the Establishment and the claim of its members to be its true representatives and the agents whom God had deployed to restore the Church of England to its pristine apostolic glory.

Relations with the Church and the Dissenters remained a constant source of tension throughout the 1740s, and indeed even until the Welsh Methodists eventually had the confidence to cut loose from the Church and ordain their own ministers in 1811. Of far more pressing concern in the early 1740s was the fragmentation taking place within the revival itself. Initially, unity had been relatively easy to maintain as many of the early Methodists were bound together by the sheer revolutionary force of their life-changing experiences. For a short while the revivalists were able to set aside their personal, theological and cultural differences and maintain a sense of common purpose in the work of reformation. Yet by late 1739, this fragile unity had begun to fragment as the initial excitement dissipated and discussions about how best to define and consolidate the work received greater attention. The fragmentation of the revival was

---

[96]   HHD 125, 19 March 1747; HHD 126, 27 March 1747; and HHD 1 April 1747.
[97]   See *DWB*, p. 1100 and Peter D. G. Thomas, ' "The Prince of Wales": Sir Watkin Williams Wynn (1693–1749)', in Thomas, *Politics in Eighteenth-century Wales*, pp. 150–77.
[98]   HHD 131a, 29 May 1748 and HHD 131a, 24 June 1748.

probably inevitable, but the speed with which it took place was both surprising and highly damaging to its long-term sustainability. In effect what had been one evangelical revival became three revivals congruent with the three leading groups that made up the English movement – the Calvinists, the Wesleyans and the Moravians. Although the Welsh Methodists never formally divided over the rival dogmas of Calvinism and Arminianism, the controversies that took place among the English Methodists forced them to align themselves with their fellow Calvinists.

The most obvious source of conflict in the earliest months of the revival was the Moravians. Initially, chiefly because of the European origins of many of their members, they were the most distinctive of all of the evangelicals who were brought together in the Fetter Lane Society. At first the Moravians and all those who had been influenced by other brands of Pietistic theology, were wholeheartedly welcomed in England. As part of the inner circle of revivalists, Harris was acutely aware of the problems in the Fetter Lane Society. He had witnessed the expulsion of John Shaw on his first visit, but this disagreement denoted much deeper problems in the society and the revival. The views of both George Whitefield and the Wesley brothers had progressed significantly in the months since John Wesley's heart-warming experience in May 1738. By early 1739 neither of them was prepared to limit his work to Fetter Lane alone. But in spite of their reservations, Harris was undoubtedly impressed by what he witnessed in the society, and his lifelong admiration for the Moravians stemmed in large part from his experiences during his first visit to London. His comments about them in his diary during May 1739 are typical; 'hearing of ye Moravian Brethren my soul was made inwardly to rejoyce in their success & to pray for their preservation – & I found ye highest esteem in my soul for them Xt honr them.'[99] However, even Harris was beginning to take notice of some of the reservations that his co-revivalists were beginning to express about the Fetter Lane Moravians. Whitefield's and Wesley's opinions forced him into taking a public position against them that firmly aligned him with their more mainstream views. This is not to say that Harris did not share some of their concerns, but it seems that his growing

99   HHD 45, 27 May 1739.

distance from the Moravians stemmed more from Whitefield's example than from any principled objection on Harris's part.

The chief issue that aroused the opposition of Whitefield, Harris and Wesley was the Moravian doctrine of 'stillness' which had been introduced into the society by Philipp Molther in 1739.[100] For the majority of the revivalists, 'stillness' seemed to strike at the foundation of their faith. Harris had of course been born again at a Communion service[101] and Wesley had had his heart strangely warmed when listening to a reading of the preface to Martin Luther's commentary on the Epistle to the Romans.[102] Closely related to their emphasis on passivity, the Moravians also held that there were no degrees of saving faith short of full and complete assurance. Once again, this contradicted all that the early revivalists knew both from their reading and from their experiences. Many of them, Harris and Whitefield in particular, had only come into a position of faith gradually, and Harris especially was often plagued by doubts about his spiritual condition. He clearly recognized the significance of the fault line that was beginning to open up between those jostling for supremacy within the society. In his diary he wrote of the 'great Division among ye Brethren – the Moravians denyg any weak faith any degrees short of assurance & full power over sin & full liberty &c. & that till faith is given no use of any ordinances'.[103] These tensions remained ever present in the revival throughout 1739 and into 1740 as the revivalists tried to come to terms with the new Moravian teaching. Whilst their eventual split from the Fetter Lane Society was as much over the alternative theological standpoints that the Wesley brothers and Whitefield had adopted, there were also strong personal rivalries within the society that made it virtually impossible for them all to cooperate at such close quarters.

Breaking point was eventually reached in April 1740 when Charles Wesley took the first step towards disrupting the fragile unity of Fetter Lane. He had become more outspoken in his opposition to Molther's stillness teaching and had begun to take

---

[100] Harris's own difficulties with 'stillness' teaching are outlined in chapter IV. See above, pp. 130–2.
[101] Bennett, *Howell Harris and the Dawn of Revival*, pp. 19–27.
[102] Curnock (ed.), *The Journal of John Wesley*, I, pp. 475–6.
[103] HHD 56, 5 May 1740.

every opportunity to speak about the necessity of regularly receiving Communion. By Easter Sunday he had been barred from attending meetings at the society and threatened with complete expulsion if he continued actively to oppose Molther.[104] Through all these events Howel Harris remained in fellowship with Molther and the Fetter Lane Moravians and, perhaps as a result of his own confusion over the issue, attempted to persuade Molther to define more clearly what he actually meant when he spoke of passively waiting for the gift of faith. At one of these meetings with Molther on 6 June 1740, both Harris and Charles Wesley came with the express desire of listening to Molther's dispassionate and reasoned account of what he believed before they took further action. Molther attempted to be as conciliatory as possible and distanced himself from some of the perfectionist tendencies of a number of his more enthusiastic followers. For Harris, though, this was hardly the main issue. He found the Moravians' insistence on there being no degrees of faith short of full assurance potentially dangerous. Throughout their discussions with Molther, both Harris and Charles Wesley attempted to relate all that he said to their own experience, and by doing so they found it severely wanting. For example, in his account of this meeting in his diary, Harris confided:

> discours'd for some time abt who was to come to ye sacrament Molther sd that those were fittest or properest to come that were in full liberty but none shd come that was not poor in spirit & hungrg & thirstg because they cd not examine themselves. I bore my testimony how I was convinced of sin & set free from sin there.[105]

The sacrament had been a converting ordinance in Harris's experience. By limiting attendance to those fully assured of their faith, Harris felt that the Moravians were stripping it of its efficacy and undermining one of its main sanctifying purposes, robbing their converts of one of the most important means of obtaining the full assurance that Molther thought so essential.

The final division at Fetter Lane took place on 16 July 1740, when John Wesley was formally barred from preaching before

---

[104] Podmore, *The Moravian Church in England*, p. 67.
[105] HHD 57, 6 June 1740.

the society.[106] He immediately celebrated Communion for the first time in his new meeting room at the Foundery, thereby establishing his own London base and proclaiming his complete independence from the Moravians. The expulsion of the Wesley brothers from the Fetter Lane Society marks a turning-point in the early development of the Methodist movement. The unity which membership of the society had originally guaranteed was shattered and for a few months there were two revivals in England, one Moravian and the other Methodist. From this date the Moravians were forced to proceed alone, slightly apart from the main current of the revival. Even so, at times their influence was felt more strongly, as conflicts with them once more caught the attention of Whitefield and the Wesleys. The Wesley brothers maintained an ambivalent attitude towards them for the rest of their lives, adopting some aspects of their theology and practices while publicly taking a very harsh and critical line against them.[107] Whitefield tended to keep his distance from them, and it seems that he was never quite as impressed with them as either Wesley or Harris had been, even during the first months of the revival when he too had regularly attended Fetter Lane.[108] In the dispute that tore the Fetter Lane Society apart, Whitefield maintained what Colin Podmore has termed a position of 'distanced neutrality',[109] but, significantly, he never formally took the further step of completely severing relations with them, a fact that was to be important in the later 1740s when, after the revival had settled into a more regular rhythm, Whitefield, with Howel Harris's help, began to attempt to mend some of the breaches that had brought the revival into disrepute and premature decline.

Of all the revivalists, Howel Harris maintained the most open relationship with the Moravians. Throughout his life he remained consistently more moderate and accommodating in his attitude towards them than any of his fellow revivalists. While in England, he was able to play an important behind-the-scenes role in trying to maintain some semblance of friendly relations between the Moravians and the Methodists, and on a number of

---

[106] Rack, *Reasonable Enthusiast*, p. 204.
[107] Podmore, *The Moravian Church in England*, pp. 73–80.
[108] Ibid., pp. 80–8, 95–6.
[109] Ibid., p. 80.

occasions in the later 1740s he was to be at the forefront of attempts to reintegrate the Moravians into the mainstream of the revival. In 1740, and unconsciously perhaps, Howel Harris had begun to develop a role for himself that ultimately proved well suited to his talents. His trusted friendships with individuals from all factions of the revival enabled him to act as a broker between them, and there can be little doubt that his efforts helped to prevent the revival from fragmenting still further through the petty jealousies and theological rivalries of its main protagonists.

Harris's role as mediator came into its own just a few months after the initial split with the Moravians when it became clear that the Arminian views of the Wesley brothers were increasingly incompatible with the moderate Calvinism of Whitefield and his followers, who at this stage still outnumbered those who had chosen to adopt the rapidly emerging alternative theology of the Wesleys. From their first meeting,[110] both parties had been impressed with each other, and it seems that Harris was able to forge a relationship of trust and respect with both Wesley brothers that was strong enough to withstand the often bitter controversies that took place between the Calvinists and the Arminians in the 1740s. It was the depth of this trust that enabled Harris to maintain their confidence and to keep them engaged in meaningful debate, despite his own alignment with Whitefield and his Calvinism.

Although tensions between the Wesleyan and Whitefieldian wings of the revival did not reach their climax until mid-1741, an air of suspicion and mistrust was present from the very earliest days of John Wesley's ministry in Bristol. Whitefield had left England for the American colonies early in 1740 and was busy fanning the flames of what later became known as the Great Awakening when Wesley's true ambitions became apparent. Whitefield had left John Wesley in control of the English revival, with particular responsibility for the oversight of his Bristol societies.[111] Herbert McGonigle has suggested that before he began preaching in the city, Wesley's views on salvation by faith and the distinction between justification and sanctification were

---

[110] See HHD 47, 18, 19 and 20 June 1739 and A. H. Williams, 'The leaders of Welsh and English Methodism, 1738–1791', *Bathafarn*, 16 (1961), 36–40.

[111] George Whitefield to John Wesley (26 March 1740), in Baker (ed.), *The Works of John Wesley, 26: Letters II: 1740–1755* (Oxford, 1982), p. 11.

still crystallizing.[112] But it was in Bristol that he finally seems to have resolved any remaining doubts. It was here that he encountered Calvinistic Methodists at first hand. Wesley's antipathy for Predestinarians, born of his mother's influence in the Epworth rectory, his own struggles over Election and Reprobation at Oxford[113] and his reading of supralapsarian high Calvinistic writers such as William Perkins (1558–1602)[114], Elisha Coles (?1608–88)[115] and the Baptist, John Gill (1697–1771)[116], led him to ignore Whitefield's warnings about speaking against Calvinism in Bristol.[117] The vacuum left by Whitefield's departure presented Wesley with the perfect opportunity to move out of the former's shadow and place his own stamp on Whitefield's converts. Sufficiently convinced of his theological position, it seems, Wesley refused to tolerate anybody holding Calvinistic views in Bristol. On 26 April 1740 he preached a sermon virulently opposing Predestination, arguing strongly in favour of a robust conception of human free will, leaving the Bristol Methodists in uproar. Tensions were raised still further when Wesley began to expel people from the society whom he suspected to be guilty of holding extreme Calvinistic views. However, it was the expulsion of John Acourt from Wesley's own Foundery society in July 1740[118] that made the difference public and drew Whitefield, albeit reluctantly, into more open conflict with Wesley.

Wesley's rapid development was mirrored in Whitefield. While in the colonies on this second visit, Whitefield's own theological opinions also underwent significant modification. By

---

[112] McGonigle, *Sufficient Saving Grace*, p. 112.

[113] Ibid., p. 113.

[114] On Perkins and his influence see *ODCC*, p. 1256; R. T. Kendall, *Calvin and English Calvinism to 1649* (Oxford, 1979), pp. 56–76; and Richard A. Muller, *Christ and the Decree: Christology and Predestination in Reformed Theology from Calvin to Perkins* (Durham, NC, 1986).

[115] The Puritan Elisha Coles was the author of the highly influential *A Practical Discourse on God's Sovereignty* (1676), which was translated into Welsh by Peter Williams (1723–96) in 1760. Evans, 'Howel Harris and the printed page', 47; R. Tudur Jones, 'Yr Hen Ymneilltuwyr, 1700–1740', in R. Tudur Jones (gol. D. Densil Morgan), *Grym y Gair a Fflam y Ffydd: Ysgrifau ar Hanes Crefydd yng Nghymru* (Bangor, 1998), pp. 136, 141.

[116] For Gill see Peter Toon, *The Emergence of Hyper-Calvinism in English Nonconformity, 1689–1765* (London, 1967), 96–100 and Peter Naylor, *Picking up a Pin for the Lord: English Particular Baptists from 1688 to the Early Nineteenth Century* (London, 1992).

[117] Dallimore, *George Whitefield*, I, p. 307.

[118] Trevecka 257, John Acourt to Howel Harris (3 July 1740).

the time he returned to England in March 1741, Whitefield had become a far more committed Calvinist and appeared to be possessed of a fresh zeal to defend Reformed orthodoxy. But he still remained reluctant to disagree with Wesley publicly, realizing the damage that any protracted theological disputation might do to the revival at large. In a letter to Wesley from America shortly after he had first heard about his anti-Calvinistic activities in Bristol, Whitefield wrote: 'I cannot bear the thoughts of opposing you: but how can I avoid it, if you go about (as your brother C— once said) to drive John *Calvin* out of *Bristol*.'[119] Whitefield's response to news of Wesley's actions is typical of his attitude to the revival. Throughout his career Whitefield tended to shy away from protracted involvement in day-to-day admin-istrative affairs, whether it was theological debate, the minutiae of the organization of the societies or ensuring publicity for his revivals. He preferred the role of the roving evangelist, or the inspirational leader who came into an area to fan the flames of revival but preferred to leave others to pick up the pieces. It was this, and the realization that he was probably ill equipped to set up a rival organization to oppose Wesley, something that he evidently felt would be inevitable if they clashed over theological issues, that dictated his initially cautious approach.

At first Whitefield reacted with a measure of incredulity that the Wesleys could espouse doctrines which seemed to have dubious pedigrees, such as human free will and the possibility of obtaining complete freedom from sin.[120] Of far more immediate seriousness though was the belligerence with which Wesley had begun to advocate his views. This had been demonstrated in the most ruthless manner when he began to take control of some of Whitefield's Bristol enterprises and to expel members whom he suspected of harbouring even the mildest Calvinistic views. Although in America, Whitefield tried to reason with Wesley and drew the obvious contrast between the fractiousness of the English revival and the unity, because of a shared commitment to a modest Calvinistic theology, which still characterized the colonial revival at this stage. He wrote:

[119] George Whitefield to John Wesley (25 August 1740), in Murray (ed.), *George Whitefield's Letters*, pp. 204–5.
[120] See for example the letter from Whitefield to John Wesley written from America on 24 May 1740, in Murray (ed.), *George Whitefield's Letters*, pp. 181–3.

I cannot entertain prejudices against your conduct and principles any longer, without informing you. The more I examine the writings of the most experienced men [. . .] the more I differ from your notions [. . .] I dread coming to England, unless you are resolved to oppose those truths with less warmth than when I was there last. I dread your coming over to America; because the work of GOD is carried on here [. . .] by doctrines quite opposite to those you hold [. . .] The work goes on without divisions: and with more success because all employed in it are of one mind.[121]

Whether Whitefield actually believed that Wesley would moderate his tone is difficult to say. What is certain is that Whitefield's conciliatory policy was intended to minimize the damage that Wesley's actions had caused. Although at this stage he does not seem to have thought about severing relations with the Wesley brothers, he was aware that if they persisted in their outspoken policy, and if John in particular took the step of publishing his highly controversial and inflammatory sermon on *Free Grace*,[122] he would be left with little option but to oppose him publicly and risk dividing the whole revival. He pleaded with John Wesley never to 'speak against election in your sermons, no one can say that I ever mentioned it in public discourses, whatever my private sentiments may be [. . .] Nothing will so much prevent a division as you being silent on this head.'[123] At this stage in their relationship, Whitefield seems to have thought that his personal friendship with John Wesley and his obvious pre-eminence within English Methodism would be sufficient to hold Wesley back from placing the whole movement in jeopardy. His naïvety was probably born of the fact that he been absent from England for almost a year and had not realized the extent to which Wesley was distancing himself from him, by attempting to wrest control of the societies in his absence. Howel Harris, who was that much closer to events and who sought to calm matters by

---

[121] Ibid., pp. 181–2.

[122] John Wesley's sermon on *Free Grace* was published in London in 1740. For a full discussion of its contents see Brown-Lawson, *John Wesley and the Anglican Evangelicals of the Eighteenth Century*, pp. 162–5. For a much more biased account of the controversy, exonerating Whitefield from any involvement in schismatic activity, see Robert Oliver, 'The Arminian controversy of eighteenth century Methodism', in *Divisions and Dissensions: Papers Read at the 1987 Westminster Conference* (London, 1988), pp. 78–93.

[123] George Whitefield to John Wesley (25 June 1740), in Murray (ed.), *George Whitefield's Letters*, pp. 189–90.

papering over some of the differences that were beginning to appear ominously irreconcilable, was forced into taking a more prominent part in the debates than he might otherwise have done. Harris seemed the ideal candidate to carry out this task. He had quickly established a close relationship with John Wesley in particular and, as he had done some months previously, he attempted, through the force of his own personality, to hold the various factions together and maintain lines of communication between Wesley and Calvinists like himself.

Almost immediately after John Acourt's dismissal from the Foundery in April 1740, Harris wrote a long and frank letter to John Wesley in which he challenged his actions and pleaded with him to temper the zeal with which he seemed determined to advocate his Arminian ideas. With characteristic bluntness, Harris challenged Wesley's attitude by appealing to him to look 'in a more cool spirit, what lay at ye bottom of this?'[124] Clearly, he thought Wesley guilty of hypocrisy because, by dismissing Acourt, he was acting 'with ye same still, unbroken, uncharitable spirit, which you do and ought to condemn in others'.[125] However, Harris's approach remained conciliatory. In all of his dealings with the Wesley brothers he attempted to pursue a middle course designed to prevent an ignominious polarization of the revival along doctrinal lines. This is not to say that he was unaware of the importance of the issues at stake or that he attempted to disguise his personal preference for Calvinism in his discussions with the Wesleys. In his letters to both John and Charles he consistently stressed that 'it is owing to special Distinguishing and irresistible grace, that those that are saved are saved'.[126]

There is no doubt that Harris and Whitefield found themselves in an impossible situation. Whilst their personal admiration for the Wesley brothers was undiminished and prevented them from severing their ties with them immediately, the increasing clarity with which Harris and Whitefield had come to Calvinistic convictions impelled them to take John Wesley's doctrinal innovations more seriously than perhaps Wesley might have expected. In Harris's mind the problems that had by this

[124] Trevecka 260, Howel Harris to John Wesley (16 July 1740).
[125] Ibid.
[126] Ibid.

time come to dominate the whole movement had the potential to stifle the revival completely. For this reason, after the débâcle over Acourt's expulsion, Harris appealed to John Wesley:

> if you exclude him (John Acourt) out of ye society, & from ye fraternity of ye Methodists, you must exclude Bro Whit—d, Bro Seward & myself and if you go as to take such methods as to let those who are without rejoice in our Divisions, will you not grieve ye Spirit of God in all ye Brethren?[127]

The impression of the controversy that emerges from the correspondence of Whitefield and Howel Harris is significantly different from the view, stemming largely from John Wesley's own accounts in his *Journals*, which has been expressed in studies of this period of the revival.[128] Often Whitefield has been portrayed as an unbending traditionalist who was not prepared to modify his rigid Calvinism in order to accommodate the far more humane Wesleyan understanding of the order of salvation. Yet from reading Whitefield's and Harris's accounts, it is clear that Wesley was the innovator, the one who was threatening the unity of the revival and, according to Harris, opposing 'what God's people feel, viz. his Electing Love and [that he made] many poor souls believe simply because you hold it'.[129] Yet the controversy was also about far more than rival theologies. It was about control of English Methodism. Whitefield's absence from England throughout most of 1740 allowed Wesley to take control of most of Whitefield's evangelical agencies in Bristol and London. Whilst at first this occurred gradually and was largely welcomed by the societies who had been left directionless by Whitefield, problems began to surface later as Wesley's lack of tolerance for the Calvinism of most of the English Methodists became apparent.

Harris's timely intervention in the Acourt case seems to have paid off in the short term, and Wesley responded to him in a letter which revealed a softening of his attitude and a more concerted attempt at easing the tensions which even he admitted

---

[127] Howel Harris to John Wesley (16 July 1740), in Baker (ed.), *The Works of John Wesley, 26*, p. 19.
[128] See for example Rack, *Reasonable Enthusiast*, pp. 198–202 and to a slightly lesser extent McGonigle, *Sufficient Saving Grace*, pp. 110–29.
[129] McGonigle, *Sufficient Saving Grace*, p. 42.

were beginning to get out of control. He responded by arguing that he did not expel John Acourt because he believed in Predestination, but because Acourt was a high Calvinist intent on propagating supralapsarian Double-Predestination and drawing Methodists towards a more extreme version of Calvinism.[130] Wesley wrote to Harris: 'You see, my brother that the reason why Mr Acourt was not admitted into our society was not holding election separate from reprobation, but "openly declaring his fixed purpose to introduce and carry on the dispute concerning reprobation whenever he came".'[131] This exchange of letters seems to have had the desired effect and defused the immediate tension. Harris also seems to have been reassured about Wesley's orthodoxy and his intentions towards Whitefield and his societies. Harris undoubtedly thought that by discussion and patient reasoning over a longer term, John Wesley could be won over to see both the correctness of Calvinistic theology and the error of his rapidly developing doctrine of sinless perfection. Over the months following the Acourt affair, Harris redoubled his efforts to placate and humour Wesley, arguing that because 'the eyes of all the nation'[132] were on him, it was essential that the welfare of the converts remained uppermost in his mind and that he avoid any actions which would bring the revival into disrepute or endanger its long-term stability.

Harris, stressing the need to avoid all unnecessary controversy and a 'wrangling spirit',[133] urged John Wesley continually to re-evaluate his theology in the light of Scripture and his own personal experience, and if he did so Harris remained convinced that Wesley would naturally come to see 'God's particular election plainly'.[134] Ready to be as conciliatory as possible, Harris seems to have still thought that the differences between the Calvinists and the Wesleyans were relatively insignificant and

---

[130] On the various forms of Predestinarian theology see *ERF*, pp. 291–3, 193–4, 360–1; Muller, *Christ and the Decree*; and D. D. Wallace, *Puritans and Predestination: Grace in English Protestant Theology, 1525–1695* (Chapel Hill, 1982). For the eighteenth-century context see Toon, *The Emergence of Hyper-Calvinism*; A. C. Clifford, *Atonement and Justification: English Evangelical Theology, 1640–1790 – An Evaluation* (Oxford, 1990).

[131] John Wesley to Howel Harris (29 July 1740), in Baker (ed.), *The Works of John Wesley, 26*, p. 22.

[132] Howel Harris to John Wesley (27 October 1740), in Baker (ed.), *The Works of John Wesley, 26*, p. 42.

[133] HHD 56, 22 May 1740.

[134] Ibid.

that they had arisen as a result of John Wesley's reluctance to clarify his somewhat ambiguous language rather than from more substantive differences. After exhorting at the Foundery Society in London in May 1740, Harris concluded: 'we differ much for want of Words to express our meaning.'[135] With hindsight it is possible to argue that Harris was being unrealistic. He was too slow to realize what John Wesley's true intentions were and he did not appreciate the extent to which Wesley's Arminianism and Perfectionism were the product of careful theological reflection. Yet his actions were typical. Harris, the self-styled peacemaker, used his close personal relationships with both Whitefield and John Wesley to ensure that the lines of communication between the two groups remained open and that any misunderstandings were dealt with as swiftly as possible to minimize the potential damage.

The major shift in Harris's thinking appears to have come in October 1740 when William Seward arrived in Wales, having recently and formally broken off relations with Charles Wesley. In a poignant letter to John Cennick, Harris conveyed the news of what had taken place. His disappointment, combined with the growing realization that any possibility of repairing the breaches was almost impossible, precipitated the gradual change in the way in which Harris related to both John and Charles Wesley. Whilst Harris was not yet prepared to sever relations with the Wesleys completely, the letter candidly outlines the barriers that he now felt lay before any recovery of trust and reunion. He wrote:

> I have long been waiting to see if Br Charles shd receive further sight or to be silent and oppose Election & Perseverance but finding no hopes thereof I begin to be stagger'd about ym wt to do – I plainly see that we preach two Gospels, one sets all on God, ye other on men, the one on God's will the other on mans will, one on God's chossing, ye other on man chossing, the one on God's distinguishing love in making one to differ from the other, the other on man's being better than another & taking more pains & being a better husband of his grace than ye other.[136]

[135] Ibid.
[136] Trevecka 282, Howel Harris to John Cennick (27 October 1740).

In spite of these major obstacles, Harris's positive attitude to the Wesley brothers remained intact and was exemplified by his willingness to continue to meet them and work alongside them as often as possible. It was against this backdrop that Charles Wesley arrived in Wales in November 1740. At the outset of the tour Harris admitted to being 'in fear least I do wrong of both sides not knowing what to do or say, fearing these Divisions and Errors'.[137] Initially he found Charles Wesley uncommonly reticent, and he confessed to being unable to get beyond thinking that Charles was a hypocrite 'under the light of making himself all things'.[138] Harris's anxieties were allayed when Charles reassured him that he believed in a form of Election, though at the same time he stressed that he believed in a general, rather than a more particular, doctrine of the extent of the atonement.[139] Some in Wales seem to have been impressed by Charles Wesley's preaching and teaching during these few days, and there is evidence to suggest that at least some in Wales felt their allegiance to Harris waver. Despite this Harris, having listened to his preaching and observing its effects, was led to conclude magnanimously that 'there is good done'[140] by the Wesley brothers.

In the aftermath of Charles Wesley's visit Harris was left in a quandary. Whilst he recognized the godly results of the Wesley brothers' ministries, he was aware of the damage that their alternative version of Methodism could wreak and the disastrous effect that two competing versions of Methodism would have on the future prospects of the evangelical revival. In his diary, Harris confessed: 'If I say the whole truth I must make Charles Wesley very black – to preach contrary to what he told me he believed and what in my hearing he preached.'[141] But Harris, unable, and probably unwilling, to lay aside his personal admiration for the Wesley brothers, remained extremely reluctant to enter publicly into a protracted controversy with them. He was content to urge caution on all sides, through his

---

[137] Tom Beynon, 'Extracts from the diaries of Howell Harris', *Bathafarn*, 4 (1949), 54.
[138] Ibid., 57.
[139] On conflicting theories of the atonement see *ODCC*, pp. 122–4; T. D. Alexander and Brian S. Rosner (eds), *New Dictionary of Biblical Theology* (Leicester, 2000), pp. 388–93; and *DMBI*, pp. 11, 52–3.
[140] Beynon, 'Extracts from the diaries of Howell Harris', 57.
[141] Ibid., 68.

correspondence and through the pages of *The Christian's Amusement* and *The Weekly History*, in the hope that in time the Wesleys would modify their views and all differences would be lost in the enthusiasm of fresh waves of revival and in their commitment to pioneer evangelism. Harris would have strongly supported the views of an anonymous correspondent whose letter John Lewis inserted in *The Christian's Amusement*:

> though we are not all of one opinion in some Particulars, yet if we have that Christian Charity which is the brightest Ornament of the Followers of JESUS, we cannot think but there are some Sincere of every particular Party: Methinks that very consideration shou'd induce us to lay aside all trifling Disputes, and join hand and heart in pulling down the Strong-holds of Satan's kingdom.[142]

The controversy finally came to a head during the early months of 1741. Throughout much of 1740, responsibility for meaningful engagement with the Wesley brothers had been left to Harris. Whitefield's return to England in March 1741 led to the rapid escalation of the controversy as events reached their climax. Whitefield returned to find the English revival, which he had left in a fairly healthy state, rapidly fragmenting. Wesley had taken control by winning over many of Whitefield's converts to his own leadership, having also by this time expelled John Cennick from the Bristol society.[143] There seems little doubt that Whitefield fully expected to be able to heal the divisions with relative ease[144] and must have been surprised when John Wesley was reluctant to meet him as soon as he arrived in England. When they did eventually meet face to face a fortnight after his arrival, Whitefield was shocked to discover just how wide a chasm had opened between them. At the meeting Whitefield informed Wesley that he thought that they now preached different Gospels and that he was no longer prepared to stand by and allow John Wesley to usurp his leadership of the English societies.[145] Whitefield's initially optimistic hopes were dashed as he was confronted with

---

[142] See the anonymous letter included in *CA* 12.
[143] See Dallimore, *George Whitefield*, II, pp. 38–40 and Rack, *Reasonable Enthusiast*, p. 199.
[144] See George Whitefield to John Wesley (24 November 1740), in Murray (ed.), *George Whitefield's Letters*, p. 225.
[145] Quoted in Dallimore, *George Whitefield*, II, p. 51.

the magnitude of the divisions between them and as he observed how the Lord was 'chiefly wounded in the house of His friends'.[146]

It was at this stage, after much discussion and considerable effort to avoid damaging controversy, that Whitefield weighed in with his response to John Wesley's sermon on *Free Grace*. Whitefield's *A Letter to the Rev. Mr John Wesley: In Answer to His Sermon Entitled 'Free Grace'*[147] was a closely reasoned answer, using well-attested Calvinistic arguments, to Wesley's criticisms of Election and Predestination. However, Whitefield's *Letter* unfortunately gained most notoriety because of the way that Whitefield revealed how John Wesley had decided whether to go ahead with the publication of his sermon by casting a lot. For Wesley this revelation was tantamount to treachery, and the embarrassment it caused him contributed as much to the breakdown in relations as anything that Whitefield said in the *Letter* itself. On the more substantive issues, Whitefield couched his reply in terms of Wesley's attempt to accuse all Calvinists of believing in supralapsarian Double-Predestination. Although Whitefield admitted that he believed in Reprobation, his conception of the doctrine was very different from Wesley's caricature. Whitefield held the moderate Calvinistic view of 'preterition' in which all men were viewed as equally fallen and sinful, but that God gratuitously elects some to life and passes by the rest, leaving them to the just consequences of their sin.[148] Whitefield went still further and reiterated his persuasion that 'none living, especially none who are desirous of salvation, can know that they are not of the number of God's elect'.[149] Whitefield's *Letter* finally delineated the exact nature of the rival interpretations of Methodist theology expounded by him and Wesley, and seemed to indicate the end of meaningful cooperation between the two factions. It was at precisely this point that Howel Harris returned to England, visiting Bristol *en route* to London.

---

[146] George Whitefield to Howel Harris (28 April 1741), in Murray (ed.), *George Whitefield's Letters*, pp. 259–60.

[147] George Whitefield, *A Letter to the Reverend Mr John Wesley: In Answer to his Sermon Entitled Free Grace* (London, 1741). For a contemporary printed copy see Murray (ed.), *George Whitefield's Journals*, pp. 564–88.

[148] See, for example, ibid., pp. 575–9.

[149] Ibid., p. 579.

On 19 June he met Charles Wesley in Bristol and confessed that he once again 'felt such love and union'[150] with him. They discussed their differences frankly, and Harris managed to get Charles to admit that the only difference between Whitefield and himself was Whitefield's apparent belief in Double-Predestination.[151] Harris brought other charges against him, but Charles vehemently denied that he believed in free will. The following day they met for further discussion, and for some reason Harris was less conciliatory than he had been the previous day. He attacked Charles for having strong sympathies with the Roman Catholic Church.[152] Charles countered by reaffirming his belief in free will, at which point Harris declared that he would have to separate from him and his brother. In his diary he wrote:

> had freedom to tell all – how I did suspect them Popishly inclined – 1st as recommendg papist Sts – 2 havg their Doctrine &c – 3 not being simple & open but he sd that all had or have or shall have freewill – I sd I must then divide from him & declare agt him on that acct.[153]

Shortly afterwards Harris discovered that Charles Wesley had been warning his followers against going to listen to him preach. This confirmed Harris's worst fears about the intentions of the Wesley brothers and led him to conclude that 'their scheme is all of ye Devil & man'.[154] The publication of Whitefield's riposte to Wesley's *Free Grace* sermon and Howel Harris's public separation from Charles Wesley seem to have marked the end of the controversy.[155] Neither Harris nor Whitefield formally separated from John Wesley; relations merely degenerated in the months immediately following Whitefield's return from America and in the aftermath of the exchange over Predestination. Subsequently, both versions of the revival coexisted relatively peacefully, although tensions between them could escalate fairly easily and accusations that each was trying to proselytize from the other were never far from the surface. For the Welsh Methodists the controversy drew them still closer to George

[150] HHD 74, 19 June 1741.
[151] Ibid.
[152] HHD 74, 20 June 1740.
[153] Ibid.
[154] HHD 74, 26 June 1740.
[155] Dallimore, *George Whitefield*, II, p. 75.

Whitefield and what from this date became English Calvinistic Methodism, until both revivals were formally united at Watford in January 1743.[156]

The fragmentation of the English revival into three factions, the Moravian, the Wesleyan and the Calvinistic, did not spell the end of interaction between the various groups. Howel Harris quickly realized the damage that had been done by the divisions, over Predestination in particular, and almost immediately began to work out strategies by which he could bring about a truce between the warring factions. The years between the summer of 1741 and John Cennick's defection to the Moravians at the end of 1745 were therefore characterized by a series of reunion attempts which owed a significant amount to the commitment and ecumenical outlook of Howel Harris.

In the aftermath of the spilt with the Wesleys, Harris became an even more common face at Whitefield's Tabernacle and among some of the other Calvinistic societies in England. He continued to spend a significant part of each year in England, dividing his time between Bristol and London and sharing the leadership of the Calvinistic revival with Whitefield and Cennick. Whitefield shared Harris's concern at the effect of the falling-out with the Wesleys and seems to have encouraged Harris in his efforts to maintain amicable relations with John Wesley in particular. When Harris met John Wesley for the first time after the split in August 1741, Harris confessed to feeling 'vast Love'[157] towards him and seemed hopeful that the 'Ld [would] remove all mountains'[158] between them. His approach in subsequent dealings with the Wesleys was typical of that which he had adopted with all the groups and individuals who had opposed the revival and with all those within the revival whose disagreements were seriously hampering its progress. Harris had of course never publicly separated from John Wesley and had only privately, after a particularly heated exchange of views, parted company with the far more volatile Charles. Throughout the controversy, and despite his obvious sympathy with Whitefield, Harris continually counselled caution and urged both sides to avoid making comments and acting in ways that would inflame matters un-

[156]   See below, pp. 214–17.
[157]   HHD 77, 30 August 1741.
[158]   Ibid.

necessarily. When tensions did finally ease, Harris was keen to resume normal relations with both Wesley brothers, although he must have realized that it would be impossible for them to recapture the spirit of the friendship they had once enjoyed.

Harris once again met John Wesley formally in September 1741. They began by airing their theological opinions, but Harris attempted to locate as much common ground with Wesley as he was able with a good conscience. Wesley must also have been in a conciliatory mood, for Harris recorded how they had agreed to start afresh and to 'forget all that is past to this Sbr [September] 10'.[159] The meeting seemed to spur Harris to still greater efforts, and in the weeks that followed he wrote to Whitefield a number of letters designed to clear away many of the misconceptions about the Wesleys that Whitefield had by now internalized. For example, after their meeting on 10 September, Harris wrote to Whitefield: 'I find ye Lord owns the Bro's Wesley's very much, and I am persuaded that what you heard of them is groundless [. . .] I am wounded when they are not counted as Brethren tho' in Errors.'[160] On the more tangible theological differences that remained between them, Harris urged Whitefield to re-examine these rationally and without prejudice, weighing all of the Wesley brothers' remarks, rather than relying merely on those spoken in the heat of argument. Harris was undoubtedly speaking from his own experience when he recommended that the Calvinists and the Wesleyans should both take a more charitable approach to one another: 'as to ye difference indeed I find, when Prejudice falls away and in love we weigh and ask each others meaning, is not as great as by some expressions it may seem to be.'[161] Harris's conciliation seems to have paid dividends and Whitefield's opposition to John Wesley subsided to such an extent that during October he wrote to Wesley in the hope of effecting some sort of reconciliation. In the letter Whitefield admitted that he had been wrong to embarrass Wesley by revealing his use of the lot when he was trying to decide whether or not to publish his *Free Grace* sermon, before going on to assure him of his admiration for his spirituality and

[159]   HHD 77, 10 September 1741.
[160]   Trevecka 638, Howel Harris to George Whitefield (11 September 1742).
[161]   Ibid.

evangelistic work.[162] When he came to theology, Whitefield, like Harris before him, attempted to build bridges. Rather than concentrate on the things that divided them, Whitefield went to great lengths to locate common ground. Thus, in reference to his views on Predestination, Whitefield reiterated his belief in the doctrine, but tempered it by assuring Wesley that he nevertheless 'offer[ed] JESUS to every individual soul'.[163] On Perfection, Whitefield professed that he was prepared to tolerate Wesley's opinions though he himself could not believe that it was possible for anybody to be entirely freed from indwelling sin in this life.[164] Although the Wesleys' teaching on the possibility of Christian perfection was opposed strongly by Whitefield and all the other Calvinistic Methodists, the issue did not figure prominently in the divisions of 1740 and 1741. At that stage it was the Wesleys' views on the doctrines of salvation that provoked the most volatile response. Perfectionism remained in the background and only occasionally forced its way to the forefront of the movement.[165]

Throughout the early 1740s, Howel Harris maintained the pressure on Whitefield, and together they seem to have come to the decision that bridging the gap between themselves and the Wesley brothers might not be completely impossible. He kept the lines of communication with John Wesley open, and during March 1742, they met during one of Wesley's brief itineraries in Wales.[166] The visit is significant because it occurred against the backdrop of a fresh exchange of letters between John Wesley and Whitefield.[167] On meeting Wesley, the affection between him and Harris was rekindled and the latter 'was humbled for any word [. . .] said against him, and finding such Benefit that I know

---

[162]   See George Whitefield to John Wesley (10 October 1741), in Murray (ed.), *George Whitefield's Letters*, p. 331.

[163]   Ibid.

[164]   Ibid.

[165]   See Rack, *Reasonable Enthusiast*, pp. 395–401; Rupert Davies, 'The people called Methodists – 1. "Our Doctrines"', in Rupert Davies and Gordon Rupp (eds), *A History of the Methodist Church in Great Britain*, I (London, 1965), pp. 169–73; and Patrick Streiff, *Reluctant Saint? A Theological Biography of Fletcher of Madeley* (London, 2001), pp. 208–11 and 288–91.

[166]   See A. H. Williams (ed.), *John Wesley in Wales, 1739–1790* (Cardiff, 1971), pp. 13–15 and HHD 86, 3–11 March 1742.

[167]   See George Whitefield to John Wesley (11 March 1742), in Baker (ed.), *The Works of John Wesley*, 26, p. 74 and George Whitefield to John Wesley (6 April 1742), in Murray (ed.), *George Whitefield's Letters*, pp. 380–1.

not how to leave him'.[168] His affection for John Wesley and Wesley's obvious trust led Harris to conclude that God had called him and provided him with the special gifts required to lead both the Wesleys and Whitefield back to union with one another.[169] More concretely, the meeting was highly significant in the history of Calvinistic and Arminian Methodism because of the theological concessions that Harris was able to extract from Wesley. At the end of Wesley's journey, Harris put together a document which outlined the areas in which the Calvinists and the Arminians were in total agreement and the areas where differences remained unresolved. The extent of their agreement was significant and included all the most fundamental articles of their faith. Their differences focused on Predestination and the precise nature of human free will.[170] Whilst there is no evidence that the document was circulated amongst the wider Methodist community, there is little doubt that it represents the most concerted effort at accommodation and compromise yet. The meeting ended amicably, and it seemed as if, for the first time for almost a year, some semblance of normality was about to return. Harris had managed to get both parties to agree not to 'meddle with Controversies anywhere'[171] and John Wesley seemed ready to repair the breach with Whitefield and rekindle the unity they once enjoyed. Responsibility for this truce lay squarely with Howel Harris. It was his skill as a mediator and his ability to grasp the real issues at stake and to work out a compromise position acceptable to all sides that enabled the Arminians and the Calvinists to coexist peacefully.

At the same time as Harris was seeking to bring Whitefield and Wesley closer together he was engaged in the more difficult task of exploring ways of easing tensions with the Moravians.[172] Although neither Whitefield nor Harris had completely severed relations with them at the same time as the Wesley brothers, their relationship with the Moravians had deteriorated markedly. Harris had quietly maintained his contacts with them, and

---

[168] Tom Beynon, 'Extracts from the diaries of Howell Harris', *Bathafarn* 6 (1951), 50.
[169] HHD 86, 3 March 1742.
[170] See HHD 87, 'The sheet reciting points of agreement and difference between Mr Harris (and Mr Whitefield and others) and Mr John Wesley, 8 March 1742' and Beynon, 'Extracts from the diaries of Howell Harris', 54–7.
[171] Beynon, 'Extracts from the diaries of Howell Harris', 52.
[172] See Podmore, *The Moravian Church in England*, pp. 78–96.

despite some reservations about their theology he began to pave the way for their eventual reintegration into the mainstream of the revival. He reasoned in his diary: 'What, shan't I love whom God loves? Though they in the Foundery and the Moravians are in errors, yet they love God and set Christ as the foundation, and give the glory to God in the best light they have.'[173] There is little doubt that reopening relations with the Moravians was far more of a risk for Whitefield than it was for Harris. Whitefield was a more prominent figure on the international stage; his every word and action were scrutinized and, more often than not, unquestioningly followed. Among his closest supporters and friends there remained considerable suspicion of the Moravians, and many of them regarded friendship with them as being only one small step away from a complete departure from orthodoxy. Nevertheless, shortly after his return to London in March 1741, Whitefield began to attend the Fetter Lane Society again and had begun discussing practical steps to facilitate cooperation with both James Hutton and August Spangenberg.[174]

The patient efforts of Harris and Whitefield came to fruition in the early months of 1743. John Cennick had first suggested the idea of a summit meeting involving all the English revivalists as early as May 1742. In a letter to Elizabeth Whitefield[175] he hoped that such a meeting would pave the way for reunion, or at the very least a rekindling of their love for one another.[176] The meeting eventually took place on 5 February, but the Moravians declined the invitation to attend at the last minute because of James Hutton's particularly vociferous opposition to any attempt to railroad them into compromise and reunion.[177] It was as a result of this meeting that Whitefield seemed to give up hope of conciliation with the Moravians, and by the 1750s he had distanced himself from them to such an extent that he was

[173]   HHD 94, 3 October 1742.
[174]   See Podmore, *The Moravian Church in England*, pp. 82–3.
[175]   Elizabeth Whitefield (née James), a widow from Abergavenny in south Wales, had married George Whitefield in November 1741, after a brief courtship with Howel Harris. Dallimore, *George Whitefield*, II, pp. 101–13; Roger Lee Brown, 'The marriage of George Whitefield at Caerphilly', *CCHMC*, 7 (1983), 24–30.
[176]   'The copy of a letter from MR CENNICK to MRS WHITEFIELD (6 May 1742)', *WH* 63 (Saturday, 19 June 1742).
[177]   Podmore, *The Moravian Church in England*, pp. 84–5.

prepared to go into print with his objections,[178] thereby making the split between them permanent. Uncharacteristically, Howel Harris was not present at the meeting, owing to even more pressing commitments in Wales, and he would have undoubtedly been disappointed at its failure. Harris did not follow Whitefield's example, remaining reluctant to distance himself from the Moravians in the months and years that followed the meeting. If anything, Harris's admiration of the Moravians became stronger, and in a number of respects he resembled them sufficiently closely for his friends in Wales to harbour serious reservations.

The February 1743 summit meeting, despite failing to reignite brotherly feeling among the three revival factions, did have one positive result. It seems to have marked the conclusion of the bitter controversies between the English Calvinists and Arminians, at least until the 1770s.[179] Although complete reunion was too difficult to achieve, the meeting at least inaugurated a truce between the warring factions. Harris was without doubt the main factor responsible for this thaw in relations, and throughout the 1740s, particularly as he grew increasingly powerful within the English revival, he consistently sought to build on the achievements of these months by means of conciliatory letters, preaching at the Foundery and meeting with the Wesley brothers at every opportunity.[180]

---

[178] Whitefield eventually spelled out his differences with the Moravians in his *Expostulatory Letter* to Count Zinzendorf which was published in 1753. See Podmore, *The Moravian Church in England*, pp. 268–75 and Dallimore, *George Whitefield*, II, pp. 325–32.

[179] Brown-Lawson, *John Wesley and the Anglican Evangelicals of the Eighteenth Century*, pp. 301–54; Rack, *Reasonable Enthusiast*, pp. 450–70 and for a more detailed discussion see Streiff, *Reluctant Saint?*, pp. 149–87, 192–214.

[180] See for example Trevecka 1343, Howel Harris to Charles Wesley (16 July 1745).

V

SETTLING TIMES: PUTTING THE 'LIVING STONES' TOGETHER

By the end of 1741 both Howel Harris and George Whitefield had realized that the controversies of the previous months had left their converts demoralized. What was now important was not the maintenance of evangelistic zeal or more debate over detailed theological points but concentration on the development of a system of pastoral supervision for those individuals who had come under their care. Consequently, in September 1742, Whitefield informed Harris that 'As the awakening seems in some measure to be over, and there are so many living stones it may be time to think of putting them together – May the great builder of His church guide and direct us.'[1] Whitefield's suggestion was testimony to the remarkable closeness that had developed between the Welsh and English Calvinistic revivals since January 1739. The Welsh revivalists had, of course, sided with Whitefield in the dispute with the Wesley brothers, and in its immediate aftermath it seemed entirely natural that the two revivals, which in any case had developed along very similar lines, should seek to formalize that relationship, binding themselves still closer to one another.

Discussions about the development of the organizational structure of the Welsh revival have tended to focus on the achievements of the Association, attended by all the main leaders of the Welsh revival and three of the most prominent leaders of the English Calvinistic revival, that took place at Watford, near Caerphilly, at the beginning of January 1743. This has led some historians[2] to exaggerate its significance and to overlook some of the longer-term processes by which the pioneer Welsh Methodists adopted a quasi-presbyterian organizational structure. As is

---

[1] 'The conclusion of the Letter begun in our last', *WH*, 80 (Saturday, 16 October 1742).
[2] Griffith T. Roberts for example talked about 'y Sasiwn enwog honno' ('that famous Association') in his 'Y Mudiad Cymreig a Diwygwyr Lloegr', in Gomer M. Roberts (ed.), *Hanes Methodistiaeth Galfinaidd Cymru, Cyfrol I: Y Deffroad Mawr* (Caernarfon, 1973), p. 307.

so often the case, responsibility for this development can be traced back to William Williams, Pantycelyn, who, in his elegy on the death of Daniel Rowland, referred to Watford as marking the birth of the great Association.[3] Though of course highly important, the true significance of the discussions at Watford cannot be adequately appreciated without taking full account of the context in which they occurred. Watford was the culmination of three years' patient work by Harris and Daniel Rowland, during which – and in response to difficulties on the ground – they, together with Whitefield, developed a structure that enabled them to regulate the beliefs and lifestyles of their converts and then launch into areas hitherto unaffected by the revival.

The bedrock of the Welsh revival was the network of small societies founded by the revivalists wherever their message was greeted with an enthusiastic response.[4] Howel Harris founded his first society in 1736,[5] and by the end of 1739 he could point to thirty societies[6] that had sprung up as a direct result of his ministry alone. When they met for the first time in March 1739 and 'took account of the several societies, and agreed on such measures as seemed most conducive to promote the common interest',[7] it was clear that the *ad hoc* establishment of societies could not continue unregulated. Although specific details about what exactly was discussed have not survived, Harris and Whitefield realized that their first face-to-face meeting established the principle of cooperation between the two revivals and marked the beginning of the process whereby the English and Welsh Calvinistic revivals were brought into close alignment.

When in Wales, Whitefield acted as an invaluable source of advice and counsel. To many in Wales, Whitefield was both a

---

[3]   'Marwnad Y Parch. Daniel Rowland, Llangeitho', in N. Cynhafal Jones (gol.), *Gweithiau Williams Pantycelyn*, I, (Trefynnon, 1887), pp. 583–4.

[4]   On the development and role of the societies within the Methodist movement see John Walsh, 'Religious societies: Methodist and evangelical, 1738–1800', in W. J. Shiels and D. Wood (eds), *Voluntary Religion*, Studies in Church History, 28 (Oxford, 1986), pp. 279–302 and Rack, 'Religious societies and the origins of Methodism'. On the specifically Welsh context see Evans, *Howell Harris*, pp. 20–9; White, *Praidd Bach y Bugail Mawr*, and White, ' "The world, the flesh and the devil" '.

[5]   Harris's first society had been founded at Y Wernos in the parish of Llandyfalle, Breconshire. See Evans, *Howell Harris*, p. 22 and Tudur, *Howell Harris*, p. 33. For Harris's own opinion of the significance of the societies see HHD 116, 15 April 1745.

[6]   Evans, *Howell Harris*, p. 22.

[7]   Murray (ed.), *George Whitefield's Journals*, p. 230.

father figure and an elder brother in the faith. In their letters to
him he was often called; 'My Dear Dear Elder Brother'[8] or 'My
dr & Eldr Bror Whd.'[9] These titles are indicative of the extent to
which the Welsh Methodists revered Whitefield and how they
clearly regarded him as the foremost figure in the entire
evangelical revival movement. Since the Act of Union had introduced primogeniture in the 1530s, the position of the elder
brother had assumed particular significance in terms of inheritance.[10] By employing this title the Welsh Methodists were symbolically elevating Whitefield to the foremost position, declaring
that they accepted his position as God's designated leader of the
revival and maybe even saying something about its ownership.
The Welsh Methodists' admiration for Whitefield was expressed
in many other ways. Harris's comments, written after one of
Whitefield's highly successful Welsh preaching tours, are typical
of the respect and esteem in which he was held: 'Many are the
good effects of your last visit to us; and tis not a few that daily
ask, When will you come again? Many of the better sort like you,
and others of them long to hear you.'[11]

The significance of the discussion of the organization of their
revivals which took place between Whitefield and Harris during
the former's first visit to Wales has not been fully appreciated.
Unfortunately, as is often the case with both Harris's diary and
Whitefield's *Journals*, events which had significant repercussions
on the movement are referred to, if at all, in the most cursory
and matter-of-fact manner. When Harris wrote to Whitefield at
the end of 1738, introducing him to the Welsh revival, he wrote
in a way that was calculated to arouse his interest and prompt
him to investigate more closely.[12] When Whitefield duly arrived
in Wales a few months later, Harris made the most of his
opportunity to question him on a number of important issues
concerning the regulation of his societies and the wider Welsh
revival.[13] Their discussions set a precedent, and by the time of

---

[8]   Trevecka 650, George Whitefield to Howel Harris (16 September 1742).
[9]   Trevecka 1152, Howel Harris to George Whitefield (19 March 1744).
[10] Glanmor Williams, *Renewal and Reformation: Wales, c.1415–1642* (Oxford,
1987), pp. 268–9 and Peter R. Roberts, 'The "Act of Union" in Welsh history',
Transactions of the Honourable Society of Cymmrodorion (1974), 49–72.
[11] Trevecka 1060, Howel Harris to George Whitefield (16 December 1743).
[12] Trevecka 136, Howel Harris to George Whitefield (8 January 1739).
[13] Murray (ed.), *George Whitefield's Journals*, pp. 229–30.

Whitefield's second visit to Wales a couple of months later their relationship had developed to such an extent that most of their time was taken up with visiting and settling the societies.[14] Whitefield's invitation to Harris to visit London was, for Harris, far more than merely the polite return of his own prior invitation. It was also intended to be more than just an opportunity for Harris to observe what was happening in London. As has already been discussed,[15] Whitefield's invitation was the pretext for Harris's introduction to the wider revival and gave him the standing he needed in the international evangelical community. These meetings were the necessary precondition for closer integration of the Welsh and English revivals. They marked the commencement of Harris and Whitefield's joint discussions on the future of their revivals. These came to full fruition when the English revival finally splintered into its various groups in 1740 and 1741, after which Whitefield attempted to secure the long-term future of his Calvinistic revival, which appeared to be in terminal decline, by attaching it to the stronger Welsh revival.

In general terms, the development of the administrative machinery of the Welsh revival corresponds broadly to the dates of the meetings at which the pioneer revivalists met to discuss the progress of their work. They were invariably occasions when the input of Whitefield was called for, and his advice often proved to be the deciding factor in settling some of the most thorny questions that were marring relations between Harris and Daniel Rowland. In the early months of the revival the Welsh revivalists, like their counterparts in England and further afield, struggled with how to organize the societies they had established. To many of them, deeply loyal to their various denominations, establishing societies within the structures of their churches could all too easily be regarded as a challenge to the pastoral efficiency of their clergy. In order to defend them against the charge of schism, Whitefield attempted to allay the fears of the Established Church by producing a detailed defence of the societies, demonstrating that they were intended to complement the ministry of the Church rather than to compete directly with it.

---

[14]   HHD 42, 5–8 April 1739.
[15]   See above, pp. 128–35.

Whitefield's defence of the societies, *The Nature and Necessity of Society in General, and of Religious Society in Particular* (1740), was little more than the edited text of a sermon that he had preached in 1737. It is probably safe to regard the position outlined by him as indicative of the views held by most of his fellow revivalists. He began by arguing that the lack of the sort of fellowship meetings that the Methodists had begun to establish was one of the overwhelming reasons for what he perceived to be 'the sad decay of true Christianity'[16] in the country. From this basis he proceeded to use verses from the Book of Ecclesiastes[17] to demonstrate both the necessity and the benefits of these fellowship meetings and to outline some of the activities with which they should be occupied. These activities, in turn, were reduced to the three essential aims of mutual reproof, exhortation and encouragement in holy living by assisting and defending one another.[18] In Whitefield's opinion the vibrancy of the societies was the secret of the success and long-term prosperity of the revival. It was to be a movement dependent on the strength and commitment of its grass-roots members and therefore the duty of every Christian 'to set on foot, establish and promote, as much as in them lies, societies of this nature', because 'if ever a spirit of true Christianity is revived in the world, it must be brought about by such means as this'.[19]

The ideas outlined in this sermon were reprised, in considerably greater detail, in Whitefield's *Letter . . . to the Religious Societies Lately Set on Foot in Several Parts of England and Wales*, which was published in 1740 and almost immediately translated into Welsh.[20] The *Letter* was written at a time when the societies faced renewed pressure from the Church of England to conform. The Church repeatedly accused the Methodists of schism and regarded the societies as conventicles

---

[16] See George Whitefield, 'The necessity and benefits of religious society', in George Whitefield, *Seventy-Five Sermons on Various Important Subjects* (London, 1812), p. 129.
[17] See Ecclesiastes 4: 9–12.
[18] Whitefield, 'The nature and benefits of religious society', pp. 137–40.
[19] Ibid., p. 140.
[20] See George Whitefield, *Llythyr Oddiwrth y Parchedig Mr George Whitefield at Societies neu Gymdeithasau Crefyddol a Osodwyd yn Ddiweddar ar Droed Mewn Amriw Leodd yng Nghymru a Lloeger* (Pontypool, 1740).

or churches within the Church and undermining its authority.[21] In response, Whitefield returned once more to the example of primitive Christianity and assured his followers that there was not 'one reason [that] can be urged against your assembling together, which will not equally hold good against all assembling together for religious purposes'.[22] In order to demonstrate the legality of the religious societies, Whitefield concentrated on one contentious area: extemporaneous prayer. He argued that the set liturgical prayers contained in the *Book of Common Prayer* were intended by their authors for use at the more formal worship services of the Church, and that a degree of latitude and freedom had always been tolerated in less formal contexts.[23] By employing this argument Whitefield hoped to demonstrate, firstly, that there had always been informal gatherings for spiritual edification within the life of the Church. Secondly, he sought to establish that these gatherings had traditionally been freer from liturgical constraints than had more formal occasions. Consequently it was the Church in its present state that was in error, not those Methodists who met in order to stir one another to greater feats of godliness. Whitefield was in effect laying justification for the societies squarely at the door of the Church and its bishops. They seemed to be more interested in indulging in what he termed 'the Diversions of the Age'[24] than with promoting initiatives that were intended to augment the 'power of Godliness'.[25] Their lack of spiritual leadership had therefore given rise to the vacuum that allowed the societies to proliferate, particularly in those areas of the country where the Church's presence was weak or ineffective.

Whitefield used the letter not only to justify the existence of societies and to answer the objections of the Church, but also to offer practical advice to society members regarding their efficient

---

[21]   See David Hempton, 'Methodism and the law, 1740–1820', *Bulletin of the John Rylands University Library of Manchester*, 70, 3 (Autumn 1988), 93–7; John Walsh, 'Methodism and the mob in the eighteenth century'; and G. J. Cumming and Derek Baker (eds), *Popular Belief and Practice*, Studies in Church History, 8 (Cambridge, 1972), pp. 213–27.
[22]   George Whitefield, *A Letter from the Reverend Mr George Whitefield to the Religious Societies Lately Set on Foot in Several Parts of England and Wales* (Edinburgh, 1740), p. 7.
[23]   Ibid., pp. 8–9.
[24]   Ibid., pp. 5–6.
[25]   Ibid.

administration. The suggestions that Whitefield made in this publication are a good indication of the development of the societies by the late 1730s. The most important point, which was reiterated with care, was the necessity of ensuring that all the members of the societies were truly converted and in possession of full assurance of their salvation. For Whitefield this was fundamental. The qualifications for admission to the societies remained forbiddingly high, with both Whitefield and Harris keen to emphasize that the additional requirement of full assurance was vital to full membership in the societies. John Wesley believed that God had raised up the Methodists in the 1730s specifically in order to recover the doctrine of assurance of salvation[26] and that it was within the confines of the societies that the way to obtain such an exalted spiritual state was explained and managed.[27] Whitefield also used the letter to remind the members of the societies of some of the central tenets of their faith and the necessity of earnestly contending for them with their many detractors. The fundamental doctrine remained justification by faith, and it was the responsibility of each steward and exhorter as well as each individual member to ensure that the doctrine was clearly understood by all and proclaimed without compromise.[28] Yet Whitefield's exhortations were tempered by injunctions to maintain fellowship with all those who shared their basic evangelical faith, whether they happened to be of the Established Church or not, or whether they happened to be Calvinists, Arminians or even Moravians.[29] Then in the final section of the letter, Whitefield addressed some more specific practical questions. He urged the societies to include time in their meetings for the confession of their faults and for testifying to their latest spiritual experiences.[30] By making these activities central Whitefield hoped that a genuine interdependence would be created, that each society member would feel responsible for his or her fellow members, and that the unity that they had

[26] McGonigle, *Sufficient Saving Grace*, p. 242.
[27] See Bebbington, *Evangelicalism in Modern Britain*, pp. 42–50 and Bebbington, 'Revival and Enlightenment in eighteenth century England', pp. 22–4. See also above, pp. 45–7 and below, pp. 291–4.
[28] Whitefield, *A Letter to the Religious Societies*, pp. 12–19.
[29] Ibid., pp. 21–2.
[30] Ibid., pp. 22–3.

enjoyed up to this date would as a result become all the more difficult to jeopardize.

Whitefield's *Letter* demands such close analysis because of its critical importance to the development of the Calvinistic revival in England and Wales. The Welsh revivalists clearly thought it was significant, otherwise they would not have translated it into Welsh so quickly. Its publication in Welsh also proves that by 1740 both the English Calvinistic societies and the Welsh Methodist societies had reached a similar stage in their development. Both groups of societies had already come under some measure of pastoral oversight, and neither body continued to meet on a merely *ad hoc* basis. There was agreement on the necessity of examining potential candidates for membership, using the twin tests of the New Birth and assurance of salvation; there was agreement on core theological beliefs and a common desire to maintain a genuine and tangible inter-revival ecumenicity. Practically, there was a measure of uniformity in the activities of the societies in both countries. By 1740 their functions had been streamlined and their day-to-day operation standardized. Whitefield and Howel Harris had pooled their resources to such an extent that the publication of Whitefield's *Letter* may be viewed almost as a manifesto. It was a statement of what had already been achieved and a programme for the future of the revival, whose strength lay in countless numbers of regenerated individuals, assured of their standing before God, and united for edification and spiritual support in societies which, it was hoped, would continue to proliferate and eventually cover all corners of England and Wales.

Up until the early 1740s the Welsh societies remained under the informal control of Howel Harris and Daniel Rowland, each assuming direct responsibility for the societies that he himself had established. However, this method of control proved inadequate as the revival expanded. Allied to this, Howel Harris was beginning to spend increasing amounts of time in England, sharing the responsibility of the English Calvinistic revival with Whitefield and John Cennick. Harris and Daniel Rowland had been meeting regularly on an informal basis since 1737,[31] and during the later 1730s they enjoyed a relationship of mutual

---

[31]   Evans, *Daniel Rowland*, pp. 51–2.

respect and genuine affection, and seeming, at least on the surface, to have no trouble in regarding one another as equals.[32]

In some prefatory remarks to the official minute book of the Welsh Association Harris, with the benefit of hindsight, constructed the accepted version of early Methodist history. Commenting on this period, he attempted to argue that the Welsh Methodists had begun to meet regularly at least two years before their famous meeting at Defynnog in October 1740, and had already started to assign exhorters to various spheres of activity before this date.[33] W. G. Hughes-Edwards has shown in his study of the Welsh Methodist society that the first concerted effort at bringing order to the societies occurred in March 1739. At that point Harris, on the eve of accompanying Whitefield to London, had assigned John Roberts, a Baptist minister at Ross, Edmund Jones, assistant minister of the Congregational church at Penmaen, Monmouthshire, and Thomas James, a layman from Breconshire, to visit his societies during his absence.[34] The first meeting specifically to discuss questions relating to the organization of the converts occurred when Harris met his three newly appointed assistants on his return to Wales, a practice that continued throughout 1739.[35] This development gradually led to the formation of the Monthly Society, which met for the first time at Mynydd Mayo, Glamorgan, in January 1740 when Harris issued the societies with a list of rules and instructed them to meet in groups of four or five every week.[36] Whilst there had been considerable effort on Harris's part to set his societies in order before 1740, there is little doubt that both Harris and Daniel Rowland were conscious that their efforts to date had been wholly insufficient. A new phase in the development of the Welsh revival was therefore entered in October 1740 when a 'Society of Ministers'[37] met in conference for the first time at Defynnog in Breconshire in order to bring their societies to an 'outward settled agreement'.[38] For Harris the necessity of the

[32]   HHD 47a, 25 June 1739; HHD 63, 25 September 1740; and HHD 49, 18 September 1739.
[33]   CMA 2945, p. 2.
[34]   W. G. Hughes-Edwards, 'The development and organisation of the Methodist Society in Wales', pp. 247–8.
[35]   See HHD 47a, 5 June 1739; HHD 47a, 5 August 1739; HHD 48, 2 September 1739; and HHD 50, 30 November 1739.
[36]   Hughes-Edwards, 'The development and organisation of the Methodist Society in Wales', p. 249.
[37]   HHD 62, 7 September 1740.
[38]   CMA 2945, p. 2.

meeting had become even more pressing during the summer of
1740 in the aftermath of the news of new awakenings in the
American colonies and Scotland.[39]

Howel Harris had been deeply impressed by Ebenezer and
Ralph Erskine, whose desire for an evangelical reformation of
the Church of Scotland had eventually led them to secede from it
and establish their own doctrinally pure 'Associate Presbytery'.
Although he did not share their secessionist tendencies, their
principled stand for the evangelical faith and their experiential
piety struck a chord with him. It was taken as further evidence
that the Welsh and English revivals were only part of a more far-
reaching revitalization of evangelical Protestantism. It was a
conviction given added weight by the revivals inspired largely by
Whitefield's intercolonial itinerancy in 1740.[40] What seemed to
impress Harris most about these revivals was the way in which
they were not confined to any particular denomination or geographical area.

At this stage, Harris was convinced that the best way to ensure
the continuation of the revival and its long-term prosperity was
to achieve some measure of rapprochement between the
Dissenters and the Anglicans, beneath the banner of an
international religious revival. Therefore, in response to the news
from various corners of the world, Harris sought to maximize the
strength of the Welsh revival by inviting all those who supported
it, both Anglican and Dissenting, to unite with him and Daniel
Rowland, and pool their resources for a fresh onslaught on the
superstition and spiritual ignorance of their compatriots.

It is to the credit of both Harris and Daniel Rowland that a
number of prominent Welsh evangelicals met at Defynnog.
Representing the Dissenters were John Oulton from Leominster
and Edmund Jones from Pontypool, both enthusiastic supporters
of the revivalists in the early days. The meeting did not live up to
Harris's high expectations. On its first day Harris declared himself
delighted at the achievement of bringing so many like-minded
brethren together. They began by discussing further the rules of
their societies, and Harris was led to hand over control of his

---

[39]   HHD 63, 1 October 1740.
[40]   Murray (ed.), *George Whitefield's Journals*, pp. 323–562; Dallimore, *George
Whitefield*, I, passim; and Stout, *The Divine Dramatist*, pp. 87–112.

societies to the care of this new administrative body,[41] but conflict between Harris and some of the Dissenters surfaced the following morning. Harris had preached a sermon on assurance, in which he seems to have used typically ambiguous language, which led to some of the more Calvinistic-minded to suspect him of teaching a modified form of sinless perfection. Edmund Jones appears to have been the most ready to challenge Harris's position on this point and actually voiced serious doubts about the possibility of any future meaningful association with the Methodists.[42]

Defynnog was clearly something of a watershed in the early development of the Welsh revival. In its aftermath, Harris concluded that further cooperation with the Dissenters would be difficult, if not wholly impossible.[43] This realization may have been one of the factors in his decision to seek ever-closer ties with Whitefield's Calvinistic Methodists. Such ties inevitably necessitated a higher profile for Whitefield in Wales and, correspondingly, a more prominent role for Harris among the English revivalists. Despite not quite ushering in a new period of interdenominational harmony, the Defynnog meeting was a great success from the point of view of the development of the organization of the Welsh revival. Its achievements stimulated Harris and Rowland to set about the task of bringing order to their societies with renewed vigour and enthusiasm. From 1741 until January 1743, the Welsh revivalists, aided by the periodic secondment of Whitefield, held a further series of gatherings at which all the leaders of the Welsh revival met and hammered out an organizational structure.

Geraint Tudur has demonstrated that even before the first of these gatherings, the famous Llandovery meeting of February 1741, Harris had virtually decided on the structure which he felt should be applied to the societies. Of the seventy societies that existed in south Wales by this date, Harris planned that groups of five or six societies from a locality should meet on a monthly basis; that all the society leaders of two counties should meet bimonthly; that all Welsh leaders, both local and national, should meet once every six months, and that the leaders of English and

---

[41] Tudur, *Howell Harris*, pp. 74–5 and Evans, *Daniel Rowland*, pp. 109–15.
[42] HHD, 1 October 1740.
[43] Evans, *Daniel Rowland*, p. 110.

Welsh Methodism should meet once every year.[44] In Harris's eyes it was to be an organizational structure based on a loose connexionalism that would thrive from the commitment of its grass-roots members. It was not, at least in its conception, intended to be a rigid presbyterial structure, and Harris was certainly not attempting to introduce presbyterianism by stealth. It was very much a bottom-up structure, with each of the monthly, bi-monthly, half-yearly and annual meetings being immediately accountable to its members.[45]

It was at the bi-monthly meeting held at Llandovery and attended by over thirty Methodists, including two Church of England and two Dissenting ministers,[46] that Howel Harris and Daniel Rowland began to make public their plans by introducing matters of greater importance into the agendas of their meetings.[47] Although Whitefield was not present on this occasion, it was on the basis of the decisions taken that White-field was able to drop in and out of the Welsh revival so frequently and with such apparent ease. The society convened over two days. Its agenda was fairly broad and ended up adopting Harris's connexional structure in its entirety. Under the presiding direction of Daniel Rowland, the ministers and exhorters examined various laymen before putting them in charge of societies throughout south Wales. They discussed their relationship with both the Church of England and the evangelical Dissenters, by whom they had so recently been ostracized, in still more detail. They enthusiastically accepted Harris's ideas, and at Llandovery agreed formally, for the first time, that their meeting in this manner should take place every two months and, as he proposed, be called the 'Public Society'.[48]

However, the meeting was perhaps most significant because of the way in which it sought to exert a measure of control over all the Welsh societies by adopting a common set of rules. The rules were hastily copied and circulated to all newly appointed society leaders. This obviously was a new development in the revival, the transition from a somewhat localized phenomenon without

[44]   See HHD 67, 29 December 1740.
[45]   HHD 67, 30 December 1740.
[46]   Evans, *Daniel Rowland*, p. 122.
[47]   Hughes-Edwards, 'The development and organisation of the Methodist Society in Wales', pp. 253–5.
[48]   HHD 69, 13 February 1741.

concerted leadership to something approaching a national movement with a unified set of rules, a sense of common purpose and a distinct identity. These rules, written in Welsh, were circulated throughout Wales and carried almost legal authority within the societies. Yet, they were typically more concerned with matters relating to Methodist spirituality than with the purely administrative matters which had been discussed more privately among the revival's leaders. After some opening remarks justifying the existence of the societies, the document outlined a series of recommendations under six broad headings:

(a) that we are to open our whole heart to one another in simplicity like little children [. . .]

(b) that we, according to the advice of our Saviour [. . .] should watch over one another's tempers and behaviour, and with gentleness reprove one another. We should confess any suspicions that lurk in our minds lest love should grow cold; [. . .]

(c) that we shall allow ourselves to be examined by one another as to our motives, purpose, and principles in all things [. . .]

(d) since we trust we are led by God's Spirit, the Lord has made us of one mind in respect to doctrine; for free grace; weak and strong faith; election; perseverance in the state of grace; dominion over sin; absolute perfection in Christ, in part in ourselves and allowing progress in degrees.

(e) as there is but one body in Christ, so opinion is not the entrance into our midst, but whoever is able to give us satisfaction that he savingly knows Christ [. . .]

(f) that we take God's Word as our rule in everything; keep one day each month for prayer and fasting, for 1. the Society; 2. for the present divisions in God's Church; 3. for faithful ministers and an increase in their number; 4. for the general success of the gospel; 5. for the sins of this kingdom and of the whole world; 6. for the supervision of the societies, the members of this conference, for godly schools, and to help advance every cause.[49]

Though they did not concentrate on practical matters, these rules laid down a number of fundamental principles. Doctrinally, the rules made clear the Welsh Methodists' adherence to Calvinistic theology and their commitment to the absolute centrality of the New Birth. It stipulated that the societies were to

[49] Quoted in Evans, *Daniel Rowland*, pp. 123–4.

be regulated by the Word of God alone and that society members were to be characterized by prayerfulness. Their prayers were to encompass all aspects of the revival as well as their own spiritual well-being. The rules enshrined the principles of openness, mutual responsibility and the absolute account-ability of each individual to his or her fellow society members.

What has often been overlooked is the extent to which inter-national matters informed much of the agenda at Llandovery. The meeting occurred against the immediate backdrop of the theological divisions that were tearing English Methodism apart, and the subject was sufficiently pressing for Harris to place it at the very top of the meeting's agenda.[50] He therefore began the conference proceedings by reading a letter that he had written to Charles Wesley in which he outlined in detail his difficulties with the Wesley brothers' Arminianism and their teaching about the possibility of entire sanctification.[51] Harris's letter was supported by a parallel letter which Whitefield had sent to John Wesley outlining his own similar objections.[52] All those present at the meeting enthusiastically backed the position set out in detail by Harris and Whitefield,[53] a decision that formally aligned the Welsh revival with Whitefield's Calvinistic Methodism. The Methodism that emerged from the Llandovery meeting was, for the first time, a self-consciously coherent movement united under the control of the Public Society, Calvinist in its doctrine and confident enough to enter into the mainstream of the evangelical movement by aligning itself with Calvinistic brethren elsewhere.

For Howel Harris the meeting acted as a springboard. In its immediate aftermath, he worked tirelessly to bind the societies in Wales together and bolster the authority of the Public Society. The meeting also seemed to Harris to indicate the Welsh Methodists' appetite for closer contact with the rest of the revival. Harris himself admitted to 'long[ing] that Bro Whitef—d & all true Sts were united to us & me to & wth them'.[54] To facilitate this Harris,

---

[50]   These are discussed in detail in Chapter V.

[51]   See Trevecka 312, Howel Harris to Charles Wesley (February, 1741). Extensive sections of the letter have also been reproduced in the *Journal of the Wesley Historical Society*, XVII, Part 3, 63–5 and in *CCHMC*, 2 (June 1959), 24–8.

[52]   In the absence of a published letter from *The Weekly History* it is likely that this letter was the one which Whitefield wrote to Wesley from Philadelphia in November 1740. See Murray (ed.), *George Whitefield's Letters*, p. 219.

[53]   HHD 69, 13 February 1741.

[54]   HHD 69, 14 February 1741.

immediately after the conclusion of the Llandovery meeting, once
again left Wales for London. However, on this occasion, his
absence aroused considerable opposition, not to say bewilderment,
among the Welsh Methodists. Thomas Price of Watford was
typical when he reprimanded Harris, telling him in no uncertain
terms that he 'ought to stay, where ye Lord has most work for you
to do',[55] and even Daniel Rowland was beginning to have doubts
about Harris's readiness to desert his Welsh responsibilities at what
seemed like a moment's notice.[56] Price's complaints were all the
more significant because they were written at a time when the
Welsh Methodists were coming under renewed scrutiny from the
Church of England and, perhaps more worryingly, at the very
moment that Griffith Jones, one of the Methodists' few genuine
friends within the Church, was attempting to distance himself
from the enthusiasm of his Methodist friends.[57] Price's complaints
are also indicative of the unease which Harris's English activities
often caused in Wales. Whilst there was plenty of enthusiasm and
commitment to the international aspects of the revival amongst all
of the leaders of the Welsh work, at times there was also a feeling
that it was very easy to become more focused on what was
occurring in other countries than on events in Wales itself. It seems
that nobody was more open to this criticism on quite as many
occasions than Howel Harris himself.

When he eventually returned to Wales in October Harris, in
an attempt to stave off further criticism, attempted to address
some of the problems upsetting the equilibrium of his revival.
However, rather than concentrating purely on Welsh issues,
Harris produced an international solution to the problems which
was designed to maximize the influence of the Welsh revival by
linking its fortunes more closely to those of fellow Methodists
everywhere. His months in London had shown him that the
problems facing the Welsh revival were far from unique and
were brought into particular focus by the fresh wave of
opposition from the Church, which was once again threatening
to undermine the whole movement. When John Wesley visited

[55]   Trevecka 363, Thomas Price to Howel Harris (8 August 1741).
[56]   'The copy of a letter from the Reverend MR DANIEL ROWLAND, a minister of the
Established Church, in the Principality of WALES, to MR HOWEL HARRIS, in LONDON (20
October 1742)', *Account*, III, I, 5.
[57]   Jenkins, 'An old and much honoured soldier', 451–2.

Wales, shortly after Harris's return in October, Harris
engineered a meeting at which the leaders of the Welsh revival
and some of the English Calvinists could meet him and discuss
the possibility of a formal union between all their societies.
Harris's ambitious proposal seems all the more breathtaking
when viewed against the backdrop of the highly damaging
divisions that had so recently torn the English Methodists apart
and pitted one-time friends and co-workers against each other.
That their discussions did not produce anything positive should
come as no surprise.[58] Many in Wales did not share Harris's
admiration for the Wesley brothers. There were fears that the
latter were being less than honest, and that rather than wishing
to put all divisions to one side and work with the Calvinists, they
were attempting to gain a foothold in Wales by stealth for their
Arminian brand of Methodism.[59]

The strongest opposition to Harris's plans came from those
English Calvinists who had recently clashed with the Wesleys.
Whitefield was reportedly strongly against any proposals that
would draw the Calvinists and the Arminians closer together. His
objections, particularly his advice that it would be better if the
Welsh Methodists remained autonomous rather than linking
with the Wesleyans, brought Harris's plans to an abrupt halt.[60]
Whitefield's influence on the course of the revival in Wales was
therefore once again decisive. Although it is extremely doubtful
whether the Welsh Methodists would have countenanced
working so closely with the Wesleys, Whitefield's intervention
acted as a curb on some of Harris's more ambitious schemes. It
would, of course, be a mistake to assume that Whitefield was
opposed to any sort of inter-revival union *per se*. His vision was
of a more pure union, based on a clear doctrinal allegiance to
Calvinism, and therefore deliberately excluded the Wesleyans. It
was in the immediate aftermath of these aborted plans that
Harris redoubled his efforts, with Whitefield's obvious blessing,
to draw English and Welsh Calvinistic Methodism closer
together. The discussions that took place during these weeks, and

---

[58]   A. H. Williams, *John Wesley in Wales, 1739–1790* (Cardiff, 1971), pp. 11–12 and
Griffith T. Roberts, 'John Wesley visits Wales (October 15th–21st, 1741)', *Bathafarn*,
XIII (1958), 47.
[59]   Williams, *John Wesley in Wales*, p. 12.
[60]   See HHD 81, 9 November 1741.

Whitefield's decisive role in them, demonstrate the extent to which the Welsh Methodists, and Howel Harris in particular, were prepared to defer to Whitefield's judgement on these matters. This was a period when Whitefield enjoyed almost apostolic authority over the Calvinistic societies of England and Wales, and it seems that the Welsh Methodists were perfectly prepared to defer to his judgement and accord him this status. It was a pattern that was to develop throughout 1742, until Whitefield's position was eventually made official in January 1743.

Faced with these difficulties and in the aftermath of Harris's attempt to unite all the English and Welsh Methodists, Harris and Rowland called the leaders of the Welsh revival to Dugoedydd, in Carmarthenshire, in January 1742. Whitefield was invited, but proved unable to join the four clergymen and eighteen exhorters who met under Daniel Rowland's chairmanship. To compensate for his absence, Whitefield wrote a letter which was in reality more of an essay, analysing the current state of the Calvinistic societies and pinpointing their weaknesses. Unlike his previously published *Letter . . . to the Religious Societies*, Whitefield's second letter was refreshing in its concentration on more practical issues 'of the utmost importance',[61] which helped to settle definitively some aspects of the final shape of the Welsh revival.

He began by addressing the question of assigning individuals to the most appropriate offices within the revival. His concern reflects the Methodists' emphasis on the correct employment of an individual's God-given gifts, and to facilitate this Whitefield drew a number of distinctions between the various offices that the revivalists had originally created to meet their immediate needs. Some people were clearly gifted to 'awaken, others to establish and build up'.[62] Whitefield's basic distinction was between public work, usually involving itinerant preaching and responsibility for a significant number of societies in a given area, and private work which was usually taken to mean the local leadership of societies on a day-to-day basis. Those called to public work were encouraged to 'give themselves wholly to the

---

[61]   George Whitefield to brethren in Wales (28 December 1741), in Murray (ed.), *George Whitefield's Letters*, p. 511.
[62]   Ibid.

work, and go without purse and scrip',[63] whilst those involved in private work were instructed to remain in their secular employment and follow their spiritual calling in their spare time. This plan did not originate entirely with Whitefield. It had been adopted by the Welsh Methodists from the beginning of their work and had developed in response to the practical needs of their converts. It was only as the number of converts began to grow in the early 1740s that the *ad hoc* system, which Harris and Daniel Rowland had developed, proved incapable of bearing the strain that was being placed upon it. What Whitefield did, under Harris's guidance, was to endorse Harris's original plan, give it clearer definition by outlining the specific roles of public and private workers, and accord it the sanction of a higher authority – that of the Welsh Methodists' 'Elder Brother'. Whitefield then went on to address the thorny question of the Methodists' relationship with the Church and the evangelical Dissenters. His advice amounted to nothing more than a reiteration of the position that they had already adopted, but on this occasion he used a notably more restrained tone, doubting whether those who were ordained in the Church would be able to continue in it for very much longer.[64] Despite this they were urged to remain loyal to the Church until they were forcibly 'cast out',[65] and they were advised to appeal to sympathetic clergy who were prepared to offer the sacrament to Methodists from outside their own parishes who were being denied admission by their local anti-Methodist clergy.[66]

It is highly significant that Whitefield then progressed to a detailed discussion of some of the more practical problems that were hindering the progress of the new Calvinistic Methodist movement in England. Whitefield drew attention to its lack of personnel and shortage of suitably qualified individuals prepared to take on responsibility for the local, and in some cases national, leadership of the work. To plug some of these gaps he suggested that Thomas Lewis[67] be allowed to help out in England on a more regular basis, but he insisted that this would not solve the

---

[63] Ibid.
[64] Ibid.
[65] Ibid.
[66] Ibid.
[67] See *DWB*, p. 561.

problem of the lack of a permanent labourer among the Calvinists at Kingswood and in Wiltshire.[68] That Whitefield was
prepared to raise these issues among the Welsh gives some
indication of the way in which the fortunes of the Calvinistic
revivals in England and Wales had by this time become
inextricably linked. Whitefield evidently did not draw too sharp a
distinction between the Welsh and English Calvinists and did not
expect the Welsh Methodists to be unconcerned about the
prospects of the English work. This was, of course, a unity based
on the similar events that had occurred in the two communities,
and was given tangible expression by Whitefield's reiteration of
the need for Methodists in both countries to maintain their
practice of communicating regularly and keeping each other up-
to-date with every fresh stirring of revival enthusiasm. To this
end, Whitefield suggested that the Welsh Methodists, following
his own recent example, which he had borrowed from the
Moravians, of establishing a monthly Letter Day in Bristol and
London,[69] set apart one day each month at which exhorters and
other labourers could report on their success to the wider
Methodist community and, vitally, send a report of proceedings
to England. Whitefield, for his part, promised that the English
Methodists would return the compliment.[70] It was thus almost in
reaction to the divisions with the Wesleys that Whitefield sought
to maximize the strength of the Calvinistic wing of the revival by
committing all the Calvinistic Methodists to a closer union. This
union would, he envisaged, operate on two levels: its leaders
would set in place a single organizational structure over their
revivals which would make it simpler for them to contribute to
one another's awakenings; and the rank and file would be drawn
closer together by the sophisticated network of communications,
which it was hoped would now fulfil its potential by ensuring that
'unity would be [. . .] promoted, love increased, and our hands
strengthened'.[71]

Naturally, this letter set the agenda for the Dugoedydd
meeting, and when they met the leaders of the Welsh revival

---

[68] Murray (ed.), *George Whitefield's Letters*, p. 512.
[69] O'Brien, 'A transatlantic community of saints', 824–7; Lambert, '*Pedlar in Divinity*', p. 141.
[70] George Whitefield to brethren in Wales (28 December 1741), in Murray (ed.), *George Whitefield's Letters*, p. 512.
[71] Ibid.

wholeheartedly endorsed all of Whitefield's recommendations.[72] However, their discussions focused mainly on the constantly recurring theme of relations with the Church of England and the Dissenters. Some Methodists in Carmarthenshire had faced fresh criticism from some of the local Dissenting ministers, while the Church authorities had censured others for receiving the sacrament in Dissenting meeting houses. Howel Harris's account of the meeting, recorded in his diary, shows the extent to which the Welsh Methodists accepted the advice which Whitefield had offered in his letter. The meeting affirmed that the Welsh Methodists were free to have fellowship with all other evangelicals in sympathy with the revival but were duty bound to take the sacrament in their parish churches unless prevented from doing so by a hostile incumbent. In such circumstances they decided that they were perfectly entitled to partake of the sacrament amongst those Dissenters prepared to offer it to them. Nevertheless, they were not to countenance any talk of leaving the Church until they were faced with no alternative but to withdraw or be ejected forcibly.[73]

The meeting, like that at Llandovery a year earlier, was an unqualified success. Harris left the gathering again reinvigorated, with a new sense of purpose and at one with his fellow Methodists. He reported to Whitefield: 'we did Read yr Letter and every one agreed with yr thoughts we had much union sweetness concord and brotherly love together.'[74] The Dugoedydd meeting marks an obvious demarcation line between the fairly random development of the Welsh revival before 1742 and the more rigorous organization to which the societies were subsequently subjected. The achievements of the meeting were consolidated at a series of further monthly meetings throughout 1742, each of which laid the foundations for the famous Watford meeting. In February the leaders of the Welsh revival met at Llwynyberllan in Carmarthenshire, where they hammered out the rules of the societies in still greater detail and, significantly, the decision was taken to publish the rules of the societies in full and circulate them throughout Wales.[75] They appeared later that

---

[72]   HHD 84, 7 January 1742.
[73]   HHD 84, 7 January 1742 and Evans, *Daniel Rowland*, pp. 176–80.
[74]   Trevecka 460, Howel Harris to George Whitefield (14 January 1742).
[75]   HHD 84, 11 February 1742 and Hughes-Edwards, 'The development and organisation of the Methodist Society in Wales', pp. 260–1.

year under the title, *Sail Dibenion, a Rheolau'r Societies neu'r Cyfarfodydd Neilltuol a ddechreusant ymgynull yn ddiweddar yng Nghymru.* The book was extremely influential; it outlined how every aspect of the societies was to be managed, from the format of meetings, the procedure for accepting new members into their ranks to more specific guidance for the leaders of the societies themselves. It became, in effect, alongside the Bible, the manual for all local and national leaders of the revival in Wales and was not superseded until William Williams eventually published his famous *Drws y Society Profiad* in 1777.[76]

Geraint Tudur has attempted to demonstrate that the achievements of the Dugoedydd and Llwynyberllan meetings left the Welsh Methodists in an unquestionably strong position, so that if they were forced out of the Church they would have been able to stand alone, having already established a quasi-denominational structure.[77] Whilst it is undoubtedly true that the Welsh Methodists would have been able if necessary to adapt to life outside the Church relatively quickly, Howel Harris preferred caution and intimated that much work still remained to be done. In the letter which he wrote to Whitefield immediately after the Dugoedydd meeting, Harris, whilst thanking Whitefield for the help already given and expressing the Welsh Methodists' indebtedness to him, reiterated his appeal for Whitefield's presence in Wales in order to finalize the work.[78] Perhaps this was partly due to Harris's own insecurities, but it was equally a result of the Welsh Methodists' need for validation by the apparently larger, stronger and more influential Whitefieldian movement. Throughout the remainder of 1742, the Welsh revivalists made increasingly frequent calls on Whitefield's time and energies – a development that was the result of a number of factors relating to some fundamental changes in the nature of the revival. By now, Whitefield clearly thought that the revivals had reached a plateau and that it was high time for the revivalists' commitment to evangelism to be supplemented with an equally intense concentration on the care and nurture of their converts, since there were 'so many living

---

[76]   Garfield H. Hughes (ed.), *Gweithiau William Williams, Pantycelyn*, II (Cardiff, 1967), pp. 181–242. For a faithful English translation see William Williams, *The Experience Meeting: An Introduction to the Welsh Societies of the Evangelical Awakening*, trans. Bethan Lloyd Jones (Bridgend, 1973) and for a brief analysis of its contents see Glyn Tegai Hughes, *Williams Pantycelyn* (Cardiff, 1983), pp. 67–70.

[77]   Tudur, *Howell Harris*, p. 85.

[78]   Trevecka 460, Howel Harris to George Whitefield (14 January 1742).

stones [that] it may be time to think of putting them together'.[79] Consequently, in two letters to Harris written during August and September, Whitefield intimated that he was prepared to come to Wales and give the movement there his undivided attention. He judged that his time would be used most effectively if the Welsh Methodists could arrange a meeting of all the leaders of their movement in conference with those leaders of the English Calvinistic revival whom Whitefield brought with him.

The strengthening of the position of the Methodist societies during 1742 predictably roused the Church of England to fresh anti-Methodist activity. Still labouring under the suspicion that they might be covert bodies for anti-Establishment ideas, the Methodist societies came into further disrepute when one of their members, Benjamin Cadman,[80] began to hold a society in his own home. Accused of establishing a conventicle, Cadman was rescued by the intervention of Whitefield, who took his case to the bishop of Bangor. He employed arguments that were to be used consistently throughout the 1740s and went a considerable way towards distancing the Methodist societies from some of the harsher criticisms that were levelled against them. Whitefield argued that the Welsh Methodists were 'loyal subjects to his Majesty, and true friends to, and attendants upon the Church of *England* service'.[81] He carefully pointed out that any further discriminatory action against them would only exacerbate the problem, driving the Methodists out of the Church altogether into the arms of the Dissenters. Indeed, feelings seem to have been running so high in Wales at this time that Whitefield was prepared to warn the bishop that if legal proceedings against Cadman were commenced it was likely that 'hundreds, if not thousands, will go in a body from the Church'.[82] In the event, Whitefield's letter smoothed over the immediate tensions, and the bishop decided to take no further action. However, the episode serves to underline the way in which the Methodists were perceived as a threat, and the relative weakness of their

---

[79] 'The conclusion of the letter begun in our last' (this was a letter written by George Whitefield to Howel Harris and dated 26 August 1742), *WH* 80 (16 October 1742).

[80] See Trevecka 1205, Benjamin Cadman to Howel Harris (28 July 1744) and Evans, *Daniel Rowland*, p. 210.

[81] George Whitefield to the bishop of Bangor (19 November 1742), in Murray (ed.), *George Whitefield's Letters*, p. 463.

[82] Ibid.

position. Despite boasting a fairly extensive network of highly committed and tightly organized societies, they remained hesitant about their position and often preferred to enlist the help of the Calvinistic revivalists from England in an effort to bolster their own confidence.

There was a further, perhaps more pressing, reason for Whitefield's decision to turn his attention to Wales towards the end of 1742. Relations between Howel Harris and Daniel Rowland had become strained. Harris's domineering and abrasive personality had begun to cause Rowland and his followers increasing offence. Never a person to tolerate levity or light-hearted conversation, Harris lashed out at those, including Daniel Rowland, who did not share his unremittingly serious and earnest temper.[83] More importantly, Rowland had also begun to harbour serious doubts about some of Harris's theological opinions. Harris, unlike Daniel Rowland and George Whitefield, was never completely comfortable with the fully-fledged Calvinistic system they had adopted.[84] Although he had sided with Whitefield in the Calvinistic controversy in 1740 and made repeated assertions protesting his orthodoxy, Harris was always more ready to experiment with different theological viewpoints than were his two nearest colleagues. These tensions boiled over in a public disagreement for the first time after the Llwynyberllan meeting, when Rowland disagreed with Harris's assertion that every Christian was meant to enjoy full assurance of his or her salvation. Harris argued that assurance was of the very essence and being of saving faith, whereas Rowland maintained that it was distinct and not necessarily the possession of every single Christian. These arguments did not lead to a separation between them at this stage, and after passions had cooled they were quickly reconciled,[85] but the seriousness of the disagreement contributed significantly to the ill feeling that already existed. It seems that it was this unfortunate incident that was the catalyst for Whitefield's decision to give his undivided attention to the problems in Wales. He lamented the spirit of 'narrowness'[86] that

---

[83]   See HHD 93, 4 September 1742 and HHD 113, 4 October 1742.
[84]   For opposing views of the strength of Harris's allegiance to reformed Calvinistic theology see Evans, *Howell Harris*, pp. 17–18 and Tudur, *Howell Harris*, pp. 38–40, 193.
[85]   HHD 86, 18 March 1742.
[86]   Quoted in Evans, *Howell Harris*, p. 46.

had come to dominate the Welsh revival. He had previously expressed his dismay at the divisions in Wales when writing from Cambuslang in August 1742, though he quickly reassured both himself and the Welsh Methodists that 'dividing times generally precede settling times'.[87]

By the eve of the Watford Association the Welsh societies had been brought under the control of the Monthly Society, but at the end of 1742 this had proved inadequate to cope with the range and complexity of the decisions that had to be taken. In response to this need, the Welsh Methodists set in place an additional tier of government, the Quarterly Association,[88] which largely superseded the monthly meeting as a decision-making forum. It was in this piecemeal way that the annual Association emerged to become the main regulatory body of the Welsh revival. Under the government of the Association a connexional, almost presbyterial system of administration had come into being within the confines of the Established Church. The Methodists divided Wales into regions, each under the oversight of a superintendent under whom there was a larger network of exhorters, who in turn were divided between those who occupied a 'public' role and those who exercised a 'private' ministry. Watford made this organization official and saw it adopted in its entirety by the English Calvinistic revivalists.

The most important Calvinistic revivalists from England and Wales congregated at Watford during the first few days of 1743.[89] Whitefield was accompanied by his assistant, John Cennick, and the laymen Joseph Humphreys and Herbert Jenkins (1721–72).[90] Harris and Rowland, together with William Williams and John Powell (1708–95),[91] represented the Welsh Methodists. Despite its prominence in many of the discussions of the organization of the Welsh revival, the Watford Association did not make any major new recommendations. It authorized a number of the decisions that had already been taken and officially adopted the policies and procedures that had been

---

[87]   'The conclusion of the letter begun in our last', *WH* 80 (Saturday, 16 October 1742).
[88]   Hughes-Edwards, 'The origin and development of the Methodist Society in Wales', pp. 267–9.
[89]   See ibid., pp. 261–5.
[90]   *DWB*, pp. 432–3.
[91]   Ibid., p. 774.

agreed previously at Dugoedydd and Llwynyberllan and published in *Sail Dibenion a Rheolau'r Societies.*

The most significant decision made by the Association was the appointment of George Whitefield to the office of Moderator. M. H. Jones has suggested that the title, with its strong Presbyterian overtones, originated with Whitefield himself, particularly in the wake of his involvement in the Presbyterian-dominated Scottish revival.[92] However, it seems that the idea actually stemmed from Howel Harris.[93] The proceedings of the Association were largely concerned with assigning offices to the leaders of the Welsh work, both locally and nationally. The most pressing of these tasks was the appointment of the public and private exhorters to the care of various groups of societies beyond which they were not to function 'without previous advice & consultation'.[94] Twenty-four private exhorters were appointed to collections of societies and instructed to meet for fellowship and support on a monthly basis. All the exhorters within a larger geographical area, usually roughly equivalent to the county boundaries, were placed under the additional government of superintendents, who were instructed to report on the state of the societies under their care at quarterly meetings. These superintendents then met in an annual Association of English and Welsh Calvinistic Methodism, under the moderatorship of George Whitefield or, in his absence, Howel Harris or Daniel Rowland. All the exhorters were to be rigorously vetted by the Association before they were accounted worthy of serving their fellow Methodists. The rather draconian manner in which exhorters were assigned to particular localities was intended to ensure that all of the revival's converts came under the oversight and, perhaps more importantly, the direct discipline of the pioneer revivalists. Yet it also ensured that each exhorter knew both his place within the wider movement and the limits of his duties, and that he was aware of the nature of the accountability which he owed to his fellow exhorters. Any deviation from these norms, which for the first time were fully prescribed, could now

[92] Jones, *The Trevecka Letters*, p. 280.
[93] Trevecka 460, Howel Harris to George Whitefield (14 January 1742); Trevecka 644, Howel Harris to Daniel Rowland (14 September 1742); Dallimore, *George Whitefield*, II, p. 157.
[94] 'An account of the proceedings at the Association held at Waterford' (5–6 January 1743), CMA 2945, pp. 5–6.

be met with the full authority of the revival which had been vested in the Association.

The Association also returned once more to the vexed question of relations with the Church of England and the Dissenters. Again the policy was reiterated of genuine cooperation with those evangelical Dissenters who were sympathetic to them, whilst they remained loyal to the Church until 'the Lord should open a plain Door for leaving her Communion'.[95] It may be that the most significant effect of the Watford meeting was the spiritual and psychological effect that the gathering of so many of the revival's most important figures was able to generate. Summit meetings like the Watford gathering became landmarks in the Methodist calendar. They were, in effect, 'feast days', usually taking place over a number of days and always renowned for both the fervency of the sermons that were preached and the heightened intensity of the Methodists' spiritual feelings. They were occasions that quickly passed into folklore as defining moments in Methodist history because of the magnitude of the decisions that were often taken and the heightened spiritual emotions that were on display. The Watford deliberations, for example, took place after those who had gathered had listened to an impassioned sermon by Daniel Rowland.[96] Psychologically, they were events that contributed substantially to the development of Welsh Methodist identity by giving tangible expression to the solidarity of the Welsh societies and reaffirming their membership of the international evangelical movement.[97]

Although at times given to dramatizing the whole process of the adoption of the revival's organizational structure and his own indispensability to it, Howel Harris was quick to recognize the full significance of the achievements of Watford. He wrote to Griffith Jones, who had by this time become far more critical of his old Methodist friends,[98] in an obvious bid to reassure him of their steadfast loyalty to his beloved Church. He assured Jones

[95]   Ibid., 6.

[96]   Evans, *Daniel Rowland*, p. 213.

[97]   See White, 'The people called Methodists', passim; E. Wyn James, ' "The New Birth of a people": Welsh language and identity and the Welsh Methodists, c.1740–1820', pp. 14–42; and Geraint Tudur, ' "Thou bold champion, where art thou": Howell Harris and the issue of Welsh identity', pp. 43–60, in Robert Pope (ed.), *Religion and National Identity: Wales and Scotland, c.1700–2000* (Cardiff, 2001).

[98]   Jenkins, 'An old and much honoured soldier', 451–3.

that the societies had now come under sufficient organizational control and discipline to prevent future irregularities or, to be more precise, any further flouting of the rules of the Established Church.[99] In the wake of the meeting Harris fully expected that the newly instituted formal union between English and Welsh Calvinistic Methodism would be the catalyst for further developments resulting in a much closer and more interdependent relationship. In particular, he hoped that the interchange of ideas and manpower that had already taken place would become more frequent and that Whitefield's influence in Wales would continue to grow.[100]

For a while this was what happened. In the six months immediately following the first Watford meeting, Whitefield maintained a close interest in Welsh matters. The organization was further developed at a meeting held at Glanyrafonddu on 1 March,[101] which prompted Harris to write to Whitefield a tantalizing letter expressing the Welsh Methodists' desire to welcome him to Wales once more. He seems to have been hoping that Whitefield would be prepared to devote a considerable amount of time to Wales in order to undertake a detailed tour of the societies under the control of their joint Association. He wrote:

> I believe you'll be detained by Jesus Christ a longer time than you think. There are 8 counties open to you, and thirsting to hear you, and opposition ceases. I believe you'll have many churches open besides 14 or more that our brethren have besides Chapels &c and some new houses going on to be built. Poor Wales! The high and lofty one of Israel has not forgotten thee! [. . .] They [the Exhorters] all salute you with the warmest affections most humbly.[102]

Whitefield duly arrived in Wales at the beginning of April for a second Joint Association held at Watford. Once again the meeting was a memorable occasion. Whitefield acted as Moderator for the second time and set the tone of the meeting by preaching a highly evocative sermon on the Old Testament

---

[99]   Trevecka 776, Howel Harris to Griffith Jones (10 January 1743).
[100]   'The copy of a letter from Bro. HOWEL HARRIS in WALES, to the Rev. MR WHITEFIELD in LONDON' (25 January 1743), *Account*, II, II, 67–8.
[101]   See 'At Glan-yrafonddu, Carmarthenshire; March 1, 1743', CMA 2945, pp. 8–12.
[102]   Trevecka 811, Howel Harris to George Whitefield (1 March 1743).

patriarch, Enoch, who had been transported into heaven before the natural time of his death.[103] In some respects the second Watford Association was even more productive than the more famous first meeting. As well as receiving reports from the exhorters and assigning others to new spheres of work, the Association took the highly significant step of setting apart William Williams to be Daniel Rowland's personal assistant in south-west Wales. The importance of this decision was to become all the more evident in the later 1740s, when the Welsh revival began to polarize between those who supported Rowland and those who continued to back the increasingly erratic Howel Harris. Daniel Rowland, with the support of Williams, was able to galvanize the majority of Methodists into supporting his own more orthodox version of Methodism in 1750 and 1751 and forcing Harris into semi-retirement with just a small rump of supporters. This was a realignment that had been made possible because of the decisions taken at Watford in April 1743 and one that ultimately saved the Welsh revival from collapse in the immediate aftermath of the loss of its most charismatic leader.

The Association also appointed Howel Harris General Superintendent, a post that meant that he served as Moderator when Whitefield was not able to be present at Associations in Wales. The Association also recognized the unique contribution that Harris had made to the wider evangelical movement by officially appointing him to joint oversight of the English and Welsh Calvinistic societies. It was a decision undoubtedly forced on the Welsh Methodists by Whitefield, who recognized Harris's organizational gifts and coveted them for his own awakening, fully realizing that they were vital if the haemorrhaging of members to the Wesleyans and Moravians was to be staunched. Between 1739 and 1743, Harris had been spending increasingly lengthy periods of each year in London. From 1743 his visits became even longer as he took on more and more responsibility for the running of the English movement, and in practice full responsibility for it during Whitefield's extended absence in the American colonies between 1744 and 1748.[104]

---

[103] See Genesis 5: 21–4.
[104] 'Association held at Waterford; April 6 and 7, 1743', CMA 2945, pp. 13–15.

Whitefield's presence at both Watford meetings, therefore, put the final seal on the organizational structure of the Welsh Methodist revival and refined the almost identical structure that Whitefield and Harris had imposed on the English Calvinistic societies, thereby ensuring that the Association could legislate for both revivals in a meaningful and even-handed way. In the immediate aftermath of the meeting, Howel Harris, who had been given responsibility for keeping the minutes of the Associations, opened a new minute book with comments which reflected on the achievements of the previous five years and gave his opinion of the significance of the two Watford meetings. He highlighted first the foundational importance of the monthly meetings, noting that through them 'everything was settled so that hitherto ye Lord visibly blesses & leads & unites & shews each his place & gives us fellowship together & gives His presence in our meetings'.[105] It was, according to Harris, through these monthly meetings that the collective will of the Welsh Methodist movement was expressed most clearly and it was here that its allegiance to reformed doctrine was forged. Harris regarded loyalty to 'ye same Things [as the] Reformers and Puritans'[106] as fundamental to the Welsh revival and part of the reason for its success hitherto. This loyalty located the Methodists firmly in the mainstream of Protestant orthodoxy at a time when many, both in the Church and among the Dissenters, harboured suspicions of the extent of the Methodists' orthodoxy and of their tendency to enthusiasm, which to many in the age of the Enlightenment seemed to border on irrationality and even in some cases on insanity.[107]

The months and years immediately following the two Watford Associations were consequently very different from those preceding them. For most of 1743 Whitefield kept a closer eye on events in

---

[105] Ibid., 50.
[106] Ibid.
[107] On 'enthusiasm' in the eighteenth century see Jon Mee, *Romanticism, Enthusiasm and Regulation: Poetics and the Policing of Culture in the Romantic Period* (Oxford, 2003). For enlightened opposition to the Methodists see R. A. Knox, *Enthusiasm* (London, 1950), pp. 422–548, passim; W. Stephen Gunter, *The Limits of 'Love Divine': John Wesley's Response to Antinomianism and Enthusiasm* (Nashville, TN, 1989), pp. 13–26; A. M. Lyles, *Methodism Mocked: The Satiric Reaction to Methodism in the Eighteenth Century* (London, 1960), pp. 32–43; Walsh, 'Methodism and the mob', passim; Hempton, 'Methodism and the Law', 97–101; and Bebbington, 'Revival and Enlightenment in eighteenth century England', passim. For the more specifically Welsh context see White, '"The world, the flesh and the devil"', 53–8.

Wales than he might normally have done, and Harris ensured, by means of the correspondence between them, that events in Wales were kept uppermost in the minds of the English Calvinistic Methodists.[108] However, what is most surprising is the relatively low profile that Whitefield subsequently enjoyed in Wales, particularly after his departure to the American colonies in 1744. In the immediate post-Watford years, Whitefield's moderatorship was taken on by Harris, as had been arranged at Watford. Wales became more prominent because of Harris's higher profile among the English Calvinistic societies rather than through Whitefield's regular visits to Wales. The interdependence of the two revivals continued, but the exact balance of their relationship underwent a fundamental change, largely because of the contrasting fortunes of the two revivals. The revival in Wales went from strength to strength at the same time as the English revival was fighting for its long-term survival.

Howel Harris's contribution to the English Calvinistic revival is a subject that has not received the attention it deserves. It has long been assumed that Harris played only the most minor of roles in the London awakening and was present only as a result of Whitefield's patronage. Even Geraint Tudur's recently published biography of Harris, though it discusses Harris's relationship with the English Methodists at certain key moments, does not do full justice to the extent to which Harris became the *de facto* leader of the London Calvinists. Even before Whitefield went to America in 1744 and John Cennick deserted the Calvinists at the end of 1745, Harris shouldered almost alone much of the burden of the day-to-day leadership of the English societies.

Harris had of course been well known among the English Methodists since 1739, and throughout the 1740s he spent significant parts of each year in London. His published itinerary shows how mobile Harris was, splitting his time almost equally between the English and Welsh revivals, and developing a genuinely transnational persona.[109] The English Calvinistic revival was never as geographically extensive as either the Wesleyan or

---

[108]   See *Account*, II, I, passim.
[109]   See Appendix 1, p. 343.

the Welsh revival. Initially it had four main centres – London, Gloucester, Kingswood (Bristol) and Wiltshire – and it was only in 1745 that the area around Plymouth in the south-west became an additional focus of Calvinistic Methodist influence. As in Wales, these centres of Whitefieldian strength were broken down into smaller, more manageable areas, each of which came under the jurisdiction of one of the English revivalists.[110] Whitefield does not seem to have felt a pressing need to bring his converts under any sort of organizational structure until well after the split with the Wesleys. After this, and alarmed at the defection of many of his converts to the Wesley brothers during late 1740 and 1741,[111] he was faced with no alternative but to subject his converts to a rigid disciplinary structure designed to enable him to keep a tight rein on the progress of his revival and prevent further secessions. The hub of the Whitefieldian revival was the Tabernacle in Moorfields, London. It consisted of a large auditorium, in which Whitefield preached most days, and a separate society room in which the large and occasionally volatile Tabernacle Society met. The society was the biggest and most influential of the Whitefieldian societies and the first to have a standardized set of rules. By 1744 it had spawned a further thirty-six societies located in twenty-five different places throughout the south and west of England.[112] They were administered on a day-to-day basis by a number of exhorters, each of whom worked in one of the four distinct local Associations that corresponded with the movement's four main provinces,[113] and a close relationship between the societies and the Association was ensured by the requirement of both the societies and the exhorters to report to the Association at regular intervals.

---

[110] The local leadership of the English Calvinistic societies was far more fluid than that of the Welsh societies because of the more rapid turnover of its membership. The constant reassignment of exhorters to different parts of the movement can be observed, for example, by comparing 'Association held at London, June 18 1746', CMA 2946, pp. 15–7, with 'Morton Hill, Gloucestershire, April 15 1747', CMA 2946, pp. 29–30.

[111] Whitefield's difficulties in rebuilding his work after the split with the Wesleys are only hinted at by Arnold Dallimore in his biography of Whitefield, *George Whitefield*, II, pp. 65–78. A more realistic impression may be gained from some of Whitefield's correspondence from these months. See George Whitefield to James Hutton (25 March 1741) and George Whitefield to John Cennick (25 March 1741), in Murray (ed.), *George Whitefield's Letters*, pp. 256–8.

[112] Dallimore, *George Whitefield*, II, p. 153.

[113] 'At an Association held at Bristol, March 20 1745', CMA 2946, pp. 1–3, and Welch, *Two Calvinistic Methodist Chapels*, p. 19.

Each of Harris's visits to England followed a similar pattern. On his way to London he invariably stopped in Gloucester, before proceeding via Oxford. On his return he usually followed a different route via Bath and Bristol, which enabled him to take stock of the condition of the revival in each of the four provinces.[114] From Harris's diary it is fairly easy to piece together a picture of his daily activities in London. Virtually every day began at the Tabernacle, either listening to Whitefield preach or exhorting himself. The remainder of his days were usually spent visiting the societies, examining their members and offering support and guidance to the exhorters.[115] This arduous routine was frequently interspersed with attendance at Associations and visits to the other factions of the revival, including the Wesleyans, the Moravians and some of the other smaller splinter groups that had separated from the main body of the revival.

There is no doubt that the inspiration for the uniting of the Welsh and Whitefieldian revivals stemmed almost exclusively from Whitefield and Howel Harris. In Wales, as has already been argued, neither Daniel Rowland nor any of the other leaders of the revival could quite match Harris's enthusiasm for inter-revival communication. Whilst it would be misleading to conclude that neither Rowland nor Howel Davies nor William Williams was uninterested in the day-to-day maintenance of the transnational communications network, it would be correct to argue that their priorities lay far closer to home. There were therefore times when Harris's contemporaries, despite agreeing to the division of his labours at Watford, found his gallivanting frustrating and his commitment to the English revival, often at the expense of the well-being of his own followers in Wales, difficult to comprehend. Daniel Rowland's plea to him to return to Wales towards the end of 1742 was typical:

> Don't you hear all the brethren in Wales, crying out loudly Help! Help! Help! Help! Brother Harris! Thou bold Champion, where art thou? What is London now in the Day of Battle! What? Has not London Champions enough to fight for her? Where are the great Wesley's, Cennick. Must poor

---

[114] For an example of Harris's usual itinerary on these trips to London see M. H. Jones, 'The itinerary of Howell Harris, Trevecka: for the years 1746–1752', *CCHMC*, 10 (December 1925), 11–12.

[115] See HHD 107, 8 February 1744 and HHD 121, 9 February 1746.

Wales afford an assistant to England? Oh poor Wales! Tis thy ingratitude altogether has been the cause of all this. Good Lord pity poor Wales.[116]

Whilst Rowland's appeals did not fundamentally alter Harris's practice of dividing his time between England and Wales, comments such as these may, in part at least, account for the constant insecurity which plagued Harris and the deteriorating relationship between the two men. Harris's emotional insecurities have been a recurring theme throughout this study, and there seems little doubt that dividing his time between the two revivals led him into further bouts of self-doubt and compounded his feeling that he was not able to fulfil his role properly in either place.[117] Yet, coupled with this, there were times when Harris's mood swung to the opposite pole, when, despite protestations of his own inferiority, he felt himself to be indispensable to the revival and made sure that everyone was aware that he was to be afforded special status, because after all he had been the first revivalist.[118]

Whilst in England, Harris was able to develop a distinctive role in the London-based evangelical communities. Although for most of the 1730s and 1740s he had no official role or title, he used the strength of his position in Wales and employed the patronage of Whitefield to maximum effect. During his early visits he acted as a guest evangelist and supplemented the activities of the English revivalists, but as the initial enthusiasm of the revival subsided, Harris found himself in the novel position of acting as a peace broker between the revival's warring factions and, once the divisions between the Moravians, Wesleyans and Calvinists had run their course, he found himself unenviably having to keep the Calvinists in mind of their responsibilities to their fellow evangelicals.[119] John Cennick took on the leadership of Calvinistic Methodism in England after Whitefield's departure to the American colonies in August 1744.[120] Harris continued to

---

[116] 'The copy of a letter from the Reverend MR DANIEL ROWLAND, a minister of the Established Church, in the Principality of WALES, to MR HOWEL HARRIS, in LONDON (20 October 1742)', *Account*, II, I, 5.

[117] See for example Beynon (ed.), *Howell Harris's Visits to London*, pp. 208–9, and 239–40; and Beynon (ed.), *Howell Harris: Reformer and Soldier*, p. 53.

[118] See Beynon (ed.), *Howell Harris's Visits to London*, pp. 207–8; and HHD 145, 17 July 1750.

[119] 'The Copy of a Letter from Mr HOWEL HARRIS in Wales to the Society at the Tabernacle, London, (12 February 1742)', *WH* 47 (20 January 1742).

[120] Dallimore, *George Whitefield*, II, pp. 173, 231.

act in the same way when in London. Despite this, the Watford Association had brought about an important change in Harris's status. The gathering was of course the first Joint Association of English and Welsh Calvinistic Methodism, and one of the most tangible ways in which this new partnership was expressed concerned the role of Harris. The Association had decided that Harris was to go to England whenever he was needed, and that he was consequently to be regarded as the joint possession of the English and the Welsh revivals.[121] Whether or not this was a calculated move to sideline Harris on the part of an increasingly ambitious Daniel Rowland, the appointment certainly dissipated Harris's labours and meant that the majority of Welsh Methodists, even those who owed their conversions to him, no longer relied on his leadership to quite the same extent.

His new role added to Harris's authority in England. Initially, he remained a loyal supporter of John Cennick's leadership and continued to be a conciliatory voice, reminding the English Whitefieldians of their responsibilities to their Wesleyan and Moravian contemporaries and continuing his pastoral role among the English societies. To the Tabernacle Society in June 1745, Harris struck his usual conciliatory note, exhorting its members: 'Let all narrowness be done away, and let the Sins of all be your Burthen before the Lord, especially of all the Churches this and the other Side of the Seas.'[122] Harris continued in this vein throughout the latter part of 1744, and much of 1745. Whitefield had left for the colonies in August 1744 and the Calvinistic revival was, for a brief period, drawn closer together as its members regrouped under the very different style of leadership deployed by the far less charismatic John Cennick. Yet these were not stagnant months. The work had been extended to the south-west with the formation of a new society in Plymouth[123] and there was a generally more optimistic tone about Harris's comments in the minutes of the English Associations.[124]

[121] 'At the Association held at Waterford, Ap. 6 and 7 1743 when the Revd. Mr Whitefield was chose Moderator', CMA 2945, p. 14.

[122] 'From Bro. Howel Harris in Wales to the SOCIETY AT THE TABERNACLE' (29 June 1745), CH, VII, IV, 15.

[123] See Dallimore, George Whitefield, II, pp. 173–5; and C. E. Welch, 'Andrew Kinsman's churches at Plymouth', Report and Transactions of the Devonshire Association for the Advancement of Science, Literature and Art, XCVII (1965), 212–36.

[124] 'An account of the origins of the Tabernacle Society 1741–1744', CMA 2946, p. 1.

However, Whitefield's appointment of Cennick was a disastrous misjudgement.[125] He had initially resisted the pressure to appoint Harris to the outright leadership of the revival possibly because of the many pressures on Harris's time and, even at this early date, because of some nagging doubts about Harris's theological and emotional stability. He therefore seems to have had little option but to opt for Cennick. Cennick was completely ill suited to the role. He was not an organizer like Harris or Whitefield, and was not able to command the respect of all of the factions that made up the increasingly fractious Tabernacle Society. He was also by this time extremely well disposed to the Moravians, a tendency of which Whitefield must have been aware before appointing him and something which would have aroused the opposition of many of the more extreme Calvinists in the society. Cennick's other-worldly piety, coupled with his somewhat depressive personality, meant that people did not gravitate to him in the same way as they did to the far more magnetic personalities of Whitefield and Harris. His lack of leadership therefore saw the Tabernacle Society descend into fresh bouts of recrimination and division, as its various factions jostled for supremacy. When the sole burden of the Whitefieldian movement was thrust upon him, it seems that Cennick's own psychological insecurities led him to find increasing solace in the warm and intimate piety of the Moravians. Always impressed by them, Cennick seems to have come to regard the Moravians as more attuned to his emotional needs, and the speed with which he resigned his leadership of the Tabernacle Society and linked with them indicates the extent of his desperation by the end of 1745.[126] Howel Harris played a vital role in the wake of the crisis and his presence at the Tabernacle ensured that it withstood the highly damaging impact of these additional secessions.

The Tabernacle Society, had, of course, always contained members who were well disposed to the Moravians. When Whitefield was present and actively committed to the leadership of the Tabernacle these differences remained largely hidden from sight. When he was absent, as he frequently was, they came to assume far greater prominence. Throughout much of 1744

[125] For more on the secession of John Cennick see Nuttall, *Howell Harris*, pp. 59–60; and Podmore, *The Moravian Church in England*, pp. 88–95.
[126] Dallimore, *George Whitefield*, II, pp. 232–4 and Podmore, *The Moravian Church in England*, pp. 88–95.

and 1745, John Cennick moved so close to the Moravians that by September 1745 he had completely repudiated his Calvinism and had adopted Arminianism, albeit in a modified form.[127] Concern from some within the society, who regarded themselves as the champions of Calvinistic orthodoxy, was voiced almost immediately, particularly because of the effect that Cennick's uncertain position was having on many other members who were beginning to attend Moravian meetings in greater numbers and with increasing frequency.[128] By this time Harris had also begun to harbour doubts about Cennick's suitability to lead the Tabernacle, and at the end of 1744 he travelled to London especially in order to quell some of the dissent that was beginning to surface within the society.[129] In January, he wrote to Whitefield informing him of the potential seriousness of the situation. In his letter he reduced Cennick's new theological position to a difference over two matters, the role of the Law in the life of the Christian and the true nature of sanctification, though at this stage he did not think that either opinion was a sufficient ground for the Tabernacle to dispense with his services.[130] Harris hoped, as was his preferred policy in such situations, that as long as each of the parties maintained open lines of communication problems could be easily overcome.

Cennick himself seems to have harboured some resentment at Whitefield's wish to leave him in total control of the Calvinistic revival. In one of his many letters to some of his Moravian friends during these months, Cennick accused Whitefield of quitting England because he suspected that the whole revival was about to collapse.[131] Colin Podmore suggests, with some justification, that this feeling was coupled with the suspicion that he was not really Whitefield's first choice to lead the movement anyway and that he had only been appointed because the time was not quite right for Harris's elevation to the leadership.[132] It would seem that the influential and domineering presence of Howel Harris loomed large in Cennick's mind throughout his ill-fated leadership of the English revival. Though there is no evidence of

---

[127] Podmore, *The Moravian Church in England*, pp. 90–1.
[128] Ibid., pp. 91–2.
[129] See HHD 115a, 2, 3, 7, 8 10 and 12 December 1744.
[130] Trevecka 1279, Howel Harris to George Whitefield (11 January 1745).
[131] Podmore, *The Moravian Church in England*, p. 91.
[132] Ibid.

any personal animosity between them, Cennick undoubtedly laboured under an acute sense of his own inferiority. The episode is yet another example of how the intense excitement of the early years of the revival masked, below the surface, tensions which duly emerged once the revival had settled into the more predictable routines of Christian discipleship.

Cennick's decision to leave the Whitefieldians came on the eve of the English Calvinistic Methodist Association in December 1745,[133] and his decision seems to have been made easier by the fact that he knew that Harris was on hand and prepared to pick up the reins. Harris remained conciliatory to the last, though he admitted to fearing that Cennick's loss would see the Tabernacle Society finally 'torn to pieces'.[134] In the event Harris reluctantly accepted the oversight of the English Calvinistic revival by default, because there was nobody else with the necessary credentials to take it on.[135] However, his diary entry following Cennick's departure hints that, because of his prior commitments in Wales, he was prepared to take on the role only until Whitefield returned from America or an alternative leader could be found.[136] Again it seems that Harris's role as the leader of the Welsh and English Calvinistic revivals prevented him from assuming outright leadership of either revival in a meaningful way. At the very moment when he was appointed to lead the English work he felt guilty at neglecting the Welsh revival and doubted whether he would be able to meet his new responsibility in the way it deserved. But at the same time, events in Wales were beginning to move out of his control as his protracted absences left a vacuum which Daniel Rowland all too readily filled.

Harris's main priority in the immediate aftermath of Cennick's departure was the care of the societies that Cennick himself had managed. At his instigation, the Association decided to hand them over to Cennick and the Moravians *en masse* with the promise that the Whitefieldian brethren would not 'labr among them witht first acquainting him & conferrg by Lettr or

---

[133] 'Proceedings at an Association held at the Tabernacle House, 4, 5, 6 and 11 December 1745', CMA 2946, p. 9.

[134] HHD 120, 25 November 1745.

[135] 'Proceedings at an Association held at the Tabernacle House, 4, 5, 6 and 11 December 1745', CMA 2946, p. 10 and Trevecka 1832, Thomas Boddington to Howel Harris (29 November 1748).

[136] HHD 120, 4 December 1745.

otherwise abt it'.[137] The loss of the Wiltshire societies together with the secession of about 400 members of the Tabernacle Society left English Calvinistic Methodism numerically and psychologically decimated. The task of regrouping and ultimately rebuilding was left in the hands of Harris and, during his absences in Wales, a small band of younger preachers such as James Beaumont,[138] Thomas Adams,[139] James Relly (1722–78),[140] Andrew Kinsman[141] and Herbert Jenkins. In effect, Whitefield's revival was left without any effective full-time leadership. In Harris's opinion, Whitefield was needed in London perhaps more than ever before, but in spite of his appeals Whitefield made no definite plans to return, leaving Harris to hold what remained of the English Calvinistic revival together largely by means of his own unbounded strength and charismatic personality.

Until Whitefield's return to England in July 1748, Harris spent the majority of his time in London[142] and struggled, along with his small band of preachers, to prevent the English Calvinistic revival from completely fragmenting. However, despite his efforts the movement continued to lose members. Both John Syms, Whitefield's secretary, and the influential Whitefieldian printer John Lewis followed Cennick's lead and transferred their allegiance to the Moravians.[143] Their reasons, apart from their obvious sympathy with Moravian theology and piety, were symptomatic of the deep-seated problems bedevilling the Whitefieldian revival. Whitefield's preference for the role of an inter-revival evangelist repeatedly left the Tabernacle Society without

---

[137] 'Proceedings at an Association held at the Tabernacle House, 4, 5, 6 and 11 December 1745', CMA 2946, pp. 9–14

[138] DWB, pp. 29–30; Roberts (ed.), Hanes Methodistiaeth Galfinaidd Cymru, Cyfrol I, pp. 223–5 and Geraint Tudur, ' "Like a right arm and a pillar": the story of James Beaumont', in Robert Pope (ed.), Honouring the Past and Shaping the Future: Religious and Biblical Studies in Wales: Essays in Honour of Gareth Lloyd Jones (Leominster, 2003), pp. 133–58.

[139] BDEB, p. 4; C. E. Watson, 'Whitefield and Congregationalism', Transactions of the Congregational Historical Society, 8, 4 (1922), 172–80 and 5 (1922), 227–45; G. F. Nuttall, 'Rowland Hill and the Rodborough Connexion 1771–1833', Transactions of the Congregational Historical Society, 21, 3 (1972), 69–73.

[140] For more on John Relly and other members of his family, see Gomer M. Roberts, 'The Moravians, John Relly and his people', CCHMC, XXXVIII, 1 (March 1953), 2–7.

[141] C. E. Welch, 'Andrew Kinsman's churches at Plymouth', passim.

[142] See Appendix 1, p. 343.

[143] On John Syms's secession see Trevecka 1279, Howel Harris to George Whitefield (11 January 1745) and Podmore, The Moravian Church in England, p. 90. For John Lewis's decision to join them see ibid., pp. 93–4.

strong leadership at a number of critical junctures. This lack of direction left many of his fellow Calvinists disillusioned with both Whitefield himself and the Calvinistic revival. Consequently, their decision to join one of the other evangelical groups that offered closer pastoral supervision and a more meaningful sense of community became all the easier.

However, to regard Harris's interim leadership of the revival as a mere stopgap measure that achieved very little would be unjust. Although he could not prevent the further secessions that took place,[144] he was able to use his new position to return to one of his favourite projects: brokering unity between the Whitefield-ians, Wesleyans and Moravians. In January 1747 Harris, together with John Wesley, presided over an important meeting of the leaders of their respective revivals at Bristol. All the leaders of the English Calvinistic revival made the journey and Wesley brought four of his most trusted preachers with him.[145] This meeting took place against the background of Harris's exhaustive efforts to pave the way for a more effective interaction between the two movements and was convened in order to 'remove any hindrances of Brotherly Love which have been'.[146] It stands out from many of the previous discussions because it addressed issues that related specifically to all the Methodist communities throughout the British Isles. It could conceivably be argued that it was at this meeting that the demarcation lines between the Calvinistic and the Wesleyan revivals were finally set in stone. There had always been a significant degree of overlap between the revival communities, with individuals regularly switching allegiances between the Calvinists, Wesleyans and Moravians as well as other more traditional Dissenting groups, but more damaging problems surfaced when groups deliberately set up rival societies expressly designed to poach members from other communities. The issue was particularly relevant because of Wesley's recent provocative activities in Neath, where, after he had preached for a few days, local Methodists felt sufficiently threatened to suspect him of attempting to split their society and founding his own Arminian group in the town, thereby gaining a

---

[144] Podmore, *The Moravian Church in England*, p. 90 and Dallimore, *George Whitefield*, II, pp. 238–9.
[145] HHD 125, 22 January 1747.
[146] 'Bristol, 22 January 1747', CMA 2946, p. 20.

more secure foothold in south Wales.[147] The gathering sought an amicable solution to the problem, firstly, by gaining from Wesley an assurance that he did not intend to cause a division in the Neath society. Wesley was clearly in an amicable mood and duly reciprocated by assuring those gathered that he had no intention of founding a rival society in Neath 'or in any Town in Wales where is a Society already',[148] and that furthermore he intended to endeavour with 'all that in me lies to prevent any such separation'.[149] On this basis discussions proved to be more frank than they might otherwise have been. The meeting managed to decide that not only should attempts to steal members from one another and compete for the same groups of unconverted souls be forbidden, but that whenever Calvinists and Wesleyans preached in each other's societies they should attempt at all times 'to strenth [sic], not to weaken, each others hands'.[150] This basically meant that they were each to avoid mentioning the doctrines that they knew would offend the other's converts. Calvinists were prevented from discussing predestination and Arminians were likewise forbidden from mentioning free will and sinless perfection.

There is no doubt that both Wesley and Harris were well intentioned in their desire to put the damaging theological wranglings of previous years behind them and to concentrate on those things that united them. If left to Harris and John Wesley, then, this might even have proved possible, but on a practical level it was completely unworkable. When Harris discussed these matters with John Wesley, he often did so without the wider support of the Calvinistic movement and tended to assume that because he and Wesley could come to a mutual understanding and place their friendship before their theological differences, his followers could and would do likewise. In reality, many of them were not prepared to do this, and many Calvinists were convinced that Wesley had ulterior motives when he preached among their ranks. The prospect of practical cooperation between the two bodies was therefore dealt a severe blow when Harris was dismissed from the London revival in 1750. Neither

---

[147] Williams, *John Wesley in Wales*, p. 25.
[148] 'Bristol, 22 January 1747', CMA 2946, pp. 21–2.
[149] Ibid., p. 22.
[150] Ibid., p. 22.

Whitefield, though he still maintained fairly amicable relations with Wesley, nor the leaders of the Welsh revival after 1750 had much sympathy with the Wesley brothers and tended to see matters in stark terms. Whitefield was clearly fearful that the numerically more powerful Wesleyan movement would overrun his English revival, whilst the Welsh remained relieved that Wesley did not see the need or have the means to develop a Welsh-speaking wing to his movement which would be able to challenge their own hegemony.

For a very brief period the concord that resulted from the Bristol conference had the effect of easing tensions between the two bodies in England. Nowhere was this more evident than in relation to the problems surrounding the new Methodist front that had been opened up in the south-west of England. Whitefield had first visited Plymouth on his way to the American colonies at the end of July 1744. He had preached in the city and at Tavistock on a number of occasions as he awaited the departure of his ship, and to his evident surprise he discovered that 'preaching at the Dock [Plymouth] is now like preaching at the Tabernacle'.[151] A Calvinistic society was established almost immediately and placed under the oversight of a local man, John Stevens.[152] The work grew rapidly under his leadership to the extent that a second society was established at nearby Devonport. In April 1746, John Wesley sent one of his preachers, John Godwin, to Plymouth. He vigorously opposed Herbert Jenkins, who had been sent from Whitefield's Tabernacle to oversee the settlement of some pressing matters within the society.[153] This had the result of splitting the Tabernacle into a number of factions, Arminian, Calvinist and Moravian, and these divisions were compounded by the rumour being circulated that Herbert Jenkins was on the verge of leading the society out of the Church of England altogether.[154] The situation was made worse when John Wesley visited Devon in September 1746. By December the Plymouth society had split, the Arminian faction concentrating its efforts on the society at Devonport and leaving the

---

[151] Quoted in Dallimore, *George Whitefield*, II, p. 175. For more on Whitefield's early ministry in Plymouth see ibid., pp. 173–6 and Welch, 'Andrew Kinsman's churches at Plymouth', 213–14.
[152] Welch, 'Andrew Kinsman's churches at Plymouth', 212–13.
[153] Ibid., 217.
[154] Ibid., 218–20.

Plymouth society to the Calvinists, who in turn had banned the Wesleyans from attending their society.

By 1747, therefore, all the problems endemic in most of the other Methodist societies were hampering the work in Plymouth. Tensions over theological matters and personality clashes had quickly surfaced, and the unity of the society was marred by a significant secession from its ranks. Matters had clearly become sufficiently serious for the issue to be raised and discussed in detail with the Wesleys at the Bristol meeting. These discussions led Harris and Wesley to agree to visit Plymouth and attempt to resolve the impasse by 'endeavouring to heal the breach there, and to insist on a spirit of love and its fruits among the people'.[155]

For Harris this attempt to rescue the Plymouth society from degenerating into recrimination and irrelevance, dragging the whole revival in the south-west of England down with it, was particularly important. His departure for the south-west immediately after the conclusion of the Bristol meeting is evidence enough of the significance he attached to these unfortunate developments. Over the preceding months he had followed the course of events in the south-west with characteristic enthusiasm, and his decision to visit, albeit in less than ideal circumstances, marked the beginning of a lengthy association with the Methodist communities in the area.[156] On meeting the Plymouth Methodists, Harris upbraided them for their fractiousness and told them that he believed that they had been overtaken by an 'evil spirit'.[157] In slightly more rational discussions with the society he reasoned that although Whitefield had commenced the work in the south-west they should not let their allegiance to him and their preference for Calvinism prevent them from benefiting from the ministry of the Wesley brothers and their followers. The fullest account of these discussions is in Harris's diary, and the vehemence of his remarks indicates both the seriousness of the situation in Plymouth and the extent to which

[155]   'Bristol, 22 January 1747', CMA 2946, p. 22.
[156]   For example, he was in the area a year later during January 1748, and his association with the south-west was reinforced when he later joined the Breconshire militia in 1759. In 1761, Harris and his company were stationed in the south-west at Bridgwater, Bideford, Barnstaple, Torrington and Plymouth itself. During these months he continued to preach and exhort and made efforts to contact Methodist societies in the area. See Tom Beynon (ed.), *Howell Harris: Reformer and Soldier, 1714–1773* (Caernarfon, 1958), pp. 58–146.
[157]   HHD 125, 10 February 1747.

he had become convinced that the Bristol meeting a fortnight earlier had ushered in a new spirit of tolerance between the Whitefieldians and the Wesleyans, in London at least:

> Called a private society and spoke of Mr Whitefield's beginning the work here, and though I differ with Mr Wesley in some points, yet I love and honour him as my brother and God's minister, and stabbing him is stabbing me. I would not have a hand in hindering him or any peaceable brother of his assistants from coming here for the world, for I invite him to our societies in Wales.[158]

Predictably, some did not accept Harris's reasoning and were still not prepared to compromise and welcome the heterodox Wesleyans into their midst. Some members left the society and formed their own society with an exclusively Calvinistic basis of faith and a more strictly separatist ecclesiology. Those who remained in the original society largely accepted Harris's point of view, and Andrew Kinsman was persuaded to remain as its leader until a measure of peace was restored.[159]

The Bristol meeting and the events that had taken place in Plymouth set the agenda for Whitefield's return to England in July 1747. Largely as a result of the dogged persistence of Howel Harris, both the Calvinistic and Wesleyan wings of the English revival were once again on speaking terms, and a fairly amicable truce between the two camps had been agreed. Harris clearly expected Whitefield to be impressed with these developments and to respond enthusiastically by re-energizing his converts and continuing negotiations with the Wesleys, in the hope that eventually they would be able to heal the breach between their two revivals. However, by the time he returned to England, Whitefield's priorities had undergone a profound change and were very different from those which Harris had anticipated. Despite Harris's efforts, Whitefield's London revival had shrunk almost beyond recognition during his absence, while Wesley's movement had grown to be the dominant expression of Methodism in England. Whitefield returned reluctant to invest

---

[158] HHD 125, 14 February 1747 and Beynon (ed.), *Howell Harris's Visits to London*, pp. 124–5.
[159] HHD 125, 12 February 1747 and Beynon (ed.), *Howell Harris's Visits to London*, p. 125.

all his energies in the reinvigoration of his London base at the risk of reopening the old divisions with the Wesleys and reviving the competitive relationship between the two movements. Therefore, in a letter to John Wesley shortly after his return to England, Whitefield put an end to speculation that a reunion was possible and signalled his intention to take a far less prominent role.[160]

Even before his arrival in England, Whitefield had decided to relinquish his role as Moderator of Calvinistic Methodism in England and Wales, so that he would be able to act with a measure of freedom in whichever revival he chose to be. His wish was strengthened by the patronage of the countess of Huntingdon, who wished to make Whitefield her personal chaplain. Boyd Schlenther, in his recently published biography of the countess, has argued that it was in response to this, rather than as a result of the persistence of Howel Harris, that Whitefield had finally returned to England.[161] However, he needed someone to take permanent control of the Calvinistic societies and shoulder the burden of the English work. Harris seemed the obvious choice. He had been doing the job in an unofficial capacity since John Cennick had left the movement, but Whitefield seems to have been reluctant to appoint him because of the fairly poor state in which he had found the London revival on his return. According to Geraint Tudur this was an important development in their relationship, and from this time onwards Whitefield began to modify his opinion of Harris's gifts and to harbour serious doubts about his long-term suitability to lead the English revival. It is likely that Whitefield had already heard about some of the problems that Harris's customary belligerence and sympathy for some aspects of Moravian piety were beginning to cause in Wales, and when this is combined with his evident disappointment over the state of the Tabernacle, it is little wonder that Whitefield's suspicions and fears were aroused.[162] None the less, in the absence of an obvious alternative, Whitefield persisted in attempting to persuade Harris to take on the full-time oversight of the English Calvinistic

---

[160] Dallimore, *George Whitefield*, II, p. 250.

[161] Schlenther, *The Queen of the Methodists*, p. 39.

[162] Geraint Tudur quotes Whitefield's remark to John Wesley in relation to his reluctance to found any more societies because of the shortage of 'proper assistants to take care of them' in support of this view. See Tudur, *Howell Harris*, pp. 185–6.

societies. By the end of July 1748, it appears that Harris was on the verge of accepting, only to change his mind and withdraw at the last minute.[163] Whitefield's concerns about Harris were at least alleviated by the extent of Harris's support among the members of the society. After a crisis meeting at the Tabernacle in November 1748, Thomas Boddington wrote to Harris urging him to reconsider his decision and assuring him of the support of the majority in the Tabernacle society:

> Mr Whitefield said, He would as far as in him lay, encourage & strengthen ye Hands of anyone who would take ye Charge of it before God. We then mentioned you [. . .] Mr Whitefield said he would be very glad for ye People sake, if you wou'd undertake it but at ye same time added he believed you was not free to labour among us in London anymore [. . .] Can you bear it should be said ye Tabernacle Society was broke up & scattered abroad like sheep without a shepherd [because] Mr Harris slighted the call of its poor members to watch over them.[164]

Harris, however, still remained reluctant to accept the will of the English Calvinists, and so Whitefield had little option but to approach two other members of the society, James Relly and Thomas Adams. There is little doubt that Harris felt pressured by Whitefield into agreeing to take on the leadership of the revival even though he had been its *de facto* leader since the end of 1745, but there was confusion over his intentions owing to his lack of self-confidence and, by this stage, his declining mental health.[165] The resulting uncertainty over his commitment to the role led Whitefield to pursue his discussions with Relly and Adams with increased urgency in September 1749 and to suggest to them that it would be better if they actually replaced Harris as leaders of the movement.[166] Harris reacted angrily to this development and threatened total withdrawal from the English revival if he was expected to share the leadership with these more

---

[163] HHD 131b, 20 July 1748.

[164] Trevecka 1832, Thomas Boddington to Howel Harris (29 November 1748).

[165] Harris's psychological state in the later 1740s has been overlooked by most of his biographers and has not been thought to have a significant impact on the disruption of the revival in 1750. For example, Eifion Evans in his biographies of Harris and Rowland makes no mention of it in his detailed studies of the divisions of 1750. See Evans, *Howell Harris*, pp. 45–57 and Evans, *Daniel Rowland*, pp. 269–80. For a more balanced analysis see Tudur, *Howell Harris*, pp. 216–17, 224–5, 231.

[166] 'Low, 27 April 1749', CMA 2946, pp. 67–8.

junior figures.[167] In his own defence he cited Relly's and Adams's earlier refusal to accept the leadership when Whitefield had tried to persuade them to share it or for one or other to take it on alone.[168] For Harris the débâcle was further proof of the weakness of the position of the English Calvinistic revival. The solution in his eyes was relatively simple. Either Relly or Adams should accept the leadership of the movement in their own right or Harris should be installed as the overall leader as soon as possible. A shared leadership was, in his opinion, entirely out of the question and a recipe for confusion, given the revival's history of attracting individuals whose personalities were often far larger than the movement itself.[169] After considerable discussion a compromise was reached. Harris was appointed to sole leadership of the movement, and Relly and Adams were instructed to act as his assistants.[170]

The debate surrounding the leadership of the English revival witnessed a decisive shift in the relationship between Harris and Whitefield. Prior to Whitefield's return from the American colonies the two had been the closest of associates and over the course of the previous ten years had shared their thoughts about every aspect of the revival. In Whitefield's absence, Harris, undoubtedly as a result of the burden of shouldering the bulk of the responsibility for the revival in England and Wales, was close to a complete mental and physical breakdown. He had become more awkward and unaccommodating, fiercely protective of his own reputation and denunciatory of all who dared to oppose him. Whitefield began to find him increasingly 'proud and arbitrary'[171] and became more ready to challenge his old friend in public as well as in private.[172] Harris also lamented this change in their relationship and complained of Whitefield's relative coldness towards him, which made him feel that perhaps he had fulfilled his usefulness in England.[173] Yet despite his misgivings, Whitefield was still prepared to defend Harris and saw little

---

[167] HHD 135, 27 April 1749.
[168] Ibid.
[169] HHD 136, 1 September 1749.
[170] 'At an Association held at London 1, 2, 4, 6 and 7 September 1749', CMA 2946, pp. 71–4; and HHD 136, 1–6 September 1749, passim.
[171] HHD 136, 4 September 1749.
[172] Ibid.
[173] HHD 136, 2 September 1749.

alternative but to make him the leader of the English revival,[174] although it was more than likely that this had more to do with Whitefield's desire to divest himself of responsibility for the English Calvinistic societies than with his waning confidence in Harris's abilities.

As Whitefield voluntarily retreated from the day-to-day affairs of the Calvinistic societies in London, Harris tried to revive his exploratory discussions with the Wesley brothers and the Moravians and, despite Whitefield's distinct lack of enthusiasm, still harboured hopes that he could 'lay a solid foundation for a lasting union'[175] with them. However, Harris's pursuit of this course became yet another cause of tension with Whitefield. Whitefield was far from convinced that a reunion with the Wesley brothers was possible or even desirable, and cited their remaining theological differences as far too substantial to be surmounted as easily as Harris anticipated. It also appears that Whitefield felt somewhat threatened by the strength of the Wesleyan movement and seems to have suspected that if there were to be a reunion it would undoubtedly mean that his societies would be further undermined and their separate identity completely compromised. The alternative to this – launching a new evangelistic enterprise aimed at attracting new members to the movement in large numbers – was undesirable and impractical, given the lack of manpower that was slowly crippling his London societies.[176]

None the less, Whitefield allowed Harris a measure of freedom and agreed to attend a meeting that Harris had arranged with the Wesleyans at Bristol in August 1749. It was a friendly occasion, characterized by something resembling the spirit that had been present among them in the early days of the revival. Harris admitted to feeling 'nearer union in spirit in singing a hymn than ever before',[177] and both factions agreed once again to avoid discussing any controversial subjects in their sermons and 'to come together to prevent the people's saying of either side we have changed our opinions'.[178] Both factions also reaffirmed their allegiance to the Established Church until such

---

[174] HHD 136, 4 September 1749.
[175] HHD 136, 7 September 1749.
[176] Dallimore, *George Whitefield*, II, pp. 250–1.
[177] HHD 136, 3 August 1749.
[178] HHD 136, 2 August 1749.

time as they were compelled to leave it.[179] For Harris the meeting was a great success:

> Our hearts were united in much love and freedom. [. . .] Shewed we don't come together from necessity, because we are now more likely to flourish than ever [. . .] I declared how I feel the need of them [the Wesley brothers], and they said they felt the need of us too, that one's excellency might be communicated to the other, and so we parted lovingly and strengthened.[180]

Harris and Whitefield left the Wesley brothers in Bristol committed to recommending that their members unhesitatingly adopt the proposals and strive to avoid anything that would bring the revival into disrepute or halt its progress. However, little actually came from the meeting. Whitefield's understandable lack of enthusiasm for further concessions to the Wesleyans was undoubtedly to blame. Harris had long suspected that Whitefield was not committed to exploring ways in which to heal the breach between their societies, and ever since Whitefield's return from America, he had seen fit, on numerous occasions, to rebuke Whitefield publicly for his attitude. Whitefield's reaction to this meeting seemed to be proof positive of his real attitude.[181] It had, by this time, become fairly deeply ingrained, to the extent that Whitefield believed, in spite of appearances to the contrary, that neither the Wesleyan movement nor the Moravian cause had a very promising long-term future.[182]

---

[179] Ibid.
[180] HHD 136, 3 August 1749.
[181] See for example HHD 135, 12 April 1749.
[182] HHD 135, 9 April 1749.

VI

'TRANSCRIPTS OF MY HEART': WELSH METHODISTS AND POPULAR PIETY

Interaction between the Welsh Methodist revival and the other awakenings that together constituted the evangelical revival was not something that took place merely between the pioneer revivalists. The rank-and-file converts of the Welsh revival found that participation in an international community of saints shaped their experience of the revival as much as did their leaders. They were as conscious of the international dimensions of their movement as the revivalists were, and often as eager to avail themselves of the opportunities for meaningful lay participation.

Rank-and-file Welsh Methodist interaction with the wider evangelical movement was complex and multi-layered. For the historian seeking to unravel some of these interrelationships it is tempting, through the accessibility of sources, to limit one's attention to the perspective of the pioneer revivalists and to be content with assigning their views to their converts, ignoring any differences that might exist in the popular appropriation of the same doctrines, experiences and events.[1] By examining some of the ways in which the rank-and-file members of the Welsh revival interacted with the wider evangelical community, it is possible to balance the view of the revival, gleaned exclusively from the writings of the revivalists, with that of those individuals who did not move in the same circles and whose day-to-day lives were lived on a far more mundane level. This balance between the 'elite' and the 'popular' experience of the revival has much to tell us of the ways in which evangelicalism developed, some of the reasons for its enthusiastic reception in society and some of the precise ways in which it met the needs of those who saw in the evangelical movement an outlet for their frustrated ambitions and an ideal platform for their intellectual and social betterment.

---

[1] Christopher Marsh, *Popular Religion in Sixteenth Century England* (London, 1998), p. 6.

The focus on popular religion, or popular piety, needs more precise definition. The term has invariably come to be used in different ways by a range of historians. For some, largely following the paradigm outlined by Keith Thomas[2] and Peter Burke,[3] 'popular religion', like its counterpart 'popular culture', is taken to mean the unofficial beliefs of the mass of the population and usually includes the folk beliefs that the more committed members of the ranks of the 'godly' would never have classified as being remotely religious. For others, 'popular religion' means no more than the religion of the laity, denoting the experience of those who constituted the rank-and-file membership of a particular religious movement.[4] It is in this second way, what Barry Reay has termed 'religion as taken up at the popular level',[5] that the term is used in this study.

David Hempton's work on Methodism and popular religion has forced historians of first-generation evangelicalism to ask far more penetrating questions about how those who responded to the message of the revivalists so enthusiastically 'heard and appropriated'[6] the message. They are questions that have only recently begun to be reflected in the work of historians of the Welsh Methodist Revival.[7] Much of the historiography of Welsh Methodism, as has been repeatedly pointed out, has been content to perpetuate an interpretation of the revival that has stemmed almost solely from the diaries and letters of Howel Harris. This is of course understandable, given their sheer volume and their coverage of all the most important events in the

---

[2]   Keith Thomas, *Religion and the Decline of Magic* (London, 1971).
[3]   Peter Burke, *Popular Culture in Early Modern Europe* (London, 1978), pp. 207–43.
[4]   For examples of historians who have adopted this latter approach see Jon Butler, *Awash in a Sea of Faith: Christianising the American People* (Cambridge, MA, 1990); John H. Wigger, *Taking Heaven by Storm: Methodism and the Rise of Popular Christianity in America* (New York, 1998); the extremely influential James Obelkevich, *Religion and Rural Society: South Lindsey, 1825–1875* (Oxford, 1976), detailing popular piety among Primitive Methodists; and the equally important Deborah M. Valenze, *Prophetic Sons and Daughters: Female Preaching and Popular Religion in Industrial England* (Princeton, 1985).
[5]   Barry Reay, 'Popular Religion', in Barry Reay (ed.), *Popular Culture in Seventeenth Century England* (London, 1985), p. 91.
[6]   David Hempton, ' "Motives, methods and margins": a comparative study of Methodist expansion in the north Atlantic world, c.1750–1900', in Hempton, *The Religion of the People*, p. 28.
[7]   See White, ' "The world, the flesh and the devil" '; White, 'Women in the early Methodist societies in Wales', 95–108; and for readers of Welsh, White, *Praidd Bach y Bugail Mawr*. Also important in this respect is Morgan, *The Great Awakening in Wales*.

history of the revival, but their use has tended to foster an approach that has failed adequately to take into account the different perspectives of some of the other Welsh revivalists, Howel Davies and Daniel Rowland in particular, and it has meant that historians have found it extremely difficult to break free from writing about the revival from any other perspective than that of the higher ranks of its leadership.

Assessing the experiences of the rank-and-file members of any religious movement is dependent on the use of the most appropriate sources. This can of course include the use of sources that social historians of religion have always deployed,[8] but it can also include examining popular literature, as opposed to the more didactic literature produced by religious elites, conversion narratives, correspondence, wills, court records and various ecclesiastical records.[9] The key to uncovering the hidden world of the rank and file usually has as much to do with the way in which these sources are used and the questions that are asked of them as with the use of radically different sources. The most obvious danger in examining the rank and file relates to historians' expectations of their beliefs. It is misleading to transfer the experience and apparent sophistication of the leaders of a religious movement to their followers and to regard those who do not measure up to the standards set by the leaders as in some way deficient or even heterodox.[10] Christopher Marsh, in the introduction to his study of popular religion in sixteenth-century England, has highlighted many of the dangers facing historians as they try to free themselves from the shackles imposed by religious elites. He warns against allowing our own perspective on the past, informed by very different presuppositions, to colour our objectivity and prevent our contextualization of religious faith in the past, and he cautions that sixteenth-century people did not always prize intellectual consistency as much as we appear to do today. Their religious convictions were consequently often far more complex than their leaders would have

---

[8]   Marsh, *Popular Religion in Sixteenth Century England*, pp. 9–12.
[9]   Tim Harris, 'Problematising popular culture', in Tim Harris (ed.), *Popular Culture in England, c.1500–1850* (London, 1995), pp. 6–10.
[10]   Natalie Zemon Davis, 'Some tasks and themes in the study of popular religion', in C. Trinkaus and H. A. Oberman (eds), *The Pursuit of Holiness in Late Medieval and Renaissance Religion* (Leiden, 1974), p. 309.

wished and historians have sometimes been prepared to countenance.[11]

Simplistic models of elite versus popular, or clergy versus lay,
are therefore not always as helpful as they might appear and
rarely reveal the complex web of human relationships in any
human organization or religious movement. For example, individuals were often attracted to religious movements, particularly
of the evangelical variety, despite their social status, and, as Tim
Harris has cautioned, the religious division that Protestantism
encouraged 'cut vertically through . . . society rather than
horizontally',[12] giving poor Methodists, for example, a stronger
sense of cultural identity with better-off Methodists than with
people of a similar social standing who did not share their
religious faith.[13] A model that stresses the collective nature of
Methodist piety or spirituality and uncovers the continuity
between the experience of the revivalists and those whom they
led may be more helpful. Spirituality, as Gordon Wakefield has
pointed out, is the amalgam of 'attitudes, beliefs and practices
which animate people's lives and help them reach out towards
supersensible realities'.[14] According to John Kent this need, what
he calls 'primary religion',[15] remains constant, but the institu-
tional means by which it is met change from generation to
generation and from country to country.[16]

Students of first-generation evangelicalism in Wales, as well as
further afield, are blessed with a surprisingly large corpus of
material with which to open a window on to the lives and

[11]   See Marsh, *Popular Religion in Sixteenth Century England*, pp. 10–3.
[12]   Harris, 'Problematising popular culture', p. 26.
[13]   Ibid., pp. 25–7.
[14]   Gordon Wakefield, 'Spirituality', in A. Richardson and J. Bowden (eds), *New
Dictionary of Theology* (London, 1983), p. 539. For an introduction to Christian
spirituality, a more detailed definition and an analysis of some of its main varieties see
Alistair E. McGrath, *Christian Spirituality: An Introduction* (Oxford, 1999).
[15]   John Kent, *Wesley and the Wesleyans: Religion in Eighteenth-Century Britain*
(Cambridge, 2002), pp. 1–9.
[16]   The historiography of evangelicalism has recently begun to look at the nature of its
own spirituality. On the role of the conversion experience see David Bebbington,
'Evangelical conversion, c. 1740–1850', *Scottish Bulletin of Evangelical Theology*, 18, 2
(Autumn, 2000), 102–27. On women's piety see Linda Wilson, *Constrained by Zeal:
Female Spirituality amongst Nonconformists, 1825–1875* (Carlisle, 2000). For
comparative purposes see Charles D. Cashdollar, *A Spiritual Home: Life in British and
American Reformed Congregations, 1830–1915* (University Park, PA, 2000); Grant
Wacker, *Heaven Below: Early Pentecostals and American Culture* (Cambridge, MA,
2001); and Ian M. Randall, *Evangelical Experiences: A Study in the Spirituality of
English Evangelicalism, 1918–1939* (Carlisle, 1999).

experiences of some of the 'ordinary' members of the Welsh Methodist community. Although it was the visionary Howel Harris who was originally responsible for introducing the Welsh revival to the international community of saints, its strength and longevity stemmed from the enthusiastic support which grass-roots evangelicals in Wales lent it, in a whole series of ways. By examining their correspondence, both published and unpublished, in the Trevecka Letters collection and in John Lewis's religious magazine between 1740 and 1748, and the literature we know they were reading, and by analysing some of the ways in which they spent their money, it is possible to reconstruct a picture of what being a Methodist meant for many otherwise anonymous people in mid-eighteenth-century Wales.

At the most fundamental level, evangelicalism, in all of its various guises, was an intensely spiritual movement, based on a radically life-changing experience that was transmitted from person to person.[17] While Methodism offered its members a coherent theology, whether it happened to be Calvinist, Arminian, Moravian or a mixture of all three, for most of its members the attraction was primarily emotional and pastoral. The revival drew individuals who shared their experience of the New Birth in common. It built on this highly individualistic foundation by moulding these twice-born saints into a community in which each member invested considerable energy and consequently felt strong bonds of attachment. These bonds were supported by close ties of kinship and by the support network that was built into the movement from its earliest days. In Wales, Methodism drew much of its resilience from the energy and commitment of its active grass-roots members.

Like their leaders, these Methodists had been drawn primarily, though not exclusively, from the middling ranks of society. They had been the main recipients of the benefits of the major advances in literacy and education that had occurred in the first decades of the eighteenth century and had, as a result, been preconditioned to accept the dynamic message of the Methodist

---

[17]   Hempton, *The Religion of the People*, p. 2.

revivalists.[18] They shared their leaders' insatiable appetite for knowledge and deep-seated concern for the spiritual plight of their fellow countrymen and women, features which ensured that the religious revival quickly became one of the most useful tools by which they could initiate the reformation and evangelistic campaign that many of their Protestant predecessors had found beyond them.[19] Evangelical religion was therefore particularly attractive to them. Its stress on an intensely emotional experience of God and the nurturing that took place within the societies became the context in which many of the middling sorts exercised autonomy over their religious lives at the same time as they were attaining independence in many other aspects of their lives.

In a sense these early evangelicals stood out from the societies in which they lived, and to talk of their religious beliefs as popular (as opposed to elite) religion can be misleading. The middling sorts were not a particularly large group in Wales. Margaret Hunt has estimated that in England as a whole between 1660 and 1730, the middling sorts did not amount to any more than about 20 per cent of the population.[20] In Wales, which did not boast a town of more than 2,000 inhabitants until after 1750,[21] the proportion of middling sorts was considerably smaller. Within the ranks of the Welsh revival the social status of the revivalists and their followers, particularly in the revival's early years, was often similar, if not identical. The first generation of Methodists were, in many cases, the parents and grandparents of the very people who in later generations became the elite, as Methodism became the strongest religious denomination in Wales. In the mid- and late eighteenth century the middling people, some of whom had been attracted to evangelical religion in the 1730s, formed what Gwyn A. Williams, in reference to the later decades of the eighteenth century, has called an alternative Welsh society.[22] It was a rival society that

---

[18]   See above, pp. 59–64.

[19]   See Schmidt, *Holy Fairs* and Ward, *The Protestant Evangelical Awakening*.

[20]   Margaret R. Hunt, *The Middling Sort: Commerce, Gender and the Family in England, 1680–1780* (Berkeley, California, 1996), p. 17.

[21]   Philip Jenkins, 'Wales', in Peter Clark (ed.), *The Cambridge Urban History of Britain, II: 1540–1840* (Cambridge, 2000), pp. 133–49 and Jenkins, *The Foundations of Modern Wales*, pp. 115–19, 285–9.

[22]   Gwyn A. Williams, *When was Wales?: A History of the Welsh* (London, 1985), p. 151.

included among its members Dissenters, antiquarians, historians, poets and radical free-thinkers whose newly acquired economic independence afforded them the opportunity to act beyond the constraints of the traditional authority structure that had excluded them for centuries.

Amongst those middling people for whom evangelical religion acted as a socially as well as a spiritually liberating experience, none benefited as much as women. Gail Malmgreen, on the basis of her study of East Cheshire Methodism, has shown that 'in modern Western cultures, religion has been a predominantly female sphere'.[23] Undoubtedly inspired by the examples of pious women in the Bible, women found in evangelicalism a natural outlet for their energies and ambitions in which they could both exercise autonomy over their religious lives and have some degree of influence over their friends and neighbours. In a solidly patriarchal society in which women had little opportunity to act independently of their husbands, evangelical religion reminded them that they were individuals fully responsible for their own eternal destinies and in control of their own spiritual lives. As well as providing them with an outlet for their energies, it integrated them into a community in which they were expected to play a full part and in which their experiences and insights were deemed to be on a par with those of their male counterparts.[24] This is not to say that they were regarded as being equal with men. In mainstream Methodism women were not usually permitted to preach or lead societies. The exceptions to this principle were due to the peculiarities of individual situations, and it was only in the more radical wings of Methodism

[23] Gail Malmgreen, 'Domestic discords: women and the family in east Cheshire Methodism, 1730–1830', in J. Obelkevich, L. Roper and R. Samuel (eds), *Disciplines of Faith: Studies on Religion, Politics and Patriarchy* (London, 1987), p. 56. See also Clive D. Field, 'The social composition of English Methodism to 1830: a membership analysis', *Bulletin of the John Rylands University Library of Manchester*, 76, 1 (Spring 1994), 155–8.

[24] See White, 'Women in the early Methodist societies in Wales', 95–108 and Eryn M. White, 'Women, religion and education in eighteenth-century Wales', in Michael Roberts and Simone Clarke (eds), *Women and Gender in Early Modern Wales* (Cardiff, 2000), pp. 210–33. For the wider context see Olwen Hufton, *The Prospect before Her: A History of Women in Western Europe, I: 1500–1800* (London, 1997), pp. 359–418; Merry E. Wiesner, *Women and Gender in Early Modern Europe* (Cambridge, 1993), pp. 179–217; Patricia Crawford, *Women and Religion in England, 1500–1720* (London, 1993); and M. J. Westerkamp, *Women and Religion in Early America, 1600–1850: The Puritan and Evangelical Traditions* (London, 1999).

that female preaching was permitted during the later eighteenth century.[25] For many women contributing to the evangelical letter-writing network became the primary means by which they supplemented the spiritual diets that they received in their local societies. For the years between 1738 and 1750, the Trevecka Letters contain almost 500 letters (25 per cent of the total) either written to, or penned by, women[26] and, in a similar way, the religious magazines contained a substantial number of letters from female correspondents.[27]

Throughout the first decade of the revival in England and Wales, there was a group of between twelve and fifteen women, some based in England at Whitefield's Tabernacle Society or at Bristol, but the majority in Wales itself, who kept up a regular correspondence with Howel Harris and one another.[28] Harris was the hub around which this correspondence network flourished. Most of its participants had been introduced to each other through their links with either Harris or one of the other revivalists. Sarah Mason, for example, was introduced to Harris by her husband, Samuel Mason, Whitefield's London-based printer, while Elizabeth Thomas, from Longhouse in Pembrokeshire, and Sarah Gwynne, from Garth, Breconshire, gained access to the correspondence network by virtue of their membership of influential Methodist families. In a sense many of these women were not typical of the revival as a whole. They tended to be women of independent means, or ones who, as a result of their well-placed evangelical connections, were able to occupy positions that would have remained closed to the majority of women. It seems quite realistic to argue that some of the letters written by this otherwise anonymous group of correspondents opens a window onto the experience of Methodists immediately below the level of the revivalists, allowing us to

---

[25]   See Valenze, *Prophetic Sons and Daughters*; Paul Wesley Chilcote, *John Wesley and the Women Preachers of Early Methodism* (Metuchen and London, 1991); and idem, *'She Offered Them Christ': The Legacy of Women Preachers in Early Methodism* (Nashville, 1991).

[26]   See Appendix 2, pp. 344–6.

[27]   See Appendix 3, pp. 347–8.

[28]   The most regular contributors to the correspondence network from the English revival included Elizabeth Clifford, Anne Dutton, Elizabeth Godwin, Jane Godwin, Sister Kiggell, Sarah Mason and Elizabeth Paul. From Wales came Mrs Bowen (Tyddyn), Elizabeth Thomas (Longhouse), Anne Williams (later Harris), Elizabeth James (later Whitefield), Sarah Gwynne and Catherine and Mary Pugh.

gauge the extent to which their experiences mirrored those of their leaders.

In reference to John Wesley's *Arminian Magazine* of the later decades of the eighteenth century, Margaret Jones has argued that the nature of the material contributed to such evangelical magazines afforded women the opportunity to make their voices heard.[29] The revivalists' adoption of the epistolary form, which encouraged individuals to relate their experiences to their contemporaries, contributed to a blurring of gender roles. By elevating the conversion experience to such critical importance and delineating the signs which proved the genuineness of each conversion, the revivalists encouraged their converts to examine their spiritual experiences in a detailed way in order to identify signs of genuine grace. This was done in a whole series of ways, most regularly within the privacy of society meetings. Those with particularly clear testimonies, or with testimonies which had involved conversion from particularly flagrant lifestyles, were often encouraged to commit their experience to paper so that their cases could be an example and a help to others. Since the conversion experience was identical in both men and women, there were no rational grounds for preventing women from penning their own accounts of their experiences.

Despite Margaret Jones's insistence that this usually meant that women adopted the style dictated by their male leaders,[30] there were subtle differences between the ways in which men and women wrote. Women were more willing to discuss the intricacies of their experiences and emotional development than their male counterparts were, and they tended to be far more honest in their accounts of their fears and doubts. This was largely due to the very different roles that they occupied in the revival. Men occupied all the most important leadership roles. There were no female revivalists, superintendents, exhorters or society stewards, for example. Men's letters therefore tended to be more concerned with issues relating directly to theological matters, administrative problems and plans for the consolidation and advancement of the revival. Denied access to the offices that

---

[29]   Margaret P. Jones, ' "The state of my soul to exalted piety": women's voices in the Arminian/Methodism Magazine, 1778–1821', pp. 273–4.

[30]   Ibid., pp. 276–7.

these men occupied, women focused more closely on issues relating to their own spiritual pilgrimages, and consequently wrote more freely about their doubts, fears, disappointments and frustrations. A select few were more confident and took it upon themselves to counsel and even exhort their leaders, contribute to theological debates and on some occasions even disagree with their supposed fathers in the faith when they perceived them to be mistaken.

What has never been adequately appreciated is the extent and range of the network of communications that operated beneath the level of the revivalists and that at times existed independent of their immediate control. The Welsh Methodists were not a collection of misfits who had retreated from the 'world' and formed an alternative society that cut them off from those who did not share their enthusiastic evangelicalism. They were a highly sophisticated group of people, literate, well read, often financially comfortably off and amongst the best-informed people in the country, belonging to a movement that forced them to look beyond their own experience and locality and to place themselves in the vanguard of what God was doing in the world.

The rank-and-file Welsh Methodists' participation in the international communications network may be approached from two perspectives. It can used to understand the nature of Welsh Methodist spirituality or popular piety. The first generation of Welsh Methodist converts followed the course of the revival through letters and magazines, learned about the true nature of New Birth, participated in some of the theological debates among their leaders, and sought advice and counsel from those more senior in the faith than themselves; their experience illustrates how they benefited from being part of a movement in which every member was expected to help others in a variety of ways. The material may also be used to uncover some of the ways in which they interacted with the wider revival community, the Christian community more broadly defined and the secular state in which they lived. It shows how they took a keen interest in all the inter-revival projects that their leaders initiated and how they sought solace from one another when it appeared that their very existence was under threat because of the consti-

tutional threats to the British state posed by the Jacobites in the
mid-1740s. Many Welsh Methodists therefore had a far more
rounded view of the world than may at first appear. On both a
spiritual and a practical level the rank-and-file Welsh evangelicals were at the forefront of the international revival, and the
contours of their movement were often decisively shaped by their
commitment to it.

Not surprisingly, rank-and-file Welsh Methodists adopted the same
terminology as their leaders when they referred to the revivals in
which they occupied such a prominent part. Many of them seemed
as aware of the international dimensions of the evangelical movement as Howel Harris and George Whitefield and at times they
even matched their enthusiasm for international news and contacts. To them also, the revival was the 'glorious Work [. . .] in
the world,'[31] and they revelled in the fact that 'in many nations the
Gospel is spreading its healing wings'.[32] Their realization that the
revival was making remarkable progress in 'Scotland, Yorkshire,
Lincolnshire, Warwickshire, Wiltshire, Germany, Prussia, New
England, Pennsylvania and many other provinces'[33] led many of
them to take every opportunity to find out more about the progress
of the Gospel. This they did through letters, those that they
themselves received from Harris or Whitefield, those they heard
read aloud in their local societies, and those they read in the pages
of *The Weekly History*. Anne Thomas from Longhouse,
Pembrokeshire, for example, was thrilled to receive some copies of
The Weekly History: 'I receivd [. . .] the Weekly Histories which
you was so kind as to send me [. . .] I think my soul has received
some Benefit in reading them. O how sweet is it to hear how the
Lord brings in his work.'[34] Thomas Jones, a clergyman from Cwm-
iou near Abergavenny in Monmouthshire,[35] wrote of the 'sensible
pleasure' he felt after reading 'such comfortable Accounts of the

[31] 'Extract of a letter from a minister in the country to his friend in LONDON' (3
February 1742), *WH* 46 (Saturday, 20 February 1742).
[32] Ibid.
[33] Trevecka 2803, Howel Harris to Herbert Jenkins (22 November 1742).
[34] 'The copy of a letter from Mrs Anne T—s of PEMBROKESHIRE in WALES to MR
HOWEL HARRIS in LONDON (Longhouse, 3 September 1742)', *WH* 80 (Saturday, 16
October 1742).
[35] See Eifion Evans, 'Thomas Jones, Cwm-iou (1689–1772)', *CCHMC* (1984),
24–31.

free Course and Success of the precious Gospel of JESUS CHRIST in Foreign Parts',[36] whilst an anonymous brother from Ashford in Kent, wrote:

> It is a Matter of Joy and Consolation to see and hear of the Progress of the Gospel [in] divers parts of this Christian Realm, and that the primitive Purity of the Gospel is reviving; that there is a breathing upon the dry bones. It is most wonderfully refreshing to read the Accounts that we have noted in the Weekly History![37]

The thirst for news about the progress of the revival was not limited to a few well-connected individuals. When the English Calvinistic Methodists met at the Tabernacle for what, at the height of the revival in the early 1740s, was a monthly Letter Day, the sheer bulk of news that was read did not seem to overwhelm them or dim their enthusiasm.[38] Their response to the news received on these occasions was often expressed in hymns that had been written specially for these evangelical feast days. The 'Hymn of intercession and thanksgiving for the progress of the Gospel in various parts of the world', which was composed in readiness for the Letter Day which took place during February 1743, and which was subsequently published in John Lewis's magazine, *An Account of the Most Remarkable Particulars Relating to the Present Progress of the Gospel*, gives some inkling of how most of the rank-and-file evangelicals perceived themselves. They sang:

> Thanks with many thousand tears
> That thy churches labourers
> Ev'ry where such fresh blessings meet;
> For this grace we kiss thy feet.
> Many in these latter days
> Have experienc'd JESU'S grace:
> Souls in Europe not a few
> Find the gospel tidings true.

---

[36] 'A letter from a clergyman in Wales, near Abergavenny: of whom MR WHITEFIELD in a former journal makes an honourable mention – It was wrote to our deceased Brother SEWARD soon after his arrival in England – Cwmyoy, 28 July 1740)', *CA* 21.

[37] 'The copy of a letter from Mr S—n T—r, near Ashford in Kent, to the printer of this book', *Account*, III, II, 47.

[38] For more on the important role of the letter days see O'Brien, ' "A transatlantic community of saints" ', 825–7.

Britain's Isle has catched the flame;
Many know and love the Lamb
Both in England and in Wales,
And in Scotland grace prevails:[39]

After interspersing verses on the progress of the revival in various parts of England, Scotland, Germany, the American colonies and even Greenland, the hymn ended on a highly optimistic note by reflecting the widely held opinion that the revival was about to usher in the ultimate triumph of the worldwide Church:

LORD, we're hearing frequently
How thy Kingdom makes its way
When the tidings reach our ears,
We could almost melt in tears
Still let more receive thy name,
O thou crucified LAMB
Out of ev'ry Land and place
Bring forth some redeem'd by grace.[40]

The way in which many of the rank-and-file evangelicals thought of themselves seems therefore to have rested on two main assumptions. The first of these concerned the role of George Whitefield. For many evangelicals, particularly after the rancorous divisions of 1740 and 1741, his ministry was the single most obvious factor linking them all together. His first-hand experience of the revivals in England, Wales, Scotland, Ireland and the American colonies led naturally to his being seen as the figure-head for all those who shared his Calvinistic interpretation of the revival. Whitefield's concerns and interests became synonymous with the concerns of the rank-and-file evangelicals and any form of contact with him became highly prized.[41] Secondly, the rank-and-file evangelicals seem to have shared the millennial speculations of the revivalists with unusual fervour. Whilst, as has already been argued, the revivalists, and Jonathan

---

[39]   For a copy of the complete hymn, which runs to twelve stanzas, see 'The hymn of intercession and thanksgiving for the progress of the Gospel in various parts of the world. – To be sung in the Association of the saints', *Account*, II, II, 76–81.

[40]   Ibid.

[41]   See for example 'The copy of a letter from a friend in the country (26 April 1742)', *WH* 55 (Saturday, 24 April 1742).

Edwards in particular, developed a theologically sophisticated prophetic calendar, among the ordinary evangelicals, millenarian expectations were more frequently, and often more crudely, voiced. They were convinced that 'the Glory of the Latter Days seems to be at hand'[42] and that God was about 'to bring our Zion to be the praise of the whole Earth'.[43] They were deeply persuaded that because of the scope and the intensity of the revival, particularly between 1739 and 1743, the climax of the history of the Kingdom of God was at hand. James Oulton, a sympathetic Dissenting minister from Leominster, on the Welsh border, gave expression to this expectation most persuasively in one of his many letters to Whitefield:

> I desire to glorify God in you; and I hope I can say, my spirit does rejoice in God my Saviour, who is surely fulfilling the Prophecies of the Latter Day Glory – What the Church of Christ has pray'd for these 1700 years, by her Lords direction viz 'Thy Kingdom come, Thy will be done on Earth as it is in Heaven'.[44]

For some of the rank-and-file Methodists a mere awareness of the existence of the wider revival and second-hand knowledge about its progress were insufficient. Many wrote to the revivalist with whom they had easiest and most regular contact requesting news about his latest activities, whilst others, more ambitiously, were inspired to contribute their own perspectives, by writing their revival narratives. In this way knowledge about the scope and success of the revival increased from the bottom up. Though they often took their inspiration from the revivalists, it was largely the response of evangelicals on the ground that ensured that knowledge about the progress of the revival proliferated, in secluded, out-of-the-way places, as well as in major centres of population like London and Bristol.

First-hand accounts of local awakenings like these operated on a number of levels. By establishing a forum for their converts to

---

[42] 'From Mr. A. T. to the Rev. MR WHITEFIELD (1 April 1742)', *WH* 55 (Saturday, 8 May 1742).

[43] 'The copy of a letter from BR HOWELL GRIFFITH, to BROTHER CENNICK (dated from Traverick-Ucha, in Llantrisant-Parish in Glamorganshire, south Wales, 3 March 1743)', *Account*, III, II, 29–33.

[44] 'The copy of a letter from the Reverend James Oulton, to the Reverend MR WHITEFIELD (Leominster, 12 November 1742)', in *Account*, II, II, 35.

report on the progress of the revival in their own localities, Whitefield and Harris provided a means by which their followers could stake a tangible claim to participation in the international revival. For those middling sorts attracted to the Welsh revival, the opportunities for influence and a relatively high profile that the communications network afforded seemed almost too good to be true. Frank Lambert has argued that Whitefield was in effect 'good business'[45] and has demonstrated how he benefited from the interest of newspaper editors and printers throughout the north Atlantic world who were committed, for commercial as much as religious reasons, to publicizing his progress.[46] What Lambert has not sufficiently emphasized is the way in which, in England and Wales at least, Whitefield relied on an army of anonymous individuals to carry out a similar task to that of the more sophisticated and far-reaching colonial press. For White-field the significance of this inter-revival journalistic activity lay in its importance to the perpetuation of the revival. In the colonies he had used reports of his preaching as advance publicity, intended to heighten the expectation of those living in the areas that he planned to visit.[47] Whilst this obviously has repercussions for our understanding of the nature of the revival itself and of the role which such carefully deployed publicity could play in awakenings in other areas, Whitefield does not seem to have seen any contradiction between such interven-tionist activity and his strictly providentialist interpretation of the revival.[48] In the British Isles, many had been conditioned to accept the evangelical message and had had their sense of expectation heightened by reading about Whitefield's exploits in his *Journals*, and in many of the letters that were hurriedly conveyed from person to person in the later 1730s.

When John Lewis, clearly acting on Whitefield's advice, issued guidelines to his readers in 1740 about the format that their letters should take if they wished them to appear in the pages of his magazine, his overriding concern was not that they should be

---

[45]   Lambert, *'Pedlar in Divinity'*, p. 110.
[46]   See ibid., pp. 103–10.
[47]   This theme forms the backbone of Frank Lambert's works on Whitefield and the Great Awakening. See Lambert, *Inventing the 'Great Awakening'* and Lambert, *'Pedlar in Divinity'*.
[48]   This is seen clearly in the writings of Jonathan Edwards. See Goen (ed.), *The Works of Jonathan Edwards, IV: The Great Awakening*, pp. 32–46.

written in a particular style or concentrate on any single subject. It was that everything written should be penned in such a way as to inspire people to work towards a similar revival in their own communities. An anonymous letter, very probably written by Howel Harris and included in one of the early editions of *The Weekly History*, elaborated on the purpose behind Methodist journalism:

> Every one of them [the Methodist converts] for the general good of the Christian Republick, to send you an account of what they have experienced of the work of God upon their souls, which they may insert in your weekly paper [. . .] I cannot recollect anything at present that will be more eternally useful for your well-disposed Readers, or attended with less Inconveniences.[49]

That many people responded in this fashion is testimony to the inspirational quality of many of the letters and the power that the revivalists enjoyed over their followers. Elizabeth Paul, for example, a member of the Tabernacle Society, confessed that she had 'been much refreshed by the good news Dear Mr Whitefield hath brought from Wales'[50] after a recent visit, and Anne Dutton, another London evangelical, wrote to Howel Harris: 'I rejoice to hear [. . .] that ye Lord's work still goes on in Wales & yt you are upheld & yr blessed labours in his Gospel.'[51] Not surprisingly, perhaps, it was Howel Harris, more than Whitefield, who was most faithful in encouraging people to draw the inevitable conclusions from these letters. He urged on his friends and followers the necessity of expecting still greater things to happen – the revival to spread even further with still more exciting and ecstatic religious experiences. Again Harris used these letters to build up his followers' expectations, creating the most fertile conditions for the rapid spread of the movement. In a letter to two London friends he wrote:

---

[49] *WH* 13 (no date). This reasoning also lay behind Isaac Watts and John Guyse's wish to print a British edition of Edwards's account of the Northampton awakening. See Jonathan Edwards, *A Faithful Narrative of the Surprising Work of God*, in Goen (ed.), *The Works of Jonathan Edwards, V: The Great Awakening*, p. 137.
[50] Trevecka 904, Elizabeth Paul to Howel Harris (7 July 1743).
[51] Trevecka 1638, Anne Dutton to Howel Harris (3 April 1747).

Remember to tell him [God] to humble and purify all the Lambs, to send his Gospel over the world. Put him in mind of his Promises to ye Jews and ye whole world. Beg of him to unite all his Lambs in one and to set ye Hearts of his Ministers on flame of fire.[52]

In the early weeks and months of the revival, before the communications network had become sophisticated enough to handle the rapid dissemination of evangelical news, many of the rank-and-file evangelicals learned about the progress of the revival by writing to one of the revivalists themselves. The anonymous writer whose speculative letter to Whitefield appeared in one of the early copies of *The Weekly History* was typical of many:

How much do I long for the pleasure of a line from you: I have written to you twice since I had any from you – But your time is much better employed. Glory be to God for the continued success of the Gospel by your Ministry.[53]

The response to letters like this contained an account of the progress of the Gospel in the area most closely associated with the revivalist to whom it was directed. Whitefield and Harris were often the exceptions to this rule. Although many of Harris's letters were full of news from Wales, they also contained a considerable amount of detail about awakenings elsewhere. A similar pattern may be seen in the letters of Whitefield, though they are naturally wider-ranging in their scope because of Whitefield's international itinerancy. They complemented each other, and the successful transmission of revival news often rested on the foundation of their closely synchronized working relationship. Harris obtained news about the progress of the revival directly from Whitefield, whether he happened to be in Bristol, the south-west, Scotland or the American colonies. That news was then mediated through Harris who selected what was most sensational, which was then distributed through his network of correspondents in Wales, England and Scotland. From this

---

[52]   'Extract of a letter from a minister in the country to his friend in LONDON (3 February 1742)', *WH* 46 (Saturday, 20 February 1742).
[53]   From Mr. A.T. to the REV. MR WHITEFIELD (1 April 1742)', *WH* 55 (Saturday, 24 April 1742).

vantage point he could write thus to Marmaduke Gwynne (?1694–1769)[54] of Garth in Breconshire, one of the few among the minor Welsh gentry who embraced Methodism: 'A glorious work is going on in the world [. . .] In many nations the Gospel is spreading its healing wings. There are above 100 ministers everywhere up and down the world now employ'd in the Great Work.'[55] Similarly he could write to Howel Davies in 1743: 'ye work of ye Lord goes on most gloriously in many Towns and villages in several Counties in this Nation, Scotland, New England, Pennsylvania Besides many provinces in Germany.'[56] The efficiency with which rank-and-file members of the revival received up-to-date revival news was aided by two highly significant developments – Letter Days and the efficient circulation of *The Weekly History*. From the earliest days of the revival, the English evangelicals, impressed by the Moravian practice of setting aside a day every month for the reading of revival letters,[57] had established their own days, though initially on a fairly infrequent basis. In 1739 John Wesley had written to the publisher James Hutton requesting 'extracts of all your foreign letters to be read out on Intercession Day'.[58] Whitefield began his own days for reading letters in London and Bristol in 1741,[59] made sure that his Welsh friends were kept informed of their success and sent details of the events that were reported.[60] Harris, who was often in London when Letter Days were held, sent back long and detailed reports to Daniel Rowland and some of the Welsh exhorters. In September 1742, for example, he wrote:

> Yesterday we had our monthly Day for readg Letters abt ye Progress of ye Gospel Every where – Such accts as we had from America & Scotland yr ears never heard of ye Power that comes on ye Congregations to awaken & to build up is such as was hardly ever known.[61]

[54]   See *DWB*, pp. 331–2; *DMBI*, p. 145; and A. H. Williams, 'The Gwynnes of Garth c.1712–1809', *Brycheiniog*, XIV (1970), 76–96.
[55]   Trevecka 708, Howel Harris to Marmaduke Gwynne (21 October 1742).
[56]   Trevecka 977, Howel Harris to Howel Davies (13 September 1743). See also Trevecka 1510, Howel Harris to Stephen Dixon (26 August 1746).
[57]   Podmore, *The Moravian Church in England*, pp. 44, 123–4.
[58]   Quoted in O'Brien, '"A transatlantic community of saints"', 825–6.
[59]   Welch, *Two Calvinistic Methodist Chapels*, p. 19.
[60]   Trevecka 450, George Whitefield to the Association (Cil-y-cwm, Carmarthenshire) (28 December 1741).
[61]   Trevecka 644, Howel Harris to Daniel Rowland (14 September 1742).

Although the Welsh Methodists did not make the Letter Day an integral part of their regular monthly programme, their network of societies and the closeness of the Welsh and English revivals ensured that the transmission of what had occurred on these days was as efficient as possible.

Despite the efficiency with which information about the Letter Days was transmitted, their usefulness for the revival as a whole was obviously limited. Only a relatively small number, when compared with the total Methodist constituency, could attend a Letter Day at Bristol or in London. It was in response to this problem that Whitefield had assumed editorial control of John Lewis's *The Christian's Amusement,* relaunching it as the official mouthpiece of the Calvinistic revival in 1741, to allow rank-and-file members of the revival to keep abreast of the latest developments in an easily assimilated format. The magazine was extremely popular in the immediate aftermath of its take-over and was, for a few months, packed with letters from converts expressing their gratitude for the copies of the magazine they had received. From Scotland, Lady Jane Hume Campbell informed Howel Harris: 'It has pleased the Lord to bless your letters in the Weekly History in a Peculiar Manner to my heart I can't resist Dear Mr Whitefield's Proposal of returning my hearty thanks for them.'[62] John Oulton, in a highly significant letter, recorded: 'With pleasure and refreshment I read ye experimental Gospel Letters in the weekly history (and hope they will be continued) Especially as they are a transcript of my own Heart respecting Sin and Grace.'[63] Oulton's letter is significant because it demonstrates the importance that many of the early Methodists attached to their participation in the communications network. That John Oulton regarded the letters as transcripts of his heart, helping him to interpret his own experiences, demonstrates the extent to which Whitefield's and Harris's vision of a vibrant transnational community of saints was a vital component of the world-view of evangelicals in England and Wales, particularly between 1740 and 1743. Many of them found within the network material vital to their spiritual development that helped

---

[62]   Trevecka 666, Lady Jane Hume Campbell to Howel Harris (28 September 1742).
[63]   Trevecka 504, John Oulton to Howel Harris (27 March 1742).

them to tackle their spiritual problems and supplemented what they received in their society meetings.

However, many Methodists were not content just to read second-hand accounts of revivals from the four corners of the evangelical world. Some took the next step and began to write about the revival in their own localities. Again, the most access-ible way was via the letter-writing network. For the majority of those who wrote, the letters tended to be spontaneous, joyful accounts of what they had experienced, more often than not directed to just one of the pioneer revivalists.[64] Others showed more self-confidence and were able to write more polished letters that they clearly expected to be included in the pages of *The Weekly History*.[65]

Perhaps the most significant contribution made by a Welsh Methodist to the communications network, apart from Howel Harris's, stemmed from Whitefield's wife, Elizabeth James. Born near Abergavenny, she had spent much of her early life in Breconshire. Having been widowed, she was briefly courted by Howel Harris, but married Whitefield in November 1741.[66] Marriage to Whitefield took her away from Wales and saw her full integration into the life of English Calvinistic Methodism at Whitefield's Tabernacle. However, her sense of identity with Wales continued, chiefly through the regular visits of Harris to the capital. By her frequent letters to him when he was in Wales, she became one of the most regular sources of revival news for many Welsh Methodists, and this was a role which she was able to fulfil to maximum effect when she accompanied Whitefield on his colonial itinerancy in 1744. Her letters from the colonies between 1744 and 1748 became the chief source of information for the majority of British Methodists about the progress of Whitefield's ministry during the early months and years of the

---

[64]   Trevecka 482, Ann Evan to Howel Harris (13 February 1742); Trevecka 727, Ann Davies to Howel Harris (6 November 1742); Trevecka 804, Isabel Allen to Howel Harris (16 February 1743); Trevecka 983, Anne Harry to Howel Harris (15 September 1743); Trevecka 1222, Elizabeth Kiggell to Howel Harris (3 September 1744).

[65]   See John Oulton to George Whitefield (19 April 1742), *WH* 60 (Saturday, 29 May 1742); James Beaumont to Howel Harris (16 August 1742), *WH* 79 (Saturday, 9 October 1742); Anne Thomas to Howel Harris (3 September 1742), *WH* 80 (Saturday, 16 October 1742); 'Herbert Jenkins to the printer of this paper' (7 October 1742), *WH* 83 (Saturday, 6 November 1742) and continued in *WH* 84 (Saturday, 13 November 1742).

[66]   Brown, 'The marriage of George Whitefield at Caerphilly'; Dallimore, *George Whitefield*, II, pp. 101–13.

event that has come to be known as the Great Awakening. In July 1745 she wrote one of her many letters to Harris and all the other members of the Tabernacle Society, from Whitefield's Orphan House at Bethesda, providing details about the progress of her husband's ministry:

> Through the goodness of God he [Whitefield] is enabled to preach three times a day & ride near twenty miles [. . .] the fields are in everywhere white & ready to harvest and great numbers flock to the word as doves to ye windows the good Lord wonderfully blesses his ministrations the Word is attended with great power and there are added to the church daily such as shall be saved [. . .] And will it not rejoice you to hear that the last time my dr Master was here that thousands were born of God there was one minister that said in company where I was that he kept account till a thousand had been sat down that was the effect of his last visit not unto us but unto thy Great name be all the Glory.[67]

It seems that Elizabeth Whitefield saw her contribution to the letter-writing network as a vital means of supporting and furthering her husband's ministry.[68] By using her Welsh contacts she was able to carve out her own niche within the revival and develop a network of interested correspondents through whom she could circulate the latest news from the colonies. By in effect acting as her husband's secretary, she was able to exert a measure of influence among the rank and file of the movement.

There were other Methodist women who acted as intermediaries between Harris and the hub of the communications network when he was in Wales. A group of printers and English exhorters regularly sent copies of the latest literature to Harris, but there were also a number of women who filled a similar role. Anne Dutton, the wife of a Baptist minister in Huntingdonshire,[69] was particularly prominent in the mid-1740s, sending regular parcels of books and letters to Harris containing the latest news from throughout the revival which Harris was then able to

---

[67] Trevecka 1340, Mrs Elizabeth Whitefield to Harris, Jenkins, Adams, and all at the Tabernacle (1 July 1745).

[68] See Trevecka 1359, Mrs Whitefield to Howel Harris (29 September 1745); Trevecka 1535, Elizabeth Whitefield to Howel Harris (6 October 1746); and Trevecka 1660, Elizabeth Whitefield to Howel Harris (30 May 1747).

[69] See Stephen J. Stein, 'A note on Anne Dutton, eighteenth-century evangelical', *Church History*, 44 (1975), 485–91.

pass to his network of exhorters scattered at strategic points through the Welsh countryside.[70] Her contribution, like that of Elizabeth Whitefield, is evidence of how some women, albeit those with powerful contacts or unusual access to one or other of the pioneer revivalists, were able, though excluded from the highest offices of evangelical leadership, to develop their own niche in the evangelical movement.

There is enough evidence to be able to suggest tentatively that the transmission of evangelical news did not always exclusively rely on an individual's immediate access to one of the pioneer revivalists. Some among the rank and file were more than capable of forming relationships with one another without the initiative of one of their leaders. For example, after a weekend spent listening to the preaching of Daniel Rowland at Llangeitho during August 1743, E—n W—ms wrote to his friend Brother L—e, in order to share with him what he had experienced and to bring him up-to-date with the latest events from his society. He wrote:

> I am newly returned from hearing that famous man of God, the Reverend Mr Rowland [. . .] There was a dozen of the Members of our Society, and exceeding sweet was the Lord to our Souls, both in our going, while there, and coming home. Wonderful was the Power Mr Rowland had on the Sabbath Day [. . .] As for our Society in particular, never did we enjoy such times as we do at present![71]

The communications network was far more than a disorganized and unrelated collection of correspondents that had evolved haphazardly during the early years of the revival. It was a highly sophisticated network that relied on the active participation of a large proportion of the converts who joined Methodist communities. Rank-and-file Methodists availed themselves of the news that was circulated through the network and in many cases they became the source of much of the information that entered the public domain. In Wales, the rank-and-file Methodists tended to rely on the initiative of Howel Harris, and information about the

---

[70]   Trevecka 1056, Anne Dutton to Howel Harris (15 December 1743); Trevecka 1325, Anne Dutton to Howel Harris (30 May 1745); Trevecka 1681, Anne Dutton to Howel Harris (23 July 1747).
[71]   'From Brother E—n W—ms, to Brother L—t (29 August 1743)', *Account*, IV, I, 76–9.

wider revival spread from him to all corners of the Welsh awakening. Yet it would be a mistake to assume that in Wales the network depended exclusively on Harris. Some made their own contributions to it independent of his initiative, so that in both ways information about the wider revival grew, as humble Methodists in Wales became as familiar with the revival in London, Bristol and Glasgow as they did with the awakenings in Breconshire and Carmarthenshire.

Many of the rank-and-file members of the revival, in Wales and elsewhere, used the communications network in far more sophisticated ways than merely to read the latest news and report on the latest movements of God's Spirit. Although this tended to be the first contact that most Methodists had with the network, many of them subsequently made more imaginative use of their initial contacts in order to maintain their spiritual vitality. They rapidly discovered that the forum could be used just as easily to compare their experiences with those of their contemporaries; offer and seek spiritual advice and counsel; discuss theological problems; seek advice in their daily lives; advertise practical services which they were prepared to place at the disposal of their evangelical brethren; and in some cases even find marriage partners.

For many of the rank-and-file Methodists the communications network was an indispensable source of guidance to every aspect of their spiritual lives. As the revival progressed the pioneer revivalists realized that the network could be transformed from a journalistic tool into a means of providing emotional and pastoral support. By comparing their experiences with the models that appeared in the pages of *The Weekly History* or were circulated in the letter-writing network, they hoped that their followers would be able to test the validity of their experiences and provide genuine spiritual assurance. The experience of the New Birth elevated the role of the individual, forcing people to assume control of their own religious destinies. This was an autonomy reinforced when evangelicals also placed responsibility for testing the authenticity of that experience squarely with each individual. The evangelicals had adapted the theology of conversion, inherited from their forebears, the Puritans, by contracting it into a very short time-frame and stressing that the experience was instantaneously available to all. This was the one theme that recurred in almost all of Whitefield's sermons, and it was reiterated in the pages of his published *Journals*. In one of his earliest printed sermons, *The Nature and Necessity of New Birth in Christ Jesus, in Order to Salvation* (1737),[72] he had reduced conversion to three stages. Consciousness of sin was the first prerequisite which was only relieved as the penitent exercised faith and experienced conversion. Whitefield then expected his converts, in the third place, to be able to rationalize their faith, comparing it to biblical norms, by using the syllogisms provided in the New Testament, and thereby reaching a degree of assurance. The genius of Whitefield's theology lay not so much in new systems or innovatory understandings, but in the way in which he took hold of the evangelical message and combined it with dramatic preaching that demanded an immediate response from its listeners.[73]

In addition to delineating the contours of genuine conversion in his sermons, Whitefield encouraged his converts to testify to their experiences in writing, the best examples of which, after being vetted by the revivalists, were circulated throughout the communications network by word of mouth, the letter-distribution network and *The Weekly History*. In April 1742, John Lewis published a letter from an anonymous correspondent that contained an account of 'a fresh Instance of the quickening, comforting Influences of the good spirit'.[74] Its author penned a dramatic and vivid account of his conversion:

> I was alone employ'd in a Branch of my worldy Business in the Twilight of the Evening, and without much Attention, or Design, revolving in my Mind these Lines,

> He will present our Souls
> Unblemish'd and compleat
> Before the Glory of his Face
> With joy divinely great.

---

[72] It was a sermon extremely influential throughout the revival. It was published in Welsh as *Angenrheidrwydd a Natur o'n Genedigaeth Newydd yng Nghrist Iesu, Mewn Trefn i Iachydwriaeth. Sef Pregeth a Bregethwyd yn Eglwys St Mary Redcliff yn Bristol* (Pontypool, 1739).

[73] Lambert, '*Pedlar in Divinity*', pp. 15–25.

[74] 'The copy of a letter from a friend in the country (26 April 1742)', *WH* 57 (Saturday, 8 May 1742).

With sudden almost as a Flash of Lightening my Soul was ravish'd with a joyful Assurance that our Blessed Saviour, my dear Jesus, will one day present my worthless Soul, polluted and vile as it now is, before the Presence of CHRIST at once filled me throughout with transporting pleasure.[75]

This narrative is typical and highlights some of the key motifs of Methodist religious experience. It begins with an indication of its author's apparent disregard for spiritual matters, before injecting a note of urgency when a verse of an apparently well-known hymn was suddenly brought to his attention, suggesting that the author had had some form of religious upbringing. The imagery employed reinforces the evangelical emphasis on the immediacy of genuine spiritual experience and the feelings that could be taken to indicate its authenticity. The writer's attention was suddenly arrested like a 'Flash of Lightening', drawing attention to the terror of sin and the reality of the wrath of God. In characteristic fashion this was not dwelt upon for too long as the writer testified to being quickly assured of acceptance and forgiveness, tangibly proven by an 'overwhelming sense' of the love of God and 'transporting pleasure'. Although there could be slight variations in this model, particularly in the time-scale and the intensity of the various phases, Methodist experience was pared down to the central themes of an awareness of personal sinfulness and a subsequent assurance of acceptance by God, easily demonstrable by signs that were almost always located in the feelings and emotions of the convert. By printing this letter, John Lewis, undoubtedly at Whitefield's behest, was ensuring that all his readers, wherever they happened to be, clearly understood the precise nature of the New Birth, so that they could examine themselves closely and compare their experiences against these benchmarks.

Very little distinction was drawn between the experiences of men and women. Indeed, the prominence that the evangelicals gave to experience ensured that gender roles would, to some extent, be blurred. Both sexes were encouraged to share their testimonies and women in particular seem to have been more ready to bare their souls and undergo close scrutiny than their

75 Ibid.

male counterparts. To illustrate: Ann Harry, from St Kennox in Pembrokeshire, offered an account of her conversion in a letter to Howel Harris. She began by describing how she felt 'full of darkness and vileness' and 'so black as hell and so full of corruptions'.[76] Such was her despair that she even at one point wondered 'how the Lord does look upon such one as me'.[77] Although her letter does not contain a complete picture of her experience, it is a useful example of the way in which some evangelicals responded to their feelings of despair and dejection. In Ann Harry's case, her despondency led her to entreat Harris 'to remember me at the throne of grace . . .[and] to pray that I may never rest till I rest in his wounds'.[78] However, she found some relief in the fact that she had already detected some signs of grace in her life, particularly that she found 'daily in my soul some seeking for the Lord Jesus'.[79] The letter was another example of the Methodists' success in reducing the conversion experience to a readily identifiable formula, backed by the series of evidences that Whitefield and Jonathan Edwards had elaborated in such detail. Ann Harry's letter concluded in exactly the same way as those of many of her contemporaries. Even while going through deep inner turmoil, she expressed her interest in the progress of the revival and her hope that 'the Lord [would] enable you and strengthen you more and more every day to call thousands and ten thousands home to the dear Lamb'.[80]

For many first-generation Welsh Methodists, involvement in the international communications network afforded them the opportunity to test their experiences. That a significant number of them found the network to be the ideal forum in which to do so illustrates both their self-confidence and the enthusiasm with which many of them responded to participation in the wider evangelical community. Yet, by their contributing accounts according to this pattern, an artificial and somewhat formulaic style was made almost inevitable. The evangelical message offered people security and certainty, supported as it was by a simply

---

[76] Trevecka Letter, 983, Anne Harry to Howel Harris (15 September 1743).
[77] Ibid.
[78] Ibid.
[79] Ibid.
[80] Ibid.

understood theology and a rigorous disciplining network. It is not surprising therefore that when they wrote about their experiences many of the early Methodists adapted the particularities of their own cases to the models with which they had been supplied.[81] In this way the experience that lay at the heart of evangelicalism was standardized and a measure of unity was engendered amongst evangelicals naturally, and almost inevitably, drawn together on account of their near-identical experiences.

Many Welsh evangelicals participated in the international communications network by seeking and, in some cases, offering spiritual advice and counsel, and it seems that many members of the revival found the proximity of the communications network an indispensable support as they endeavoured to maintain a faithful testimony to their newly discovered faith. Letters written by women concentrated on matters relating to the internal dynamics of the spiritual life in a way that those written by their male counterparts often did not. Many women also seemed more willing to seek counsel and found the proximity of the communications network indispensable in this. Their letters betray their reliance on the network and their readiness to use it in order to relate their post-conversion experiences and discuss some of their problems and difficulties. Religious experience was of course a great leveller, and there was no obvious reason to prevent women from testifying to their experiences within the confines of the Methodist societies or the pages of Methodist epistolary.[82] Men tended to be more interested in questions relating to the progress of the revival, theology and the consolidation of their movement, particularly after the divisions of 1740 and 1741.[83]

The overwhelming bulk of this correspondence was directed to Howel Harris, and it seems that many of the rank-and-file converts found him to be the most sympathetic of all the revivalists. Harris appears to have been aware of this, and

[81]   D. Bruce Hindmarsh, ' "My chains fell off, my heart was free": early Methodist conversion narrative in England', 910–29; Ward and Heitzenrater, 'Introduction' in Ward and Heitzenrater (eds), *The Works of John Wesley*, 18, pp. 1–36.

[82]   Compare with Gail Malmgreen, 'Domestic discords: women and family in east Cheshire Methodism', pp. 55–70.

[83]   On this contrast see Jones, ' "From the state of my soul" ', p. 276 and White, 'Women in early Methodist societies in Wales', 104–7.

throughout his career he attached particular importance to being 'made instrumental to comfort any of the poor dear precious Lambs that are equally dear to the dear shepherd, with the strongest and bravest soldier'.[84] By such letters to Harris, many of the concerns that preoccupied rank-and-file Welsh Methodists came to receive far wider attention. His unrivalled knowledge of the issues and problems confronting the Methodists on the ground in England and Wales led him to use the letter-writing network and the revivalist magazine to address many of these issues. It is probably not an exaggeration to say that in the 1740s the communications network acted as an evangelical confessional. Its contents therefore can be used to uncover many otherwise hidden aspects of early Methodist spirituality and obtain an insight into their mindset.

It is likely that many of those who wrote to Howel Harris did so with little or no expectation of a reply. Many wrote purely because of the therapeutic effect of unburdening themselves to someone they knew to be sympathetic. In February 1742 Ann Evan, a member of the Tabernacle Society in London, wrote a letter to Harris which typifies the way in which many rank-and-file Methodists used their relationships with the pioneer revivalists to share their problems. It seems that she wrote to Harris shortly after he had returned to Wales after one of his extended visits to London. She had evidently heard him preach at the Tabernacle on a number of occasions and seems to have felt on this basis that he would be sympathetic to her needs. She began by assuring Harris that she had 'longed for an opportunity to let you know what our Dear Dear Lord hath Done for my soul since you left us'.[85] She then described a period of doubt and uncertainty over her spiritual state in the three weeks that had elapsed since Harris left London, which had culminated when she stopped attending the Tabernacle 'being grievously harried about by the enemy'.[86] Her condition had been eased listening to John Cennick preach and by reading a letter that Harris had written to another member of the Tabernacle society, Sister Hart. This is highly significant and demonstrates how the letter-

---

[84]   'The copy of a letter from MR. HOWEL Harris, to Mrs E.P. in LONDON (4 February 1742)', *WH* 46 (Saturday, 4 February 1742).
[85]   Trevecka 482, Ann Evan to Howel Harris (13 February 1742).
[86]   Ibid.

writing network could encompass more individuals than those who actually penned letters. It shows how Harris's pastoral letters, often written to individuals whose circumstances on one level seemed unique, had a far wider relevance than perhaps even he realized. Ann Evan concluded her letter hoping that she would have further contact with Harris and that his letter-writing ministry would continue: 'O that my Lord would be pleased once more to let me see you and hear the joyful sound of the glorious gospel from you [. . .] your letters are made so great youse to me so were your preaching.'[87]

This pattern of writing is mirrored in the letters of other correspondents who wrote to Harris in similar circumstances. Alice Powell wrote, after having received a letter from Harris, to say:

> Your kind Remembrance of me a poor unworthy, proud, foolish, rebellious Child caused praise to be offered to my dear Saviour [. . .] I am still in the field of battell and find while I keep my eye upon my Captain nothing moveth me but when I look on the Creature in any Sheep I am shaken tho I am rooted and grounded and established upon the Rock, Christ.[88]

Similarly, Isabel Allen wrote:

> My promise puts me now upon writing to you! Oh wt a sinfull Dulness & backwardness there is in me to speak of any of ye merciful Dealings of ye Lord towards me yet at ye same time I believe there is not one has greater reason as I to be continually Blessing and Praising his Holy Name.[89]

Ann Davies wrote in order to unburden herself and tell Harris about her latest batch of spiritual trials:

> It has often been in my mind since you left Bristol to write to you but want of time has in some measure hindered me but I must confess that ye Chief Thing was because I had nothing but clouds and Heaviness and temptations to tell you of.[90]

---

[87] Ibid.
[88] Trevecka 841, Alice Powell to Howel Harris (no date).
[89] Trevecka 804, Isabel Allen to Howel Harris (16 February 1743).
[90] Trevecka 727, Ann Davies to Howel Harris (6 November 1742).

She continued by describing her spiritual depression at some considerable length, convincing herself as the letter progressed of the reality of her spiritual life. She, like some others who wrote to Harris, seems to have used letter-writing as a primitive form of therapy. By merely putting pen to paper some of these Methodists began the long process of spiritual healing and renewal and for many of them recovery was speeded up by an unexpected reply from Harris himself.

Throughout his career Howel Harris seems to have attached particular importance to his role as a spiritual adviser and confidant.[91] His replies to letters from distressed souls were written graciously and with the immediate circumstances of the recipient in mind. His letters were therefore not merely general responses to abstract case studies and they were not simply packed with scriptural proof texts and well-worn clichés. Rather, they were characterized by a sympathetic and heartfelt pastoral concern.[92] To Sister Molly Jenkins, for example, he wrote inquiring 'how tis with thy dr soul'[93] and to another anonymous sister he wrote reminding her that 'our dear Lord does not suffer ungrateful Me to forget [you]',[94] before going on to encourage her to remain steadfast in the faith despite her present trials: 'I find the Days of my mourning are not yet ended. You are taught to wait all your appointed time, till your Charge come. – He will come, and will not tarry: and the lower he humbles us, the higher he raises us up again.'[95] To Catherine Poyer he wrote in a similar manner, 'long[ing] to see thee plunged in the wounds of ye Lamb'[96] and with the prayer that she would become 'more Intimately acquainted with Him & leaning on his sacred Bosom'.[97]

---

[91]   'The copy of a letter from MR HOWEL HARRIS, to Mrs E.P. in LONDON (4 February 1742)', WH 46, (Saturday, 4 February 1742).

[92]   See Trevecka 797, Howel Harris to Elizabeth Thomas (10 February 1743); Trevecka 864, Howel Harris to Anne Dutton (9 May 1743); Trevecka 883, Howel Harris to Elizabeth Wood (4 June 1743); Trevecka 894, Howel Harris to Catherine Poyer (19 June 1743); Trevecka 1029, Howel Harris to Sister Aubery (3 November 1743); Trevecka 1030, Howel Harris to Anne Bowen (3 November 1743); and 'From Bro Howel Harris, in Wales to a sister in London', CH, VII, IV, 25–8.

[93]   Trevecka 884, Howel Harris to Molly Jenkins (4 June 1743).

[94]   'A letter from Mr Howel Harris, to a sister under trials', WH 53 (Saturday, 10 April 1742).

[95]   Ibid.

[96]   Trevecka 894, Howel Harris to Catherine Poyer (19 June 1743).

[97]   Ibid.

Harris's slightly longer letter to Mrs J. Godwin, written in March 1743, is typical of his approach to pastoral counselling. He began his letter with a general consideration of her particular difficulty, then proceeded with advice on how best to deal with it, before turning to what he felt to be the underlying cause of her depression:

> You are by sore conflicts brought to see the vanity of every thing besides God in Christ and this lesson is worth learning let it be ever so bitter in the learning of it [. . .] What still all you[r] appointed Time remembering that all even the worse that we can meet with here is better than Hell [. . .] As soon as we become clay in the Potters Hands, we are happy and shall feel our Souls renew'd after his image daily.[98]

Despite his somewhat crude approach and the simplistic reasoning that he often deployed, there is little doubt that Harris's advice was widely sought and that there were many who genuinely benefited from it. Throughout Harris counselled against morbid introspection and, in an effort to warn people of this danger, he used news about the success of the revival to demonstrate to depressed souls that their God was all-powerful and that he was accomplishing great things in the light of which they had little to fear or be depressed about. This argument from the greater to the lesser obviously worked remarkably well. After having read Harris's direct advice, Mrs J. Godwin, for example, was treated to a whistle-stop tour of the Welsh revival complete with evidence of how 'the work goes still sweeter and sweeter in most Places'.[99]

Although much of the initiative for the effective operation of this international counselling network stemmed from Howel Harris, there are enough examples of rank-and-file Welsh Methodists writing similar letters to fellow evangelicals in England to be able to broaden its scope. The usual way in which ordinary Methodists struck up these correspondences was by responding to those letters that caught their attention in the pages of *The Weekly History* or that had been read aloud at society meetings. In 1744, an anonymous convert from

---

[98]   Trevecka 827, Howel Harris to Mrs J. Godwin (25 March 1743).
[99]   Ibid.

Cardiganshire wrote to a member of the Calvinistic Methodist society at Deptford, which contained many London-Welsh members:

> I am glad to hear that you are well – I hope that you do glorify God in your Health, by denying yourself, and departing from all Iniquity. And that you have the Holy Spirit to lead, guide and govern you; and that your Eye is fix'd on eternal Happiness. It is this that will make you long more and more to be there, and to walk with God continually while here.[100]

Others among the Welsh Methodists contributed letters to *The Weekly History* and its two successors; they were originally intended to be letters of pastoral counsel to private individuals. In addition to Howel Harris, Daniel Rowland contributed a few letters to the network, particularly to former members of his congregation who had moved to London or who were visiting the capital for an extended period. His letters tended to have a recurring theme. He warned his converts to flee from the temptations of life in the city and to be careful lest they slide back into a life of worldliness and ungodliness. To two anonymous Welsh sisters who had moved to London he wrote:

> May the Great God lift up the light of his countenance upon you. But where have you been all this while? What are you doing? – Who do you hear? What conscience do you make of secret prayer? Do you greedily run after the Blessed Ordinances? Do you join in publick and private worship with other Sisters? The neglecting of such Means will dry up your spirit.[101]

Far-sighted Welsh Methodists wrote letters with an eye to their publication or at the very least their being read by a wider readership. Some letters dealt with subjects that were considered relevant to a broader readership and were drafted in less personal terms to ensure a broader audience. In one of the earliest issues of *The Christian's Amusement*, John Lewis included a letter from a person 'whom God hath wounded, but

---

[100] 'From a person in Wales, to one at Deptford (11 August 1744)', *Account*, IV, II, 34–5.
[101] 'From the REVEREND MR DANIEL ROWLAND (a Church of England minister) in Wales to two Welsh Sisters of his flock in LONDON', *Account*, IV, II, 13–16.

he hath since apply'd to the Devil to be cured'.[102] Its otherwise
anonymous author explained the pastoral motivation that lay
behind the letter: 'I thought to have written a private penny post
letter; but as I consider'd others might possibly be in the like
Case, I imagin'd a more publick disposition of it might be more
convenient and useful [. . .]'[103] The letter consisted of advice to a
person who had had some limited contact with evangelical
religion, but who had sought to alleviate the effects of acute
conviction of sin by turning to alcohol. Whether the details of the
letter are true or not, it was undoubtedly intended to be a case
study offering guidance to others in a similar situation and
warning the faithful against some of the pitfalls into which it was
possible to fall. The letter, continuing in the best traditions of
Puritan casuistry,[104] demonstrates the uses to which the communications network could be put. Even for those who had no
intention of writing to its editor or any of the revivalists, the
network could and did contain material particularly suited to
them, addressing some of their particular problems.

There are also a few instances of rank-and-file Methodists who
encouraged, advised and even, in some instances, rebuked their
fellow members. Howel Harris in particular benefited from the
advice that he received on a number of occasions from a small
group of female supporters who seemed to have had unusual
access to him. In June 1743, for example, Harris wrote to a sister
from London expressing his gratitude for a recent letter: 'I can't
forget the Favour of yours to me. It was much blessed to me. I
believe our Lord used your pen to send some sweet messages
to my poor Soul: and when this is manifest, our Call is clear
to write frequently.'[105] Harris seems to have prized the small
group of women who persisted in writing to him regularly in the
early years of his career. In many of these letters some of his
closest friends were able to be completely honest with him. They

---

[102]   'A letter to a person whom GOD hath wounded, but he hath since apply'd to the
devil to be cured', *CA* 19.
[103]   Ibid.
[104]   Sargent Bush Jr., 'Epistolary counseling in the Puritan movement: the example of
John Cotton', in Francis J. Bremer (ed.), *Puritanism: Transatlantic Perspectives on a
Seventeenth-Century Anglo-American Faith* (Boston, 1993), pp. 127–46 and Charles
Lloyd Cohen, *God's Caress: The Psychology of Puritan Religious Experience* (Oxford,
1986).
[105]   'The copy of a letter from Howel Harris to a sister in London (8 June 1743)',
Account, III, III, 22.

encouraged him during his frequent periods of depression and continually assured him that he occupied the foremost place in their intercessory prayers. In a letter to one of these women in 1743, Anne Bowen, Harris expressed his indebtedness to her for fulfilling this kind of role and, significantly, gave some indication of the esteem in which he held her as a result: 'I can say you have been a means far beyond anyone in England and Wales of strengthening my Hands and that several ways – you are a Mother a Phoebe – a pillar indeed.'[106] Harris's language is indicative of the important place that she occupied in his ministry. The imagery employed in this letter has a threefold connotation. By referring to her as a mother he was echoing the biblical description of the Old Testament prophetess Deborah, described as 'a Mother in Israel'.[107] By comparing her to a pillar[108] he was adopting a scriptural metaphor to commend her spiritual strength and steadfastness. However, it is the allusion to Phoebe that is most interesting. Phoebe was the 'deaconess' mentioned by the apostle Paul in his letter to the Church at Rome.[109] By making this comparison Harris was demonstrating to her the validity of her own largely unsung and behind-the-scenes ministry and reminding her of her indispensability to the success of his own ministry. For women deprived of the opportunity to occupy the highest offices in the revival, Harris's comments represent evidence of the high regard in which he held the unofficial semi-public ministries of a number of influential women, and they are an indication of his relatively enlightened attitude to the role of women in religious communities more generally.

For many of the rank-and-file Welsh Methodists who wrote to Howel Harris in order to testify to their conversion experiences, their foray into the international evangelical communications network was just the beginning of their involvement. They soon discovered that not only did the network alter their view of the world and the way they thought about their movement, but that it introduced them to a very different world in which each member felt some measure of responsibility for his or her

---

[106]   Trevecka 1030, Howel Harris to Anne Bowen (3 November 1743).
[107]   Judges 5: 7.
[108]   See Exodus 13: 21 and 1 Timothy 3: 15.
[109]   Romans 16: 1.

spiritual brothers and sisters. Fellow-feeling was quickly engendered as converts shared their difficulties and sought advice,
and in this way the experiences subsequent to conversion were
discussed and analysed. Those who needed education in the
fundamentals of the faith received guidance; those who doubted
their faith were reassured and those who were just lonely were
introduced to a new circle of potential friends. Together they
ensured that the network developed far beyond a forum for the
transmission of revival news, into something that resembled a
self-help group, from which there was a realistic expectation that
anybody could seek and gain help and advice.

For many Welsh Methodists the communications network
became the means by which they learned of the wider issues that
affected the revival at certain key moments in its early
development. It was the means by which many Calvinistic
Methodists in Wales came into contact with some of the varying
versions of evangelicalism that were competing for space in the
London revival during the early months of the movement. Many
of the letters included in *The Weekly History* during 1740 and
1741 focus on the controversy between Whitefield and Wesley,
and they show the extent of the crisis threatening the future of
the revival and provide a valuable insight into the way some of
the rank and file reacted to it.

Whilst not immediately involved in the theological debates
between the Moravians, the Calvinists and the Wesleyans, which
assumed massive proportions during these months,[110] many
Welsh Methodists none the less found themselves in a position
where they had to choose which version of the revival they
wanted to adopt. Most were content to accept the judgement of
the revivalists to whom they owed their conversion and did not
bother over much with the intricacies of these controversies.
However, there are enough examples to be able to suggest that
some Welsh Methodists were independently minded enough to
read Wesley and the Moravians for themselves and had sufficient
confidence and theological education to follow the course of the

[110] The course of these discussions and the issues that were at stake have already been
discussed at length in Chapter IV. See above, pp. 168–85.

debates closely, and even in some cases to make their own contributions to them.

Perhaps the most significant contribution made by a Methodist of Welsh origin stemmed from the relatively neglected work of the London-Welsh printer, John Lewis. Lewis remains a shadowy figure in the early history of the revival, coming to prominence initially as the printer and editor of the revivalist magazine, *The Christian's Amusement,* and then subsequently as the printer, under Whitefield's strict editorial guidance, of *The Weekly History* and its two successors. In the course of publishing *The Christian's Amusement,* Lewis had final say over the material that was to be included in its pages every week. Throughout its year in print, Lewis peppered every issue with his editorial comments, designed to inform his readers of the latest events and interpreting them for the benefit of the rank and file. During 1740 the majority of his comments concentrated on the theological debates that were dominating the English revival, and through them Lewis attempted to act as a conciliator between the Moravians, the Calvinists and the followers of John Wesley. The idea of using the magazine in this way appears to have come from Howel Harris. In one of its first issues Lewis wrote: 'The strict charge of promoting unity, Brotherly Love and true Christian Charity which Brother Harris has given me in his letter sticks close to my soul.'[111] In other comments he frequently chided the Calvinists and the Wesleyans for their lack of tolerance,[112] and in one important instance he held up the example of Howel Harris's relationship with Charles Wesley as a perfect illustration of how brothers with major doctrinal differences could and should behave towards one another:

It is a bleeding prospect to observe the Divisions and Contentions that are among us; [. . .] I fear (God forgive me if I judge wrong) that some carnal Predestinarians are the Tools of Satan made use of to execute his dark designs [. . .] Instances of their rudeness I and hundred more have seen at the Foundery more than once, where they have insulted the Preacher because he was not of their Opinion. Are these marks of Election? I say, nay, they are quite the reverse [. . .] I find tis this sort of Opinionists that have bely'd Mr John WESLEY in saying that he preaches Personal

[111]   'Editorial comments by John Lewis on promoting unity', *CA* 5.
[112]   See also *CA* 1, *CA* 7 and *CA* 15.

Perfection. But I am acquainted with many Predestinarians who are truly pious souls [. . .] I have heard (and I doubt not the truth of it) that the Rev Mr CHARLES WESLEY hath lately been to visit Brother HOWEL HARRIS in Wales. When they met, they most tenderly and most affectionately embrac'd each other, when neither of them cou'd speak a Word for excess of joy – These, these my Brethren are the true marks of true Christianity.[113]

Such passages did not prevent some, particularly among the Wesleyans, from suspecting that Lewis was taking sides in the debates and using his privileged position to defend Whitefield's Calvinistic opinions. After one such accusation he responded by protesting: 'My Brethren, though we are not all of one Opinion in some Particulars, yet if we have that Christian Charity which is the brightest ornament of the followers of JESUS, we cannot think but there are some sincere of every particular party.'[114] Ignoring these comments as best he could, Lewis continued to devote considerable effort in subsequent months to keeping both sides of the predestinarian debate on speaking terms. Whilst the immediate impact of his efforts was not felt quite so keenly among the leading revivalists, his contribution seems to have been appreciated by rank-and-file Methodists, who still regarded him as the interpreter of the complexities of their leaders' disputes. Among them his calls for tolerance, together with his policy of printing revival narratives written by Calvinists, Wesleyans and Moravians, received a more friendly response:

The Divisions we have among us, are certainly very grievous to those who desire peace and love; the obtaining of which, I plainly see is not the work of Man but of God [. . .] May my God keep me and all those who believe in Him, free from all Error and Delusion.[115]

Many of the individuals who wrote to Howel Harris reflected the preoccupations of John Lewis. They gave expression to their exasperation at what had happened to their revival, fearing that if events proceeded unchecked the very future of the revival

---

[113] 'Editorial comments by John Lewis', *CA* 11.
[114] 'John Lewis's editorial comments', *CA* 12.
[115] 'John Lewis's editorial comments', *CA* 6.

would be placed in jeopardy.[116] Sarah Mason, the wife of printer and bookseller, Samuel Mason, one of Whitefield's closest London friends, in a typically impassioned letter to Harris in February 1741, voiced her concerns about the ability of the revival to recover from such bitter and hostile arguments unless there was a resolution among all the revivalists to focus on the many things on which they were agreed rather than the relatively peripheral matters which forced them apart:

> I believe it [the revival] would be much more flourishing than it is, was not Satan suffer'd to sow the seeds of discord amongst Brethren on account of different sentiments. O when shall particular opinions be swallowed up in vital Religion and the important truths in which all sincere Christians and true Believers agree become more the subject of pulpit and private discourse.[117]

For others these theological divisions triggered a crisis of conscience and forced them to re-evaluate what they believed and why they believed it. Again Howel Harris received numerous letters in which some of his friends and contacts expressed doubts about the Calvinism they had inherited from him. Some of these letters bear eloquent testimony to the sophistication of many rank-and-file converts and demonstrate how a popular religious movement afforded people the opportunity to contribute way beyond the confines of their own communities. Elizabeth Clifford, a member of the Tabernacle Society, wrote Harris a letter which is an outstanding example of the way in which some women converts developed clear views on theological subjects and felt able to challenge the opinions of their leaders in highly articulate and persuasive terms. Her reason for writing was to discuss John Wesley's doctrine of Christian Perfection. While not fully accepting the doctrine herself, Elizabeth Clifford attempted to highlight the areas where she agreed with Wesley and those which she found less convincing. To her the crux of the issue was the possibility that the new teaching held out 'much greater degrees of grace and

---

[116]   See for example the anonymous letter from a young woman in *CA* 12; Trevecka 307, Samuel Mason to Howel Harris (23 June 1741); and Trevecka 363, Thomas Price to Howel Harris (8 August 1741).
[117]   Trevecka 316, Sarah Mason to Howel Harris (28 February 1741).

holiness to be obtained in this life than Christians generally thought of'.[118] Her letter can be read as an example of the way in which some rank-and-file Methodists felt dissatisfied with the theology that was on offer in the particular revival community to which they belonged, and as an illustration of the way in which some, on contact with other versions of the Methodist message, found that these versions often contained doctrines or patterns of spirituality which met their deepest spiritual needs in unanticipated ways. Despite her obvious ability to interact with varying theological viewpoints and to come to balanced conclusions about their relative merits, Clifford's letter shows some of the limitations of the spiritual autonomy of women in early Methodism. After outlining her opinions about Christian Perfection in detail, she ended her letter by submitting to the opinions of Harris, albeit that he was led to those by the Holy Spirit!

> I sought ye Lord that he would send me a word by you for I did not receive you in your name but in ye Name of Christ in ye name of a Prophet [. . .] I desire you will seriously consider these things & go to the Throne of Grace in my behalf there intreat ye Lord to put into your heart a suitable word for me O may he give you ye spirit to plead and wrestle with him [. . .] then I desire you will write to me if you find me in an error, endeavour to convince me if in a fault reprove me don't spair me or else ye Lord shall direct you to.[119]

Despite the ability of Clifford, and other early Methodist women, to think for themselves and in some instances to debate theology with the revivalists and occasionally question some of their actions,[120] most women, in Welsh and English Calvinistic Methodism in particular, continued to accept, more often than not without question, the traditional gender divisions and to bow to what they thought to be the superior wisdom of their male leaders.[121]

---

[118] Trevecka 265, Elizabeth Clifford to Howel Harris (9 August 1740).
[119] Ibid.
[120] See also Trevecka 1325, Anne Dutton to Howel Harris (30 May 1745).
[121] Some of the limits to women's involvement in early Methodism and evangelicalism have been explored in Chilcote, *John Wesley and the Women Preachers of Early Methodism*, pp. 49–113; Westerkamp, *Women and Religion in Early America*, passim; and White, 'Women in the early Methodist societies in Wales', 95–108. Also helpful, chiefly by way of comparison, is Wilson, *Constrained by Zeal*.

In his increasingly lonely attempts to maintain a conciliatory approach in his dealings with Whitefield, Wesley and the Moravians, Harris came to rely on the support of a number of Welsh Methodists who shared his vision. None was more committed to keeping the lines of communication with the Wesley brothers open than Thomas Price from Watford.[122] In August 1740 he had written to Harris and cautioned him to 'beware of endless & dire Disputings about strange Doctrines',[123] and, on hearing that Harris intended to go into print with an open letter to John Wesley, outlining his disagreements with his theological position. Price urged caution: 'I have heard yt you wrote 2 sheets against the Wesleys which I hope are Children of God & if not do not dispute but preach you ye Gospel & let every one stand or fall to his own Master.'[124] After the split between Whitefield and Wesley had occurred and the dust finally settled, Price remained committed to keeping the lines of communication between the Calvinists and the Wesleyans open, and after a meeting with Charles Wesley in Cardiff at the end of August 1742 he told Harris:

> The Lord I hope is uniting us more and more. Brother C—s W—y has been in the Country last week – I was to hear him on Monday last – I could not agree with him in some Things he said, I told him of it – He answered that he knew very well, but that he was not in the least straitened towards me; and bid me hold fast what I attained, and what I saw erroneous in him, to pray for him, that the Lord would enlighten, and shew him which is the true Gospel Spirit.[125]

However, Harris's conciliatory role in England was not supported with quite the same enthusiasm by some of the more Calvinistically committed members of the Welsh and English revivals. Joseph Humphreys,[126] for example, after having heard John Wesley preach, and re-examining the sermon in the light of

---

[122] James Davies, 'Caerphilly and early Methodism', *CCHMC*, XXI, 4 (December 1936), 103–13; D. Emrys Williams, 'Teulu Thomas Price, Plas Y Watfford', *CCHMC*, LVI, 1 (March 1971), 3–7.
[123] Trevecka 363, Thomas Price to Howel Harris (8 August 1741).
[124] Trevecka 597, Thomas Price to Howel Harris (12 August 1742).
[125] Ibid.
[126] See *BDEB*, p. 582 and G. F. Nuttall, 'George Whitefield's "curate": Gloucestershire Dissent and the revival', *Journal of Ecclesiastical History*, 27, 4 (1976), 369–86.

the New Testament, became even more belligerently Calvinistic
and still more outspoken in his opposition to those with whom he
disagreed. In a letter to John Wesley he wrote:

> I was reading the latter Part of the Eighth to the Romans. It immediately
> darted into my mind, that nothing could by any means separate those
> whom god hath justify'd from the Love of Christ [. . .] No reasonings or
> Arguments could have prevailed with me; but when God overpower'd me
> with love, what was I that I should withstand God![127]

For much of 1740 and 1741, the theological disputes between
the Calvinists and the Wesleyans focused the attention of rank-
and-file members of the revival above everything else. Once the
split between the two factions had finally occurred, interest in the
differences between the groups naturally declined, although
there were a number of occasions in the mid- and later 1740s
when some felt sufficiently strongly to write to Harris and protest
at the incursions of the Wesleys into Wales and various aspects of
their distinctive theology, and to express concern at the
proselytizing zeal with which Wesley was beginning to act in
some parts of south Wales.[128] By this stage the majority of Welsh
Methodists were content to leave detailed theological wranglings
to the revivalists. Many grew increasingly weary of theological
bickering and backbiting, and gave expression to the hope that
relatively minor theological issues could be overlooked, especially
when placed in the context of the revival as a whole and all that
it seemed to presage. When the subject of the division in the
movement appeared in their letters it was usually in the form of a
wistful longing for the days when all divisions would be overcome and all Christians would be able to coexist in love and
harmony. An anonymous letter printed in *The Christian's
Amusement* gave expression to this longing in a particularly clear
and vivid manner:

> My Brethren the Sins of the Times are upon us! By these Divisions it
> appears that judgement is began at the House of God and what will the

---

[127] 'The copy of a letter from MR HUMPHREYS to the REV MR JOHN WESLEY (5 April
1741)', *WH* 11.
[128] See above, pp. 229–31.

End be? [. . .] But notwithstanding, tho' the Lord will approve his Churches, yet blessed be his holy Name, he will preserve himself a Church without Spot or wrinkle: He will come down as in the Days of old, in his strength, as Lord of Hosts, and will fight for Mount Zion, and for the Hill thereof.[129]

For the majority of Welsh Methodists their knowledge of the international evangelical community and their participation in its communications network operated on a strictly spiritual and therefore, at times, slightly intangible level. In the earliest months of the revival there was far more fluidity in the way in which the evangelical communications network operated on a day-to-day basis. As has already been repeatedly stressed, the network's existence depended on the commitment of the grass-roots Methodist converts to make it viable, and it was their use of it to flesh out every aspect of their daily Christian lives that made it so relevant to them. There is sufficient evidence to be able to demonstrate that in the later 1730s, Methodists attempted to pool their resources, taking advantage of the consumer oppor- tunities in the middle years of the eighteenth century,[130] in an attempt to recapture the true spirit of primitive Christianity[131] and give expression to the spiritual unity that many of them were persuaded had already sprung into existence.

In London, John Lewis, as editor of *The Christian's Amuse- ment*, encouraged his readers to notify him of any practical services that they could put at the disposal of their fellow Methodists. He wrote:

> I shall be willing to advertise for any Brother or Sister, in this Paper, gratis: for I would they should assist one another: For if you do but begin to be in earnest about Religion you will soon find the Frowns of an ill-natured world. And some have lost their Bread for Conscience sake.[132]

[129] 'Letter from a friend', *CA* 12.
[130] See Neil McKendrick, 'The consumer revolution in eighteenth-century England', in Neil McKendrick, John Brewer and J. H. Plumb, *The Birth of a Consumer Society: The Commercialisation of Eighteenth-Century England* (Bloomington, 1982), pp. 9–33; Woodruff D. Smith, *Consumption and the Making of Respectability 1600–1800* (London, 2002), pp. 5–24; and Lambert, *'Pedlar in Divinity'*, pp. 25–36.
[131] See John Walsh, 'John Wesley and the community of goods', in Keith Robbins (ed.), *Protestant Evangelicalism: Britain, Ireland, Germany and America, c.1750–1950: Essays in Honour of W. R. Ward* (Oxford, 1990), pp. 25–50 and Eamon Duffy, 'Primitive Christianity revived: religious renewal in Augustan England', pp. 287–300.
[132] 'Editorial comments', *CA* 12.

As a result Lewis advertised the services of Sister Betty Angus, who owned a clothes shop,[133] and Jacob Humphreys, who was a watch- and clock-maker.[134] Whilst in London, Harris benefited on a number of occasions from the generosity of these entrepreneurial Methodists, receiving various gifts from a new suit of clothes[135] to a watch.[136] Other Methodists were able to offer practical assistance on a more local level. In Wales, Anne Thomas and Sister Bowen took the initiative in drawing up itineraries for the preaching tour of the revivalists, organizing suitable locations for their meetings and arranging comfortable hospitality for them *en route*.[137] What John Lewis was attempting to create was a network of sympathetic contacts that the rank-and-file members of the revival could use for the provision of their practical daily requirements. The significance of this development lies in the revivalists' awareness of the practical sacrifice that membership of the revival often entailed for many of their followers. The revivalists usually had sufficient resources and contacts to enable them to surmount this problem, but they were conscious that many of their converts, often living in small, remote rural communities, did not have access to sympathetically inclined shopkeepers and tradespeople as they did. This also undoubtedly reflected the early Methodists' preoccupation with the simplicity and communitarian spirit that characterized the apostolic Church. When they read that the first Christians practised community of goods,[138] the Methodists, as they strove to follow the apostolic pattern closely, sought to do likewise. Despite its initial success, it turned out to be a very short-lived project. As the revival expanded outside its main areas of strength and then split into various factions, there was less opportunity for sharing practical resources as individuals were pitted against one another. This is not to say that the communitarian ideal evaporated altogether, but any attempt to pursue it on a inter-revival level proved impossible.

---

[133]   Ibid.
[134]   Ibid.
[135]   HHD 41, 13–15 March 1739.
[136]   Trevecka 404, George Whitefield to Howel Harris (28 November 1741). See also Trevecka 2811, Howel Harris to Anne Williams (18 February 1744).
[137]   See Howell, *The Rural Poor*, p. 153 and White, 'Women and the Methodist revival in Wales', 104–5.
[138]   Acts 2: 41–7.

For most rank-and-file Methodists, participation in the commercial side of the communications network took place most
frequently when they responded to the advertisements which
appeared in *The Weekly History*. Most of these were for books
and printed sermons, and it was mainly by responding to them
that many Welsh Methodists got their hands on the newly
printed works of evangelical writers like Jonathan Edwards,
Ralph and Ebenezer Erskine and, of course, George Whitefield
himself.[139] Others received the newly published works by joining
the literature distribution network that Howel Harris attempted
to establish. Throughout south Wales, Harris had woven
together a network of Methodists, usually local exhorters and
society leaders, to whom he sent parcels of books which were
then distributed among the local Methodist population.[140]
Thomas Bowen, Tyddyn, Llandinam, was one such recipient. In
March 1743, he wrote to Harris requesting copies of some of the
works of the Erskine brothers and a copy of John Cennick's
hymns. When he was in Wales, Harris relied on the activities of
friends in London to keep him up to date with the most recent
publications and send him enough copies to satisfy the demands
of his Welsh followers. In December 1743, one of these friends,
Anne Dutton, sent Harris a parcel containing: 'Of Brief Acct &c
2d Part, Seven [. . .] Of Gentleman's Letter Book, Seven, [. . .]
Of Meditations &c Seven [. . .] Of Chastisement &c seven [. . .]
Of letter to those that Love Christ &c seven [. . .] Of Hurt of Sin,
one.'[141] These books were to be distributed by Harris to anybody
who was interested, and Harris was instructed to 'keep a seventh
Part of the Money for yr Trouble'.[142]

The frequency with which the Welsh Methodists requested the
latest books to emerge from the pens of the most articulate
defenders of the new evangelical movement and the enthusiasm
with which these were distributed to fellow converts are further
evidence of the Methodists' eagerness to support the inter-

---

[139] See *CA* 2; *CA* 10; *WH* 44 (Saturday, 6 February 1742); *WH* 46 (Saturday, 20
February 1742); *WH* 53 (Saturday, 10 April 1742); and *WH* 62 (Saturday, 12 June 1742).
[140] Trevecka 293, Howell Harris to Anne and Elizabeth Thomas, Longhouse (10
December 1740); Trevecka 315, Howel Harris to anonymous (16 February 1741);
Trevecka 475, David Thomas to Howel Harris (9 February 1742); Trevecka 1432,
Richard Jones to Howel Harris (22 March 1746); Trevecka 1815, Evan Williams to John
Sucket (29 August 1748).
[141] Trevecka 1056, Anne Dutton to Howel Harris (15 December 1743).
[142] Ibid.

national revival and keep abreast of the latest thinking on the nature and the future direction of their movement. The international Methodist book trade reinforced all the other methods by which the evangelical awakenings were kept together and ensured that, despite doctrinal differences, many of them developed along similar lines. However, it is also an indication of the extent to which participation in the international communications network could free many of the grass-roots Methodists from over-reliance on the initiative of their leaders.

For some Methodists participation in this international evangelical community was the means by which they found their marriage partners. Despite the revivalists' preference for purely spiritual matters and their often less than enthusiastic attitude to marriage,[143] their followers did not always share their coyness. The two best-known examples of 'ordinary' Methodists finding marriage partners as a result of involvement in the wider revival are those of Elizabeth James and Sarah Gwynne. Elizabeth James married George Whitefield in November 1741.[144] Their meeting and the circumstances of their marriage developed from Whitefield's close friendship with Howel Harris. Harris, it seems, had been 'courting' Elizabeth James for a number of months and seemed to have been on the verge of proposing marriage when he learned that Whitefield was looking for a wife! After considerable heart-searching and a protracted season of prayer, Harris felt compelled to renounce his romantic interest in her and allow Whitefield the opportunity to court her.[145] The two were married shortly after. Sarah Gwynne, the daughter of Marmaduke Gwynne, of Garth, Breconshire,[146] married Charles Wesley. The Gwynnes were a prominent Welsh landowning family and among the few supporters that Wesley could count on in Wales. Both John and Charles Wesley used their Breconshire home as a base for preaching tours of the few parts of south Wales that welcomed them, and it seems that it was on one of these occasions that

[143]   Henry D. Rack, '"But Lord, let it be Betsy": love and marriage in early Methodism', *Proceedings of the Wesley Historical Society*, 53, 1 (February 2001), 1–13 and Bufford W. Coe, *John Wesley and Marriage* (Bethlehem, PA, 1996).

[144]   Roger Lee Brown, 'The marriage of George Whitefield at Caerphilly', *CCHMC*, 7 (1983), 24–30.

[145]   Beynon, *Howell Harris's Visits to London*, p. 28.

[146]   Frederick C. Gill, *Charles Wesley: The First Methodist* (London, 1964), pp. 125–42; Richard P. Heitzenrater, *Wesley and the People called Methodists* (Nashville, 1995), p. 172.

Charles Wesley first met Sarah in August 1747. A close friendship quickly developed, leading to their marriage two years later, an event that, much to his brother's disapproval, precipitated Charles's subsequent withdrawal from the life of an itinerant evangelist.[147] These two marriages are exceptional; not every Welsh Methodist married one of the revivalists. Others married partners that they met in their local societies or at the various local and national Methodist gatherings at which converts from a wider geographical area met. Crucially, many of these marriages did not take place without Harris's recommendation. Elizabeth Thomas's marriage to John Sims in January 1746 only went ahead when Howel Harris had assured her father of Sims's good character.[148] Similarly, Watkin Watkins felt that he had to ask Harris's opinion before he married Hester Parry in 1744.[149]

These marriages are indicative of some of the most powerful motives compelling grass-roots evangelicals to participate in the revival – namely fellowship, friendship and the security of a finely honed support network. The fact that participation in the revival introduced converts to new potential friends was one of the chief contributory factors in its longer-term sustainability.[150] Joining the revival had often entailed considerable sacrifice, and so the communitarian spirit of the communications network compensated for the early Methodists' dislocation and provided converts with a meaningful context within which to carry on their daily lives. New friends, new opportunities, and in some cases the redirection of their lives as they took on responsibility for local leadership of the revival, were usually very attractive in a society where the monotony and harshness of everyday life was often unrelenting. The close friendship of like-minded people, together with the knowledge that they were part of an international renewal movement, added considerable zest and colour to the lives of many in the first generation of the Welsh Methodist revival's converts.

[147]   Rack, *Reasonable Enthusiast*, pp. 253–5. Excellent on the relationship between Charles and John Wesley is Gareth Lloyd, 'Charles Wesley: a new evaluation of his life and ministry' (Ph.D., University of Liverpool, 2002).
[148]   Trevecka 1348, Howel Harris to John Thomas (5 August 1745).
[149]   Trevecka 1158, Watkin Watkins to Howel Harris (March 1744?). See also the case of the marriage between Catherine James and John Williams, in White, *Praidd Bach y Bugail Mawr*, p. 85.
[150]   White, 'The world, the flesh and the devil', 55, and White, 'Women in the early Methodist societies in Wales', 103–4.

VII

'THE REDEEMER'S KINGDOM ABROAD': WELSH METHODISTS AND THE WIDER WORLD

In order to gain a more complete picture of the Welsh Methodists' participation in the international evangelical community in the 1740s it is necessary to widen the focus to consider how wider events informed the world-view of the first generation of rank-and-file Welsh Methodists. The Welsh Methodists' knowledge of the English revival, as has been demonstrated, was often detailed and up to date because of the close working relationship that existed between Calvinistic Methodism in both countries. However, the extent to which the rank-and-file members of the Welsh revival were exposed to influences from other national awakenings is more difficult to assess.

The American colonies exercised a remarkably strong hold on the minds of many Welsh Methodists throughout the revival's first decade. The awakening at Northampton in New England in 1734–5, superintended by Jonathan Edwards, presaged the more remarkable emergence of evangelical Protestantism a few years later. After Edwards's highly influential account of the revival, *A Narrative of Surprising Conversions*, was published in Britain for the first time in 1737, the Northampton awakening came to be seen as the benchmark against which the authenticity of all other awakenings was to be tested. Whitefield's extended visit to the colonies in 1740 and 1741, which fanned the flames of revival and gave birth to the event that historians have dubbed the Great Awakening,[1] was followed in Wales with intense interest

---

[1] The term 'Great Awakening' was coined by Joseph Tracy in his *The Great Awakening: A History of the Revival of Religion in the time of Edwards and Whitefield* (1842; reprinted Edinburgh, 1976). His description has cast a long shadow over studies of the colonial revivals. For an analysis of its defects see Jon Butler, 'Enthusiasm described and decried: the Great Awakening as interpretative fiction', *Journal of American History*, 69 (September 1982), 305–25. The notion of a Great Awakening was defended by Alan Heimert and Perry Miller in the introduction to their anthology, *The Great Awakening* (Indianapolis, 1967), pp. xiii–xv. More recently, the term has again been rehabilitated by Frank Lambert in his *Inventing the 'Great Awakening'*. For a summary of the debate see Allen C. Guelzo, 'God's designs: the literature of the colonial revivals of religion, 1735–1760', in Harry S. Stout and D. G. Hart (eds), *New Directions in American Religious History* (New York, 1997), pp. 141–72.

through the letters that were circulated by means of the communications network and those printed in *The Weekly History* and its successors.

Welsh fascination with the progress of colonial events is more difficult to explain than the interest in either Scottish[2] or even English evangelicals. Emigration to the colonies from Wales had not occurred on as large a scale as from Scotland and England, and those who left Welsh shores had usually done so in small numbers and for strictly religious reasons.[3] The majority of Welsh emigrants had been Quakers, most of whom settled on 40,000 acres of land, known as the Welsh Tract or New Wales, in Pennsylvania, which had been set aside for them by William Penn himself. It has been estimated that between 1688 and 1722 only about 2,000 Welsh people sought a new beginning in the colonies.[4] Attitudes to them tended to be unsympathetic. Robert Jones, the Methodist leader, prominent at the end of the eighteenth century, thought that emigration to the colonies was sheer escapism and that it was 'folly to think that there exists in America any place to hide from the punishment of Him against whom we have sinned'.[5]

First-generation Methodists had a very different attitude to America. Part of the reason for this surely lies in the changing nature of Britain's relationship with the colonies, with a culture based on commercialism, led by the entrepreneurial spirit of the newly influential middling sorts, coming to dominate all aspects of English and colonial society.[6] Commercialism and the

---

[2]   On the complexity of the relationship between Scotland and the colonies see Schmidt, *Holy Fairs*; Westerkamp, *Triumph of the Laity*; Crawford, *Seasons of Grace*; and Simonson, 'Jonathan Edwards and his Scottish connections', 353–70.

[3]   James Horn, 'British diaspora: emigration from Britain, 1680–1815', in P. J. Marshall (ed.), *The Oxford History of the British Empire, II: The Eighteenth Century* (Oxford, 1998), pp. 28–52; Glanmor Williams, 'A prospect of paradise? Wales and the United States of America, 1716–1914', in Glanmor Williams, *Religion, Language and Nationality in Wales* (Cardiff, 1979), pp. 217–36; Hywel M. Davies, *Transatlantic Brethren: Rev. Samuel Jones (1735–1814) and his Friends* (Bethlehem, PA, 1995); Boyd S. Schlenther, ' "The English is swallowing up their language": Welsh ethnic ambivalence in colonial Pennsylvania and the experience of David Evans', *The Pennsylvania Magazine of History and Biography*, CXIV, 2 (April 1990), 201–28.

[4]   Elwyn T. Ashton, *The Welsh in the United States* (London, 1984), p. 43.

[5]   Williams, 'A prospect of paradise', p. 217.

[6]   Neil McKendrick, 'The consumer revolution of eighteenth-century England', in N. McKendrick, J. Brewer and J. H. Plumb (eds), *The Birth of a Consumer Society: The Commercialisation of Eighteenth-Century England* (Bloomington, 1982), pp. 9–33; T. H. Breen ' "Baubles of Britain": the American and consumer revolutions of the eighteenth century', *Past and Present*, CXIX (May 1988), 73–104; Boyd S. Schlenther, 'Religious faith and commercial empire', pp. 128–50.

consumer-driven mentality empowered individuals to take possession of their lives and destinies, make their own choices and try as best they could to improve their lot. It was an attitude that introduced a new spirit of individualism into the religious realm as competition between the various branches of Christianity in the British Isles and the American colonies was encouraged as never before and Churches were forced to compete for souls in the open market.[7]

Whitefield, as has already been pointed out, exemplified this new commercial spirit in many respects. He adopted the language and many of the techniques of the commercial world, and allowed his personality and message to be sold by the rapidly developing popular press and a variety of innovative promotional methods.[8] By acting, in effect, as an inter-revival evangelist, Whitefield was able to ensure that all the individual local and national awakenings were loosely bound together by virtue of their common interest in his itinerancy. His absorption in the colonial revival ensured that all those who looked to him for leadership became participants, in varying degrees and at various levels, in the Great Awakening and that influences from the colonies came to have a disproportionate effect on the revivals in the British Isles.

The leaders of the Welsh Methodist revival responded enthusiastically to the news and ideas that emanated from the colonies. They were deeply influenced by Jonathan Edwards's pneumatalogical theology of the revival, developed chiefly in the aftermath of the ground-breaking events at Northampton in 1735–6, and at times they drew direct comparisons between their revival and what had happened there. Writing to Daniel Rowland in 1738, for example, Howel Harris, having just read Edwards's account of the Northampton awakening, enthusiastically remarked: 'Surely the time here is like New England.'[9] As the revival progressed, comments such as these were fleshed out and became more discriminating, whilst fascination with the colonies remained undimmed.

Despite this fascination, both Harris and his fellow Methodists in Wales had only very limited first-hand links with the colonies.

---

[7] Schlenther, 'Religious faith and commercial empire', p. 149.
[8] Lambert, '*Pedlar in Divinity*', pp. 52–94.
[9] HHD 35, 22 November 1738.

There is evidence that Harris received at least one letter from an American correspondent, Abiel Walley, in January 1745. The letter appears to have been penned at the suggestion of George Whitefield. It contains very little news about the progress of the colonial revival and, disappointingly, gives no indication of the extent of Walley's knowledge about events in Wales. He seems to have been content simply to offer some general comments on the progress of the revival and some exhortations to Harris to remain faithful. He wrote: '[It is a] matter of great joy to hear of ye flourishing of the Redeemers kingdom abroad, and is a ground of praise and thanksgiving when we are worshipping at his footstool.'[10] There is no evidence that any of the rank-and-file Welsh Methodists enjoyed a meaningful correspondence with any of their colonial counterparts. We can only surmise that among those who had emigrated to the colonies, some were caught up in the revival and wrote to family and friends back home.[11] What is far easier to establish is that the progress of the Welsh revival was followed in the colonies, and that the names of some of its leading figures, Howel Harris and Daniel Rowland in particular, were fairly widely known. A colonial correspondent of Whitefield's could write to him in 1743 and express how

> It much rejoices my soul to hear what great things our Lord is doing by your ministry in England, Scotland and Wales, and wherever he is pleased to send you. [. . .] Be pleased to greet very heartily the dear Servants of the Lamb, Mr Harris and Mr Cennick. I love them very much.[12]

Although this letter shows that the Welsh revival was known in the colonies, it also shows how important George Whitefield was to the propagation of information about the wider revival among the colonists. The flow of information worked well in the opposite direction. For the rank and file, news from the colonies depended just as much on the initiative of Whitefield, who, when in the colonies, maintained his practice of writing regular letters outlining the highs and, less frequently, the lows of his itinerary.

[10]   Trevecka 1273, Abiel Walley to Howel Harris (4 January 1745).
[11]   We know that this occurred among evangelicals of Scottish origin, for example. David Cressy, *Coming Over: Migration and Communication between England and New England in the Seventeenth Century* (Cambridge, 1987).
[12]   'The Copy of a Letter from Mr E. E.— to the Reverend MR WHITEFIELD (26 September 1743)', *Account*, IV, III, 19–24.

The letters which he or one of his secretaries, usually his wife Elizabeth during most of the 1740s, wrote back to the British Isles were, more often than not, directed to Howel Harris, who from the vantage point of Whitefield's London Tabernacle distributed them to the various Methodist centres in England and Wales. The overwhelming majority of the letters were fairly spontaneous accounts of local colonial awakenings, and their frequency tended to reflect the progress of Whitefield's own itinerancy. In the early 1740s, Whitefield's letters were supplemented by extracts from colonial newspapers such as the *Boston Gazette*[13] and the *Charles-town Gazette*[14] which were reprinted in *The Christian's Amusement* and *The Weekly History*. Through these accounts Welsh Methodists became increasingly familiar with the names of Jonathan Edwards, Gilbert and William Tennant, James Davenport, Samuel Davies and Thomas Prince, and could, on occasion, be more aware of events in places like Boston, Charlestown, Philadelphia and Georgia than in many places closer to home.

Perhaps the most interesting element in many of the letters about the colonial revival that made their way to Welsh Methodists was the way in which they included comparisons between the awakenings in America and Wales. In the early years of his colonial itinerancy Whitefield, as he had done after visiting Wales for the first time,[15] thought that Americans were far more susceptible to revival and to experimental religion than were many of his fellow countrymen in England. In a letter to Howel Harris, he extolled the virtues of his colonial congregations, comparing them with the coldness of his congregations in England: 'JESUS manifests forth his glory daily in these parts [. . .] America, ere long, will be more famous for Christians. Surely the candlestick will shortly be removed from England.'[16] Whilst these comments tell us as much about the negative impact which the arguments raging between the Calvinists, the

---

[13] 'From the Boston Gazette, 28 June 1740', *CA*, 1.
[14] 'From the Charles-Town Gazette, 18 July 1740', *CA* 3 and 'From the Charles-Town Gazette, from Saturday 6 September to Saturday, 13 September 1740', *WH*, 13. There were also numerous extracts from other colonial newspapers. See 'A Postscript to the South-Carolina Gazette, No. 361', *WH*, 7.
[15] Murray (ed.), *George Whitefield's Journals*, pp. 229–30.
[16] George Whitefield to Howel Harris (9 November 1740), in Murray (ed.), *George Whitefield's Letters*, p. 220.

Arminians and the Wesleyans had on the day-to-day response to Whitefield's ministry, they and many other similar comments[17] also tell us something about the ease with which Whitefield made the transition from English revivalist to colonial itinerant. Whether Whitefield's enthusiasm for his colonial hearers owed more – in New England at least – to their more orthodox Calvinist heritage, the better mobilization of advance publicity or, more likely, their independence of mind, conditioned by being far enough removed from Britain to be able to respond more enthusiastically to a message that put all of its emphasis on each individual's spiritual autonomy. Significantly, the radical sounding tone of the evangelical message appeared to strike a chord with those in the colonies who were thinking, more clearly than ever before, about achieving political autonomy.[18]

By sending home such positive comments about his colonial congregations Whitefield, it seems, was trying to achieve a number of things. He was showing to his followers in the British Isles the potential of their own awakening, which was, as he wrote, being threatened by the self-interest of a few in the over-heated atmosphere of the London awakening. As rank-and-file Welsh Methodists read such comments, it is inconceivable that they would not have been inspired to continue in their newly discovered faith with renewed vigour, in spite of the problems that their movement seemed to be facing. In effect, Whitefield was attempting to turn the attention of his English and Welsh followers away from their seemingly petty arguments over Predestination, provoking them to focus on more important matters. Whitefield and Harris also realized the benefits that reading so many positive reports from the colonies could have,[19] and they never tired of reminding their followers of the influence that they might gain if only they were all prepared to focus on the revival's core aims.

---

[17] 'Extract of a letter from the Rev. Mr Whitefield to Mr Seward: dated May 19 1740. On board the Savannah sloop bound from Pennsylvania to Georgia', *CA*, 1.

[18] Mark A. Noll, *America's God: From Jonathan Edwards to Abraham Lincoln* (New York, 2002), pp. 43–4.

[19] 'The copy of a letter from the Rev. Mr Whitefield, dated Charles-town, July 18, 1740', *CA* 6 and 'A letter from the Rev. Mr Whitefield, dated from Boston, October 10, 1740', *CA* 15.

Whitefield's unbounded enthusiasm for the colonies predictably cooled in the same way as many of his other enthusiasms were dissipated when the novelty of his activities had passed and criticisms began to be voiced more stridently. Comments eulogizing his colonial congregations and praising his own contribution became less frequent and hyperbolic. In their place appeared much more realistic comments on the pressing spiritual needs of his listeners, which Whitefield quickly came to feel were in actual fact often more acute than in the British Isles. In 1745, for example, Elizabeth Whitefield reported to Harris: 'the fields are in everywhere white and ready to harvest and great numbers flock to the Word as doves to ye windows.'[20] By 1747, Whitefield's reports had become far more downbeat as he viewed the thousands and thousands in these American parts who, as to spiritual things, 'know not their Right Hand from their left'.[21]

Probably the single most important influence emanating from the colonial revival was the writings of Jonathan Edwards.[22] Edwards, as has already been mentioned, was the chief theological apologist of the revival. His writings reached all parts of the movement and were used, to a greater or lesser degree, by all the revivalists.[23] In his three works, *A Faithful Narrative of the Surprising Work of God* (1736), *The Distinguishing Marks of a Work of the Spirit of God* (1741) and *A Treatise Concerning the Religious Affections* (1746), all loosely connected to the subject of revival by their concentration on the broader theme of religious experience and using information and case studies gathered over the years when the revival was at its most intense, Edwards constructed a theology which sought to explain the highly emotional spiritual experiences that lay at the heart of the movement. However, despite the importance of Edwards's writings, tracing the precise way in which his influence was felt in Wales is difficult.

[20] Trevecka 1340, Elizabeth Whitefield to Howel Harris, Herbert Jenkins, Thomas Adams and all at the Tabernacle (July 1745).

[21] 'From the REV MR WHITEFIELD to Mr Howel Harris (30 May 1747), *CH*, 1747, 114.

[22] The introductions and critical texts in Perry Miller, John E. Smith and Harry S. Stout (eds), *The Works of Jonathan Edwards* (New Haven, 1957–) are the essential places to begin a study of Edwards's thought. For detailed study of his life and development see Marsden, *Jonathan Edwards* and for analysis of his writings on revival and religious experience Goen (ed.), *The Works of Jonathan Edwards*, IV, pp. 1–95 and Crawford, *Seasons of Grace*, pp. 180–90.

[23] On parallels between Edwards and John Wesley see Richard B. Steele, *'Gracious Affection' and 'True Virtue' According to Jonathan Edwards and John Wesley* (Metuchen, N.J, 1994).

Of his three books it was *A Faithful Narrative* that was read by the greatest number of Methodists in the British Isles, and as such it casts an extremely long shadow over the evangelical revival and furthermore over the subsequent history of the evangelical movement, in that its description became, in the words of Michael Crawford, the 'prototype'[24] for all subsequent revivals. Whilst Edwards himself warned of the danger of too formulaic an understanding of religious revivals and evangelical conversion,[25] there is little doubt that many who read his work, having neither his theological understanding nor pastoral sagacity, applied it to the letter. In Edwards's account Howel Harris would have read about the progress of the Northampton revival and, for the first time, read his detailed reflections on the conversion process. The almost scientific observation of conversions in the town during 1734–5 had led Edwards to posit a threefold pattern of conversion corresponding roughly to the stages of deep conviction of sin and despair at the hopelessness of one's spiritual condition, which invariably and finally culminated in rapturous release in the New Birth experience itself. It was a pattern with which Harris would have been familiar through his similar observations in and around Trefeca and from reading Whitefield's sermon, *The Nature and Necessity of New Birth in Christ Jesus, in order to Salvation* (1737).

Whilst there were differences between Edwards's *Faithful Narrative* and the accounts written about awakenings in the British Isles, particularly the congregational context in which revival in the colonies tended to occur, as opposed to the extra-parochial gatherings of the Methodists,[26] the similarities between his account and what was occurring in Wales were too striking to escape Harris's attention.[27] *The Faithful Narrative* was intended by Edwards to be nothing more than a record of his observations on the Northampton awakening. Its contents[28] were mirrored closely in the revival narratives written by evangelicals in the

---

[24]   Crawford, *Seasons of Grace*, p. 132.
[25]   See Conrad Cherry, *The Theology of Jonathan Edwards: A Reappraisal* (New York, 1966), p. 65 and Goen (ed.), *The Works of Jonathan Edwards, IV*, pp. 28–30.
[26]   Crawford, *Seasons of Grace*, pp. 189–90.
[27]   HHD 35, 27 November 1738.
[28]   For an analysis of its contents see Crawford, *Seasons of Grace*, p. 185.

British Isles. However, it is difficult to trace this trend directly to Edwards. He and the Methodists borrowed from the long tradition of Puritan conversion narratives, and it is not surprising that when they wrote about their revivals they followed in that tradition, adapting it to suit their particular circumstances.[29] Whitefield as much as Edwards, in an English context at least, was equally influential in formulating the boundaries of the conversion process. It is possible to demonstrate the way in which narratives from the two countries overlapped, highlighting some of the common themes that made up the conversion process and how they helped in the wider creation of a new evangelical climate.

The first generation of Welsh pioneer revivalists, it has to be admitted, had neither the gifts nor, it would appear, the wish to recast Edwards's theology in a Welsh context. This was something achieved piecemeal over thirty years later by William Williams, who almost single-handedly produced a distinctively Welsh experiential theology of revival, drawing from his own experience and that of his fellow Welsh revivalists as well as from writers like Jonathan Edwards.[30] In the early years of the revival the influence of Edwards's writings is only detectable indirectly. People tended to write descriptions of revival experiences that mirrored Edwards's precisely because those experiences were so similar, rather than because they were consciously following his example.[31]

Some Welsh Methodists were reading Edwards at an early date. Howel Harris and Daniel Rowland had discussed *A Faithful Narrative* when they met at Defynnog during November

---

[29]   On the Methodist adaptation of this genre see Hindmarsh, ' "My chains fell off, my heart was free": early Methodist conversion narrative in England', 910–29 and Hindmarsh, 'The Olney autobiographers: English conversion narrative in the mid-eighteenth century', 61–84.

[30]   The overwhelming majority of William Williams's writings are in Welsh. The standard edition of his works is Gomer M. Roberts (gol.), *Gweithiau William Williams Pantycelyn*, I (Cardiff, 1964) and G. H. Hughes (gol.), *Gweithiau William Williams Pantycelyn*, II (Cardiff, 1967). For English translations of some of these see Williams, *The Experience Meeting* and Eifion Evans, *Pursued by God: A Selective Translation with Notes of the Welsh Religious Classic, Theomemphus by William Williams of Pantycelyn* (Bridgend, 1996). For a useful single-volume analysis of Williams's thought see Derec Llwyd Morgan (gol.), *Meddwl a Dychymyg Williams Pantycelyn* (Llandysul, 1991).

[31]   For a brief comparison see Evans, *Daniel Rowland*, pp. 69–78.

1738.[32] Subsequently we know that advertisements for Edwards's works appeared from time to time in *The Weekly History*,[33] and it would be inconceivable to imagine that the Welsh Methodists, who usually responded so enthusiastically to such advertisements, would not have taken advantage of the opportunity to acquire some of Edwards's works. By the mid-1740s, when the initial excitement and turmoil of the revival had abated and the Welsh revivalists were devoting increasingly large amounts of their time to the consolidation of their converts, the works of Edwards were turned to afresh. William Williams was reading *The Distinguishing Marks of a Work of the Spirit of God* at the end of 1745 and thought that it was the 'best book I have Seen to that purpose'.[34] Towards the end of the decade, Thomas Bowen, the exhorter from Llandinam, who was undoubtedly one of the most widely read of all the Welsh Methodists, was also discussing Edwards's ideas in a letter to Harris.[35] Therefore, whilst it is difficult to adduce concrete evidence that the Welsh Methodists adopted Edwards's theology verbatim, it would not be an exaggeration to claim that Edwards's writing remained part of the core canon of evangelical writings with which those who led societies or played a role in the administration of the revival were expected to be familiar.

For many rank-and-file Welsh Methodists their most tangible link with the American colonies was the orphanage that Whitefield established in Georgia.[36] The Orphan House was the one element of the international revival in which ordinary Welsh Methodists had a direct stake. Whitefield's vision of a home for orphaned children in the recently established colony of Georgia was something that he took with him on his itineraries throughout the revival, and it became a project that took up an increasing amount of his time and energy in the 1740s as it lurched from one financial catastrophe to another. To keep its

---

[32] HHD 35, 27 November 1738.
[33] See for example *WH* 56 (Saturday, 1 May 1742).
[34] Trevecka 1381, William Williams to Howel Harris (7 December 1745).
[35] Trevecka 1847, Thomas Bowen to Howel Harris (30 January 1749).
[36] See Neil J. O'Connell, 'George Whitefield and Bethesda Orphan-House', *Georgia Historical Quarterly*, 54 (1970), 41–62; Dallimore, *George Whitefield*, I and II, passim; and Schlenther, *Queen of the Methodists*, pp. 83–95.

doors open, Whitefield used his itinerant ministry as a means of raising funds by way of collections for the orphans at the conclusion of his sermons throughout the revival.

The Georgia colony had been established in 1733 as a philanthropic venture at the instigation of James Oglethorpe (1696–1785).[37] From its beginning, the southernmost of the American colonies had exercised an almost hypnotic hold on the minds of many evangelicals. John Wesley had famously gone there as a colonial missionary in 1735, only to return dejected little more than a year later.[38] None the less the colony continued to appeal to those evangelicals who had come under the influence of Pietism and the writings of August Herman Francke, the Halle Lutheran Pietist, whose this-worldly Pietism had resulted in a flood of philanthropic ventures, including the building of an orphanage.[39] Francke's example had been particularly important to Whitefield, who was ready to admit his indebtedness to him on a number of occasions.[40] His reasons for the foundation of the Georgia Orphan House had obvious parallels with Francke's. According to Whitefield, the idea for its establishment had taken root on his first visit to the colony in 1738, when he observed 'so many objects of charity [. . .] [including] orphans [and] [. . .] poor people's children'.[41] Whitefield had apparently made inquiries about the orphan problem and seems to have decided very quickly that it was up to him to do what he could to alleviate it.[42] In keeping with his evangelicalism, however, Whitefield turned the Orphan House into a faith ministry. It was intended primarily to be a place of refuge for orphans but it was also designed to be a place at which it would be possible to 'preach chiefly to children's hearts . . . [and] instruct them by the Church of England's Articles'.[43] Its funding depended on the energy and enthusiasm of his fellow Methodists,

[37]   Daniel Boorstin, *The Americans: The Colonial Experience* (New York, 1958), pp. 73–96; Harold E. Davis, *The Fledgling Province: Social and Cultural Life in Colonial Georgia, 1733–1776* (Williamsburg, and Chapel Hill, 1976), pp. 7–32; and Phinizy Spalding, *Oglethorpe in America* (Chicago, 1997), pp. 1–17.

[38]   Rack, *Reasonable Enthusiast*, pp. 107–36; Richard P. Heitzenrater, 'John Wesley in America', *Proceedings of the Wesley Historical Society*, 54, 3 (October 2003), 87–91.

[39]   Ward, *The Protestant Evangelical Awakening*, pp. 61–3; Nuttall, 'Continental Pietism and the evangelical movement in Britain'; Brunner, *Halle Pietists in England*, passim.

[40]   See Murray (ed.), *George Whitefield's Journals*, p. 334.

[41]   Lambert, '*Pedlar in Divinity*', p. 58.

[42]   Murray (ed.), *George Whitefield's Journals*, p. 156.

[43]   Lambert, '*Pedlar in Divinity*', p. 156.

who were encouraged to give what they could as regularly as they could in support of the project. Whitefield presented the project to them in terms of their Christian responsibility to those less fortunate than themselves.[44]

Funding the Orphan House through voluntary subscriptions necessitated placing it at the forefront of his itinerant ministry, and during his life the Orphan House took up increasing amounts of Whitefield's time and energy as he sought to publicize its activities and stir up his followers to maintain their high levels of financial support of the work. Frank Lambert has argued that Whitefield's commitment to the Orphan House plunged him 'deep into the Atlantic commercial world, requiring him to develop many of the entrepreneurial skills demanded of merchants in far flung trade'.[45] Firstly, he used his high profile to good effect by wedding his fund-raising activities to his preaching. On almost every occasion, Whitefield concluded his sermons with news from the Orphan House and an impassioned appeal for financial support. Alongside this, and to reach an ever wider public, he used one of his favourite techniques, advertisements disguised as religious journalism, to particularly profitable effect. Using the international communications network, particularly *The Weekly History* and its sister publications in Scotland and the colonies, Whitefield posted regular news bulletins about the progress of events in Georgia, thereby keeping the project constantly before his fellow Methodists and ensuring the steady flow of cash into the coffers.

The Welsh Methodists responded enthusiastically to White-field's appeals and throughout the 1740s they played a particularly prominent part in supporting the Orphan House, chiefly through the fund-raising activities of Howel Harris. Like Whitefield, Harris had also been influenced by the writings of Pietists such as Francke and concurred wholeheartedly with Whitefield's desire for a more tangible, practical outworking of evangelical zeal along Pietistic lines. Harris's attempts to ensure that the Welsh societies became genuine havens in which members would be supported both spiritually and materially by their leaders and, perhaps more importantly, by one another

[44]   Murray (ed.), *George Whitefield's Journals*, p. 156.
[45]   Lambert, '*Pedlar in Divinity*', p. 58.

can, to some extent, be taken as an indication of his desire to implement an intensely practical Christianity.[46] Harris had also attempted, unsuccessfully, to establish a collection for the poor in 1743,[47] an idea that was revived in 1749, following the example set by Whitefield's Tabernacle;[48] he managed to convince his fellow revivalists of the necessity of a system of weekly collections intended for the help of those facing acute financial difficulties.[49] The true extent to which Harris was influenced by Francke did not become apparent until the mid-1750s when, freed of all his Methodist responsibilities, he established his religious community at Trefeca.[50] Amongst the rank-and-file Methodists in Wales there is plenty of evidence of the depth of their social concern. Eryn White, in her examination of some of their wills, has discovered that among the more prosperous members there were some prepared to use their prosperity for the benefit of their fellow Methodists.[51] Some of them contributed liberally to the building of meeting houses for societies that had outgrown the local farmhouse kitchen[52] and others gave in support of fellow members facing court cases and persecution on account of their faith.[53] The Orphan House was another philanthropic venture along the same lines that they were prepared to support. The fact that it was located on another continent seemed to make very little difference to saints who were intensely proud of the internationalism of their revival.

Harris's own commitment to the Orphan House project was of an altogether different order. Always interested in the colonies, he had considered becoming a colonial missionary a number of times during the 1740s. He had read Whitefield's

[46]   See for example *Sail, Dibenion, a Rheolau'r Societies Neu'r Cyfarfodydd Neullduol a ddechreassant ymgynull yn ddiweddar yn Nghymru* (Bristol, 1742), p. 3.

[47]   'Glan-yrafonddu, Carmarthenshire, 1 March 1743', CMA 2945, pp. 10–11.

[48]   Trevecka 1305, James Erskine to John Edwards (19 March 1745).

[49]   HHD 134, 12 March 1749. On Methodist attitudes to provision for the poor see Joanna Innes, 'The "mixed economy of welfare" in early modern England: assessments of the options from Hale to Malthus (c.1683–1803)', in Martin Daunton (ed.), *Charity, Self-Interest and Welfare in the English Past* (London, 1996), pp. 153–60 and R. P. Heitzenrater (ed.), *The Poor and the People Called Methodists, 1729–1999* (Nashville, 2002).

[50]   Alun Wynne Owen, 'A study of Howell Harris and the Trevecka "family" (1752–1760) based upon the Trevecka letters and diaries and other Methodist archives at the NLW' (MA, University of Wales, 1957).

[51]   White, *Praidd Bach y Bugail Mawr*, pp. 137–8.

[52]   HHD 134, 12 March 1749.

[53]   White, *Praidd Bach y Bugail Mawr*, p. 138.

Journals account of his first visit to the American colonies and
was particularly interested in the Moravian and Salzburger
settlements in Georgia and their evangelistic work among the
native Indian population. In November 1739 he confided to his
diary his desire to go to preach among them: 'I was much melted
down wth Love to ye Indians & cd find myself out of pity to them
made willg to suffr anything for them & long to be wth them &
do them good.'[54] Despite this idea coming to nothing, the
American colonies continued to attract Harris. For a time he
considered accompanying Whitefield as his assistant during his
extended visits,[55] but his indispensability to the Welsh revival and
his rising profile among the English Calvinistic Methodists meant
that by 1742 the idea had retreated to the back of Harris's mind.
He contented himself with being the chief spokesperson and
fund-raiser for the orphans in England and Wales.[56]

He did this by using his partnership with John Lewis to ensure
that *The Weekly History* and its successors contained regular
updates on the work of the Orphan House. These letters became
the chief source of information for many rank-and-file Methodists, who were able to keep track of the use to which their
financial contributions were being put. The letters usually contained a significant amount of practical material, information
about the building of the house, its staffing, the constant problem
of obtaining adequate provisions, and issues relating to the
recruitment of residents and staff. When Georgia was under
threat from a Spanish embargo at the end of 1741 and during
the early months of 1742,[57] letters regarding the shortage of
provisions at the Orphan House became more frequent, and as
the embargo continued with little hope of abatement letters
became more desperate as supplies got lower and lower. At the
beginning of 1742, James Habersham, the superintendent at
Bethesda, wrote that the residents at the house 'have been

[54]   HHD 50, 9 November 1739.
[55]   HHD 73, 6 and 13 June 1741 and Trevecka 376, Griffith Twyning to Howell
Harris (28 August 1741).
[56]   See for example HHD 77, 29 August 1741.
[57]   Bruce Lenman, 'Colonial wars and imperial instability, 1688–1793', in Marshall
(ed.), *The Oxford History of the British Empire*, II, pp. 157–8; Spalding, *Oglethorpe in
America*, pp. 127–50; and Harvey H. Jackson III, 'Behind the lines: Oglethorpe,
Savannah, and the War of Jenkins's Ear', in John C. Inscoe (ed.), *James Edward
Oglethorpe: New Perspectives on his Life and Legacy: A Tercentenary Commemoration*
(Savannah, 1997), pp. 71–91.

plentifully supplied all the summer, while many about us have lacked',[58] but later 'our stores are [. . .] pretty far spent.'[59] Such appeals were certain to bring in floods of contributions.

Interested parties in the British Isles were also kept closely informed of the fluctuations in the numbers of orphans being cared for and the turnover of personnel, which at times seemed extremely rapid. In January 1742, for example, a report printed in *The Weekly History* informed the Orphan House's supporters that the enterprise consisted of:

> 84 Persons Men, women and children, and 19 more employed about us, and 5 in the Infirmary. The latter have a Doctor and Nurse and other Necessaries found them gratis at the Orphan-House expense – We have 58 Children, 32 of them belong to the Colony, 6 to Parisborough, who are I think as great objects of Charity as any in Georgia.[60]

Very few of the letters that were printed in the revivalist magazine discussed its problems. The contentment of its residents, proved by the fact that 'they are of one Heart and one Mind [and that] there is no grudging or repining one against another',[61] seemed sufficient evidence that 'this House is so much of God that He will never let it fall'.[62] As if to fend off potential criticism, these glowing reports were supported by accounts of the Orphan House written by independent observers. Josiah Smith, the influential minister at Charlestown, South Carolina, writing to his friend and colleague, William Cooper of Boston, testified, in a letter later reprinted by John Lewis, that he 'was wonderfully pleas'd with the Situation and admirable Contrivance of the House, with the many Accommodations within, and improvements without'.[63] Letters like this had the effect of reassuring those who were contributing fairly sizeable financial sums to the project on a regular basis that their monies were

---

[58] 'A letter from James Habersham, at the Orphanhouse in Georgia, to a friend (Bethesda, September 1 1741)', *WH* 39.
[59] Ibid.
[60] 'The conclusion of the letter concerning the Orphan-house in Georgia', *WH* 40.
[61] 'From Mr J—s E—ds, of the Orphanhouse in Georgia, to the Rev. Mr Whitefield (3 September 1743)', *CH*, V, I, 54.
[62] Ibid., 55.
[63] 'From the Reverend Josiah Smith, minister of the Gospel, in Charlestown, South Carolina; to the Reverend Mr William Cooper, in Boston, New England (5 June 1743)', *Account*, IV, I, 50.

being put to good use. It also provided Whitefield with the sort of independent verification that he needed. His practice of requesting donations at the end of his sermons had led some to accuse him of abusing his position and using it to line his own pocket.[64] Letters from influential colonial ministers showed the contrary and demonstrated, to Whitefield's satisfaction at least, that all the money that he collected was put to the best possible use.

However, the overwhelming majority of letters about the Orphan House that appeared in *The Weekly History* were about the spiritual well-being of its residents. Whitefield was aware that its most emotive selling point was the success of the evangelistic work among the orphans. For many of the Orphan House's most ardent supporters, this not only gave them the opportunity to contribute to the physical needs of the poor but also to support a frontier mission station. In a letter from the Orphan House during April 1743, signs of a fresh quickening of religious enthusiasm were given pride of place by John Lewis: 'A Glorious Work has begun at Bethesda about two months ago. Since which Time several Souls have been savingly converted, and other[s] remain still under Concern [. . .] Blessed be God, that he sets his Seal to the Foundation of Bethesda.'[65] This change in the religious climate at the Orphan House was one of many reported during the 1740s. Usually, as in the case just mentioned, reports came from one of the superintendents or assistants at the Orphan House. More powerful were the letters that occasionally came from the orphans themselves. The letter from a ten-year-old resident in March 1741 is typical: 'I hope the Lord hath begun a good Work in my Soul, and I hope he will carry it on to a sound Conversion, and never let it weare of.'[66] Whilst the way in which these letters were written and their conformity to the formulaic patterns of conversion narratives raise questions about their authenticity, for current purposes they were significant because of their fund-raising power. Nothing was calculated to

---

[64] Lambert, '*Pedlar in Divinity*', pp. 176–82.
[65] 'An extract of a letter from a Mr Grant, one of the assistants at the Orphanage in Georgia, to Mr S. M—n (7 April 1743)', *Account*, III, I, 84.
[66] 'From a boy about 10 years of age (23 March 1741)', *WH* 21 (Saturday, 29 August 1741). See also 'Copies of several letters wrote by the children at the Orphan House, to the Reverend Mr Whitefield', *WH* 20 (Saturday, 22 August 1741) and 'From a young maiden about 17 years of age (25 March 1741)', *WH* 22 (Saturday, 5 September 1741).

evoke more sympathy for the Georgia project than news of orphans experiencing the New Birth. It appears, that, at the time, no one from within the ranks of the movement was prepared to question whether letters, supposedly written by young children in fairly sophisticated theological language, were genuine. The money continued to flow in steadily, confirming observers' opinions that the Orphan House really was 'a Place where the Lord delights to dwell'.[67]

In Wales, Howel Harris used such letters to publicize the Orphan House project and to stimulate people to contribute to it liberally. His usual practice seems to have involved raising the issue of the Orphan House at the conclusion of one of his sermons, reporting on the latest news from it and maybe even reading a letter from one of its staff or residents. This highly emotive ploy was then followed by an appeal for money, which was passed on to Whitefield's agents in London who saw that it reached the orphans. Visiting south-west Wales in February 1748, Harris used this method of fund-raising to particularly good effect. After visiting the society at Maesnonni in Carmarthenshire he wrote:

> Last Night aftr Bro Wms preachd I discoursed a little [. . .] I opend abt ye Orphan House & made a collectn here & gatherd some many aftr openg ye Mattr & shewg home how God has placd us in various stations in this Life to some poor & some rich &c shewd how I was free to beg for God's poor opend [. . .] ye orphan house.[68]

Two days later at Penywennallt, Harris again spoke at length about the Georgia orphans: 'Afterwd I lay ye case of ye orphn House before them & collected 1–11–6 &c.'[69] From Penywennallt Harris 'went hence gatherg to ye orphn House every where'.[70] In his diary for February 1748, he made a record of all the money that he collected on his tour in south and south-west Wales, recording that he had collected the admirable sum of £41 12s. ½d. from the members of just thirty-six societies.[71] By

---

67 'From Mr J— M— to the REV MR WHITEFIELD (2 September 1743)', *CH*, V, I, 56.
68 HHD 129, 5 February 1748.
69 HHD 129, 7 February 1748.
70 HHD 129, 9 February 1748.
71 HHD 129 (inside front cover).

contributing financially to this transatlantic philanthropic venture, rank-and-file Welsh Methodists were claiming a stake in the world-wide propagation of the evangelical faith in a frontier environment.[72] Their financial sacrifices were repaid by their receipt of regular, up-to-date information about the way in which their money was being used. The Orphan House rapidly became the most tangible link that many ordinary Welsh Methodists enjoyed with the international revival, and certainly with the revival in the colonies.

The way in which rank-and-file Methodists in Wales interacted with other awakenings mirrors, albeit on a smaller scale, their relationship with the revival in the American colonies. Despite having no direct contacts with any Scottish evangelicals, rank-and-file Welsh Methodists were intensely interested in the progress of the Scottish revival and remarkably well informed about its progress, particularly during its most expansionist phase in 1742.[73] Their knowledge of its progress came from the usual sources, mediated through their leaders and the material that they saw fit to include in the international communications network.

Once again Howel Harris was the conduit through which correspondence from and about Scotland found its way to Wales. Despite his frequent longings for inter-revival travel, Harris turned down the chance to visit Scotland in 1742 because of his responsibilities in the English and Welsh revivals:

> As for my coming to Scotland, indeed I freely would, but as tis so well provided with such able men fitted for the great work, and as we have so few Labourers and such a great harvest, and the people young and ignorant that here such an Ignorant Novice as me may be made useful, which I cannot bear the Thoughts of without an immediate call amidst so many worthy labourers in Scotland.[74]

[72] For further examples of rank-and-file contributions to the Orphan House see Trevecka 1521, Howel Harris to Thomas Adams (6 September 1746); Trevecka 1522, Howel Harris to George Whitefield (8 September 1746); and Trevecka 1745, Howel Harris to George Whitefield (17 December 1747).

[73] John MacInnes, *The Evangelical Movement in the Highlands of Scotland* (Aberdeen, 1951), pp. 154–66; Callum Brown, *The Social History of Religion in Scotland since 1730* (London, 1987); Fawcett, *The Cambuslang Revival*.

[74] Trevecka 736, Howel Harris to a minister in Scotland (23 November 1742).

The real reason for his lack of enthusiasm for visiting Scotland probably had as much to do with his own feelings of inferiority, because of his lack of ordination, as it did with his other evangelical commitments. It is likely that the presence of the unordained Harris in Scotland would have aroused considerable opposition from the resolutely Presbyterian religious establishment. Therefore in an effort to avoid the sort of controversy that could easily hamper the progress of the Scottish revival, Harris swallowed his pride and made the undoubtedly painful decision to remain at home.

To compensate he coordinated the distribution of the letters that Whitefield sent from Scotland, ensuring that the Scottish revival received almost saturation coverage in the evangelical print network. Whitefield's Scottish letters tended to be more straightforward and journalistic in tone than many of those he wrote on other occasions. Nearly all concentrated on the enthusiasm with which his preaching was greeted and on the success of the Scottish revival. The letters that appeared in *The Weekly History* were of two kinds. To add to the sense of immediacy and excitement, John Lewis appended brief bulletins containing up-to-date synopses of Whitefield's latest activities.[75] These were usually unedited accounts of Whitefield's preaching in various towns and villages, and were calculated to capture some of the intensity and enthusiasm with which he was greeted. In July 1742, for example, John Lewis printed the following bulletin:

> Last Saturday Evening, the Rev. Mr Whitefield, came to this City from the west, where he preach'd all the next week, viz. on Monday twice at Paisley, six mile[s] from Glasgow. On Tuesday twice at the Mearns, sixteen Miles from that. On Friday three times at Cumbernauld, and on Saturday twice at Falkirk, in his Way to Edinburgh. In every place there have been the greatest Commotions among the people as has been known. Their mourning in most places, was like unto peoples mourning for their firstborn. The Auditories were very large, and the Work of God seems to be spreading more and more. On Sabbath last, he preach'd twice in the park, and once in the church; and every Day since twice [. . .] [He] purposes, God willing to go to Cambuslang Tomorrow, in order to assist at the Communion; and to preach at various places westward.[76]

[75] See *WH* 68 (Saturday, 24 July 1742); *WH* 70 (Saturday, 7 August 1742); and *WH* 76 (Saturday, 18 September 1742).
[76] *WH* 68 (Saturday, 24 July 1742).

More common were the letters that Whitefield sent to his fellow revivalists. Whilst in Scotland, Whitefield followed his usual practice of writing to a select band of supporters, most of whom were based in London, in the knowledge that they, as some of the most mobile of all the early evangelicals, would either distribute or print his accounts. Once more the majority of the letters that Whitefield penned were buoyant in tone, capturing something of the enthusiasm that met Whitefield's preaching. From Edinburgh he wrote that 'it would make your heart leap for joy'[77] to witness the revival under way, whilst from Aberdeen he confessed that 'God appeared for me in an extraordinary manner'[78] and at Cambuslang he had preached to what he estimated to be 20,000 people.[79] Whilst most of these letters were circulated in the usual way through the letter-writing network, some of those considered most valuable were printed in *The Weekly History.* As if to stress the significance of this latest burst of revival activity and to whip up fresh enthusiasm amongst the beleaguered London evangelicals, John Lewis printed a special double issue of his magazine on 10 July 1742 that was devoted to news from Scotland. The issue included a series of characteristic letters from Whitefield, the master publicist, regaling his readers with a blow-by-blow account of his success:

> I know not where to begin, or how to end telling you what is doing in Scotland – Last Lords Day I preach'd in the Morning in the Park at Edinburgh, to a very great multitude. Afterward I attended, and partook of the Holy Sacrament, and served four Tables, and preached in the Afternoon in the Church-yard, to a far greater Number [. . .] Oh it was a Day never to be forgotten. – On Monday I preach'd again at Edinburgh with great Power – On Tuesday I preach'd twice at Kilsyth, twenty-seven miles westward, to ten thousand. But such a commotion I believe you never saw [. . .] Last night God brought me thither [Glasgow] – A friend met me without the Town and welcomed me in the Name of Twenty thousand – The streets were alarmed. By three in the morning People were coming to hear the Word of God – By Seven I preached to many many thousands and again this Evening [. . .] The Work is spreading exceedingly

⁷⁷ 'The Rev. Mr Whitefield to Mr H. Harris (15 August 1741)', *WH* 21 (Saturday, 29 August 1741).
⁷⁸ 'The copy of a letter from the Rev Mr Whitefield in Scotland, to Mr Cennick in London (17 October 1741)', *WH* 30 (Saturday, 31 October 1741).
⁷⁹ 'Extract of a letter from the Rev Mr Whitefield to Mr Cennick (14 July 1742)', *WH* 75 (Saturday, 11 September 1742).

– It flies from parish to parish [. . .] Publish this on the House top. And exhort ALL to give THANKS.[80]

The relationship with Scotland was not merely one-way. The revival in Wales was well known among the readers of the Scottish revivalist magazine, *The Glasgow Weekly History*, edited by William McCulloch and published between December 1741 and December 1742.[81] McCulloch's paper differed from the English and Welsh versions in that it merely contained letters culled from the pages of its longer-running sister publication. McCulloch maintained a regular correspondence with Howel Harris throughout much of 1742 and 1743, and Harris was obviously the source for many of the letters that he reprinted including those about Wales, even though he had turned down McCulloch's original request for a historical account of the Welsh revival.[82] The Welsh letters reprinted towards the end of 1742 appeared in the immediate aftermath of the Cambuslang awakening when the attention of the Scottish evangelicals was most likely to be engaged by news from Wales. The three letters included one from an anonymous Dissenting minister that contained a comprehensive account of the Welsh revival complete with background comments on Wales itself and its spiritual history.[83] The other two were from Daniel Rowland and Herbert Jenkins, one providing details of the revival in south-west Wales[84] and the other containing exhortations on the duty of Christians of different persuasions to maintain good relations with one another.[85] Once the magazine reached the end of its run, news from Wales became much more scarce as the Scottish revival

---

[80] 'The Copy of a Letter from the REV MR WHITEFIELD to MR CENNICK (16 June 1742)', *WH* 66 (Saturday, 10 July 1742).

[81] Durden, 'A study of the first evangelical magazines, 1740–1748', 257–8.

[82] See Trevecka 736, Howel Harris to a minister in Scotland (23 November 1742) and Trevecka 854, Howel Harris to William McCulloch (15 April 1743).

[83] 'Extract of a letter to Mr M'C—, from a Dissenting minister in Wales, relating to the state of religion there (26 October 1742)', *The Glasgow Weekly History Relating to the Late Progress of the Gospel at Home and Abroad: Being a Collection of Letters Partly Reprinted from the London-Weekly-History* (ed. William McCulloch), 48.

[84] 'The copy of a letter from the Reverend Mr Daniel Rowland, a minister of the Establish'd Church in the Principality of Wales, to Mr Howell Harris, in London (20 October 1742)', *The Glasgow-Weekly-History*, 49.

[85] 'The copy a letter from Brother Herbert Jenkins in Wales, to Brother P. in London', *The Glasgow-Weekly-History*, 49.

subsided and became much less important to the wider
international community.

Most of what appeared in *The Weekly History* about
Whitefield's Scottish itineraries during 1742 was overwhelmingly
positive. The only negative reporting concerned the attitude of
Ralph and Ebenezer Erskine. Initially, they had been the first
Scottish evangelicals to respond positively to Whitefield's
preaching and had invited him to Scotland in 1739.[86] However,
when Whitefield failed to support their secessionist Associate
Presbytery, founded when they split from the Church of
Scotland over the issue of patronage in 1733,[87] they turned
against him bitterly, organizing a fast day in September 1742 to
pray against the Scottish revival.[88] It was the way in which this
division was reported in *The Weekly History* that is most
interesting. Whitefield portrayed himself as the genuine
ecumenist, putting the success of the revival and the evangelical
cause before denominational and party squabbles. A Glasgow
correspondent assured the London evangelicals that Whitefield's
'Doctrine and practice seems to be calculated for bringing souls
to Christ, and building up his body, not for making a party in
that Body.'[89] It seems that Whitefield, in the immediate aftermath of the highly damaging divisions that had so recently taken
place in the English revival, was at pains to avoid getting dragged
into another theological or confessional conflict. He therefore
studiously avoided too close an identification with any group that
challenged the Established Church, whether in England or
Scotland. His portrayal of the problems in his relations with the
Erskine brothers was therefore carefully choreographed to
demonstrate to the wider evangelical community the ill effects
that an overconcentration on ephemeral issues could have.
When Whitefield recommended the printing of a letter from an
anonymous Scottish correspondent, praising his aloofness from
theological arguments, we can be sure that the letter reflected his
attitude perfectly.

[86]   Ward, *The Protestant Evangelical Awakening*, pp. 329–32 and Dallimore, *George Whitefield*, II, pp. 84–90.

[87]   Ward, *The Protestant Evangelical Awakening*, p. 329.

[88]   'The copy of a letter from the REV MR WHITEFIELD in Scotland, to MR HOWEL HARRIS in London (26 August 1742)', *WH* 79 (Saturday, 9 October 1742).

[89]   'Extract of a letter from a gentleman at Glasgow to his friend in Edinburgh (21 October 1741)', *WH* 32 (Saturday, 14 November 1741).

If Christians were united and more concerned in propagating practical
Religion, than in spending Time in contending about the Externals of it
[. . .] Antichrists kingdom would not have such support as it has plainly got
from the Strife and Contention of those who are agreed in the Essentials of
Christianity but differ in externals.[90]

Despite their obvious disappointment at the Erskine brothers'
lack of enthusiasm for the revival, many Methodists devoured
their books and sermons with great relish. One of the ironies of
the Welsh Methodists' relationship with the Scottish revival is the
fact that the most tangible link between them was the writings of
the two brothers, who, despite their clear evangelicalism, were
deeply critical of Methodist ecclesiology. Whilst Eifion Evans
might be overstating the case when he argues that their writings
were the most significant literary influence on the Welsh
Methodists,[91] the Erskines were undoubtedly of major importance to a significant number of rank-and-file Welsh evangelicals.
At times when the Welsh revivalists were grappling with abstruse
theological issues they turned with gratitude to the clearly
expressed covenantal, Reformed theology of the Erskines.
During much of 1742 and 1743, for example, controversies over
the place of the Law in the life of the Christian dominated some
of the Welsh Methodists' Association meetings. At the meeting at
Dugoedydd in May 1743, the revivalists discussed the possibility
of funding the translation and printing of a series of Ralph
Erskine's sermons, *Law–Death, Gospel–Life* (1724),[92] which they
hoped would help those of their number who were confused over
this issue. Many more of the Erskines' works were translated into
Welsh in the following years,[93] chiefly at the behest of Daniel
Rowland, who it seems was concerned to raise the theological
understanding of Welsh Methodists, particularly once the
excitement of the early months and years of the revival had
abated.[94]

The degree to which the majority of rank-and-file Welsh
Methodists shared Rowland's vision is harder to ascertain.

[90] Ibid.
[91] Evans, *Daniel Rowland*, p. 250.
[92] 'At the Monthly Association held at Dygoedydd, May 25, 1743', CMA 2945, p.
17.
[93] See Rees (ed.), *Libri Walliæ*, pp. 229–31.
[94] Morgan, *The Great Awakening in Wales*, p. 158.

Whilst Harris, Rowland and William Williams freely expressed their debt to the Erskines' writings, others were not so keen. There is plenty of evidence to demonstrate that many Methodists read the Erskines' works. Many of them requested their works from Howel Harris,[95] but when they published *Siccrwydd Ffydd* in 1759, a translation of some of Ebenezer Erskine's sermons on assurance, over 300 copies remained unsold in 1764.[96] The explanation for this probably lies in the fairly academic nature of some of the Erskine brothers' writings and the over-optimistic number of volumes that the Methodists printed. The lack of enthusiasm must also reflect the limits of Welsh Methodist interest in the wider revival by this stage. Despite being highly theologically literate, many Welsh Methodists evidently found the Erskines' books unhelpful and probably too impractical, concerned as they often were with obscure points of applied theology and wedded to a more radical Presbyterian ecclesiology than many in Wales were prepared to countenance. It must also be borne in mind that although literacy rates among the early Methodists were high, there just were not enough Methodists scattered around the country to take advantage of the relatively large number of books that were optimistically printed.

Most rank-and-file Welsh Methodists had little if any contact with continental evangelicals, whose contribution to the Welsh revival tended to be far more indirect, mediated through Howel Harris, who, as has been reiterated throughout this study, was influenced by the Pietism of Francke and the Moravians to a greater extent than perhaps any of the other revivalists. Yet, unlike John Wesley who had visited Herrnhut in 1738,[97] and despite his friendships with many of the most prominent London-based Moravians, Harris does not seem to have expressed any interest in visiting either Herrnhut or Halle.

[95]   Trevecka 715, Howel Harris to Richard Jenkins (25 October 1742); Trevecka 811, Howel Harris to George Whitefield (1 March 1743); Trevecka 826, Thomas Bowen to Howel Harris (24 March 1743); Trevecka 1072, Howel Harris to Griffith Jones (4 January 1744).

[96]   Morgan, *The Great Awakening in Wales*, pp. 159–60. See also Trevecka 1257, John Morgan to Howel Harris (31 December 1744).

[97]   Ward, *The Protestant Evangelical Awakening*, p. 312 and Podmore, *The Moravian Church in England*, pp. 42–3.

Methodists who did have contact with continental Protestants were limited to those who encountered them in the mid-1740s when they attempted to gain a foothold in Wales, firstly in Pembrokeshire and Carmarthenshire and then later in Caernarfonshire.[98] When the Welsh revival split in 1750, small numbers of Daniel Rowland's followers found their way into some of these Moravian communities, but on the whole they were a remote group whose direct influence remained negligible and all but evaporated once Howel Harris had been ousted from the revival.

The only other evangelical community that played any part in the regular experience of rank-and-file Welsh Methodists during the 1740s was the revival in Ireland. Whitefield had visited Ireland for the first time in November 1738 as he returned from Georgia,[99] and throughout his life he made regular visits to Irish Methodists at the beginning and end of his many Atlantic crossings.[100] The revival in Ireland had reached the attention of the wider evangelical community when John Cennick, the former Whitefieldian, became a Moravian missionary, first in Dublin and then in Ulster from 1746 until his death in 1755.[101] John Wesley, not wishing to be left out, quickly established his own foothold in Ireland in 1747 and over the next forty years made Ireland an integral part of his own personal circuit, visiting the country on twenty-one separate occasions.[102]

Remarkably Howel Harris, as far as we know, did not dream about going to Ireland, although William Williams did have

---

[98] R. T. Jenkins, 'The Moravian brethren in north Wales: an episode in the religious history of Wales', *Y Cymmrodor*, XLV (London, 1938); Roberts, 'The Moravians and John Relly and his people', 2–7; Richard Brinkley, 'Religion and education, 1660–1815', in Brian Howells (ed.), *Pembrokeshire County History, III: Early Modern Pembrokeshire, 1536–1815* (Haverfordwest, 1987), pp. 254–5.

[99] Murray (ed.), *George Whitefield's Journals*, pp. 180–5.

[100] For details of some of these visits see Dallimore, *George Whitefield*, II, pp. 339–42 and 395–9.

[101] Hempton and Hill, *Evangelical Protestantism in Ulster Society*, pp. 5–8; Podmore, *The Moravian Church in England*, pp. 88–95, 195–200; Cooper (ed.), *Extracts from the Journal of John Cennick: Moravian Evangelist*.

[102] For Wesleyan Methodism in Ireland more generally see D. A. L. Cooney, 'Irish Methodism', in Brendan Bradshaw and Dáire Keogh (eds), *Christianity in Ireland: Revisiting the Story* (Dublin, 2002), pp. 144–54 and David Hempton, 'Methodism in Irish society 1770–1830', *Transactions of the Royal Historical Society*, XXXVI (1986), 117–42.

'strong thoughts about going' there for a short time in 1746[103] and was keen to include mention of the Irish revival in the catalogue of revival sites in his *Aurora Borealis* in 1777.[104] Harris, as with every other episode in Whitefield's transatlantic itinerary, followed the course of his visits to Ireland with keen interest and conveyed news about them to some of the Welsh exhorters. In September 1742, when Whitefield was planning an itinerary that included both the Isle of Man and Ireland, Harris informed him of his enthusiastic support for the decision, assured him of his ardent prayers on his behalf[105] and immediately set about informing some of his most trusted and interested Welsh lieutenants about the exciting news which he expected them to convey to the societies in their care.[106] Ireland remained fairly prominent in the minds of some of the Welsh Methodists because of Whitefield's practice of visiting Ireland at the beginning and end of his voyages to the colonies, particularly in the mid- and late 1740s. It seems that Whitefield, particularly when his commitments in the American colonies became his main priority, began to include both Ireland and Wales in his itiner-aries on the western fringes of Britain. In 1744, for example, he was planning an itinerary beginning in Lichfield, before moving south to Birmingham, then further south to Exeter before coming back to Wales and then travelling through to Ireland.[107]

Despite John Cennick's decision to leave the Calvinists for the Moravians in 1745, Harris maintained his correspondence with him, and when he settled in Ireland in 1746 letters between them continued, albeit more sporadically.[108] None the less, Cennick remained a key source of news about evangelical activity in Ireland, and Harris would have doubtless followed the course of

---

[103] Trevecka 1471, William Williams to Howel Harris (5 June 1746). See also White, 'The people called "Methodists": early Welsh Methodists and the question of identity', 10.

[104] William Williams, *Aurora Borealis*, in Garfield H. Hughes (ed.), *Gweithiau William Williams Pantycelyn*, II (Cardiff, 1967), p. 178.

[105] Trevecka 649, Howel Harris to George Whitefield (16 September 1742); Trevecka 658, Howel Harris to George Whitefield (23 September 1742); Trevecka 669, Howel Harris to George Whitefield (29 September 1742).

[106] Trevecka 510, Howel Harris to Thomas Bowen (no date) and Trevecka 656, Howel Harris to Thomas James (21 September 1742).

[107] Trevecka 1096, Howel Harris to Daniel Rowland (31 January 1744).

[108] Trevecka 1517, Howel Harris to John Cennick (30 August 1746); Trevecka 1849, John Cennick to Howel Harris (5 March 1749); and Trevecka 1938, Howel Harris to John Cennick (5 June 1750).

his efforts to establish a Moravian community at Gracehill in Ulster with particular interest.[109] So, whilst accounts of revival in Ireland did not figure as prominently in the world-view of many rank-and-file Welsh Methodists as the revivals in the American colonies or in Scotland, Whitefield's prominence and Harris's commitment to every mile of Whitefield's itinerancy ensured that amongst the best-informed of the Welsh Methodists, the Irish were known and, still more importantly, prayed for on a regular basis.

It was their realization of the importance of prayer for one another that led many of the revivalists in the later 1740s to attempt to create an international prayer network, designed to quicken expectations and create the right atmosphere for a new wave of awakenings. By the mid-1740s, when the initial revival had subsided and many of the converts had been settled in societies under the watchful eye of a sophisticated connexional structure, when Whitefield's colonial ministry had settled into a regular pattern and the excitement in Scotland had abated, the revivalists, realizing that they had lost some of their old energy, turned their attention increasingly to schemes aimed at re-kindling the fires of religious enthusiasm once again. For a brief period it seemed as though the English Calvinistic revival, the Welsh revival and the Scottish and colonial awakenings were about to come together in a remarkable show of evangelical unity and inspire fresh revivals by their plans to inaugurate special seasons of prayer designed to quicken the expectations of the by this stage slightly demoralized evangelical communities.

Prayer Days[110] had become an increasingly important evangelical technique for reviving interest in the possibility of fresh awakenings by the early 1740s. Michael J. Crawford has shown how in 1712 London Dissenters had called on British and American Protestants to agree on a common time at which to intercede for the Church.[111] For the Methodists, calling for

---

[109] Hempton and Hill, *Evangelical Protestantism in Ulster Society*, p. 8; Cooper (ed.), *Extracts from the Journal of John Cennick*, pp. 35–9; Geoffrey and Margaret Stead, *The Exotic Plant: A History of the Moravian Church in Great Britain, 1742–2000* (Peterborough, 2003), pp. 53–5.

[110] See Simonson, 'Jonathan Edwards and his Scottish connections, 372–6; Lambert, *Inventing the 'Great Awakening'*, pp. 164–5; and O'Brien, ' "A transatlantic community of saints" ', 824–7.

[111] Crawford, *Seasons of Grace*, p. 229.

similar days when the revival had apparently lost its way was a reversion to the maxim, widely assumed in the preceding half-century, that seasons of concerted prayer invariably gave birth to fresh awakenings. This particular innovation had its origins in Glasgow when a group of 'awakened' ministers, led by John MacLaurin (1693–1754),[112] set aside part of every Saturday evening and Sunday morning and the first Tuesday of the last month of each quarter of the year for earnest intercessory prayer for fresh outpourings of the Spirit. Rapidly Methodists in England, including John Wesley,[113] were invited to join, as were the colonial evangelicals, Gilbert Tennant and Jonathan Edwards. However, it was Edwards, with his *A Humble Attempt to Promote Explicit Agreement and Visible Union of God's People in Extraordinary Prayers* (1747),[114] who transformed the idea from a private agreement between like-minded ministers to a more broadly based international solution to the problems confronting the revival. George Marsden has demonstrated how Edwards took a Scottish proposal and turned it into an international network, legitimized by his conviction that extra-ordinary prayer meetings were inextricably linked to fresh awakenings, which in turn would usher in the dawn of the millennium.[115] In his initial response to the idea in a letter to the Scottish minister who first suggested the Concert for Prayer, Edwards argued:

> I am persuaded that such an agreement of the people of God in different parts, to unite together, to pray for the Holy Spirit, is lovely in the eyes of Jesus Christ the glorious head of the church. And if endeavours are used to uphold, and promote, and enlarge such a Concert, who knows what it may come to at last?[116]

---

[112] *DSCHT*, pp. 527–8.

[113] John Wesley to James Erskine, Lord Grange (16 March 1745), in Baker (ed.), *The Works of John Wesley*, 26, p. 128.

[114] For a modern edition of the work see Stephen J. Stein (ed.), *The Works of Jonathan Edwards, V: Apocalyptic Writings* (New Haven, 1977).

[115] Marsden, *Jonathan Edwards*, pp. 334–5; Helen P. Westra, 'Divinity's design: Edwards and the history of the work of revival', in Sang Hyun Lee and Allen C. Guelzo (eds), *Edwards in Our Time: Jonathan Edwards and the Shaping of American Religion* (Grand Rapids, 1999), pp. 155–7; Simonson, 'Jonathan Edwards and his Scottish connections', 373–4.

[116] 'Jonathan Edwards to a correspondent in Scotland (November 1745)', in Claghorn (ed.), *The Works of Jonathan Edwards*, XVI, p. 183.

In Wales the idea of unified days of prayer was initially welcomed with enthusiasm. Indeed, its acceptance in Wales as late as 1747 is evidence of the extent to which the communications network still operated successfully and of the reality of the international dimension of the revival. Proposals for Welsh participation in the network were first discussed at an Association at Trefeca in March 1745. Harris, acting as Moderator and following the proposals of MacLaurin closely, recommended that a regular day of prayer should be instituted once every three months and that Sunday mornings should be set aside 'on account of ye late work in England, Scotland, Wales & America, both to praise God for it & intercede & Pray for it[s] furtherance & to be humbled for ye sin that attended it'.[117] Despite Harris's advocacy, by the end of the decade enthusiasm had dimmed to the point of indifference.[118] Yet this apathy should not be seen as an indication of any loss of interest in the progress of the wider revival itself. By the late 1740s the Welsh revivalists were facing too many of their own problems to justify devoting a significant amount of time to this new project. Howel Harris and Daniel Rowland were finding it almost impossible to work together by 1747, and there was already something approaching a polarization between their followers. It is not unlikely that by this stage any idea emanating from Harris would have been greeted with suspicion and even outright hostility by some of Rowland's followers, who by 1750 made up the overwhelming majority of Welsh Methodists.

From its beginning the Methodist revival aroused grave suspicion in both secular and ecclesiastical authorities. Although for many rank-and-file Welsh Methodists participation in the evangelical communications network operated on a purely spiritual level, for others it became the place where they reacted to being suspected of subversion and the forum in which they shared their experiences of persecution and repression.[119] By joining the Methodist

---

[117] 'At an Association held at Trevecka, 29 March 1745', CMA 2915, p. 145.

[118] Trevecka 1312, Howel Harris to James Erskine (12 April 1745).

[119] On the wider significance of persecution see John Coffey, *Persecution and Toleration in Protestant England, 1558–1689* (London, 2000), pp. 21–46 and Walsham, *Providence in Early Modern England*, pp. 100–3. On the more specific Methodist experience see John Walsh, 'Methodism and the mob in the eighteenth century', pp. 215–27; Hempton, 'Methodism and the law, 1740–1820', 93–107 and D. Dunn Wilson, 'Hanoverian government and Methodist persecution', *Proceedings of the Wesley Historical Society*, 23, 5 (March 1962), 94–9.

movement, converts immediately exposed themselves to the antagonism and derision of their contemporaries in both Church and state. Enthusiasm was distrusted by the Church of England and the state in equal measure, and the emergence of the Methodist movement appeared to many to be a reversion to the anarchy of the Interregnum when the abolition of the Established Church and the introduction of freedom of choice in religious matters had resulted in the proliferation of myriad millenarian sects and the destruction of the whole concept of an 'official' state religion and meaningful religious conformity.[120]

Fears that the Methodists might represent a reversion to this kind of individualistic religious anarchy were rife in the 1730s and 1740s, and had their origins in the precarious position of the Hanoverian monarchy. When Queen Anne died in 1714 leaving no heir, there seemed to be a high probability that the exiled Stuarts would attempt to recapture the throne, plunging the country into anarchy as in the mid-seventeenth century. A solution had been brokered when the Protestant elector of Hanover was invited to take the throne, becoming George I in 1714. The new Hanoverian dynasty remained weak in its first decades and faced a series of potentially destabilizing threats from the newly confident Jacobite Stuarts.[121] The first rising in 1715 fortunately turned out to be an unmitigated disaster for the poorly organized and dishevelled Jacobites[122] and had very little impact on a remote and bewildered Wales,[123] which had responded with muted resignation to the multiple changes in the succession and religion of the British Isles during the previous century and a half. The rising did however leave what has been called a 'waning romantic ideology',[124] evidenced in clandestine meetings and ritualistic displays of Jacobite loyalty among Welshmen who retained their Catholicism and support for the

---

[120] See Knox, *Enthusiasm* (London, 1950) and Mee, *Romanticism, Enthusiasm and Regulation*, pp. 23–81.

[121] The best introduction to the Jacobite threat is undoubtedly Murray G. H. Pittock, *Jacobitism* (London, 1998). See also J. C. D. Clark, *English Society, 1688–1832: Religion, Ideology and Politics during the 'Ancien Regime'* (Cambridge, 2000); Bruce Lenman, *The Jacobite Risings in Britain, 1689–1746* (Aberdeen, 1980); and Paul Kléber Monod, *Jacobitism and the English People, 1688–1788* (Cambridge, 1989).

[122] Pittock, *Jacobitism*, pp. 36–66; Lenman, *The Jacobite Risings in Britain*, pp. 107–54.

[123] For Jacobitism in Wales see Thomas, *Politics in Eighteenth Century Wales*, pp. 133–49 and Jenkins, *Foundations of Modern Wales*, pp. 149–52, 309–12.

[124] Jenkins, *The Foundations of Modern Wales*, p. 151.

exiled Stuarts. Yet in Wales such feelings were not often translated into political action. Accusations of Jacobitism and the full force of state repression tended to be reserved for those groups which seemed to be the heirs of the apparently subversive religious and political groups of the previous century. The Methodists, with their international communications network, disciplined groups of societies under a connexional organization, the use of an army of itinerant evangelists, lay and ordained, who regularly preached outside the walls and therefore the juris-diction of the Church, were an obvious target for accusations that they were closet Catholics, political subversives or even covert practitioners of all sorts of vice and immorality.

The beginning of the evangelical revival in the mid-1730s unfortunately coincided with a particularly dramatic upsurge in political tension. In 1740 England declared war on Spain over the disputed Austrian succession.[125] The 1741 general election had precipitated the downfall of the prime minister, Robert Walpole,[126] and Britain entered war with France once more in 1744.[127] These tensions were overshadowed by potentially the most dangerous Jacobite rising of all in 1745, when Bonnie Prince Charlie landed in Scotland. His army swept south through much of the north of England in the knowledge that the French had agreed to land an army in Britain to wrest the English throne back finally for the Stuarts.[128] These events led to fresh waves of anti-Stuart, anti-Catholic and anti-French propa-ganda and rioting against those suspected of having sympathies with the Stuarts. All this dramatically curtailed the activities of groups that seemed to be a challenge to the existing order. Increased tensions led to renewed accusations that the Method-ists were in fact 'crypto-papists, bold Jacobites, or servants of Satan'.[129] Such accusations were supported in many cases by mob violence aimed particularly at those exhorters and preachers who in many communities were seen as interlopers

[125] Jeremy Black, *The Rise of the European Powers, 1679–1793* (London, 1990), pp. 101–7; Jeremy Black, *Britain as a Military Power, 1688–1815* (London, 1999), pp. 62–70.
[126] Eveline Cruickshanks, 'The political management of Sir Robert Walpole, 1720–42', in Jeremy Black (ed.), *Britain in the Age of Walpole* (Basingstoke, 1984), pp. 42–3.
[127] Bruce Lenman, *Britain's Colonial Wars, 1688–1783* (London, 2001), pp. 70–8.
[128] Pittock, *Jacobitism*, pp. 93–122; Lenman, *The Jacobite Risings in Britain*, pp. 231–59; Michael Lynch (ed.), *Jacobitism and the '45* (London, 1995).
[129] Jenkins, *The Foundations of Modern Wales*, pp. 326–7.

intent on upsetting the natural order of village life by calling on individuals to settle their own religious destinies, in many instances without the assistance of the Church.

Being a Methodist in the 1740s entailed considerable personal sacrifice on many levels. Many Methodists were prepared to accept with little complaint the derision and persecution directed at them from the Church. What was far more difficult to tolerate was the alienation that membership often caused within families, between husbands and wives and parents and children. In its early years, membership of the revival therefore required remark-able single-mindedness and copious reserves of stamina and resilience; but, surprisingly, responses to this sort of persecution are largely absent from the communications network. This need not necessarily mean that it did not play a particularly prominent part in people's lives. Rather, it shows that for many this kind of daily opposition and ostracism – which might be felt in a wide variety of ways, from the loss of old friends, gossip among neighbours or, more seriously, the loss of one's job or even home, all of which were far more obvious in the small close-knit village communities in which most Methodists lived – was usually regarded as an inevitable part of the evangelical lifestyle.[130]

What the communications network does demonstrate is the extent to which some Methodists lived with the threat of more overt forms of physical violence and intimidation. Many, particu-larly among the exhorters, faced such persecution with steadfast-ness and heroism and attempted to rationalize the experience by reverting to a favourite evangelical habit, drawing parallels between themselves and the martyrs of the first Christian communities. In doing this, the revivalists sought to construct a theology of persecution that stressed its positive benefits and its inevitability in a life of consistent godliness. In the second issue of *The Christian's Amusement* in 1740, for example, John Lewis reminded his readers: 'those whom the Lord calls thus to suffer, will be strengthened with power from on high to fight the Lord's Battles.'[131] His comments occurred within the context of the theological disagreements between the Moravians, Wesleyans and Whitefieldians that were beginning to tear the English revival

---

[130] Walsh, 'Methodism and the mob in the eighteenth century', p. 213.
[131] *CA*, 2.

apart, and they seemed to coincide with fresh outbursts of disorder and mob violence at Methodist gatherings. The mobs varied in size and sophistication, and could range from a group of high-spirited youths intent on causing mischief to the more organized and threatening urban crowds that assaulted worshippers, particularly during open-air gatherings in London and Bristol. This activity was rarely the result of mindless violence. Mobs were often highly organized and in many cases were stirred up by the local clergy or gentry who felt their authority in the community to be under threat by, as Henry Rack has pointed out, 'individuals with strange accents, with no apparent means of support, singing hymns to gather a crowd and preaching a strange message, in some cases condemning the local clergy and popular customs'.[132]

The religious magazines bear ample testimony to the damage such mobs could do to the infant Methodist communities. John Lewis, for example, printed a letter about William Seward's ill-fated preaching tour of Monmouthshire in September 1740 which outlined his experiences at the hands of hostile anti-Methodist mobs. Seward is an important figure in the history of anti-Methodist persecution. He was one of the earliest supporters of the revival, after having achieved financial independence by means of wise investments in the stock market. He became one of Whitefield's main English supporters, coordinating his publicity machine from London and sending news of the revival in England and Wales to all corners of the international evangelical community.[133] However, he gained almost iconic status as the revival's first and only martyr. He was killed by an angry mob at Hay-on-Wye in October 1740 after being struck with a stone hurled as he stood alongside Howel Harris, who was preaching at the cross in the middle of the town.[134] The death of such a high-profile figure sent shock waves through the revival. Many rank-and-file Methodists struggled to come to terms with his death and found it difficult to understand why someone so apparently indispensible to the movement could be sacrificed so cheaply. Sarah Mason, in an almost poetic letter, expressed her bewilderment at this tragic loss,

---

[132] Rack, *Reasonable Enthusiast*, p. 273.
[133] For Seward's contribution to the early development of the revival see *DMBI*, p. 313; Lambert, '*Pedlar in Divinity*', pp. 52–5.
[134] Geoffrey L. Fairs, 'Notes on the death of William Seward at Hay, 1740', *CCHMC*, LVIII, I (March 1973), 12–18.

but her letter also demonstrates how the early Methodists were clearly indebted to Puritan and Calvinistic ideas of Divine Providence[135] that stressed God's ultimate sovereignty and intimate ordering of every aspect of life and death:

> The death of Mr Seward was awfully surprising [. . .] Why did blessed Seward leave this world so soon, why did so bright a star thus set at noon. But stay what bold enquirer asks to know [. . .] can we fathom wisdoms deep design. By our undiminished reasons [. . .] let all agree in silence to adore and by remarking querys sin no more But humbly wait the Glorious Rich display of God's Perfection in the rising way. They'll brightly shine in one eternal Ray Amen Hallelujah.[136]

Accounts of persecution, and in this instance martyrdom, were intended to have a sanctifying effect. Like many Protestants before them, the Methodists prized these accounts because they enabled them to trace the hand of Providence more clearly. Accounts like this were what Alexandra Walsham has called 'a sort of Morse code or semaphore between the Soul and its Saviour',[137] and when they were interpreted and fitted together they began to represent a catalogue of God's dealings with his Methodist saints and became essential in the Methodists' desire to discern what God's will for the future of their movement might be. In Seward's case his death conferred on Methodism a certain degree of legitimacy in the eyes of its early members. It was interpreted as evidence that the Methodists were making inroads and therefore proof that God was attesting their message and lifestyle. Persecution, which on the surface apparently threatened the future of the whole movement, was thus turned into something positive, to be welcomed, however reluctantly, from the hands of a Providence that had repeatedly intimated that true Christianity would always set people at variance with one another, husbands against wives, children against parents and neighbours against neighbours.

Although martyrdom was exceptional in the early history of the revival, many evangelicals experienced overt persecution in

---

[135] For more on the prevalence of the Puritan doctrine of Divine Providence see Walsham, *Providence in Early Modern England*, pp. 8–32 and Alistair E. McGrath, *Reformation Thought: An Introduction* (Oxford, 1988), pp. 86–93.

[136] Trevecka 316, Sarah Mason to Howel Harris (28 February 1741).

[137] Walsham, *Providence in Early Modern England*, p. 15.

various forms and to varying degrees, and penned accounts of their experiences for the edification of their fellow evangelicals. Throughout the 1740s, *The Weekly History* and its successors were packed with colourful details of close scrapes with angry mobs and skirmishes with ecclesiastical and secular officials. For many, persecution was often fairly innocuous, resulting in nothing more than mild embarrassment and inconvenience. For example, two Methodists were ambushed by a rope stretched across a bridge and thrown into the river below as they returned from their society meeting one evening in November 1744,[138] and in another instance three exhorters were overcharged as they tried to cross the river Wye in Breconshire on their way to a society meeting.[139]

Others were less fortunate and became a target for the censure of the authorities and the mindless violence of more organized mobs. The name that occurs with most frequency in this respect is James Beaumont.[140] On two occasions in the second half of 1742 he found himself threatened with imprisonment in the stocks after the heckling of an assembled mob failed to put an end to his preaching. Whilst the motivation for this kind of harassment often arose from the belligerence and sheer un-pleasantness of some of the local leaders of the revival, there is little doubt that at times it arose because of the threat that they posed to the traditional way of life in villages and towns. On the two occasions just mentioned, James Beaumont preached at social gatherings where people had congregated for reasons other than to listen to sermons – at the convening of the Presteigne assizes and at a wake, both occasions marked by gatherings of large numbers of people, the consumption of large amounts of alcohol and considerable conviviality besides. Preaching in such a confrontational manner at such events was often a deliberate policy, calculated to arouse an impassioned response from those who usually bore the brunt of a preacher's denunciations. James Beaumont's accounts of these confront-ations were cast in the context of the cosmic struggle between the

---

[138] 'Mr J.W. to Brother J.E. (20 November 1744)', *CH*, VI, IV, 69–72.
[139] 'The copy of a letter from Brother J—s to Brother Cennick (26 March 1743)', *Account*, III, II, 3–6.
[140] For Beaumont see Geraint Tudur, '"Like a right arm and a pillar": the story of James Beaumont', in Pope (ed.), *Honouring the Past and Shaping the Future*, pp. 133–58.

Kingdom of God and the Kingdom of the devil and they invariably showed how the Kingdom of God was triumphing and being extended into new areas. The accounts were always positive, rarely dwelling on the actual violence suffered and always ending with a positive reiteration of the ultimate triumph of the evangelical Gospel. Writing about his experiences at Presteigne, Beaumont concluded: 'The Lord was with me of a Truth [. . .] The Lord gave me uncommon strength [. . .] and [. . .] great Power to Discourse [. . .] insomuch that the People seem'd unwilling to go away.'[141]

The Methodists were deeply disliked by many because of their antipathy to traditional beliefs and cultural practices.[142] Whilst it is too early in these formative years to speak of Methodism acting as an agent of social control, there is little doubt that the revival was largely successful in replacing its converts' beliefs in magic and superstition and weaning them away from popular entertainments like theatres, dancing, cock-fighting and bull-baiting. Although many contemporary historians have been quick to condemn them for clamping down on such festivities, Methodists usually replaced them with what was for many a more attractive alternative society. Evangelical religion was, as John Rule has pointed out, a 'counterattractive, as well as a counteractive force'.[143] Its alternative culture of highly emotional religious revivals, communal gatherings to hear famous preachers like Howel Harris and Daniel Rowland and its small and intimate society meetings which offered members a close-knit and caring atmosphere in which to develop their faith and base their spiritual and social lives was, for many, deeply attractive.[144] So, despite arousing the opposition of many who wished to defend their way of life, Methodism attracted others, predominantly

---

[141] 'The copy of a letter from Mr James Beaumont, an exhorter in Pembrokeshire, directed to Mr John Lewis, printer in Bartholemew-Close, London (11 September 1742)', *WH* 75 (Saturday, 11 September 1742).

[142] For an indication of the prevalence of these practices in Wales in the early eighteenth century see Geraint H. Jenkins, 'Popular beliefs in Wales from Restoration to Methodism', *The Bulletin of the Board of Celtic Studies*, XXVII, III (November, 1977), 440–62.

[143] John Rule, 'Methodism, popular beliefs and village culture in Cornwall', in R. D. Storch (ed.), *Popular Culture and Religion in Nineteenth Century England* (London, 1982), pp. 48–70. See also Eryn M. White, ' "The world, the flesh and the devil" ', 55.

[144] See David Hempton and John Walsh, 'E. P. Thompson and Methodism', in Mark A. Noll (ed.), *God and Mammon: Protestants, Money, and the Market, 1790–1860* (New York, 2001), pp. 108–10.

from the middling sorts, who were ready to abandon a traditional culture for one that was literate and intelligent and which offered plenty of opportunity for self-improvement.

Although he was a particularly abrasive personality who, one suspects, enjoyed the cut and thrust of close brushes with the authorities and their mobs, the experiences of James Beaumont were far from unique. In England, Whitefield was used to competing with the jeers of crowds out to cause trouble, with trumpet players who attempted to drown out the sound of his voice and with crowds keen to pelt him with rotten vegetables and dead animals. John Cennick, an altogether more timorous and peaceable character, was also frequently plagued by threats from unruly mobs intent on silencing him.[145] Others in Wales encountered similar problems. Thomas James, while preaching in Breconshire on one occasion, aroused the opposition of the local alehouse keeper, who stirred up a mob who pelted him and his congregation 'with Dung and Clay and slung sticks at us'.[146] Thomas Lewis, on a preaching tour of Gloucestershire and Somerset, also provoked the opposition of the mob on a number of occasions and was repeatedly attacked with stones and sticks.[147]

For others in Wales, Methodist membership involved considerable personal sacrifice. James Ingram, Harris's servant and travelling companion, taken by the press gang to Brecon gaol, faced imprisonment stoically and with equanimity, and on his release lived with the possibility of being press-ganged into military service at any time.[148] Elinor Cadman, Benjamin Cadman's mother, was summoned for allowing the society at Llanidloes to meet in her house.[149] Howel Harris was closely involved in the legal proceedings taken against her, and encouraged her to appear before the ecclesiastical courts to plead her case in person.[150] Her case is important not only because it contributes to our understanding of the attitude of the ecclesiastical authorities but because it demonstrates how a fairly 'ordinary' female Methodist was prepared to

---

[145] See 'A letter from Mr Cennick to Mr Howel Harris (15 August 1741)', *WH* 23 (Saturday 12 September 1741).

[146] 'Thomas James to Howel Harris (9 October 1742)', *Account*, vol. II, no. I, 51.

[147] 'Brother Thomas Lewis to the printer of this book (2 February 1743)', *Account*, II, III, 30–9.

[148] 'From Brother James Ingram, a Welch exhorter, to a brother in London (19 June 1744)', *CH*, V, IV, 68–9.

[149] Trevecka 1065, Elinor Cadman to Chancellor Owen (31 December 1743).

[150] Trevecka 1087, Howel Harris to Anne Bowen (21 January 1744).

challenge the authority of the Church and defend the Methodist cause against the Church's policy of restricting Methodists' freedom and suppressing any ecclesiastical irregularities.

For the majority of rank-and-file Methodists, the threat of outright violence and the possibility of being hauled before the Church courts remained an ever-present reminder of the precariousness of their position during the revival's first decade. That so many letters on the subject were circulated throughout the communications network and printed in *The Weekly History* is evidence in and of itself of the prevalence of violence and, perhaps more importantly, of the premium that the revivalists put upon a correct understanding of the purpose behind such persecution and on a proper response to it. To this end they used the written accounts as preventative measures against depression and despair. Their semi-heroic terminology, with their copious references to the experiences of the Christians in the New Testament, far from discouraging them, worked as an encouragement as they were reminded of the fact that they were being counted worthy enough to suffer persecution. Such accounts also gave the early Methodists their own distinct martyrology, drawn from all corners of the revival, which seemed to enable them to bear whatever experiences came their way with admirable fortitude.

All this is not to say that all the early Methodists courted persecution. Some like James Beaumont tended to do so, but this was in spite of the revivalists' endeavours to remove the potential for persecution by stressing over and over again their loyalty to the King and the Church of England and their opposition to the Stuarts. During the early 1740s the revivalists engaged in a programme of damage limitation by instilling in their followers a deep attachment to the monarchy and the Protestant establishment. Howel Harris, when he was in England as well as in Wales, was tireless in his efforts to remind his converts of their responsibilities as faithful subjects of George II. When national events looked particularly precarious in 1744 and 1745, Harris was amongst the first to urge his fellow Methodists to set aside time for prayer and fasting for the deliverance of the nation from the judgements which it was under, according to Harris as a result of national apostasy.[151]

---

[151] Trevecka 1281, Howel Harris to James Erskine (14 January 1745); Trevecka 1335, Howel Harris to The Tabernacle Society (29 June 1745); and Trevecka 1372, Howel Harris to George Whitefield (8 November 1745).

The political anxiety of the early and mid-1740s resulted in a wave of renewed intolerance on the part of the Church of England and a determination to suppress those groups that challenged its authority. Opposition to the Methodists in Wales consequently became far more blatant and difficult to bear. William Williams, for example, serving as a curate in Breconshire, felt the full force of the local ecclesiastical hierarchy as he faced being hauled before the bishop of St David's in June 1742.[152] A number of Radnorshire Methodists,[153] and another group of 'ordinary' Methodists from neighbouring Montgomeryshire,[154] were accused of holding illegal gatherings, what were in effect conventicles,[155] and endured the opposition of violent mobs often stirred up by local clergy. Montgomeryshire Methodists seemed to suffer significantly more interference than many of their contemporaries, the result, no doubt, of the overzealous bishop of Bangor, under whose ecclesiastical jurisdiction they fell. Howel Harris himself had been arrested for preaching in the parish of Cemais and had been accused of being a papist, a Presbyterian and a Quaker, all at the same time![156] Compelled by these developments and the subsequent excommunication of some of the Montgomeryshire Methodists,[157] at the end of 1742 Daniel Rowland turned to Whitefield for help.[158] After consultations with the archbishop of Canterbury and the bishop of London in September 1742,[159] Whitefield formally intervened with an open letter to the bishop of Bangor.[160] Written at the end of November, the letter attempted to prove that, far from being illegal, the Methodist societies were thoroughly biblical and in no way intended to be a challenge to the Church. The threat of

---

[152] Evans, *Daniel Rowland*, pp. 209–10.
[153] See 'The copy of a letter from MR JAMES BEAUMONT, an exhorter in RADNORSHIRE, directed to MR JOHN LEWIS, printer, in BARTHOLOMEW-CLOSE, london (Presteign, 4 September 1742)', *WH* 75 (Saturday, 11 September 1742) and 'The copy of a letter from Brother JAMES BEAUMONT in WALES, to Brother J. G——ce, in LONDON (29 November 1742), *Account*, II, I, 76–80.
[154] Trevecka 705, Daniel Rowland to Howel Harris (20 October 1742).
[155] See Watts, *The Dissenters*, I, pp. 226, 259–60. On the impact of its repeal see J. S. Simon, 'The repeal of the Conventicle Act', *Proceedings of the Wesley Historical Society*, XI (1902), 103–8.
[156] HHD 52, 11 February 1740.
[157] Trevecka 705, Daniel Rowland to Howel Harris (20 October 1742).
[158] Ibid.
[159] Trevecka 644, Howel Harris to Daniel Rowland (14 September 1742).
[160] George Whitefield to the bishop of Bangor (19 November 1742), in Murray (ed.), *George Whitefield's Letters*, pp. 462–3.

excommunication, which the bishop seemed all too ready to prosecute, was, according to Whitefield, wholly inappropriate. However, what is perhaps most significant about the letter is Whitefield's tacit admission that the societies and the administrative structure that regulated them could be misconstrued as being a nascent Church within the Church. Consequently, he spent much of the letter labouring the point that the Methodists were 'loyal subjects to his Majesty, and true friends to, and attendants upon the Church of England service'.[161] If persecution continued unabated he had no hesitation in warning the bishop: 'Hundreds, if not thousands, will go in a body from the Church.'[162]

The attitude of the Church continued to harden, particularly in the immediate aftermath of Britain's entry into conflict with some of the major European powers. Spanish attacks on the American colonies in 1742 brought home to many Methodists the precariousness of their position, and the threat posed to Whitefield's Orphan House in Georgia seemed to sum up the danger in particularly stark terms. Howel Harris took upon himself the responsibility for keeping his fellow Methodists informed about the progress of the conflicts and filled the correspondence network with letters reporting the latest news, concentrating on the fortunes of the inhabitants of the Orphan House. To James Beaumont, in Wales, he wrote: 'This morning I heard that Georgia is taken by ye Spaniards, sure this will send you with strong cries to ye Lord for ye poor Dear Orphans. But the Lord will remember his Covenant, and give them strength according to the Day.'[163] When the conflict was resolved fairly speedily[164] Harris, in a show of triumphalistic jingoism, urged his Methodists to set aside a day in which they could record their gratitude to God for his providential deliverance of the Georgia orphans and the Protestant King George II.[165]

The most concerted effort at portraying a more loyal public image took place on either side of the most serious Jacobite Rising in 1745. During these months the correspondence net-

[161] Ibid., p. 463.
[162] Ibid.
[163] Trevecka 641, Howel Harris to James Beaumont (11 September 1742).
[164] Lenman, 'Colonial wars and imperial instability, 1688–1793', p. 157.
[165] 'See ORDER for a thanksgiving to ALMIGHTY GOD, for having put an end to the SPANISH INVASION of Georgia', Account, II, II, 19–23.

work teemed with letters declaring the Methodists' loyalty and commitment to the Protestant establishment.[166] They proclaimed their loyalty and exemplary citizenship in a number of ways. John Lewis, in his position as the editor of what by then had become *The Christian History*, began to include letters from soldiers fighting the French in the Low Countries. Most of these correspondents seem to have been members of the Tabernacle Society at one time or another and were written with an obvious eye to their publication in the evangelical magazine. The letters astonishingly contain very few details about the day-to-day routine of military life and very little about the progress of the war itself.[167] The majority of them are full of the testimonies of soldiers and news about the state of their spiritual lives.[168] The most frequent correspondent was Anthony Conjuet, a drummer in the British army who wrote a number of letters from the battlefield reporting on his evangelistic work among his fellow soldiers. In June 1744 he told John Cennick about the sizeable congregations that he had been able to attract to his informal exhorting,[169] and in April 1745 he wrote at length about the societies which he had been able to establish at Bruges as a consequence of this exhorting:

> In my Way to Ghent I called at Bruges, where I saw Brother Hymms the Dragoon, an old friend of mine [. . .] He has a sweet Society of about an hundred, who I believe are sincere hearers of the dear Lamb [. . .] We have three Societies in Ghent; one is held by Brother Clements, the other

---

[166] David Hempton, *Methodism and Politics in British Society, 1750–1850* (London, 1984), pp. 32–3; David Butler, *Methodists and Papists: John Wesley and the Catholic Church in the Eighteenth Century* (London, 1995), pp. 31–41; D. Dunn Wilson, *Many Waters Cannot Quench: A Study of the Sufferings of Eighteenth-Century Methodism and their Significance for John Wesley and the First Methodists* (London, 1969), pp. 69–70; David Hempton, 'John Wesley and England's "Ancien Régime"', in David Hempton, *The Religion of the Heart*, p. 79–80; Ward, *The Protestant Evangelical Awakening*, pp. 332–5.

[167] See 'The copy of a letter from Bro ANTHONY CONJUET, a drummer in the English camp in Flanders, to his wife in LONDON (26 May 1745)', *CH*, VII, IV, 3–9 and 'Extract of a letter from a soldier in FLANDERS, to his FRIEND in the county of SUFFOLK, ENGLAND: since the late battle with the French at FONTENOY (31 May 1745)', *CH*, VII, IV, 52–5.

[168] 'The copy of a letter from P. STAGG (dated from GHENT in FLANDERS) to Mr CENNICK (29 January 1744)', *CH*, Volume V, Number III, 3–9; 'The copy of a letter from a person at GHENT in FLANDERS, to his friend in LONDON (25 January 1745)', *CH*, V, IV, 56–60.

[169] 'From BROTHER ANTHONY CONJUET the drummer, at the English camp, near GHENT, in the Netherlands, to MR JOHN CENNICK, and the society at LONDON (20 June 1744)', *CH*, V, IV, 45–9.

by Brother Wells, and the third is held by a Person unknown to me [. . .] I was at Brother Clements, who has a large Society; I believe the Number is about an Hundred, if not more.[170]

As the rank-and-file converts in Wales read these letters they would have been struck once again by the significance of the international events that were occurring around them.

Harris drove home their significance repeatedly. The days of prayer, which he thought so necessary, were presented as occasions during which Methodists were to intercede for the progress of the Gospel and for the success of the war which would safeguard the Protestant establishment and the religious toleration that had been won with such difficulty in 1689. In February 1744 Harris wrote to James Beaumont:

> We are like to be called to the Field of Blood soon [. . .] the French fleet now lay at anchor in one of our Ports being come over with a firm Resolution to dethrone his Majesty & set the Pretenders Son on the Throne of England & consequently not only take away all Toleration & liberty of Protestants but establish Popery again [. . .] Next Monday we have settled for fasting and prayer for the Kg & Nation we all hold it our Duty to preach loyalty to the King set over us by the Ld & as he is a Protestant & tolerates the true Religion & as he is laid deeply on our hearts too.[171]

It was the guarantee of freedom to practise their religion, a freedom which the Protestant Hanoverians ensured, that led the Methodists, like all other Protestants, to protest their loyalty to George II vehemently. In a sense old tensions with the Church of England were forgotten during these months as erstwhile opponents came together against a common enemy. Linda Colley has argued that the prevalence of popular and elite anti-Catholicism during these years, born of repeated conflict with France and other European Catholic powers, worked to focus the attention of many people on the elements that united them rather than on those that drove them apart. The most potent unifying factor of all was undoubtedly Protestantism, and when

---

[170] 'From BROTHER CONJUET, a drummer, at GHENT in FLANDERS, to BRO. CENNICK (4 April 1745)', *CH*, VII, II, 61–2.

[171] Trevecka 1118, Howel Harris to James Beaumont (18 February 1744).

that appeared to be most at threat, people clung to it and were prepared to defend it with incredible vigour.[172] When in the immediate aftermath of the 1745 rising, the Welsh Methodists held their day of thanksgiving, Harris's protestations of loyalty to the king is compelling evidence of the soundness of Colley's argument and of how far the Methodists had travelled. From being widely suspected of subversion, Jacobitism and even Popery they had reinvented themselves as model subjects of the British state. Harris wrote:

> This day I was in our parish church, to join in the prayers and I had some freedom with the Lord: and I had some Love yet for this nation, that the Lord will erect his standard here [. . .] I found much liberty to wrestle for King George [. . .] I find our national trials have been hitherto great blessings: they have been instrumental in turning the hearts of many to the King.[173]

It was comments such as this that have led some historians to assume that Harris and his Methodists had an underdeveloped sense of their Welshness. For many first-generation Welsh Methodists identity was a complex issue. Geraint Tudur has amply demonstrated that Harris was deeply conscious of his Welshness and remained committed, despite many additional responsibilities, to Wales and his Welsh converts.[174] Yet Harris was able to move in a number of circles with apparent ease. At various times he professed to be a Methodist, a Calvinist, a Protestant and a Christian, all labels that indicate various national and international allegiances. Despite some recent attempts to argue that the Welsh Methodists had a far more positive attitude to Welsh culture than has been usually assumed,[175] it remains a fact that the majority of them preferred

---

[172] Linda Colley, *Britons: Forging the Nation, 1707–1837* (London, 1992); Colin Haydon, *Anti-Catholicism in Eighteenth-Century England: A Political and Social Study* (Manchester, 1993), pp. 129–63.

[173] 'From Mr Howel Harris, at Trevecca, near the Hay, in Breconshire, south Wales to Mr Thomas Adams, at the Tabernacle House, near Moorfields, London', *CH*, 1747, 21–3.

[174] Geraint Tudur, ' "Thou bold champion, where art thou": Howell Harris and the issue of Welsh identity', in Pope (ed.), *Religion and National Identity: Wales and Scotland, c.1700–2000*, pp.43–60.

[175] E. Wyn James, ' "The New Birth of a people": Welsh language and identity and the Welsh Methodists, c. 1740–1820', in Pope (ed.), *Religion and National Identity*, p. 19.

to celebrate their membership of an international evangelical community of saints that was both transnational and transatlantic, rather than their Welshness.[176] Perhaps most importantly they saw themselves as cogs in the great cosmic drama of redemption. They were citizens of the kingdom of God and fully expected all temporary national and denominational divisions to be subsumed once the millennial age had dawned, an age that many of them firmly believed was just around the corner.

---

[176] For a more balanced analysis of some of the issues relating to early Welsh Methodist identity see White, 'The people called "Methodists" ', 1–14.

CONCLUSION: THE SIGNIFICANCE OF 1750

By 1750 the Welsh Methodists' expectation that the evangelical revival would usher in the millennial reign of Christ had been replaced by fears that the revival was in grave danger and that its future was far from secure. This can be seen particularly clearly in the Welsh Methodists' relations with the wider evangelical community. Between 1739 and 1750 Howel Harris had been the focus of their interaction with the wider evangelical revival. Capitalizing on his friendship with George Whitefield, he had introduced them to this evangelical community and had publicized the Welsh awakening at every conceivable opportunity. Although much of this activity had occurred on Harris's initiative, he had been able to transmit his infectious enthusiasm to many of his followers. In this way the rank-and-file members of the Welsh revival discovered a whole range of ways in which they could participate in the collective understanding of the experience of revival and engage with a community that had far wider boundaries than their own immediate localities. Yet by the late 1740s Welsh participation in this vibrant community was under threat. Its chief supporter in Wales, Howel Harris, had become the focus of considerable controversy. When he was eventually dismissed from the leadership of the English revival at the beginning of 1750 and was ousted from his position in Wales later that same year, the international communications network in Wales atrophied. Daniel Rowland, as has been pointed out, had never accorded it the same priority as Harris, and without Harris's network of contacts many 'ordinary' Welsh Methodists lost much of their interest in the wider movement, as they became engrossed in the struggle for their own survival.

Harris had finally accepted the leadership of English Calvinistic Methodism in April 1749, after having deputized for Whitefield for the previous four years. Prospects for the revival initially seemed good. In July, Harris testified to a renewal of his evangelistic zeal and was full of expectation regarding the future. On 29 July 1749 he recorded in his diary:

> Last Night I continued singing and preaching all night with Mrs Griffith and maid. I never felt the like before, for 6 days the Lord has filled my heart and mouth so as I never had before, and 'tis impossible to express with words [. . .] I see 'tis some fresh glory God gives me, I am raised out of the corrupt nature more than ever, and out of the flesh and unclean spirit, so as I have not been for several years, and my love made more and more pure indeed.[1]

The following day at an Association at Llangeitho he testified to having received his old authority back.[2] However, Harris's optimism was seriously misplaced. His Welsh co-revivalists had grown impatient with his increasingly erratic behaviour. Whitefield himself had only appointed Harris as a last resort and was the first among the leaders of the revival to take a principled stand against him by expelling him from the Tabernacle in December 1749. Howel Harris's expulsion from the evangelical revival was not an exclusively Welsh matter. It occurred within the context of the international evangelical community and had significant ramifications far beyond Wales.

Difficulties surrounding Howel Harris had surfaced before 1749. The later 1740s witnessed the full realization of a number of potentially divisive issues that had lain below the surface of the Welsh revival since its early days. At the same time as Harris was making his massive contributions to both the Welsh and English revivals, he was being closely watched by his co-revivalists, who were becoming concerned about his irregular and inexplicable mood swings. By the mid-1740s, Daniel Rowland had become fearful of the direction in which Harris was attempting to lead the movement. By 1749, Harris had been involved in evangelical activity for almost fifteen years. He had preached practically every day, often more than once, and had travelled many thousands of miles throughout England and Wales. By the later 1740s he was physically and emotionally exhausted. As early as 1744 he had begun to complain about ill health and fatigue, a condition that was seriously affecting his relations with his co-

---

[1] HHD 135a, 29 July 1749.
[2] HHD 135a, 30 July 1749.

revivalists and his attitude towards his own work. In February 1744 he confided to his diary: 'I find I am decayed in person and though but 30 years of age, yet look old and decaying, and have done nothing comparatively for the Lord.'[3]

In the early years of the revival, Harris and Daniel Rowland had been so engrossed in their work that they found it relatively easy to work together. However, as the initial excitement of the revival subsided and they had to spend more time in one another's company, they found it more difficult to cooperate. Many of the tensions between them undoubtedly stemmed from Harris's inferiority complex on account of his unordained status. Though there is no evidence to think that Rowland thought Harris's lack of clerical status problematic, Harris regularly felt the need to reiterate his supremacy. One of the most frequent ways in which he did this was by reminding his co-revivalists that it had been he who had begun the revival. He repeatedly styled himself as 'the first of all the Brethren'[4] and 'the first to sound the Trumpet about the Country'.[5] Technically this was true, and Harris used the fact to full advantage, arguing that his primacy gave him special authority. So long as the revivalists concentrated on pioneer evangelistic work, his domineering spirit was overlooked. However, when he began to adopt ambiguous theological language and act in an irrational and inconsistent manner, his belligerence became a major stumbling block for his colleagues, who found it almost impossible to reason with him and, ultimately, to work with him in any capacity whatsoever.

Prior to 1744, the relationship between Harris and Rowland had been one of mutual respect and admiration. There had been conflicts, but these had been smoothed over, and very little long-term damage had been done. At Llwynyberllan in March 1742, Rowland had disagreed with Harris over the doctrine of assurance. Harris, following what he had heard from John Wesley, argued that assurance was an essential part of Christian profession and that without it an individual was not truly converted. Rowland, as George Whitefield had done in England, disagreed strongly and argued that an individual could be a Christian without experiencing full assurance of faith. After

---

[3]   HHD 107, 6 February 1744.
[4]   HHD 125, 20 January 1747.
[5]   Quoted in Tudur, *Howell Harris*, p. 153.

heated disagreements Harris spoke of leaving the revival, but when he realized how little support he had amongst the ex-horters, he backed down and apologized to Rowland, where-upon unity was preserved and the revival continued. Such confrontations were not unusual in the early years of the revival. Differences between Harris and Rowland often produced heated disagreements, but permanent divisions were avoided when the revivalists calmly considered the wider implications of the positions they were adopting.

Geraint Tudur has argued that 1744 marked a critical watershed in the relationship between Harris and Rowland because it was during this year that the influence of Moravian theology on Harris, particularly patripassianism,[6] became more pronounced.[7] During his time in London in November and December he was once again impressed with the depth of spirituality possessed by the Moravians. This he attributed to their emphasis on the virtues of the blood of Christ, and he became convinced that his own lack of emphasis on this particular theme accounted for his weakness and what he regarded as the powerlessness of his ministry. After attending a Moravian Letter Day, Harris wrote: 'Hearing all these letters about experience of the Blood of Christ, how that it is all, I saw them gone before me far in faith and strength and the divine life.'[8] The following day he made a resolution that he would 'love all that preach this Blood alike of all sects and countries'.[9]

Harris returned to Wales with an emphasis markedly different from when he had left. He soon began to talk about the power of Christ's blood in his sermons. The difference did not go unnoticed. At an Association during June 1745 Rowland dis-agreed with him, criticizing his overemphasis on the power of the actual physical blood of Christ. Similarly in London, members of the Tabernacle became increasingly perturbed at some of Harris's strange and confused language. In May 1746 some members of the Tabernacle Society had been so concerned that

---

[6]   Patripassianism was a teaching that involved confusion over the functions of the different members of the Trinity. Literally, it means the suffering of the Father and it is usually used in the case of individuals who claim that it was God the Father who suffered and died on the cross as well as God the Son. *ODCC*, pp. 1233, 1434.

[7]   Tudur, *Howell Harris*, p. 160.

[8]   HHD 115a, 3 December 1744.

[9]   HHD 115a, 4 December 1744.

they expressed their protest by walking out while Harris was
exhorting, specifically because of the Moravian-type language
that he had adopted.[10] From this time onwards, Harris's doctrinal aberrations, together with his increased insecurity regarding his position within the movement, led to a gradual
deterioration in his reputation and eventually to the disruption of
the Welsh Methodist revival.

Between 1745 and July 1748, Harris moved between the
English and Welsh revivals. Forced to act as Whitefield's deputy
and feeling that the Welsh revival was past its peak, Harris
devoted more and more of his time to the work in England,
where he felt he was appreciated far more. Harris undoubtedly
found his extended visits to London a relief. Whilst there, he had
more freedom than in Wales, with no eagle-eyed Daniel
Rowland to watch him, and it seems that Harris found his duties
in the English revival to be a useful diversion when affairs in
Wales began to go against him.

In Wales, Rowland grew increasingly frustrated. At an
Association in June 1746 the differences surfaced publicly for the
first time as Harris and Rowland clashed openly. Rowland
furiously questioned Harris's orthodoxy, accusing him of using
ambiguous statements about the blood of Christ and of being an
antinomian.[11] Harris attempted unsuccessfully to defend himself,
issuing an explicit denial of the charge that he believed that God
had suffered on the Cross.[12] The Association had shown for the
first time the real extent of the suspicion in which Harris was now
held. However, a division did not immediately follow. At another
meeting at Watford in October, there was a reconciliation.
Rowland backed down with the proviso that Harris renounce any
sympathy for Moravian teachings. Harris gladly did so, and in his
diary at the end of the meeting recorded his gratitude to God that
peace had been restored. He wrote: 'Many of the Brethren, I find,
despise me more and more on my infirmities and I am enabled to
commit it all to God to see to keep me in my Place and to suit me
with all Grace and Gifts.'[13] Yet this truce was fragile. Throughout
1747 Harris became increasingly arrogant and outspoken. His

[10] HHD 122, 26 May 1746.
[11] Tudur, *Howell Harris*, pp. 170–1.
[12] HHD 123, 27–8 June 1746.
[13] HHD 124, 19 October 1746.

claims to supremacy became more vehement and were reinforced by his status as leader of the English movement. When in Wales, Harris attempted to strengthen his position by purging the societies of those individuals whom he thought lukewarm and lacking in spiritual discernment. In reality this was a cover for his practice of casting out those who objected to his Moravian language and his emphasis on the blood of Christ. Predictably, the Welsh converts became impatient and found it increasingly difficult to cooperate with him. Harris responded in his usual way, rejecting all criticism and becoming more and more isolated in his assertion that his new theological emphases had been revealed to him by God directly. This belief gave him an authority above those who tried to counsel him, like Rowland and later Whitefield. He was able to dismiss their objections, accusing them of relying on their carnal reasoning and not being as spiritually mature as he felt himself to be.

The events surrounding the final disruption of the Welsh Methodist revival have been fairly fully documented.[14] However, what has not been widely appreciated is the extent to which Harris's fall from grace occurred within a transnational context. The first to make a final decision about Harris was George Whitefield. Whitefield had returned from the American colonies in July 1748, determined to relinquish permanently his Moderatorship of English and Welsh Calvinistic Methodism and take up a far freer role. Upon his return he clearly hoped that Harris would step into the breach and accept the leadership of the movement.[15] Yet the Harris that he met in London was not the Harris that he had left four years previously. Whitefield's suspicions were initially roused by the poor condition in which he discovered his societies. They had witnessed a number of secessions and were both numerically and spiritually weak. Whitefield also encountered a Harris more defensive and belligerent, sounding remarkably like a Moravian and intent on securing his acceptance of a union between his movement and that of the Wesleys. During his time in America Whitefield had also undergone a significant change in his attitudes

[14] See Tudur, *Howell Harris*, pp. 151–228; Geraint Tudur, 'The king's daughter: a reassessment of Anne Harris of Trefeca', *JWRH*, 7 (1999), 64–75; and Tudur, 'Like a right arm and a pillar', in Pope (ed.), *Honouring the Past and Shaping the Future*, pp. 133–58.

[15] For a detailed discussion of the process by which Harris accepted the leadership see above, pp. 234–7.

towards some of the more exceptional manifestations of the revival. He had witnessed the confusion that a number of enthusiasts had sown throughout the American revival, and his caution about Harris's new emphases and approach prevented him from wholeheartedly endorsing Harris's previous three years' labours. In his diary Harris recorded that Whitefield was

> determined not to join with any to preach (after the delusion and abomination he had seen through young ones going out rashly in a wild fire) till he should be fully satisfied of the teachable, of their tempers, and if they are willing to use all means to improve themselves.[16]

Harris was sufficiently worried by this development and by Whitefield's initial coolness towards the idea of a reunion with the Wesleys to consider his own position in England. At a meeting with the Whitefieldian preachers he 'Opened [my] mind that I would not come to England more, but that I would come to the Association, and found it in my hand to strengthen their hands all I could – and to come and help them here I was ready.'[17] Against the background of difficulties in Wales, Harris began to feel that his closest associates were beginning to turn against him. In July 1748 he recorded in his diary that he felt that Whitefield and Rowland had both 'withdrawn'[18] from him.

It was at this delicate point that Harris met Madam Sidney Griffith for the first time. It was her presence at Harris's side through the latter half of 1749 that finally precipitated his ejection from the movement. Harris became totally besotted with Madam Griffith. The precise nature of the relationship between them has been one of the most controversial issues in Welsh Methodist historiography. The debate has become polarized between those who see clear evidence of adultery and those who have sought to explain the relationship in the light of Harris's enthusiasm and lack of judgement. Geraint H. Jenkins has drawn the inevitable conclusion from Harris's language in reference to Madam Griffith that the relationship was almost certainly adulterous.[19] Yet Geraint Tudur in his recently published study

[16]   HHD 131b, 21 July 1748.
[17]   HHD 131b, 22 July 1748.
[18]   Ibid.
[19]   See Jenkins, *The Foundations of Modern Wales*, p. 346.

of the diaries of Harris has argued convincingly that there is no definite proof of an adulterous relationship, but plenty of evidence that Harris was torn between his 'physical lust and spiritual duty'.[20] Whether Harris's relationship with Madam Griffith involved actual physical adultery is probably impossible to say with absolute certainty. Whilst Harris's language certainly suggests this, especially when he wrote in his diary that he 'felt a superior love to Mrs Griffith over all, even Anne',[21] determining the precise context in which he used these words is considerably more difficult than might at first appear.

An understanding of the role that Harris believed Madam Griffith deserved is undoubtedly the key to understanding their highly unusual relationship. After she moved into Trefeca with Harris and his wife, Anne,[22] he attempted to integrate her into the daily life of the revival by claiming that she possessed special spiritual gifts and that God had begun to reveal his will for Harris's life, and thus for the Welsh revival, through his new prophetess. To Harris, Madam Griffith was God's channel who regularly received fresh revelations.[23] It was this fact that led Harris to think of her in a class apart from all of his other associates, even at times his own wife. For Rowland and Whitefield this development, together with the potential for public misunderstanding of the relationship, was completely unacceptable and became the catalyst for the final disruption of the Welsh revival and Harris's retreat to Trefeca.

The full implications of the relationship did not immediately become apparent. In April 1749 Harris was once again in London and finally accepted the leadership of the Whitefieldian societies. His new position did not put an end to Whitefield's doubts about his orthodoxy. In April 1749 Harris had publicly reprimanded Whitefield for 'speaking so free against the brethren [the Moravians] before everybody'[24] and had reiterated his own 'esteem of the Moravians [because] they have the main and great

---

[20]   Tudur, *Howell Harris*, p. 295.
[21]   HHD 138, 17 October 1749. For Anne Harris's response to Sidney Griffith, see Tudur, 'The king's daughter: a reassessment of Anne Harris of Trefeca', 64–75.
[22]   Harris had married Anne Williams, from Skreen (Ynys-grin), near Erwood, Radnorshire, in June 1744. Tudur, 'The king's daughter', 56.
[23]   HHD 137, 8 October 1749.
[24]   HHD 135, 12 April 1749.

thing – the saving knowledge of Christ and His glory'.[25] By the end of this visit to London Harris realized that Whitefield was beginning to have serious reservations about his long-term place as leader of the movement and had come to the conclusion that it 'was necessity and not choice'[26] that had made Whitefield appoint him in the first place. In his diary he recorded: 'Mr Whitefield thought the people would not receive me and perhaps thought I had too great an esteem for the Moravians.'[27]

Harris returned to Wales discouraged and depressed, once again in confusion regarding his future role in the international revival. It was Madam Sidney Griffith who came to his aid, so that when he returned to London three months later he testified to being 'raised to a new life with God, in everything'.[28] Yet in London he discovered that attitudes had hardened against him. He seems to have come on this occasion with the intention of reasserting his position in the English revival. In discussions at the Tabernacle regarding the future direction of the societies, he criticized Whitefield's leadership, suggesting that 'the work has been more shattered since Mr Whitefield came over than before'.[29] His answer to the situation was assumption of outright leadership of the revival, enabling him to act independently of Whitefield.[30] Whitefield was predictably cool about Harris's proposals, and when he failed to take them up Harris's usual feelings of inferiority and self-doubt quickly resurfaced. He returned to the fact that Whitefield had only appointed him to the leadership as a last resort and began to question his very presence in London. He wrote in his diary that he no longer knew 'What I am called here for. My place in Wales I see and know. I believe Mr Whitefield himself thinks me selfish, and is not from his heart for my taking the care of it.'[31]

It seems that Harris increasingly came to the opinion that Whitefield no longer trusted him to lead the English societies. At another conference of the English brethren, Whitefield openly disagreed with Harris, and walked out of the meeting.[32] White-

[25]   Ibid.
[26]   HHD 135, 7 May 1749.
[27]   Ibid.
[28]   HHD 136, 21 August 1749.
[29]   HHD 136, 31 August 1749.
[30]   Ibid.
[31]   HHD 136, 2 September 1749.
[32]   HHD 136, 4 September 1749.

field had been influenced by some Dissenters, who in their attempts to help him free the movement from charges of 'enthusiasm,' had counselled him that Harris's presence at its head would eventually cause the societies to collapse. As a result he began to make arrangements to deprive Harris of his leadership. Initially he argued that it was necessary for the societies to have a full-time leader and singled out Thomas Adams as the most appropriate candidate, with Harris assisting at periodic intervals. Harris, more isolated than ever before, returned to Wales and to Madam Griffith, who once again sought to rebuild his confidence by reminding him of their joint divine commission. By this time Harris was acting almost alone. In Wales, the relationship between him and Rowland had been irreparably damaged, and sordid rumours were rife about the precise nature of his association with Madam Griffith.[33] He continued to attempt to bolster his position in Wales by excluding those who, he concluded, were spiritually deficient. Once again, this policy only seemed to alienate him further from his followers. His harshness, coupled with his unshakeable confidence in the rightness of his own actions and their divine sanction by Madam Griffith, contributed to the impression that Harris was now actually hindering the progress of the revival and bringing it into widespread disrepute.

Harris arrived in London as the leader of English Calvinistic Methodism for the last time at the beginning of December 1749. Whitefield practically ignored him. Almost immediately, Harris recognized that Whitefield had finally turned against him. He confronted him and protested at being left 'to spend my time idle after coming so far'.[34] It took Whitefield five days to invite Harris to preach at the Tabernacle, a snub that Harris found impossible to forgive. He quickly began to turn against Whitefield, his reasons being a mixture of personal attacks and understandable grievances. He began to question Whitefield's integrity, accusing him of 'not growing in the knowledge of Christ'[35] and sinning by 'not going to the little places to preach'.[36] More concretely, Harris returned to the fact that Whitefield did not really want

[33] See Tudur, *Howell Harris*, p. 209.
[34] HHD 139, 11 December 1749.
[35] HHD 140, 20 December 1749.
[36] Ibid.

him at the head of the English revival anyway and that he had offered it to him only after three other men had refused.

Underlying everything, Harris came back to his biggest source of insecurity by concluding that Whitefield was prejudiced against him on account of his unordained status. Harris justified his ministry in his usual manner by stressing that 'God sent me out by myself as well as him before I knew him'.[37] Harris, encouraged by Madam Griffith, had become uncontrollable. Accepting nobody's authority if it contradicted his own, he insulated himself against all criticism by arguing that his steps were uniquely ordered by God and were thus to be heeded at the expense of everybody else. The final break came in early January 1750. On 1 January Harris recorded in his diary that Whitefield had succumbed to the influence of his wife, recording a conversation that he had had with Mrs Whitefield in September 1749 in which he told her of her

> pride in not submitting her judgement to Mr Whitefield. My fears about her being prejudiced against the Moravians, and Mr Whitefield, and that she is to meddle no more with us and our affairs than to give her judgement about a thing and then leave it, not retain somewhat in her mind and so bring it out continually.[38]

Later he also blamed the Dissenters.[39] By the end of the day Whitefield had turned him out of the English Calvinistic movement. A few days later Harris gave up his rooms at the Tabernacle House and finally parted company with Whitefield. He stayed in London for a further three weeks but discovered that everywhere he went the 'rage'[40] against him was 'amazing'[41] on account of his being 'Suspected as a Moravian, my preaching Christ crucified, my catholic love to Mr Wesley, my standing ground for the authority given me and judged proud'.[42]

Despite all the controversy that Harris's presence in London caused, he continued to meet some of the London evangelicals and to argue that the future of the revival in England would be

37   Ibid.
38   HHD 137, 14 September 1749.
39   HHD 140, 1 January 1750.
40   Tom Beynon, *Howell Harris's Visits to London*, p. 257.
41   Ibid.
42   HHD 140, 22 December 1749.

best served by a union between Wesley and Whitefield and by their preaching among one another's societies and converts. That Whitefield and Wesley did eventually agree to preach for each other undoubtedly owed much to Harris's conciliatory work over the previous five years.[43] It was only as Harris was being forced out of the English revival that the project that had been closest to his heart, and for which he had worked for so long, began to reach its fruition. It was possibly Harris's greatest legacy to the English Methodist movement.

As he returned to Wales, Harris must have feared that Daniel Rowland would seize the opportunity to take immediate action against him. He once more attempted to rally his supporters, but to no avail. In May, Harris and Rowland met in an Association at Llanidloes for the last time for over a decade. Harris protested that he could not accept Rowland's authority, and from Llanidloes the two men finally went their separate ways. Their separation was confirmed at an Association the following month at Trefeca, after which date the converts split according to which of the two revivalists they favoured. That the overwhelming majority of Welsh Methodists sided with Daniel Rowland was ample testimony to the isolation and weakness of Harris's position and the extent to which his personal reputation lay in tatters.

Harris quickly realized that his place in the revival had been lost. His last desperate attempts to garner support among the societies proved futile, and when Madam Sidney Griffith unexpectedly died in 1752, Harris began to withdraw from public life altogether. His retreat was accompanied by a marked decline in the Welsh Methodists' involvement in the international evangelical community. Many of Harris's chief associates throughout the community severed their relations with him and many Welsh Methodists gave up contributing to the transnational network when they lost his constant encouragement.

Yet it would be a mistake to assume that the Welsh Methodists completely lost sight of the international dimension of their movement, even during the years of crisis and retrenchment in the 1750s. Harris himself used his retirement to fulfil his ambition of founding a Pietistic community based on the ideals

---

[43]   See Dallimore, *George Whitefield*, II, pp. 335–53.

of August Hermann Francke.[44] Daniel Rowland kept in fairly close contact with George Whitefield. In September 1750, Whitefield considered making a tour of Wales, but decided that it had 'better be deferred to the cool of the day'.[45] Whitefield waited until May and June 1758 to return to Wales. He toured south Wales but made no attempt to seek out Harris. Of the other pioneer revivalists, John Wesley maintained the closest relationship with Harris during these years. He visited Trefeca in 1756 but found Harris depressed and talking about his imminent demise. His spirits were little altered from the description he had given in a letter to Wesley in January 1753:

> I have been expecting to be at the marriage supper of the Lamb before this. O my dear brother, honour His blood and death and He will honour you. I send this as my dying and loving request to you for the Lord's sake, for your own sake, and for the sake of the thousands that attend your ministry.[46]

By 1758 there was a general feeling among the leaders of the Welsh revival that Harris's exile had been long enough and that his presence in the revival was once again necessary. However, reconciliation was delayed by Harris's enrolment in the Breconshire militia during the Seven Years War.[47] Whilst enrolled, Harris rediscovered some of his old enthusiasm, especially when he began exhorting once more during his posting in the southwest of England. Harris was eventually reconciled to his fellow Welsh Methodists in early 1763,[48] at the same time as a new revival broke out in Llangeitho.[49] Harris rebuilt some of his transnational connections and was at an Association in Bristol as early as March 1763.[50] His greatest contribution to the international revival during these years came out of his relationship

---

[44]   The best study of Harris's Trefeca community remains the unpublished thesis of Alun Wynne Owen, 'A study of Howel Harris and the Trevecca "family" (1752–1760) based upon the Trevecca letters and diaries and other Methodist archives at the National Library of Wales' (MA, Wales, 1957).
[45]   Quoted in Evans, *Howell Harris*, p. 58.
[46]   Trevecka 2042, Howel Harris to John Wesley (1 January 1753).
[47]   Tom Beynon, *Howell Harris: Reformer and Soldier, 1714–1773* (Caernarfon, 1958), pp. 58–146, passim.
[48]   HHD 240, 15–16 February 1763.
[49]   See R. Geraint Gruffudd, 'Diwygiad 1762 a William Williams o Bantycelyn', *CCHMC*, LIV, 3 (October 1969), 68–75 and LV, 1 (March, 1970), 4–13.
[50]   HHD 240, 5–10 March 1763.

with the countess of Huntingdon. In August 1768 a Methodist academy[51] was opened at Trefeca to train men for the Calvinistic Methodist ministry. The opening day, 24 August, was another Methodist landmark. All of the leaders of the British movement were present, including Whitefield and John Wesley, and the meeting was reminiscent of the unity that had characterized the revival in the later 1730s. Yet in reality the Harris that had re-entered the revival in 1763 was very different from the one who had occupied such a prominent position in the international evangelical community during the later 1730s and the 1740s. He had lost much of his enthusiasm and could never quite free himself from the taint of past misdemeanours. Harris was not able to recapture his early zeal, and for ten years occupied a fairly inconspicuous place in a movement that had moved on in his absence.

The ability of the revival to operate without Harris's influence throughout the 1750s is testimony to the strength of the movement which he and Daniel Rowland had created. Whilst his contemporaries recognized that he was essential to the ongoing success of the revival, in reality the detailed organizational structure that he had been instrumental in setting up in the early 1740s ensured that the movement was not totally dependent on the presence of a single charismatic personality. It was for this reason that the loss of Harris did not completely fragment the work, but forced its members to reorientate the revival and consolidate their achievements until they were re-energized by a fresh 'pouring out of the Spirit' at Llangeitho in 1762.

---

[51] Schlenther, *Queen of the Methodists*, pp. 56–82; Geoffrey F. Nuttall, 'The students of Trevecca College, 1768–1791', *Transactions of the Honourable Society of Cymmrodorion* (1968), 249–69; Edwin Welch, *Spiritual Pilgrim: A Reassessment of the Life of the Countess of Huntingdon* (Cardiff, 1995), pp. 111–30.

APPENDIX 1
HOWEL HARRIS'S VISITS TO THE ENGLISH REVIVAL, 1739–50

10 April–20 June 1739 (Gloucester, Cheltenham, Evesham, Oxford, London and Bristol).

1 May–18 June 1740 (Gloucester, Oxford, London and Gloucester).

20 June–12 October 1741 (Gloucester, Bristol, London, Wiltshire and Bristol).

19 August–15 November 1742 (Bristol, London, Wiltshire and Bristol).

17 August–30 September 1743 (Bristol, Wiltshire, London, Oxford and Gloucester).

12 January–17 March 1744 (Gloucester, London and Gloucester).

1–5 June 1744 (Bristol).

27 November–29 December 1744 (Gloucester and London).

21–25 March 1745 (Bristol and Bath).

23 May–20 June 1745 (Gloucester, London, Bath and Bristol).

20 November–16 December 1745 (Gloucester, Oxford, London, Oxford and Gloucester).

30 January–7 March 1746 (Gloucester, London and Bristol).

7 May–23 June 1746 (Gloucester, Oxford, London and Gloucester).

8 August–23 September 1746 (Gloucester, London, Oxford and Gloucester).

10 March–17 April 1747 (Gloucester, Oxford, London and Gloucester).

26 May –17 July 1747 (Gloucester, London, Birmingham and Hereford).

12 November–23 December 1747 (Gloucester, London, Oxford and Gloucester).

1–28 January 1748 (Bristol, Bath, Exeter, Plymouth, Exeter, Bristol, Bath and Bristol).

18 May–28 July 1748 (Gloucestershire, Oxford, London, Oxford and Gloucester);

2 April–10 May 1749 (Gloucester, London, Oxford, Gloucester).

16 August–22 September 1749 (Gloucester, London, Oxford and Gloucester).

29 November 1749–27 January 1750 (Gloucester, London and Oxfordshire).

APPENDIX 2
FEMALE PARTICIPANTS IN THE LETTER-WRITING NETWORK, 1738–50

The figures in square brackets refer to the number of letters that each correspondent contributed to the network.

Adams, Elizabeth [1]
Adams, Mrs Thomas [3]
Allen, Isabel [1]
Alleim, Sister [1]
Antel, Ann [1]
Aubery, Sister (Hay) [1]
Barnsley, Elizabeth [11]
Barton, Sarah (Bristol) [1]
Beebee, Miss (Prestatyn) [1]
Biggs, Mary [10]
Bishop, Mary [1]
Bowen, Ann (Tyfyn) [3]
Burton, Sarah [3]
Cadman, Eleanor (Llanidloes) [1]
Chatwin, Elizabeth [1]
Clifford, Elizabeth [2]
Cooke, Elizabeth (Stoke Newington) [2]
Cripps, Sister [1]
Crossland, Elizabeth [1]
Davies, Ann (Bristol) [2]
Davies, Sarah [3]
Davis, Mary [1]
Dinah, Sister [1]
Dobe, Rachel (London) [1]
Doyle, Mrs [1]
Dutton, Anne (London) [9]
Evan, Anne [1]
Godwin, Elizabeth (London) [4]
Godwin, Mrs J. (London) [24]
Griffith, Madam Sidney [6]
Griffiths, Sister Mary [1]
Gwynne, Sarah [4]

Harris, Ann (wife of Joseph Harris) [1]
Harris/Williams, Anne [108]
Harry, Ann (St Kennox) [2]
Hart, Sister [1]
Hilling, Ann [1]
Howells, Elizabeth [3]
Huntingdon, Lady [5]
James, Elizabeth [1]
Jenkins, Sister Molly [1]
Johnson, Isabella [2]
Kiggell, Elizabeth [9]
Lady in Scotland [2]
Lewis, ?Miss [1]
Mason, Sarah (London) [5]
Orn, Sister (London) [2]
P., Mrs G. [1]
Page, Mary Ann [5]
Parry, Sister Elizabeth [1]
Parsons, Ann [1]
Paul, Elizabeth [23]
Perkins, Mary [1]
Powell, Alice [1]
Poyer, Catherine [6]
Price, Amy [1]
Price, Elizabeth [1]
Price, Nancy (Llangamach) [1]
Pugh, Catherine [2]
Pugh, Elizabeth [1]
Pugh, Kate [1]
Pugh, Mary [1]
Pugh, Peggy [2]
Richard, Mary [1]
Rowlands, Mrs Dolly (London) [1]
Saunders, Mrs [1]
Stevens, Ann (Plymouth) [1]
Taylor, Anna [2]
Thomas, Ann (Longhouse) [1]
Thomas, Anne [1]
Thomas, Elizabeth (Longhouse) [18]
Towl, Martha [1]
Underhill, Martha [1]
Watkins, Mary [3]
Watson, Grace [1]

Wealch, Ann [1]
Whitefield/James, Elizabeth [35]
Wildman, Ann [1]
Wilkins, Elizabeth [1]
Williams, Molly (Erwood) [3]
Williams, Sarah (Builth) [3]
Wood, Elizabeth [15]

ANONYMOUS LETTERS

Anon. (Pontypool) [1]
Anon. (Mrs —, Watford) [1]
Anon. (daughter of Thomas Price, Watford) [1]
Honoured Madam [1]
Madam — (Herefordshire) [1]

APPENDIX 3
FEMALE CONTRIBUTORS TO THE RELIGIOUS
MAGAZINES, 1740–8

The figures in the square brackets refer to the number of letters a
correspondent had printed in the magazines.

A—ng, A. (Society at Kingswood) [1]
A—, Mrs T. [3]
B—, Mrs [1]
B., Mrs E. [1]
B—p, Sister [1]
B—r, Mrs S—h [1]
B—y, Mrs (Orphanhouse in Georgia) [1]
C—, Mrs [1]
C—, Mrs S— [1]
C—, Sister S— [2]
Dutton, Anne (London) [1]
E., Mrs [1]
H., Mrs M. [1]
H-D, Sister (Brinkworth) [1]
J., Mrs E. [1]
K—, A— (a young girl in the Merchants' Hospital, Edinburgh) [1]
L., Mrs E. [1]
L—e, Mrs E-h (Swindon) [2]
L—y M—t (a young girl in the Merchants' Hospital, Edinburgh) [1]
M—, Mrs F— [1]
M—, Sister [1]
P., Mrs A. [1]
P., Mrs E [1]
Paul, Elizabeth (London) [1]
Rowe, Mrs [1]
S. Mrs [2]
S—n, Mrs [1]
Thomas, Mrs Anne (Longhouse) [1]
W—, Sister (Cambridge) [1]
Whitefield, Elizabeth [3]

ANONYMOUS CORRESPONDENTS

Gentlewoman in the Country [1]
Sister at Bath [3]
Sister in Chinnor, Oxfordshire [1]
Sister in darkness [1]
Sister in London [1]
Sister at Inworth [1]
Sister to the Tabernacle Society [1]
Sister in Walsall, Staffordshire [1]
Sister under trials [1]
One in the country to her Sister [1]
Young lady at Bath [1]

SELECT BIBLIOGRAPHY

Original Sources

A. *Unpublished*

1. *Calvinistic Methodist Archives, National Library of Wales, Aberystwyth*

(i) Trevecka Group
1–1966 The Trevecka Letters, 1725–1751.
2788–2823 Additional Letters 1740–1751.
2945 Records of Associations, 1.
2946 Records of Associations, 2.

(ii) The Diaries of Howel Harris, 1739–63.

(iii) Calvinist Methodist Archive 170–80.

2. *The John Rylands University of Manchester Library*

(i) Methodist Church Archives.
John Wesley's Letters: MAM. JW. 3. 40

B. *Published*

Baker, Frank, *The Works of John Wesley, 25: Letters, I: 1721–1739* (Oxford, 1980).
——, *The Works of John Wesley, 26: Letters, II: 1740–1755* (Oxford, 1982).
Beynon, Tom, *Howell Harris: Reformer and Soldier, 1714–1773* (Caernarfon, 1958).
——, *Howell Harris's Visits to London* (Aberystwyth, 1960).
——, *Howell Harris's Visits to Pembrokeshire* (Aberystwyth, 1966).
Claghorn, George S. (ed.), *The Works of Jonathan Edwards, XVI: Letters and Personal Writings* (New Haven, 1998).

Clement, Mary (ed.), *The Correspondence and Minutes of the S.P.C.K to Wales, 1699–1740* (Cardiff, 1952).

Curnock, Nehemiah (ed.), *The Journal of the Rev. John Wesley, A.M.*, 8 vols (London, 1938).

Erskine, Ebenezer and Erskine, Ralph, *Crist ym Mreichiau'r Credadyn Wedi Ei Osod Allan Mewn Pregeth ar Luc. ii, 28 . . . Hefyd, Odi ar Waith a Dadl y Nefoedd Wedi ei Gymmeryd Allan o'r Llyfr . . . 'Gospel Sonnets.' Newydd eu Cyfieithu i'r Gymraeg* (Caerfyrddin, 1744).

Erskine, Ralph, *Traethawd am Farw i'r Ddeddf a Byw i Dduw . . .* [gan. Ralph Erskine, cyf. gan, John Morgan]; *at Ba Un y Chwanegwyd Chwech o Hymnau . . . o Waith Daniel Rowland* (Bristol, 1743).

Goen, C. C. (ed.), *The Works of Jonathan Edwards, IV: The Great Awakening* (New Haven Conn., 1972).

Hughes, Garfield H., *Gweithiau William Williams*, II (Cardiff, 1967).

Jay, Elizabeth (ed.), *The Journal of John Wesley: A Selection* (Oxford, 1987).

Jones, M. H., *The Trevecka Letters* (Caernarfon, 1932).

Jones, N. Cynhafal (ed.), *Gweithiau Williams Pantycelyn*, I (1887).

Lewis, John (ed.), *The Christian's Amusement: Containing Letter's Concerning the Progress of the Gospel Both at Home and Abroad &c. Together with an Account of the Waldenses and Albigenses: People that Never Fell into the Popish Errors, but Retained the Truth of the Gospel from the Time of the Apostles, under all the Popish Persecutions down to the Reformation*, 1–27 (September 1740–March 1741).

——, *The Weekly History: or An Account of the Most Remarkable Particulars Relating to the Present Progress of the Gospel, by the Encouragement of the Rev. Mr Whitefield*, 1–84 (11 April 1741–13 November 1742).

——, *An Account of the Most Remarkable Particulars Relating to the Present Progress of the Gospel*, vol. II, nos. I, II and III; vol. III, nos. I, II and III and vol. IV, nos. I, II and III (Autumn 1742–Autumn 1748).

——, *The Christian History: Or a General Account of the Progress of the Gospel, in England, Wales, Scotland and America: So Far as the Rev. Mr Whitefield, His Fellow-Labourers, and Assistants are Concern'd*, vol. V, nos. I, II, III and IV; vol. VI, nos. I, II, III and IV; vol. VII, nos. I, II, III and IV and vol. VII (Autumn 1743–June 1748).

McCulloch, William (ed.), *The Glasgow Weekly History Relating to the Late Progress of the Gospel at Home and Abroad: Being a Collection of Letters Partly Reprinted from the London-Weekly-History* (printed by William Duncan, Glasgow, 1742) (University of Glasgow Library).

Murray, Iain H. (ed.), *George Whitefield's Journals* (London, 1960).

——, *George Whitefield's Letters, 1734–1742* (Edinburgh, 1976).

Roberts, Gomer M. (ed.), *Gweithiau William Williams, Pantycelyn*, I (Cardiff, 1964).

——, *Selected Trevecka Letters, 1742–1747* (Caernarfon, 1956).

——, *Selected Trevecka Letters, 1747–1794* (Caernarfon, 1962).

Sail, Dibenion, a Rheolau'r Societies Neu'r Cyfarfodydd Neullduol a ddechreassant ymgynull yn ddiweddar yn Nghymru (Bristol, 1742).

Stein, Stephen J. (ed.), *The Works of Jonathan Edwards, V: Apocalyptic Writings* (New Haven, 1977).

Thickens, John (ed.), *Howel Harris yn Llundain* (Caernarfon, 1934).

Thomas, Graham C. G. (ed.), 'George Whitefield and friends: the correspondence of some early Methodists', *National Library of Wales Journal*, 26, III (Summer 1990), 251–80; 26, IV (Winter 1990), 367–96; 27, I (Summer 1991), 65–96; 27, II (Winter 1991), 175–203; 27, III (Summer 1992), 289–318; 27, IV (Winter 1992), 431–52.

Ward, W. R. and Heitzenrater, R. P. (eds), *The Works of John Wesley, 28: Journal and Diaries, I (1735–38)* (Nashville, 1988).

Welch, Edwin, (ed.), *Two Calvinistic Methodist Chapels 1743–1811: The London Tabernacle and Spa Fields Chapel* (London, 1975).

Whitefield, George, *Angenrheidrwydd a Natur o'n Genedigaeth Newydd yng Nghrist Iesu, Mewn Trefn i Iachydwriaeth. Sef Pregeth a Bregethwyd yn Eglwys St. Mary Redcliff yn Bristol* (Bristol, 1739).

——, *Atteb y Parchedig Mr Whitefield, i Lythyr Bugeilaidd Diweddaf Esgob Llundain* (cyf. John Lewis, 1740).

——, *A Letter from the Reverend Mr George Whitefield to the Religious Societies Lately Set on Foot in Several Parts of England and Wales* (Edinburgh 1740).

——, *Llythyr Oddiwrth y Parchedig Mr George Whitefield at Societies neu Gymdeithasau Crefyddol a Osodwyd yn Ddiweddar ar Droed Mewn Amriw Leodd yng Nghymru a Lloeger* (Pontypool, 1740).

——, *The Nature and Necessity of Society in General, and of Religious Society in Particular* (Bristol, 1740).

——, *A Letter to the Reverend Mr John Wesley: In Answer to his Sermon Entitled Free Grace* (London, 1741).

——, *The Works of George Whitefield*, 6 vols (London, 1771–2).

——, 'The necessity and benefits of religious society', in *George Whitefield, Seventy-Five Sermons on Various Important Subjects*, 1 (London, 1812).

Williams, A. H., 'The leaders of English and Welsh Methodism', *Bathafarn*, 16 (1961), 23–40; 17 (1962), 5–26; 22 (1967), 24–36; 23 (1968), 7–13; 24 (1969), 20–5.

——, *John Wesley in Wales, 1739–1790* (Cardiff, 1971).

Williams, William, *The Experience Meeting: An Introduction to the Welsh Societies of the Evangelical Awakening*, trans. Bethan Lloyd Jones (Bridgend, 1973).

Wilson, J. F. (ed.), *The Works of Jonathan Edwards, IX: A History of the Work of Redemption* (New Haven, 1989).

SECONDARY WORKS

Alexander, T. D. and Rosner, Brian S. (eds), *New Dictionary of Biblical Theology* (Leicester, 2000).

Amory, Hugh and Hall, David D. (eds), *The History of the Book in America, I: The Colonial Book in the Atlantic World* (Cambridge, 2000).

Anderson, Howard and Ehrenpreis, Irvin, 'The familiar letter in the eighteenth century: some generalisations', in Howard Anderson, Philip B. Daghlion and Irvin Ehrenpreis (eds), *The Familiar Letter in the Eighteenth Century* (Lawrence, Kansas, 1966), pp. 269–82.

Armitage, David and Braddick, Michael J. (eds), *The British Atlantic World, 1500–1800* (Basingstoke, 2002).

Armstrong, A., *The Church of England, the Methodists and Society, 1700–1850* (London, 1973).

Asch, Ronald G., *The Thirty Years War: The Holy Roman Empire and Europe, 1618–48* (London, 1997).

Ashton, Elwyn T., *The Welsh in the United States* (London, 1984).

Baker, Frank, *John Wesley and the Church of England* (London, 1970).

——, 'Whitefield's break with the Wesleys', *The Church Quarterly*, 3, 2 (1971), 103–13.

Barker, Hannah, *Newspapers, Politics, and Public Opinion in Late Eighteenth Century England* (Oxford, 1998).

Barnard, John, McKenzie, D. F. and Bell, Maureen (eds), *The Cambridge History of the Book in Britain, IV: 1557–1696* (Cambridge, 2000).

Barnes, David Russell, *People of Seion: Patterns of Nonconformity in Cardiganshire and Carmarthenshire in the Century Preceding the Religious Census of 1851* (Llandysul, 1995).

Barry, Jonathan and Brooks, Christopher (eds), *The Middling Sort of People: Culture, Society and Politics in England, 1550–1800* (London, 1994).

—— and Morgan, Kenneth (eds), *Revival and Reformation in Eighteenth Century Bristol* (Bristol, 1994).

Bassett, T. M., *The Welsh Baptists* (Swansea, 1977).

Baumann, G., *The Written Word: Literacy in Transition* (Oxford, 1986).

Bebbington, D. W., *Evangelicalism in Modern Britain: A History from the 1730s to the 1990s* (London, 1989).

——, 'Revival and Enlightenment in eighteenth-century England', in Edith Blumhofer and Randall Balmer (eds), *Modern Christian Revivals* (Chicago, 1993), pp. 17–41.

——, 'Evangelical conversion, c. 1740–1850', *Scottish Bulletin of Evangelical Theology*, 18, 2 (Autumn, 2000), 102–27.

Benedict, Philip, *Christ's Churches Purely Reformed: A Social History of Calvinism* (New Haven, 2002).

Bennett, Richard (trans.), *The Early Life of Howell Harris* (London, 1962).

Black, Jeremy, *Britain in the Age of Walpole* (Basingstoke, 1984).

——, *The English Press in the Eighteenth Century* (London, 1987).

——, *Eighteenth Century Europe, 1700–1789* (London, 1990).

——, *The Rise of the European Powers, 1679–1793* (London, 1990).

——, *Britain as a Military Power, 1688–1815* (London, 1999).

—— and Porter, Roy, *The Penguin Dictionary of Eighteenth-Century History* (Harmondsworth, 1994).

Bloch, Ruth, *The Visionary Republic: Millennial Themes in American Thought, 1756–1800* (Cambridge, 1985).

Bonomi, Patricia, *Under the Cope of Heaven: Religion, Society and Politics in Colonial America* (New York, 1986).

Boorstin, Daniel J., *The Americans: The Colonial Experience* (New York, 1958).

Bradley, James E. and Muller, Richard A., *Church History: An Introduction to Research, Reference Works, and Methods* (Grand Rapids, 1995).

Bradshaw, Brendan and Keogh, Dáire (eds), *Christianity in Ireland: Revisiting the Story* (Dublin, 2002).

Bradshaw, B. and Roberts, Peter (eds), *British Consciousness and Identity: The Making of Britain, 1533–1707* (Cambridge, 1998).

Brantley, R. E., *Locke, Wesley and the Method of English Romanticism* (Gainesville, Florida, 1984).

Breen, T. H., ' "Baubles of Britain": the American and consumer revolutions of the eighteenth century', *Past and Present*, 119 (May 1980), 73–104.

——, 'An empire of goods: the Anglicisation of colonial America, 1690–1770', *Journal of British Studies*, 25 (October 1986), 467–99.

Bremer, Francis J. (ed.), *Puritanism: Transatlantic Perspectives on a Seventeenth-Century Anglo-American Faith* (Boston, 1993).

Breward, Ian, 'William Perkins and the Origins of reformed casuistry', *The Evangelical Quarterly*, XL, I (1968), 3–20.

Brewer, John, *The Pleasures of the Imagination: English Culture in the Eighteenth Century* (London, 1997).

Bridenbaugh, Carl, *Mitre and Sceptre: Transatlantic Faiths, Ideas, Personalities and Problems, 1689–1775* (New York, 1962).

Brown, C. G., *The Social History of Religion in Scotland since 1730* (London, 1987).

Brown, Richard, *Church and State in Modern Britain, 1700–1850* (London, 1991).

Brown, Roger Lee, 'The marriage of George Whitefield at Caerphilly', *Cylchgrawn Cymdeithas Hanes y Methodistiaid Calfinaidd*, 7 (1983), 24–30.

Bruce, Steve, 'Social change and collective behaviour: the revival in eighteenth-century Ross-shire', *The British Journal of Sociology*, XXXIV, 4 (1988), 554–72.

Brunner, Daniel L., *Halle Pietists in England: Anthony William Boehme and the Society for Promoting Christian Knowledge* (Göttingen, 1993).

Burke, Peter, *Popular Culture in Early Modern Europe* (London, 1978).

Butler, David, *Methodists and Papists: John Wesley and the Catholic Church in the Eighteenth Century* (London, 1995).

Butler, Jon, 'Enthusiasm described and decried: the Great Awakening as interpretative fiction', *Journal of American History*, 69 (September 1982), 305–25.

——, *Awash in a Sea of Faith: Christianising the American People* (Cambridge, MA, 1990).

Caldwell, Patricia, *The Puritan Conversion Narrative: The Beginnings of American Expression* (Cambridge, 1982).

Cameron, Nigel M. de S. (ed.), *The Dictionary of Scottish Church History and Theology* (Edinburgh, 1993).

Campbell, Ted A., *The Religion of the Heart: A Study of European Religious Life in the Seventeenth and Eighteenth Centuries* (Columbia, SC, 1991).

Cannon, John (ed.), *The Oxford Companion to British History* (Oxford, 1997).

Carwardine, Richard, *Trans-Atlantic Revivalism: Popular Evangelicalism in Britain and America, 1790–1865* (Westport, CT, 1978).

Cashdollar, Charles D., *A Spiritual Home: Life in British and American Reformed Congregations, 1830–1915* (University Park, PA, 2000).

Cavanagh, F. A., *The Life and Work of Griffith Jones of Llanddowror* (Cardiff, 1930).

Chai, Leon, *Jonathan Edwards and the Limits of Enlightenment Philosophy* (New York, 1998).

Chilcote, Paul Wesley, *'She Offered Them Christ': The Legacy of Women Preachers in Early Methodism* (Nashville, TN, 1993).

Clark, J. C. D., *English Society, 1660–1832: Religion, Ideology and Politics during the 'Ancien Regime'* (Cambridge, 2000).

Clarkson, George E., *George Whitefield and Welsh Calvinistic Methodism* (New York and Lampeter, 1996).

Claydon, T. and McBride, I. (eds), *Protestantism and National Identity: Britain and Ireland, c.1650–c.1850* (Cambridge, 1998).

Clement, M., *The S.P.C.K. and Wales, 1699–1740* (London, 1954).

Clifford, Alan C., *Atonement and Justification: English Evangelical Theology, 1640–1790 – An Evaluation* (Oxford, 1990).

Coalter, M. J., *Gilbert Tennant, Son of Thunder: A Case Study of Continental Pietism's Impact on the First Great Awakening in the Middle Colonies* (New York, 1986).

Coffey, John, *Persecution and Toleration in Protestant England, 1558–1689* (London, 2000).

Cohen, Charles Lloyd, *God's Caress: The Psychology of Puritan Religious Experience* (Oxford, 1986).

Coleman, Kenneth, *Colonial Georgia: A History* (New York, 1976).

Colley, Linda, *In Defence of Oligarchy: The Tory Party, 1714–60* (Cambridge, 1982).

——, *Britons: Forging the Nation, 1707–1837* (London, 1992).

Collins, Kenneth J. and Tyson, J. H. (eds), *Conversion in the Wesleyan Tradition* (Nashville, 2001).

Collinson, Patrick, *Godly People* (London, 1982).

——, *The Religion of Protestants* (Oxford, 1982).

——, *The Elizabethan Puritan Movement* (Oxford, 1990).

Cook, Elizabeth Heckendorn, *Epistolary Bodies: Gender and Genre in the Eighteenth-Century Republic of Letters* (Stanford, 1996).

Cooper, J. H. (ed.), *Extracts From the Journals of John Cennick: Moravian Evangelist* (Glengormley, 1996).

Crawford, Michael J., 'Origins of the eighteenth century evangelical revival: England and New England compared', *Journal of British Studies*, 26 (1987), 361–97.

——, *Seasons of Grace: Colonial New England's Revival Tradition in its British Context* (New York, 1991).

Crawford, Patricia, *Women and Religion in England, 1500–1720* (London, 1993).

Cressy, David, *Education in Tudor and Stuart England* (London, 1975).

——, *Literacy and the Social Order: Reading and Writing in Tudor and Stuart England* (Cambridge, 1980).

——, *Coming Over: Migration and Communication between England and New England in the Seventeenth Century* (Cambridge, 1987).

Cross, F. L. and Livingstone, E. A. (eds), *The Oxford Dictionary of the Christian Church* (Oxford, 1997).

Dallimore, Arnold A., *George Whitefield: The Life and Times of the Great Evangelist of the Eighteenth Century Revival*, 2 vols (Edinburgh, 1970, 1980).

Davidoff, L. and Hall, C. *Family Fortunes: Men and Women of the English Middle Class, 1780–1850* (London, 1987).

Davidson, James West, *The Logic of Millennial Thought: Eighteenth Century New England* (New Haven, 1977).

Davies, G. C. B., *The Early Cornish Evangelicals, 1735–60: A Study of Walker of Truro and Others* (London, 1951).

Davies, Horton, *Worship and Theology in England: From Watts and Wesley to Maurice, 1690–1850* (Grand Rapids, 1996).

Davies, Hywel M., *Transatlantic Brethren: Rev. Samuel Jones (1735–1814) and his Friends* (Bethlehem, PA, 1995).

Davies, John, *A History of Wales* (Cardiff, 1994).

Davies, R. E. and Rupp, E. G. (eds), *A History of the Methodist Church in Great Britain, I* (London, 1965).

Davies, Sioned, 'Performing from the pulpit: an introduction to preaching in nineteenth-century Wales', in Joseph Falaky Nagy (ed.), *Identifying the 'Celtic'* (Dublin, 2002), pp. 115–40.

Davis, Harold E., *The Fledgling Province: Social and Cultural Life in Colonial Georgia, 1733–1776* (New York, 1976).

Davis, Natalie Zemon, 'Some tasks and themes in the study of popular religion', in C. Trinkaus and H. Oberman (eds), *The Pursuit of Holiness in Late Medieval and Renaissance Religion: Studies in Medieval and Reformation Thought* (Leiden, 1974), pp. 307–36.

Dearnley, Moira, *Distant Fields: Eighteenth-Century Fictions of Wales* (Cardiff, 2001).

Dickinson, H. T. (ed.), *A Companion to Eighteenth Century Britain* (Oxford, 2002).

Ditchfield, G. M., *The Evangelical Revival* (London, 1998).

Dodd, A. H., 'New England influences in early Welsh Puritanism', *Bulletin of the Board of Celtic Studies*, 16 (1954), 30–7.

Drummond, Andrew L. and Bulloch, James, *The Scottish Church 1688–1843: The Age of the Moderates* (Edinburgh, 1973).

Duffy, Eamon, 'Primitive Christianity revived: religious renewal in Augustan England', in Derek Baker (ed.), *Renaissance and Renewal in Christian History*, Studies in Church History, 14 (Oxford, 1977), pp. 287–300.

Durden, Susan, 'A study of the first evangelical magazines, 1740–1748,' in *Journal of Ecclesiastical History*, 27, 3 (1976), 255–75.

Eales, J., *Women in Early Modern England, 1500–1700* (London, 1998).

Earle, Peter, *The Making of the English Middle Class: Business, Society and Family Life in London, 1660–1730* (London, 1989).

Earle, Rebecca (ed.), *Epistolary Slaves: Letters and Letter-Writing, 1600–1945* (Aldershot, 1999).

Ellis, Steven G. and Barber, Sarah, *Conquest and Union: Fashioning a British State 1485–1725* (London, 1995).

Elwell, Walter A. (ed.), *The Evangelical Dictionary of Theology* (Carlisle, 1984).

Ettinger, Amos Aschbach, *James Edward Oglethorpe: Imperial Idealist* (Oxford, 1968).

Evans, Eifion, *Howell Harris: Evangelist, 1714–1773* (Cardiff, 1974).

——, 'Thomas Jones, Cwmiou (1689–1772)', *Cylchgrawn Cymdeithas Hanes y Methodistiaid Calfinaidd*, 8 (1984), 24–31.

——, *Daniel Rowland and the Great Evangelical Awakening in Wales* (Edinburgh, 1985).

——, *Fire in the Thatch: The True Nature of Religious Revival* (Bridgend, 1996).

——, *Pursued by God: A Selective Translation with Notes of the Welsh Religious Classic, Theomemphus by William Williams of Pantycelyn* (Bridgend, 1996).

——, 'Howell Harris and the printed page', *Cylchgrawn Cymdeithas Hanes y Methodistiaid Calfinaidd*, 23 (1999), 33–62.

Evans, Nesta, *Religion and Politics in Mid-Eighteenth Century Anglesey* (Cardiff, 1953).

Fairs, George L., 'Notes on the death of William Seward at Hay, 1740',

Cylchgrawn Cymdeithas Hanes y Methodistiaid Calfinaidd, LVIII, I (March 1973), 12–17.

Fawcett, Arthur, *The Cambuslang Revival: The Scottish Evangelical Revival of the Eighteenth Century* (Edinburgh, 1971).

Feather, John, *The Provincial Book Trade in Eighteenth-Century England* (Cambridge, 1985).

——, *A History of British Publishing* (London, 1988).

Field, C. D., 'Adam and Eve: gender in the English Free Church tradition', *Journal of Ecclesiastical History*, 44 (1993), 63–79.

——, 'The social composition of English Methodism to 1830: a membership analysis', *Bulletin of John Rylands University of Manchester Library*, 76 (Spring 1994), 153–69.

Fiering, Norman, 'The rationalist foundations of Jonathan Edwards's metaphysics', in Nathan O. Hatch and Harry S. Stout (eds), *Jonathan Edwards and the American Experience* (New York, 1988), pp. 73–101.

Foster, H. J., 'Westley Hall', *Proceedings of the Wesley Historical Society*, 5 (1906), 146–51.

Fryde, E. B., Greenaway, D. E., Porter, S. and Roy, I. (eds), *Handbook of British Chronology* (London, 1986).

Garrett, Jane and Matthews, Colin (eds), *Revival and Religion since 1700: Essay for John Wesley* (Oxford, 1993).

Gawthrop, Richard L., *Pietism and the Making of Eighteenth-Century Prussia* (Cambridge, 1993).

Gibson, William, *Church, State and Society, 1760–1850* (London, 1994).

—— (ed.), *Religion and Society in England and Wales, 1689–1800* (Leicester, 1998).

Gilbert, A. D., *Religion and Society in Industrial England: Church, Chapel and Social Change, 1740–1914* (London, 1970).

Gildrie, Richard P., *The Profane, the Civil and the Godly: The Reformation of Manners in Orthodox New England, 1679–1749* (University Park, PA, 1994).

Gill, Frederick C., *Charles Wesley: The First Methodist* (London, 1964).

Gillies, John, *Memoirs of George Whitefield* (New Ipswich, NH, 1993).

Gilmore, W. J., *Reading Becomes a Necessity of Life: Material and Cultural Life in Rural New England, 1780–1835* (Knoxville, 1989).

Goodwin, Charles H., 'John Wesley's indebtedness to Jonathan Edwards', *Epworth Review*, 25, 2 (April 1998), 89–96.

Green, Ian, *Print and Protestantism in Early Modern England* (Oxford, 2000).

Gregory, Jeremy and Chamberlain, Jeffrey S. (eds), *The National Church in Local Perspective: the Church of England and the Regions, 1660–1800* (Woodbridge, 2003).

Greyerz, C. von, *Religion and Society in Early Modern Europe, 1500–1800* (London, 1984).

Griffiths, Rhidian, 'Howel Davies: Apostol Sir Benfro', *Cylchgrawn Cymdeithas Hanes y Methodistiaid Calfinaidd*, 11 (1987), 2–14.

Gruffudd, R. Geraint, 'Diwygiad 1762 a William Williams o Bantycelyn', *Cylchgrawn Cymdeithas Hanes y Methodistiaid Calfinaidd*, LIV, 3 (October 1969), 68–75; LV, 1 (March 1970), 4–13.

——, 'In that Gentile Country': The Beginnings of Puritan Nonconformity in *Wales* (Bridgend, 1976).

Gunter, W. Stephen, *The Limits of 'Love Divine': John Wesley's Response to Antinomianism and Enthusiasm* (Nashville, TN, 1989).

Guy, John, *Tudor England* (Oxford, 1988).

Halévy, É., *The Birth of Methodism in England* (trans. B. Semmel, Chicago, 1971).

Hall, David D., *Worlds of Wonder, Days of Judgement: Popular Religious Belief in Early New England* (Cambridge, MA, 1990).

Hambrick-Stowe, Charles E., *The Practice of Piety: Puritan Devotional Disciplines in Seventeenth-Century New England* (Chapel Hill, 1982).

Harris, Michael and Lee, Alan (eds), *The Press in English Society from the Seventeenth to Nineteenth Centuries* (London, 1986).

Harris, Tim (ed.), *Popular Culture in England, c.1500–1800* (London, 1995).

Hartmann. E. G., *Americans from Wales* (New York, 1978).

Harvey, John, *The Art of Piety: The Visual Culture of Welsh Nonconformity* (Cardiff, 1995).

Hatch, Nathan O., *The Democratization of American Christianity* (New Haven, 1989).

Hattersley, Roy, *A Brand from the Burning: The Life of John Wesley* (London, 2002).

Hechter, M., *Internal Colonialism: The Celtic Fringe in British National Development, 1536–1966* (London, 1975).

Heimert, Alan, *Religion and the American Mind from the Great Awakening to the Revolution* (Cambridge, MA, 1966).

Heitzenrater, R. P., *Wesley and the People Called Methodists* (Nashville, 1995).

——, *The Poor and the People Called Methodists, 1729–1999* (Nashville, 2002).

——, 'Wesley in America', *Proceedings of the Wesley Historical Society*, 54, 3 (October 2003), 85–114.

Hempton, D., 'Evangelicalism and eschatology', *Journal of Ecclesiastical History*, 31, 2 (April 1980), 179–94.

——, *Methodism and Politics in British Society, 1750–1850* (London, 1984).

——, 'Methodism and the law, 1740–1820', *Bulletin of the John Rylands University Library of Manchester*, 70, 3 (1988), 93–107.

——, *Religion and Political Culture in Britain and Ireland: From the Glorious Revolution to the Decline of Empire* (Cambridge, 1996).

——, *The Religion of the People: Methodism and Popular Religion, c.1750–1900* (London, 1996).

——, 'Established Churches and the growth of religious pluralism: a case study of Christianisation and secularisation in England since 1700', in Hugh McLeod and Werner Ustorf (eds), *The Decline of Christendom in Western Europe, 1750–2000* (Cambridge, 2003), pp. 81–98.

—— and Hill, Myrtle, *Evangelical Protestantism in Ulster Society, 1740–1890* (London, 1992).

—— and Walsh, John, 'E. P. Thompson and Methodism', in Mark A. Noll (ed.), *God and Mammon: Protestants, Money and the Market, 1790–1860* (New York, 2001), pp. 99–120.

Hill, Christopher, *The Century of Revolution, 1603–1714* (London, 1961).

——, 'Propagating the Gospel', in H. E. Bell and R. L. Ollard (eds), *Historical Essays, 1600–1750: Presented to David Ogg* (London, 1963), pp. 35–59.

——, *Society and Puritanism in Pre-revolutionary England* (London, 1964).

——, *The World Turned Upside Down: Radical Ideas During the English Revolution* (London, 1972).

——, 'Puritans and the "dark corners of the land" ', in Christopher Hill (ed.), *Change and Continuity in Seventeenth Century England* (London, 1974), pp. 3–47.

——, 'History and denominational history', in Christopher Hill, *The Collected Essays of Christopher Hill, II: Religion and Politics in Seventeenth Century England* (Brighton, 1986), pp. 3–10.

Hilton, Boyd, *The Age of Atonement: The Influence of Evangelicalism on Social and Economic Thought, 1785–1865* (Oxford, 1988).

Hindmarsh, D. Bruce, *John Newton and the English Evangelical Tradition* (Cambridge, 1996).

——, 'The Olney autobiographers: English conversion narrative in the mid-eighteenth century', *Journal of Ecclesiastical History*, 49, 1 (January, 1998), 61–84.

——, ' "My chains fell off, my heart was free": early Methodist conversion narrative in England', *Church History: Studies in Christianity and Culture*, 68, 4 (December 1999), 910–29.

Holmes, Geoffrey, *The Making of a Great Power: Late Stuart and Early Georgian Britain, 1660–1722* (London, 1993).

—— and Szechi, D., *The Age of Oligarchy: Pre-industrial Britain, 1722–1783* (London, 1995).

Houston, R. A., *Literacy in Early Modern Europe: Culture and Education, 1500–1800* (London, 1988).

Howell, David, W., *Patriarchs and Parasites: The Gentry of South-West Wales in the Eighteenth Century* (Cardiff, 1986).

——, *The Rural Poor in Eighteenth-Century Wales* (Cardiff, 2000).

Howells, Brian (ed.), *Pembrokeshire County History, III: Early Modern Pembrokeshire, 1536–1815* (Haverfordwest, 1987).

Hufton, Olwen, *The Prospect Before Her: A History of Women in Western Europe, 1: 1500–1800* (London, 1995).

Hughes, Dewi Arwel, 'William Williams Pantycelyn's eschatology as seen in his *Aurora Borealis* of 1774', *Scottish Bulletin of Evangelical Theology*, IV, I (1986), 49–63.

Hughes, G. Tegai, *Williams Pantycelyn* (Cardiff, 1983).

Hughes, Hugh J., *Life of Howell Harris: The Welsh Reformer* (London, 1892).

Humphreys Melvin, *The Crisis of Community: Montgomeryshire, 1680–1815* (Cardiff, 1996).

Hunt, Margaret R., *The Middling Sort: Commerce, Gender and the Family in England, 1680–1780* (Berkeley, CA, 1996).

Hutton, J. E., *A History of the Moravian Church* (London, 1909).

Hylson-Smith, K., *Evangelicals in the Church of England, 1734–1843* (Edinburgh, 1989).

Innes, Joanna, 'The "mixed economy of welfare" in early modern England: assessments of the options from Hale to Malthus (c. 1683–1803)', in Martin Daunton (ed.), *Charity, Self-Interest, and Welfare in the English Past* (London, 1996), pp. 139–80.

Inscoe, John C. (ed.), *James Edward Oglethorpe: New Perspectives on his Life and Legacy: A Tercentenary Commemoration* (Savannah, GA, 1997).

Jacob, W., *Lay People and Religion in the Early Eighteenth Century* (Cambridge, 1996).

Jarvis, Branwen (ed.), *A Guide to Welsh Literature, c.1700–1800* (Cardiff, 2000).

Jenkins, D. E. *Calvinistic Methodist Holy Orders* (Caernarfon, 1911).

Jenkins, Geraint H., 'Popular beliefs in Wales from the Restoration to Methodism', *Bulletin of the Board of Celtic Studies*, XXVII, III (November, 1977), 440–62.

——, *Literature, Religion and Society in Wales, 1660–1730* (Cardiff, 1978).

——, '"An old and much honoured soldier:" Griffith Jones, Llanddowror,' *Welsh History Review* (1983), 449–68.

——, *Cadw Tŷ Mewn Cwmwl Tystion: Ysgrifau Hanesyddol ar Grefydd a Diwylliant* (Llandysul, 1990).

——, *Protestant Dissenters in Wales, 1639–1689* (Cardiff, 1992).

——, *The Foundations of Modern Wales, 1642–1780* (Cardiff, 1993).

—— (ed.), *The Welsh Language before the Industrial Revolution* (Cardiff, 1997).

Jenkins, Philip, *A History of Modern Wales, 1536–1990* (London, 1992).

——, 'The Anglican Church and the unity of Britain: the Welsh experience, 1560–1714', in Steven G. Ellis and Sarah Barker (eds), *Conquest and Union: Fashioning a British State, 1485–1725* (London, 1995), pp. 115–38.

——, 'Church, nation and language: the Welsh Church, 1660–1800', in Jeremy Gregory and Jeffrey S. Chamberlain (eds), *The National Church in Local Perspective: The Church of England and the Regions, 1660–1800* (Woodbridge, 2003), pp. 265–84.

Jenkins, R. T., 'The Moravian brethren in North Wales: an episode in the religious history of Wales', *Y Cymmrodor*, XLV (London, 1938).

Jones, David, *The Life and Times of Griffith Jones of Llanddowror* (London, 1902; reprinted, Clonmel, 1995).

Jones, D. J. Odwyn, *Daniel Rowland, Llangeitho* (Llandysul, 1938).

Jones, Emrys (ed.), *The Welsh in London, 1500–2000* (Cardiff, 2001).

Jones, Euros W., 'Nathaniel Rowland (1749–1831)', *Cylchgrawn Cymdeithas Hanes y Methodistiaid Calfinaidd*, 7 (1983), 35–42.

Jones, J. Gwynfor, 'Bishop William Morgan: defender of Church and faith', *Journal of Welsh Ecclesiastical History*, 5 (1988), 1–30.

——, 'John Penry: government, order and the "perishing souls" of Wales', *Transactions of the Honourable Society of Cymmrodorion* (1993), 47–81.

——, *Early Modern Wales, c.1525–1640* (London, 1994).

——, *The Welsh Gentry, 1536–1640* (Cardiff, 1998).

——, 'Welsh gentlewomen: piety and Christian conduct, c.1560–1730', *Journal of Welsh Religious History*, 7 (1999), 1–37.

——, 'Some Puritan influences on the Anglican Church in Wales in the early seventeenth century', *Journal of Welsh Religious History*, 2 (2002), 19–50.

Jones, Margaret P., 'From "the state of my soul" to "exalted piety": women's voices in the Arminian/Methodist Magazine, 1778–1821', in R. N. Swanson (ed.), *Gender and Christian Religion*, Studies in Church History, 34 (Woodbridge, 1998), pp. 273–86.

Jones, M. G., *The Charity School Movement: A Study of Eighteenth Century Puritanism in Action* (Cambridge, 1938).

Jones, M. H., 'The Christian's Amusement: a review', *Cylchgrawn Cymdeithas Hanes y Methodistiaid Calfinaidd*, 2 (December 1916), 47–54.

——, 'The Christian's Amusement and the Weekly History', *Cylchgrawn Cymdeithas Hanes y Methodistiaid Calfinaidd*, 3 (March 1917), 78–82.

——, 'The Weekly History', *Cylchgrawn Cymdeithas Hanes y Methodistiaid Calfinaidd*, 4 (January 1919), 59–65.

——, 'John Lewis, the printer of the Weekly History', *Cylchgrawn Cymdeithas Hanes y Methodistiaid Calfinaidd*, 4 (June 1919), 84–92.

——, 'The itinerary of Howel Harris, Trevecka: for the years 1735–1745', *Cylchgrawn Cymdeithas Hanes y Methodistiaid Calfinaidd*, 8 (December 1923), 11–64.

——, 'The itinerary of Howel Harris, Trevecka: for the years 1746–1752', *Cylchgrawn Cymdeithas Hanes y Methodistiaid Calfinaidd*, 10 (December 1925), 3–51.

Jones, P. H. (ed.), *A Bibliography of the History of Wales* (microfiche, 1988)

—— and Rees, Eiluned (eds), *A Nation and its Books: A History of the Book in Wales* (Aberystwyth, 1998).

Jones, R. Brinley, *William Salesbury* (Cardiff, 1994).

Jones, R. Tudur, *Congregationalism in England, 1662–1962* (London, 1962).

——, 'The healing herb and the rose of love: the piety of two Welsh Puritans', in R. B. Knox (ed.), *Reformation, Conformity and Dissent: Essays in Honour of Geoffrey Nuttall* (London, 1977), pp. 154–79.

——, 'The evangelical revival in Wales: a study in spirituality', in J. Mackey (ed.), *An Introduction to Celtic Christianity* (London, 1989), pp. 237–67.

——, *Grym y Gair a Fflam y Ffydd: Ysgrifau ar Hanes Crefydd yng Nghymru* (Bangor, 1998).

Kendall, R. T., *Calvin and English Calvinism to 1649* (Oxford, 1979).

Kenney, William H., 'George Whitefield: Dissenter priest of the Great Awakening, 1739–1741', *William and Mary Quarterly*, 26 (1969), 75–93.

Kent, John, *Wesley and the Wesleyans: Religion in Eighteenth-Century Britain* (Cambridge, 2002).

Knowles, Anne K., *Calvinists Incorporated: Welsh Immigration on Ohio's Industrial Frontier* (Chicago, 1997).

Knox, R. A., *Enthusiasm: A Chapter in the History of Religion with Special Reference to the XVII and XVIII Centuries* (Oxford, 1950).

Knox, R. B., 'Howell Harris and his doctrine of the Church', *Cylchgrawn Cymdeithas Hanes y Methodistiaid Calfinaidd*, 49–50 (1964–5), 61–78; 1–18.

——, 'Howell Harris, 1714–1773: a bicentenary survey', *Cylchgrawn Cymdeithas Hanes y Methodistiaid Calfinaidd*, 58 (July 1973), 38–56.

Lambert, Frank, ' "Pedlar in divinity": George Whitefield and the Great Awakening, 1737–1745', *Journal of American History*, 77 (1990), 812–37.

——, 'The Great Awakening as artifact: George Whitefield and the construction of an inter-colonial revival, 1739–1745', *Church History*, 60 (June 1991), 223–46.

——, *'Pedlar in Divinity': George Whitefield and the Transatlantic Revivals* (Princeton, 1994).

——, *Inventing the 'Great Awakening'* (Princeton, 1999).

——, *The Founding Fathers and the Place of Religion in America* (Princeton, 2003).

Landsman, Ned, 'Evangelists and their hearers: popular interpretation of revivalist preaching in eighteenth-century Scotland', *Journal of British Studies*, 28 (1989), 120–49.

——, 'Presbyterians and provincial society: the evangelical enlightenment in the west of Scotland, 1740–1775', in J. Dwyer and R. B. Sher (eds), *Sociability and Society in Eighteenth-Century Scotland* (Edinburgh, 1993), pp. 194–209.

Langford, Paul, *A Polite and Commercial People: England, 1727–1783* (Oxford, 1989).

Larsen, Timothy (ed.), *Biographical Dictionary of Evangelicals* (Leicester, 2003).

Laslett, Peter, *The World We Have Lost: Further Explored* (London, 1971).

LaTrobe, Benjamin, *A Brief Account of the Life of Howell Harris Extracted from Papers Written by Himself. To which is Added a Concise Collection of his Letters from the Year 1738 to 1772* (Trevecka, 1791).

Lawson, A. Brown, *John Wesley and the Anglican Evangelicals of the Eighteenth Century* (Durham, 1994).

Leach, William, 'John Cennick, 1718–1755: a bicentenary appreciation', *Proceedings of the Wesley Historical Society*, XXX, 2 (June 1955), 30–7.

Lee, Sang Hyun and Guelzo, Allen C. (eds), *Edwards in our Time: Jonathan Edwards and the Shaping of American Religion* (Grand Rapids, 1999).

Lenman, Buce, *The Jacobite Risings in Britain, 1689–1746* (Aberdeen, 1980).

——, *Britain's Colonial Wars, 1688–1783* (London, 2001).

Letham, Robert and Macleod, Donald, 'Is evangelicalism Christian?', *The Evangelical Quarterly*, 67, 1 (January 1995), 3–33.

Lewis, A. J., *Zinzendorf, the Ecumenical Pioneer: A Study in the Moravian Contribution to Christian Mission and Unity* (London, 1962).

Lewis, D. M. (ed.), *The Blackwell Dictionary of Evangelical Biography, 1730–1860*, 2 vols (Oxford, 1995).

Lindsey, J. O. (ed.), *The New Cambridge Modern History, VII: The Old Regime, 1713–63* (Cambridge, 1957).

Lloyd, J. T and Jenkins, R. T. (eds), *The Dictionary of Welsh Biography down to 1940: Under the Auspices of the 'Honourable Society of Cymmrodorion'* (London, 1959).

Lord, Peter, *Words with Pictures: Welsh Images and Images of Wales in the Popular Press, 1640–1860* (Aberystwyth, 1995).

Lovegrove, Deryck W., *Established Church, Sectarian People: Itinerancy and the Transformation of English Dissent, 1780–1830* (Cambridge, 1988).

Lovejoy, David, *Religious Enthusiasm in the New World* (Cambridge, 1985).

Lyles, A. M., *Methodism Mocked: The Satiric Reaction to Methodism in the Eighteenth Century* (London, 1960).

Lynch, Michael (ed.), *Jacobitism and the '45* (London, 1995).

MacInnes, J., *The Evangelical Movement in the Highlands of Scotland, 1688 to 1800* (Aberdeen, 1951).

Madden, Lionel (ed.), *Methodism in Wales: A Short History of the Wesley Tradition* (Llandudno, 2003).

Malcolmson, Robert W., ' "A set of ungovernable people": the Kingswood colliers in the eighteenth century', in J. Brewer and J. Styles (eds), *An Ungovernable People: The English and their Law in the Seventeenth and Eighteenth Centuries* (London, 1980), pp. 85–127.

Malmgreen, G. (ed.), *Religion in the Lives of English Women, 1760–1930* (London, 1986).

Mandleson, P. and Crawford, P. (eds), *Women in Early Modern England, 1550–1720* (Oxford, 1999).

Manning, B. L., *The Protestant Dissenting Deputies* (Cambridge, 1952).

Marsden, George M., *Jonathan Edwards: A Life* (New Haven, 2003).

Marsh, Christopher, *Popular Religion in Sixteenth Century England* (London, 1998).

Marshall, P. J. (ed.), *The Oxford History of the British Empire, II: The Eighteenth Century* (Oxford, 1998).

Mascuch, Michael, *Origins of the Individualist Self: Autobiography and Self Identity in England, 1591–1791* (London, 1997).

Mason, J. C. S., *The Moravian Church and the Missionary Awakening in England 1760–1800* (London, 2001).

McCalman, Iain (ed.), *An Oxford Companion to the Romantic Age: British Culture, 1776–1832* (Oxford, 1999).

McGonigle, Herbert Boyd, *Sufficient Saving Grace: John Wesley's Evangelical Arminianism* (Carlisle, 2001).

McGrath, Alistair E., *Reformation Thought: An Introduction* (Oxford, 1988).

——, *Christian Spirituality: An Introduction* (Oxford, 1999).

McIntosh, J. R., *Church and Theology in Enlightenment Scotland: The Popular Party, 1740–1800* (East Linton, 1998).

McKendrick, N., Brewer, J. and Plumb, J. H. (eds), *The Birth of a Consumer Society: The Commercialisation of Eighteenth-Century England* (Bloomington, 1982).

McKim, Donald (ed.), *Encyclopaedia of the Reformed Faith* (Louisville, KY, and Edinburgh, 1992).

Mee, Jon, *Romanticism, Enthusiasm and Regulation: Poetics and the Policing of Culture in the Romantic Period* (Oxford, 2003).

Milburn, Geoffrey and Batty, Margaret (eds), *Workaday Preachers: The Story of Methodist Local Preaching* (Peterborough, 1995).

Monod, Paul Kléber, *Jacobitism and the English People, 1688–1788* (Cambridge, 1989).

Morgan, Derec Llwyd, *The Great Awakening in Wales* (London, 1988).

—— (ed.), *Meddwl a Dychymyg Williams Pantycelyn* (Llandysul, 1991).

Morgan, Edward, *The Life and Times of Howel Harris, Esq.* (Holywell, 1852).

Morgan, Prys, 'Wild Wales: civilising the Welsh from the sixteenth to the nineteenth centuries', in Peter Burke, Brian Harrison and Paul Slack (eds), *Civil Histories: Essays Presented to Sir Keith Thomas* (Oxford, 2000), pp. 265–83.

Muirhead, Ian A., 'The revival as a dimension of Scottish Church history', *Records of the Scottish Church Society,* 20 (1980), 179–96.

Muller, R. A., *Christ and the Decree: Christology and Predestination in Reformed Theology from Calvin to Perkins* (Durham, NC, 1986).

Murray, Iain H., *Jonathan Edwards: A New Biography* (Edinburgh, 1987).

Naylor, Peter, *Picking up a Pin for the Lord: English Particular Baptists from 1688 to the Early Nineteenth Century* (London, 1992).

Newport, Kenneth G. C., 'Methodists and the millennium: Eschatological expectation and the interpretation of biblical prophecy in early British Methodism', *Bulletin of the John Rylands University Library of Manchester*, 78 (1996), 103–22.

Noll, Mark A., *American Evangelical Christianity: An Introduction* (Oxford, 2001).

——, Bebbington, D. W. and Rawlyk, G. A. (eds), *Evangelicalism: Comparative Studies of Popular Protestantism in North America, the British Isles, and Beyond, 1700–1990* (Oxford, 1994).

—— (ed.), *God and Mammon: Protestants, Money and the Market, 1790–1860* (New York, 2001).

——, *America's God: From Jonathan Edwards to Abraham Lincoln* (New York, 2002).

——, *The Old Religion in a New World: The History of North American Christianity* (Grand Rapids, 2002).

——, *The Rise of Evangelism: The Age of Edwards, Whitefield and the Wesleys* (Leicester, 2004).

Nuttall, G. F., *The Welsh Saints, 1640–1660* (Cardiff, 1957).

——, *Howell Harris, 1714–1773: The Last Enthusiast* (Cardiff, 1965).

——, 'The students of Trevecca College, 1768–1791', *Transactions of the Honourable Society of Cymmrodorion* (1968), 249–69.

——, 'Rowland Hill and the Rodborough Connexion, 1771–1833', *Transactions of the Congregational Historical Society*, 21, 3 (1972), 69–73.

——, 'George Whitefield's "curate": Gloucestershire Dissent and the revival', *Journal of Ecclesiastical History*, 27, 4 (1976), 369–86.

——, 'Continental pietism and the evangelical movement in Britain', in J. van den Berg and J. P. van Dooren (eds), *Pietism und Reveil* (Leiden, 1978), pp. 208–36.

——, 'Methodism and the older Dissent: some perspectives', *The Journal of the United Reformed Church History Society*, 2, 18 (October 1981), 259–74.

——, 'Howell Harris and "the Grand Table": a note on religion and politics, 1744–50', *Journal of Ecclesiastical History*, 39, 4 (October 1988), 531–44.

Obelkevich, James, *Religion and Rural Society: South Lindsey, 1825–1875* (Oxford, 1976).

——, Roper, L. and Samuel, R. (eds), *Disciplines of Faith: Studies in Religion, Politics and Patriarchy* (London, 1987).

O'Brien, S., 'A transatlantic community of saints: the Great Awakening and the first Evangelical network, 1735–1755', *American Historical Review*, 91 (1986), 811–32.

O'Collins, G. and Farrugia, E. G. (eds), *A Concise Dictionary of Theology* (Edinburgh, 2000).

O'Connell, Neil J., 'George Whitefield and Bethesda Orphan-House,' *The Georgia Historical Quarterly*, 54 (1970), 41–62.

Parker, Geoffrey, *The Thirty Years' War* (London, 1984).

Pettit, Norman, *The Heart Prepared: Grace and Conversion in Puritan Spiritual Life* (New Haven, 1966).

Phillips, Edgar, *Edmund Jones: The Old Prophet* (London, 1959).

Pinnington, John, 'Moravian and Anglican: a new look at the circumstances surrounding the arrival of the Renewed Brethren in England', *Bulletin of the John Rylands Library*, 52 (Autumn 1969), 200–17.

Pittock, Murray G. H., *Investing and Resisting Britain: Cultural Identities in Britain and Ireland, 1685–1789* (London, 1997).

——, *Jacobitism* (London, 1998).

Podmore, Colin, *The Moravian Church in England, 1728–1760* (Oxford, 1998).

Pope, Robert (ed.), *Religion and National Identity: Wales and Scotland, c. 1700–2000* (Cardiff, 2001).

Porter, Roy, 'The Enlightenment in England', in R. Porter and M. Teich (eds), *The Enlightenment in National Context* (Cambridge, 1981), pp. 1–18.

——, *English Society in the Eighteenth Century* (London, 1982).

——, *Enlightenment: Britain and the Creation of the Modern World* (Oxford, 2000).

Prestwich, Menna (ed.), *International Calvinism, 1541–1715* (Oxford, 1985).

Questier, Michael C., *Conversion, Politics and Religion in England, 1580–1625* (Cambridge, 1996).

Rack, H. D., 'Religious societies and the origins of Methodism', *Journal of Ecclesiastical History*, 38 (1987), 582–95.

——, *Reasonable Enthusiast: John Wesley and the Rise of Methodism* (London, 1989).

——, ' "But Lord, let it be Betsy": love and marriage in early Methodism', *Proceedings of the Wesley Historical Society*, 53, 1 (February 2001), 1–13.

Randall, Ian M., *Evangelical Experiences: A Study in the Spirituality of English Evangelicalism, 1918–1939* (Carlisle, 1999).

Rawlyk, George A. and Noll, Mark A. (eds), *Amazing Grace: Evangelicalism in Australia, Britain, Canada and the United States* (Grand Rapids, 1993).

Reay, Barry (ed.), *Popular Culture in Seventeenth Century England* (London, 1985).

Rees, Eiluned, *Libri Walliae: A Catalogue of Welsh Books and Books Printed in Wales, 1546–1820*, 2 vols (Aberystwyth, 1987).

Reist, Irwin W., 'John Wesley and George Whitefield: a study in the integrity of two theologies of grace', *The Evangelical Quarterly*, XLVII, 1 (1975), 26–40.

Rivers, Isabel, ' "Strangers and pilgrims": sources and patterns of Methodist narrative', in J. C. Hilson, M. M. B. Jones and J. R. Watson (eds), *Augustan Worlds: Essays in Honour of A. R. Humphreys* (Leicester, 1978), pp. 189–203.

—— (ed.), *Books and their Readers in Eighteenth Century England* (Leicester, 1982).

——, *Reason, Grace and Sentiment: A Study in the Language of Religion and Ethics in England, 1660–1780, I: Whichcote to Wesley* (Cambridge, 1991).

—— (ed.), *Books and their Readers in Eighteenth-Century England: New Essays* (London, 2001).

Robbins, K., 'Religion and identity in modern British history', in S. Mews (ed.), *Religion and National Identity*, Studies in Church History, 18 (London, 1982), pp. 465–87.

—— (ed.), *Protestant Evangelicalism: Britain, Ireland, Germany and America, c.1750–1950: Essays in Honour of W. R. Ward* (Oxford, 1990).

——, 'Welsh religious history', *Journal of Welsh Religious History*, 2 (1994), 3–13.

——, *Great Britain: Identities, Institution and the Idea of Britishness* (London, 1998).

Roberts, Gomer M., 'The Moravians, John Relly and his people', *Cylchgrawn Cymdeithas Hanes y Methodistiaid Calfinaidd*, XXXVII, 1 (March, 1953), 2–6.

—— (ed.), *Hanes Methodistiaeth Galfinaidd Cymru, Cyfrol I: Y Deffroad Mawr* (Caernarfon, 1973).

——, *Hanes Methodistiaeth Galfinaidd Cymru, Cyfrol II: Cynnydd y Corff* (Caernarfon, 1978).

Roberts, Griffith T., *Howell Harris* (London, 1951).

Roberts, Michael and Clarke, Simone (eds), *Women and Gender in Early Modern Wales* (Cardiff, 2000).

Roberts, P. R., 'The Union with England and the identity of "Anglican" Wales', *Transactions of the Royal Historical Society*, 22 (1972), 49–70.

——, 'The "Act of Union" in Welsh history', *Transactions of the Honourable Society of Cymmrodorion* (1974), 49–72.

Rowell, G., 'The origins and history of universalist societies in Britain, 1750–1850', *Journal of Ecclesiastical History*, 2 (1871), 35–56.

Rule, John, 'Methodism, popular beliefs and village culture in Cornwall', in R. D. Storch (ed.), *Popular Culture and Religion in Nineteenth Century England* (London, 1982), pp. 48–70.

——, *Albion's People: English Society, 1714–1815* (London, 1992).

——, *The Vital Century: England's Developing Economy, 1714–1815* (London, 1992).

Schlenther, Boyd S., ' "The English is swallowing up their language": Welsh ethnic ambivalence in colonial Pennsylvania and the experience of David Evans', *The Pennsylvania Magazine of History and Biography*, CXIV (April 1990), 201–28.

——, *Queen of the Methodists: The Countess of Huntingdon and the Eighteenth-Century Crisis of Faith and Society* (Durham, 1997).

—— and White, E. M., *A Calendar of the Trevecka Letters* (Aberystwyth, 2003).

Schmidt, Leigh E., *Holy Fairs: Scottish Communions and American Revivals in the Early Modern Period* (Princeton, 1989).

——, *Hearing Things: Religion, Illusion and the American Enlightenment* (Cambridge, MA, 2000).

Scribner, Bob and Johnson, Trevor (eds), *Popular Religion in Germany and Central Europe, 1400–1800* (London, 1996).

Sell, A. P. F., *The Great Debate: Calvinism, Arminianism and Salvation* (Worthing, 1982).

Semmel, B., *The Methodist Revolution* (London, 1974).

Sharpe, J. A., *Early Modern England: A Social History, 1550–1750* (London, 1987).

Shaw, Jane and Kreider, Alan (eds), *Culture and the Nonconformist Tradition* (Cardiff, 1999).

Simon, J. S., 'The repeal of the Conventicle Act', *Proceedings of the Wesley Historical Society*, XI (1902), 103–8.

Simonson, Harold P., 'Jonathan Edwards and his Scottish connections', *Journal of American Studies*, 21, 3 (1987), 353–70.

Smout, T. C., 'Born again at Cambuslang: new evidence on popular religion and literacy in eighteenth century Scotland', *Past and Present*, 97 (1982), 114–27.

Spalding, Phinizy, *Oglethorpe in America* (Chicago, 1997).

Speck, W. A., *British America, 1707–1776* (London, 1985).

Spufford, M., *Contrasting Communities: English Villages in the Sixteenth and Seventeenth Centuries* (Cambridge, 1979).

—— (ed.), *The World of Rural Dissenters, 1520–1725* (Cambridge, 1995).

Spurr, John, *The Restoration Church of England, 1646–1689* (New Haven, 1991).

Stead, Geoffrey and Margaret, *The Exotic Plant: A History of the Moravian Church in Great Britain, 1742–2000* (Peterborough, 2003).

Steele, Ian K., *The English Atlantic, 1675–1740: An Exploration of Communication and Community* (New York, 1986).

Steele, Richard B., *'Gracious Affection' and 'True Virtue' according to Jonathan Edwards and John Wesley* (Metuchen, NJ, 1994).

Stein, Stephen J., 'A note on Anne Dutton, eighteenth century Evangelical', *Church History*, 44 (1975), 485–91.

Stephens, Meic (ed.), *The New Companion to the Literature of Wales* (Cardiff, 1998).

Stout, Harry S., *The New England Soul: Preaching and Religious Culture in Colonial New England* (New York, 1986).

——, *The Divine Dramatist: George Whitefield and the Rise of Modern Evangelicalism* (Grand Rapids, 1991).

—— and Hart, D. G. (eds), *New Directions in American Religious History* (New York, 1997).

Streiff, Patrick, *Reluctant Saint? A Theological Biography of Fletcher of Madeley* (London, 2001).

Sturdy, David J., *Fractured Europe, 1600–1721* (Oxford, 2002).

Suggett, Richard and White, Eryn, 'Language, literacy and aspects of identity in early modern Wales', in Adam Fox and Daniel Woolf (eds), *The Spoken Word: Oral Culture in Britain, 1500–1800* (Manchester, 2002), pp. 52–83.

Sweet, Leonard I. (ed.), *Communication and Change in American Religious History* (Grand Rapids, 1993).

Sykes, Norman, *Edmund Gibson, Bishop of London, 1699–1748: A Study in Politics and Religion in the Eighteenth Century* (Oxford, 1926).

Thomas, Hugh, *A History of Wales, 1485–1660* (Cardiff, 1972).

Thomas, Keith, *Religion and the Decline of Magic* (London, 1971).

——, 'The meaning of literacy in early modern England', in Gerd Baumann (ed.), *The Written Word: Literacy in Transition* (Oxford, 1986), pp. 97–131.

Thomas, M. Wynn, *Morgan Llwyd* (Cardiff, 1984).

Thomas, Peter D. G., *Politics in Eighteenth-century Wales* (Cardiff, 1998).

Thomas, W. S. K., *Stuart Wales* (Llandysul, 1988).

Thompson, E. P., *The Making of the English Working Class* (London, 1963).

Toon, Peter, *The Emergence of Hyper-Calvinism in English Nonconformity, 1689–1765* (London, 1967).

Towlson, C. W., *Moravian and Methodist: Relationships and Influences in the Eighteenth Century* (London, 1957).

Tracy, Joseph, *The Great Awakening: A History of the Revival of Religion in the time of Edwards and Whitefield* (1842: reprinted Edinburgh, 1976).

Tudur, Geraint, 'The king's daughter: a reassessment of Anne Harris of Trefeca', *Journal of Welsh Religious History*, 7 (1999), 55–75.

——, *Howell Harris: From Conversion to Separation, 1735–1750* (Cardiff, 2000).

——, ' "Like a right arm and a pillar": the story of James Beaumont', in Robert Pope (ed.), *Honouring the Past and Shaping the Future: Religious and Biblical Studies in Wales: Essays in Honour of Gareth Lloyd Jones* (Leominster, 2003), pp. 133–58.

Turner, John Munsey, *John Wesley: The Evangelical Revival and the Rise of Methodism in England* (London, 2002).

Tyacke, Nicholas (ed.), *England's Long Reformation, 1500–1800* (London, 1998).

Tyerman, Luke, *The Oxford Methodists: Memoirs of the Rev. Messrs. Clayton, Ingham, Gambold, Hervey, and Broughton* (London, 1873).

——, *The Life and Times of the Rev. George Whitefield*, 2 vols (London, 1876).

Tyson, John R. (ed.), *Charles Wesley: A Reader* (Oxford, 1989).

Valenze, Deborah M., *Prophetic Sons and Daughters: Female Preaching and Popular Religion in Industrial England* (Princeton, 1985).

Vickers, John, *Dictionary of Methodism in Britain and Ireland* (London, 2001).

Vincent, David, *Literacy and Popular Culture; England, 1750–1914* (Cambridge, 1989).

Virgin, Peter, *The Church in an Age of Negligence: Ecclesiastical Structure and Problems of Church Reform, 1700–1840* (Cambridge, 1989).

Walker, Andrew and Aune, Kristin (eds), *On Revival: A Critical Examination* (Carlisle, 2003).

Walker, David (ed.), *A History of the Church in Wales* (Penarth, 1976).

Wallace, D. D., *Puritans and Predestination: Grace in English Protestant Thought, 1525–1695* (Chapel Hill, 1982).

Walsh, J. D., 'Origins of the evangelical revival', in G. V. Bennett and J. D. Walsh (eds), *Essays in Modern English Church History: In Memory of Norman Sykes* (London, 1966), pp. 141–61.

——, 'Methodism and the mob in the eighteenth century', in G. J. Cuming and D. Baker (eds), *Popular Belief and Practice*, Studies in Church History, 8 (Cambridge, 1972), pp. 215–27.

——, 'The Cambridge Methodists', in Peter Brooks (ed.), *Christian Spirituality: Essays in Honour of Gordon Rupp* (London, 1975), pp. 251–83.

——, 'Élie Halévy and the birth of Methodism', *Transactions of the Royal Historical Society*, 25 (1975), 1–20.

——, 'Religious societies: Methodist and evangelical, 1738–1800', in W. J. Sheils and D. Wood (eds), *Voluntary Religion*, Studies in Church History, 23 (Oxford, 1986), pp. 279–302.

——, 'John Wesley and the community of goods', in Keith Robbins (ed.), *Protestant Evangelicalism: Britain, Ireland, Germany and America, c. 1750–1950: Essays in Honour of W. R. Ward*, Studies in Church History, Subsidia, 7 (Oxford, 1990), pp. 25–50.

——, Haydon, C. and Taylor, S. (eds), *The Church of England, c.1689–c.1833: From Toleration to Tractarianism* (Cambridge, 1993).

Walsham, Alexandra, *Providence in Early Modern England* (Oxford, 1999).

Ward, W. R., 'The relations of Enlightenment and religious revival in central Europe and in the English-speaking world', in Derek Baker (ed.), *Reform and the Reformation: England and the Continent, c.1500–c.1750*, Studies in Church History, Subsidia, 2, (1979), pp. 281–305.

——, 'Power and piety: the origins of the religious revival in the early eighteenth century', *Bulletin of the John Rylands Library*, 63 (1980), 231–52.

——, 'The renewed unity of the Brethren: ancient church, new sect or interconfessional movement?', *Bulletin of the John Rylands University Library of Manchester*, 70, 3 (Autumn 1988), 77–92.

——, *The Protestant Evangelical Awakening* (Cambridge, 1992):

——, *Christianity under the Ancien Régime, 1648–1789* (Cambridge, 1999).

Warner, Michael, *The Letters of the Republic: Publication and the Public Sphere in Eighteenth Century America* (Cambridge, MA, 1990).

Watkins, Owen C., *The Puritan Experience* (London, 1972).

Watson, C. E., 'Whitefield and Congregationalism', *Transactions of the Congregational Historical Society*, 8, no. 4 (1922), 172–80.

Watts, M. R., *The Dissenters, I: From the Reformation to the French Revolution* (Oxford, 1978).

——, *The Dissenters, II: The Expansion of Evangelical Nonconformity* (Oxford, 1995).

Welch, C. E., 'Andrew Kinsman's churches at Plymouth', *Report and Transactions of the Devonshire Association for the Advancement of Science, Literature and Art*, XCVII (1965), 212–36.

——, 'The correspondence of Nathaniel Rowland and Lady Huntingdon, 1781–90', *Cylchgrawn Cymdeithas Hanes y Methodistiaid Calfinaidd*, 2 (1978), 26–37.

——, *Spiritual Pilgrim: A Reassessment of the Life of the Countess of Huntingdon* (Cardiff, 1995).

Westerkamp, M. J., *Triumph of the Laity: Scots-Irish Piety and the Great Awakening, 1625–1760* (New York, 1988).

——, *Women and Religion in Early America, 1600–1850: The Puritan and Evangelical Traditions* (London, 1999).

Wetering, John E. van de, 'The Christian history of the Great Awakening', *Journal of Presbyterian History*, 44 (1966), 122–9.

Whilebrooke, J. C., 'Wesley and William Cudworth', *Proceedings of the Wesley Historical Society*, XII (1919), 34–6.

White, Eryn M., ' "Little female lambs": women in the Methodist societies of Carmarthenshire, 1737–1750', *Carmarthenshire Antiquary*, XXVII (1991), 31–6.

——, *Praidd Bach y Bugail Mawr: Seiadau Methodistaidd De-Orllewin Cymru* (Llandysul, 1995).

——, ' "The world, the flesh and the devil" and the early Methodist societies of south west Wales', *Transactions of the Honourable Society of Cymmrodorion*, 3 (1997), 45–61.

——, 'Women in the early Methodist societies in Wales', *Journal of Welsh Religious History*, 7 (1999), 95–108.

——, 'The people called "Methodists": early Welsh Methodism and the question of identity', *Journal of Welsh Religious History*, 1 (2001), 1–14.

Wiesner, Merry E., *Women and Gender in Early Modern Europe* (Cambridge, 1993).

Wigger, John, *Taking Heaven by Storm: Methodism and the Rise of Popular Christianity in America* (New York, 1998).

Wiles, Maurice, *Archytapal Heresy: Arianism through the Centuries* (Oxford, 1996).

Williams, A. H., 'The Gwynnes of Garth, c. 1712–1809', *Brycheiniog*, XIV (1970), 79–96.

Williams, Glanmor, *Welsh Reformation Essays* (Cardiff, 1967).

——, *Religion, Language and Nationality in Wales* (Cardiff, 1979).

——, *Renewal and Reformation: Wales, c.1415–1642* (Cardiff, 1987).

——, *The Welsh and their Religion: Historical Essays by Glanmor Williams* (Cardiff, 1991).

——, *Wales and the Reformation* (Cardiff, 1997).

Williams, Gwyn A., *The Search for Beulah Land: The Welsh and the Atlantic Revolution* (London, 1980).

——, *When was Wales?: A History of the Welsh* (London, 1985).

Williams, William, *Welsh Calvinistic Methodism: A Historical Sketch of the Presbyterian Church of Wales* (London, 1872; new edition ed. Gwyn Davies, Bridgend, 1998).

Wilson, D. Dunn, 'Hanoverian government and Methodist persecution', *Proceedings of the Wesley Historical Society*, 33, 5 (1962), 94–9.

——, *Many Waters Cannot Quench: A Study of the Sufferings of Eighteenth-Century Methodism and their Significance for John Wesley and the First Methodists* (London, 1969).

Wilson, John F., 'History, redemption and the millennium', in Nathan O. Hatch and Harry S. Stout (eds), *Jonathan Edwards and the American Experience* (New York, 1988), pp. 131–41.

Wilson, Linda, *Constrained by Zeal: Female Spirituality amongst Nonconformists, 1825–1875* (Carlisle, 2000).

Wolffe, J. (ed.), *Evangelical Faith and Public Zeal: Evangelicals and Society in Britain, 1780–1980* (London, 1995).

Wood, A. Skevington, *The Inextinguishable Blaze* (Exeter, 1960).

Wood, Craig D., 'The Welsh response to the Glorious Revolution of 1688', *Journal of Welsh Religious History*, 1 (2001), 15–33.

Wright, S, *Parish, Church and People: Local Studies in Lay Religion, 1350–1750* (London, 1988).

Wrightson, Keith, *English Society, 1580–1680* (London, 1982).

Young, B. W., *Religion and Enlightenment in Eighteenth-Century England* (Oxford, 1998).

UNPUBLISHED THESES

Durden, D. S., 'Transatlantic communications and influence during the Great Awakening: a comparative study of British and American revivalism, 1730–1760' (Ph.D., University of Hull, 1978).

Evans, R. W., 'The eighteenth century Welsh awakening, with its relationship to the contemporary English evangelical revival' (Ph.D., University of Edinburgh, 1956).

Guy, J. R., 'An investigation into the pattern and nature of patronage, plurality and non-residence in the old diocese of Llandaff between 1660 and the beginning of the nineteenth century' (Ph.D., University of Wales, 1983).

Hughes-Edwards, W. G., 'The development and organisation of the Methodist Society in Wales, 1735–50' (MA, University of Wales, 1966).

Jones, David Ceri, 'Welsh Methodism and the international evangelical revival, 1735–1750' (Ph.D., University of Wales, 2001).

Lloyd, Gareth, 'Charles Wesley: a new evaluation of his life and ministry' (Ph.D., University of Liverpool, 2002).

Owen Alun W., 'A study of Howell Harris and the Trevecka "family" (1752–1760), based upon the Trevecca letters and diaries and other Methodist archives at the National Library of Wales' (MA, University of Wales, 1957).

Thomas, S. R., 'The diocese of St. David's in the eighteenth century: the working of the diocese in a period of criticism' (MA, University of Wales, 1983).

Tudur, Geraint, 'A critical study, based on his own diaries, of the life and work of Howell Harris and his contribution to the revival in Wales between 1735 and 1750' (D.Phil., University of Oxford, 1989).

Walsh, J. D., 'The Yorkshire evangelicals in the eighteenth century with special reference to Methodism' (Ph.D., University of Cambridge, 1956).

INDEX